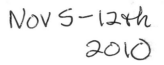

# VANCOUVER

**Discovery**
CHANNEL

**APA PUBLICATIONS** L
Part of the Langenscheidt Publishing Group

## ✳ INSIGHT GUIDE
# VANCOUVER

*Editor*
**Cathy Muscat**
*Art Editor*
**Ian Spick**
*Picture Editor*
**Hilary Genin**
*Cartography Editor*
**Zoë Goodwin**
*Production*
**Kenneth Chan**
*Editorial Director*
**Brian Bell**

### Distribution

*United States*
**Langenscheidt Publishers, Inc.**
36–36 33rd Street 4th Floor
Long Island City, NY 11106
Fax: (1) 718 784-0640

*UK & Ireland*
**GeoCenter International Ltd**
Meridian House, Churchill Way West
Basingstoke, Hampshire RG21 6YR
Fax: (44) 1256-817988

*Australia*
**Universal Publishers**
1 Waterloo Road
Macquarie Park, NSW 2113
Fax: (61) 2 9888 9074

*New Zealand*
**Hema Maps New Zealand Ltd (HNZ)**
Unit 2, 10 Cryers Road
East Tamaki, Auckland 2013
Fax: (64) 9 273 6479

*Worldwide*
**Apa Publications GmbH & Co.**
**Verlag KG (Singapore branch)**
38 Joo Koon Road, Singapore 628990
Tel: (65) 6865-1600. Fax: (65) 6861-6438

### Printing

**Insight Print Services (Pte) Ltd**
38 Joo Koon Road, Singapore 628990
Tel: (65) 6865-1600. Fax: (65) 6861-6438

©2007 Apa Publications GmbH & Co.
Verlag KG (Singapore branch)
*All Rights Reserved*

*First Edition 2007*
*Reprinted 2009*

# ABOUT THIS BOOK

The first Insight Guide pioneered the use of creative full-colour photography in guidebooks in 1970. Since then, we have expanded our range to cater for our readers' need not only for reliable information about their chosen destination but also for a real understanding of that destination. Now, when the internet can supply inexhaustible (but not always reliable) facts, our books marry text and pictures to provide that much more elusive quality: knowledge. To achieve this, they rely heavily on the authority of locally based writers and photographers.

### How to use this book

The book is carefully structured both to convey an understanding of the city and its culture and to guide readers through its sights and activities:

◆ To understand Vancouver today, you need to know something of the city's past. The first section covers its history and culture in lively, authoritative essays written by specialists.

◆ The Places section provides a full run-down of all the attractions worth seeing. The main places of interest are coordinated by number with full-colour maps. Margin notes provide background information and tips on special places and events.

◆ The Travel Tips listings section provides a point of reference for information on travel, hotels, restaurants, shops and festivals. Information may be located quickly by using the index printed on the back cover flap – and the flaps are designed to serve as bookmarks.

◆ Photographs are chosen not only to illustrate geography and buildings

but also to convey the moods of the city and the life of its people.

◆ A separate pull-out map highlights more than 50 restaurants carefully chosen by local experts.

### The contributors

The principal author of this new *Insight Guide to Vancouver* is travel writer **Anthony Lambert**. His partner is a Vancouverite and he has visited and explored the city and province of British Columbia countless times over the last 20 years. He is the author of several travel books and a frequent contributor to a variety of magazines and newspapers.

As well as writing all the places chapters, Lambert gives a vivid account of the city's history in the *Making of Vancouver*, and an insightful portrait of its people in *Living in*

*Vancouver*. He also compiled the Travel Tips section.

A team of Vancouver-based writers, all experts in their fields, supplied additional essays and features on all aspects of Vancouver life. Award-winning author and constant traveller, **Constance Brissenden**, penned the chapters on *The Great Outdoors* and *Flora and Fauna*. **Donna Spencer**, artistic producer of the Firehall Arts Centre, provided an overview of Vancouver's multicultural arts scene.

Food and wine writer **Gael Arthur** paints an appetising picture of the city's many gourmet attractions, while travel writers and wine experts **Dona Sturmanis** and **Michael Botner** contributed the enlightening feature on the increasingly prestigious BC wines. **Nick Rockel** also shares his expertise on Vancouver's microbreweries.

Award-winning journalist, and regular contributor to the *Georgia Straight*, **Guy Babineau** gives the lowdown on Gay Vancouver. Most of the photography was taken by talented West Coast photographer **Tim Thompson** with additional pictures by Anthony Lambert and **Cathy Muscat**, the editor of this book. Additional thanks go to **James Oakes** and **Anthony Norfolk** who offered valuable advice and insights, and to **Marilyn Inglis** who shared a great amount of the research. Proof-reading was by **Neil Titman** and the index was by **Helen Peters**.

**CONTACTING THE EDITORS**

We would appreciate it if readers would alert us to errors or outdated information by writing to:

**Insight Guides, P.O. Box 7910, London SE1 1WE, England.
Fax: (44) 20 7403-0290.
email: insight@apaguide.co.uk**

**NO** part of this book may be reproduced, stored in a retrieval system or transmitted in any form or means electronic, mechanical, photocopying, recording or otherwise, without prior written permission of *Apa Publications*. Brief text quotations with use of photographs are exempted for book review purposes only. Information has been obtained from sources believed to be reliable, but its accuracy and completeness, and the opinions based thereon, are not guaranteed.

**www.insightguides.com**

# Contents

# THE BEST OF VANCOUVER

Unique attractions, nature, culture, food and festivals...
Here, at a glance, are our recommendations for your visit

## ONLY IN VANCOUVER

- **The steam clock** Watch it as it steams and whistles. *See page 91.*
- **Sunbathe and ski** on the same day. *See page 47.*
- **SkyTrain tours**. A high-level tour of Greater Vancouver. *See page 234.*
- **Capilano Suspension Bridge** Wobble across the deep Capilano gorge on a historic bridge above the trees. *See page 167.*
- **The Aquarium**. Watch Beluga whales and sea otters swimming. *See page 115.*
- **Carol Ship Parade of Lights**. The spirit of Christmas in a dazzling display on water. *See page 249.*

- **Cycle round Stanley Park**. Or jog, or rollerblade... or watch a game of cricket and have tea. *See page 109.*
- **Flight in a seaplane**. Experience the West Coast's common form of transport – fly to Victoria Island, or take a scenic flight at Tofino. *See pages 196 and 232.*
- **Whale-watching**. See whales at their most impressive. *See page 253.*
- **Bears**. Orphaned bears in safe captivity on Grouse Mountain. *See pages 172–3.*

**ABOVE:** English Bay from Burrard Bridge.
**RIGHT:** crossing the Capilano Suspension Bridge.

## BEST VIEWS OF THE CITY

- **Sunset over English Bay from Sequoia Grill**. Great food in a sensational location. *See page 114.*
- **Harbour Centre Tower – Vancouver Lookout!** The best orientation viewpoint in the city. *See page 92.*
- **Grouse Mountain**. The lights of the city spread out below one

of its best restaurants. *See page 172.*
- **Queen Elizabeth Park**. The finest views over the mountains of North Vancouver. *See pages 142–3.*
- **Burrard and Granville bridges**. Looking down on English Bay and Vanier Park or the busy scene of False Creek. *See page 128.*

## BEST MUSEUMS

- **Museum of Anthropology.** A museum of international renown for its building and contents. *See page 132.*
- **Vancouver Museum.** Lively introduction to the city's history and development. *See page 130.*
- **Vancouver Maritime Museum.** Worth a visit just to see the *St Roch* and hear the story of its epic voyage. *See page 131.*
- **Vancouver Art Gallery.** Important collection of modern art and photographs, as well as temporary exhibitions. *See pages 77–8.*

- **Burnaby Village Museum.** Recreated buildings in a lovely wooded setting. *See pages 152–3.*
- **Fort Langley National Historical Site.** The best way to gain an insight into the lives of the early pioneers. *See pages 217–18.*
- **Irving House** One of Vancouver's oldest homes, with much of its original furniture. *See pages 150–1.*

**ABOVE RIGHT:** rowing in the harbour. **BELOW:** First Nations carvings in the Museum of Anthropology. **BELOW RIGHT:** fruit stall in Granville Market.

## BEST BOAT TRIPS

- **AquaBus.** For a different perspective, see the city from the water. *See page 234.*
- **Sunset dinner cruise around the harbour.** A romantic way to watch the sun go down and enjoy Vancouver's incomparable setting. *See page 235.*
- **West Coast whale-watching.** Any boat trip along the West Coast of Vancouver

Island is a scenic delight, whales or not. *See page 253.*
- **Kayaking in English Bay, False Creek or the Burrard Inlet.** Sheltered and beautiful waters for paddling. *See page 252.*
- **Ferry from Tsawwassen to Swartz Bay.** Weave through the Gulf Islands. *See page 235.*

## BEST SHOPPING

- **Granville Market.** Fantastic produce and the best concentration of craft shops and galleries. *See page 121.*
- **Robson Street.** The place to go for clothes and fashion. *See page 83.*
- **Kids' Market.** Paradise for ankle-biters. *See page 123.*

- **West 4th Avenue, Kitsilano.** Exactly what a neighbourhood shopping area should be, with good places to eat or have coffee. *See page 129.*
- **Lonsdale Quay Market.** Smaller-scale version of Granville Market. *See page 166.*

## BEST RESTAURANTS

- **Aurora**. Trendy atmosphere and imaginative use of local produce and wines. *See page 145.*
- **Il Giardino**. Fantastic courtyard and wonderfully authentic Italian cuisine. *See page 84.*
- **Lumière**. Serious gastronomy for a special occasion. *See page 134.*
- **Raincity Grill**. Casual feel but great attention is paid to food sourcing; makes the most of what the West Coast offers. *See page 85.*
- **West**. Elegant dining room with world-class chef who really knows his stuff. *See page 145.*
- **Fish Café**. Fresh fish and seafood at great prices, in a pleasant informal atmosphere. *See page 134.*

## BEST BUILDINGS

- **Marine Building**. Iconic Art Deco building with exceptionally fine detailing. *See page 75.*
- **Vancouver Law Courts**. Arthur Erickson's tour de force in the heart of the city. *See page 77.*
- **Hotel Vancouver**. The grande dame of Vancouver's hotels retains the unique ambience and style of the Canadian Pacific Railway's legendary hotels. *See page 76.*
- **Canada Place**. The perfect match of form and function on its seafront location. *See page 74.*
- **Fairacres – Burnaby Art Gallery**. Arts and Crafts house in a lovely garden setting. *See page 152.*
- **Roedde House**. Rare middle-class Queen Anne-style house of 1890. *See pages 81–2.*

## BEST FOR CHILDREN

- **La Casa Gelato**. With 218 flavours of ice-cream on offer. *See page 107.*
- **The Waterpark**. Near the Kids' Market; a great place to let off steam. *See page 124.*
- **Sutcliffe Park**. Adventure playground next to Waterpark. *See page 124.*
- **H.R. MacMillan Space Centre**. Fun and education combine in this colourful attraction. *See page 130.*
- **Science World**. An object lesson in how to keep children amused for hours, while teaching them useful skills and information. *See page 103.*
- **Maplewood Farm**. Meet farm animals in a pretty setting. *See page 171.*
- **Kitsilano Pool**. Huge saltwater pool beside the sea. *See page 127.*
- **Miniature railway**. Stanley Park ride with tunnel. *See page 114.*
- **The Aquarium**. Sea otter feeding time is hugely popular. *See page 115.*

**ABOVE:** tempting appetizers in the Raincity Grill.
**LEFT:** Vancouver Hotel.
**BELOW:** Maplewood Farm.

## BEST WALKS

- **The seawall**. The one walk everyone should do. *See page 109.*
- **Lynn Canyon**. The nearest place to get a feel for BC's forests. *See pages 168–9.*
- **Grouse Grind**. Great exercise and views, with cable car for the descent. *See page 172.*
- **Lighthouse Park**. Sea views and rainforest. *See page 176.*
- **Baden Powell Trail**. Serious walking for the experienced and fit. *See page 176.*

## BEST GARDENS

- **Stanley Park**. Rose garden and colourful mass planting in large beds. *See pages 109–15.*
- **Van Dusen Botanical Garden**. Outstanding collection of plants and trees in beautifully designed and individual settings. *See pages 141–2.*
- **Dr Sun Yat-Sen Chinese Garden**. Classic garden with series of rooms and spaces. *See page 98.*
- **UBC Botanical Garden**. A plantsman's garden. *See page 132.*
- **Queen Elizabeth Park**. Large expanse of gardens and parkland with spectacular effects in two quarries. *See pages 142–3.*

**ABOVE:** jogging and cycling in Stanley Park. **LEFT:** the Van Dusen Botanical Garden. **ABOVE RIGHT:** Celebration of Light festival.

## BEST FESTIVALS

- **Bard on the Beach**. Four Shakespeare plays in Vanier Park. *See page 248.*
- **HSBC Celebration of Light**. Two-week international firework competition lights up summer evenings. *See page 248.*
- **International Jazz Festival**. Ten days of jazz in venues around the city. *See page 248.*
- **Folk Music Festival**. International performers at Jericho Beach. *See page 248.*
- **International Film Festival**. 300 films from 50 countries. *See page 248.*

## OUT OF TOWN

**Victoria** BC's capital has some world-class museums, a more relaxed pace of life, great restaurants and some of the best buildings from the early years of BC's history. *See pages 183–91.*

**Tofino and Ucluelet** Pristine beaches, boat trips along the coast and spectacular seas in winter. *See pages 195–6.*

**Steveston** An attractive town still redolent of the importance of the sea to the BC economy, with cannery museum, working boats and historic ship-repair yards. *See pages 159–62.*

**Salt Spring Island** Laid-back atmosphere with some major artists and artisans who attract collectors from around the world. *See pages 200–2.*

**Butchart Gardens** Vancouver Island's most popular garden with dazzling displays. *See page 192.*

**Squamish/Garibaldi Provincial Park** Popular area for climbing, hiking, mountain biking and cross-country skiing. *See pages 210–12.*

**Wine Country** The Okanagan should be on any wine lover's itinerary. *See pages 221–2.*

**Whistler** Canada's best-known ski resort is gaining the benefit of Olympic facilities. *See pages 211–12.*

**Kettle Valley Steam Railway** The region's best heritage steam railway. *See page 222.*

# CITY OF GLASS

**Back in 1939, King George VI took his leave of the young city with the comment: "I think Vancouver is the place to live." He would say the same today: thoroughly modern Vancouver is one of Canada's most vibrant cities**

O nce you've been to Vancouver it comes as no surprise to read of the city's almost annual roll-call of awards for best city to visit or live in, from *Condé Nast Traveler* magazine to the Mercer Quality of Life index. Broaden the tourist criteria of ambience, friendliness, culture and sights, restaurants, accommodation, environment and shopping to include issues of importance to residents, and it's ranked the world's most liveable city by the Economic Intelligence Unit.

For visitors, Vancouver's principal attraction has to be its location. This is one of the few places in the world where you can ski in the morning, sunbathe by the sea in the afternoon and eat at a world-class restaurant in the evening. Apart from the many wet days of winter, life in Vancouver is lived out of doors. Its terrific beaches, parks and the scenic seawall path are thronged with walkers, cyclists and rollerbladers at weekends.

Take away the sea and the mountains and much of Vancouver's immediate appeal would disappear. Only on closer acquaintance would the city's other virtues become apparent. Foremost would be the fantastic restaurants, bars and cafés, which make the place a gastronomic joy – not only for the inventiveness and competence of chefs, but also the quality of ingredients, with a growing emphasis on organic origin and healthy combinations. Twenty years ago, the wines of British Columbia were barely drinkable; today there's no need to drink anything else. The friendliness of Vancouverites is another big plus. Pull out a map on a street corner and chances are someone will stop to help you on your way.

From its foundation, Vancouver has been a cosmopolitan city, and its multiculturalism lends it added vitality in such areas as Chinatown and Punjabi Market. With all this going for it, it is little wonder that Vancouver thinks of itself as a world-class city, and in many ways it is, though the nearest art gallery of international renown is 791 miles (1,273 km) away in San Francisco, and for opera and concerts you rely on seasons rather than year-round programmes. But the city has vibrant theatres and dance companies, plenty of great venues for jazz and other music, and festivals galore to delight the 22 million annual visitors to BC. ❑

---

**PRECEDING PAGES:** the view across the Burrard Inlet to the North Shore from Harbour Centre Tower; Mayne Island. **LEFT:** a cruise ship sails out to sea.

# THE MAKING OF VANCOUVER

Vancouver's history began long before the arrival of intrepid
mariners, fur trappers and gold prospectors. The land that
now supports a diverse population of more than 2 million
was settled by First Nations tribes 10,000 years ago

The story of the European settlement of
Vancouver occupies a tiny fraction of the
human history of the area. Over 3,000
years ago, and probably much longer, First
Nations people from the ancient Musqueam
("people of the grass") and Squamish ("strong
winds") cultures lived in what is now the West
End of Vancouver. As recently as the 1930s,
there were still elderly First Nations people
who could remember the location of villages
and houses they had known as children.

## First Nations

The first inhabitants of the region are thought
to have been ancient Mongolian tribes who
came across the Bering Strait about 10,000
years ago. Their descendants formed the West
Coast tribes which based their livelihoods on
the abundant salmon migrations and the cedar
tree from which they built large plankhouses
along the shores of Burrard Inlet; about 20,000
people are thought to have lived in them.

The fecundity of the region and the harmonious balance the First Nations people maintained with nature and the environment are
reflected in the thousands of years they lived
in this way.

The artistic traditions of these West Coast
natives found expression in their prominent
totem poles, elaborate masks, decorated
boxes, longboats and other wooden artefacts.
Some artwork was created to proclaim and

record family clan rights which would be
asserted through the unique ceremony of the
potlatch. These were elaborate and costly
events, and an important elder would host
only two or three in his lifetime. During the
two-week ceremony, trials or marriages might
be conducted, property rights granted, feuds
settled and noble births proclaimed.

In a society without written records, the
potlatch served as a means of impressing these
transactions and occasions on the collective
memory. This was formalised by certain people being asked to bear future witness to them,
should the need arise. In return, they were
given gifts such as longboats, chests and

---

**LEFT:** mother carrying her baby in a papoose.
**RIGHT:** woodcut illustrating the traditional houses and
dress of Vancouver's First Nations people *c.*1890.

slaves, as well as being royally entertained. So extravagant and wasteful did these presents become that the Canadian government banned potlatches between 1924 and 1952, even imprisoning elders and confiscating their regalia, though it is also argued that this was merely a pretext in the pursuit of compulsory assimiliation.

Before Europeans arrived in BC, at least 80,000 native people lived in the region; by 1885 their population had been reduced to 28,000 by disease, firearms and alcohol. Small-pox was the worst killer, since the First Nations people had no immunity; for example, it killed a third of the native population of Victoria.

## Venture capitalists

Long before the first European came to the west coast of Canada or George Vancouver was born, a company was founded in London that would have a profound effect on the development of Canada and the settlement of the West Coast. The Hudson's Bay Company (HBC) is the oldest incorporated joint-stock merchandising company in the English-speaking world, and it was given its royal charter by Charles II on 2 May 1670. To his cousin Prince Rupert and his associates, Charles granted 3.9 million square km (1½ million square miles) of land in western and northern Canada, to be known as "Rupert's Land". Charles believed it was his to

### GEORGE VANCOUVER

George Vancouver was born in 1757, the son of a customs officer at the thriving port of King's Lynn on England's east coast. He had the sea in his blood, being descended on his mother's side from the Elizabethan seafarer Sir Richard Grenville, whose death on the *Revenge* was one of the most heroic actions in British naval history.

Through his maritime connections, George's father secured his son a place on Cook's second voyage (1772–5), which gave him an unparalleled training in seamanship, navigation and surveying. After serving on Cook's third voyage (1776–80), Vancouver was appointed lieutenant and served in the West Indies. In 1790 he com-

manded an expedition making a detailed survey of the northwest coast of America from California to Alaska. To try to ascertain once and for all whether an entry to a Northwest Passage existed, Vancouver spent three years surveying the coast, during which time he named over 400 topographical features, most of which remain in use, and concluded that a Northwest Passage did not exist.

Vancouver returned to England in 1795, having sailed about 105,000km (65,600 miles) with the loss of only five of the 180 crew during the four years, a quite exceptional achievement for the time which reflects his care for his men. He died in 1798, aged just 40.

give away because no other Christian monarch had claimed it.

The company's primary object was to make money by wresting control of the fur trade from the French, who had enjoyed a monopoly over it during the 17th century.

The HBC's success was unchallenged until the formal establishment of the North West Company in Montreal in 1783, with the explicit intention of breaking the HBC's stranglehold on the fur trade. It looked to develop trade in areas not covered by the HBC's charter, dispatching expeditions led by Alexander Mackenzie, Simon Fraser and David Thompson to explore and map the western territories.

west Passage to link the Atlantic and Pacific oceans, long the dream of navigators. Parliament had offered a reward of £20,000 to anyone discovering such a passage, and its western exit was the purpose of James Cook's third and final voyage.

Cook left England in the summer of 1776, and in March 1778 he put into Nootka Sound on Vancouver Island for repairs. With him were William Bligh as master of the *Resolution* (and later of the infamous *Bounty*) and midshipman George Vancouver. When Cook's ships reached China on the return voyage, the 1,500 beaver and otter pelts they had acquired at Nootka Sound in exchange for trifles

British hegemony over the West Coast was no foregone conclusion. Spanish and British mapping expeditions had both cordial and hostile meetings along Vancouver Island. The Spanish are thought to have reached as far inland as the Okanagan, where the last of their depleted band were killed.

## Voyages of discovery

Part of the impetus for naval exploration of the region was the search for the elusive North-

**LEFT:** HMS *Discovery* and HMS *Chatham* exploring the shores of Burrard Inlet in 1792.
**ABOVE:** scene in a Hudson Bay trading store.

fetched upwards of $100 each – equal to two years' pay for an ordinary seaman. As a plaque in Vancouver's Christ Church Cathedral says, it was Cook's expedition that revealed the wealth of the region. It also led later to the hunting of otters to near extinction. It was on the way home on 14 February 1779 that Cook was killed by natives on the Sandwich Islands (now Hawaii).

Fourteen years later, George Vancouver was sent by the Admiralty in two ships, the *Discovery* and the *Chatham*, to receive the formal surrender from Spain of land the Spanish had seized around Nootka Sound on Vancouver Island. He sailed from Falmouth on

1 April 1791 and, travelling by way of the Cape of Good Hope, Australia and Hawaii, first sighted the northwest coast of America on 17 April 1792. It was on this voyage that Vancouver explored what would be named Burrard Inlet, writing that it "requires only to be enriched by the industry of man with villages, mansions, cottages, and other buildings to render it the most lovely country that can be imagined…"

## Approaches from the east

While Vancouver was mapping the West Coast, emissaries of the North West Company were exploring the river systems that they

1862), was the first-known European to travel the river that took his name to its mouth, in 1808. The object of his journey was to find a river link between Lake Ontario and the fur-trading posts on the lower Columbia river.

A party of 24 in four canoes left Fort George on Lake Ontario in May 1808, quickly discovering that the warnings given by the native inhabitants about the river were all too justified. Hauling the canoes around the rapids was extremely difficult too, leading the party to abandon them above present-day Lillooet after just 13 days' slog through several mountain ranges. They reached the coast on foot, occasionally borrowing canoes from local

knew must flow west to the Pacific, with a view to assessing their trading potential. In 1792–5 Alexander Mackenzie (1764–1820) made a trip from the North West Company's fort at Fort Chipewyan on Lake Athabasca to the Pacific, using a 7.5-metre (25-ft) birchbark canoe of exceptional strength. He crossed the Great Divide and came down a tributary of the Fraser, later named by Simon Faser, eventually completing his journey to the Pacific on foot, reaching the coast on 20 July 1793 by the Bela Coola river. He then returned to the fort by the Peace river.

Another Scotsman in the employment of the North West Company, Simon Fraser (1776–

tribes with whom Fraser established good relationships.

But at the lower reaches of the river, near today's Vancouver, the Musqueam people gave chase, denying Fraser more than a glimpse of the Strait of Georgia. By this point, however, he had realised that the river he had been following was not the Columbia but an entirely different river. It was Fraser who gave the name of New Caledonia to part of today's BC.

The squabbles and skirmishes between the two fur-trading companies came to an end in 1821 with the forced merger of the North West and Hudson's Bay companies.

Just before Christmas 1824 a party of 40 men led by a Hudson's Bay Company Chief Factor, James McMillan, explored the lower reaches of the Nicomekl, Salmon and Fraser rivers, McMillan marking a tree at what is now Langley. Over two years later, on 27 July 1827, he was back at the tree with orders to build a fort. Within five years, Fort Langley was shipping out over 2,000 beaver pelts a year, trapped by the local Kwantlen people.

Salted salmon soon became another major industry, with much of it going to the Sandwich Islands (now Hawaii). In 1839 the fort was abandoned and moved to its present site *(see page 217)*.

requesting a single company of infantry. The response was the dispatch of four vessels carrying a corps of Royal Engineers (the Columbia Detachment) under the command of Col. Richard Moody. A further response was a parliamentary Act creating the new mainland colony of British Columbia, and Douglas was offered the governorship providing he severed his links with the fur trade. That agreed, he was inaugurated as governor at Fort Langley.

Col. Moody, his wife and four children travelled via Panama, crossed the Isthmus over land (the Canal was not opened until 1914), and arrived in Victoria after a two-month journey. Moody and his sappers (a

## Gold fever

Vancouver Island had been declared a crown colony in 1849, but the future governance of the region was transformed by an event in 1858, when gold was discovered along the banks of the Fraser river. Not everyone was thrilled. The idea of prospectors invading the fur-trading grounds aroused the proprietorial instincts of HBC officials, and the Chief Factor, James Douglas, wrote to Sir Edward Bulwer-Lytton at the Colonial Office in London, even

word derived from the spade Royal Engineers used to dig trenches) accomplished an astonishing amount of work during their four years based at the site he chose for the new capital of New Westminster.

Within a year he had built a road through the forest linking New Westminster with Port Moody on ice-free Burrard Inlet, ensuring that the capital would not be cut off during a severe winter. He surveyed suitable sites for settlement, including a good part of what became downtown Vancouver, and built the Cariboo and Hope– Simalkameen roads.

Douglas's fears about the impact of the gold rush were justified. By July 1858 there were

**LEFT:** Fort Langley, where many an unsuccessful gold miner ended up.

**ABOVE:** an outfitter's store for gold diggers.

about 30,000 miners in the colony, most of them "the worst of the population of San Francisco – the very dregs in fact of society" as Douglas put it. The first ship to carry prospectors was the *Surprise*, a sternwheeler from California which entered the Fraser river on 5 June 1858 and reached Fort Hope the next day. The rapids claimed many lives before roads were built, but that first summer of 1858 saw claims on every creek and sandbar from Hope to Lytton.

History repeated itself three years later when reports leaked of Ned Campbell finding 900 ounces of gold in a day, this time in Cariboo country around Barkerville. Both gold rushes encouraged the establishment of farms around today's Burnaby and Delta and further north in Cariboo country to provide milk and meat for the hungry miners.

## Real estate

Disappointed miners formed the nucleus of many a settlement and business, none more famously than a Yorkshire potter named John Morton and two fellow countrymen, Sam Brighouse and William Hailstone. In 1862 they pooled their resources to buy 225 hectares (550 acres) of what became the West End of Vancouver, with a view to making bricks on the site. Neither this nor any of their

### THE PEOPLE BEHIND THE PLACE NAMES

Many of Vancouver's landmarks carry the names of the explorers and pioneers who opened the region up to Europe. Naming the young town after George Vancouver *(see page 18)* was the idea of the Canadian Pacific Railway's president, who maintained that Vancouver was more famous for his exploits in the region than Granville, after whom the city was originally named.

Simon Fraser began exploring the country west of the Rockies in the early 19th century, establishing trading posts and trade routes. In 1808 he travelled down the river that now bears his name with a view to taking possession of that country and setting up forts along the way.

In 1788, Scotsman Alexander Mackenzie founded Fort Chipewyan, the first settlement in Alberta. Information about local waterways gleaned from First Nations people encouraged Mackenzie to follow the river that was later to bear his name, only to discover that it did not flow into Cook Inlet in Alaska as he had hoped but to the Arctic Ocean.

In 1858 Col. Richard Moody of the Royal Engineers was appointed Chief Commissioner of Lands and Works and Lieutenant Governor of the new colony of BC. Moody's name was given to the port on Burrard Inlet which was chosen as the original western terminus of the Canadian Pacific Railway.

other money-making ideas came to much, but they still owned the land when the Canadian Pacific Railway (CPR) directors decided to extend the transcontinental line beyond the original terminus of Port Moody to Burrard Inlet, transforming the value of their land. The water at Port Moody was too shallow for ever-larger ocean-going ships.

Another Yorkshireman, Jack Deighton *(see page 93)* started the fledgling community's first bar and hotel in 1867, the same year that nearby Hastings Mill began processing timber and the year that three eastern British colonies formed the Confederation of Canada. The boundaries of districts such as Langley,

making other investments" because "it is only once in a lifetime that the public have such a chance as the present."

## The Great Fire

Vancouver became a city by royal assent on 6 April 1886, and within three months 500 buildings had been erected. The sounds of two-man saws and axes could be heard around the city's edges as the hemlocks and firs were felled, but the frenetic pace of forest clearance brought a nemesis: on 13 June a fire to burn brushwood went out of control and in 45 minutes destroyed almost everything that had been built, though sparing Hastings Mill. City Hall

Maple Ridge, Surrey, Delta and Richmond were laid out during the 1870s. But even by the beginning of the 1880s, the population of Granville (later Vancouver – *see panel*) was still in the low hundreds. Electric light arrived first on the north shore in 1882 in the village of Moodyville that grew up around a mill owned by an American, Sewell Moody (no relation to the Royal Engineer). A prescient writer for the Portland-based *West Shore Magazine* advised "those who have money to investigate the merits of Vancouver…before

was relegated to a tent where the city was replanned, using stone and brick rather than wood. Six months later, the city boasted 23 hotels, 51 stores, a church, a school, hospital, livery stable and opera house, bank and new City Hall. The population was over 8,000.

Support for the colony of British Columbia joining Canada was orchestrated by the Confederation League. Fear of annexation by the United States was a significant factor in its arguments, as was the debt burden created by developing the infrastructure needed to cope with the rapid population increase. Moreover, the economy needed to be placed on a firmer footing than the fly-by-night enterprises

**LEFT:** first Vancouver City Council meeting after the fire, 1886. **ABOVE:** Canadian Pacific Railway train.

engendered by the gold rush; its end had been followed by an inevitable depression.

Vancouver's future was secured when the Prime Minister, Sir John A. MacDonald, promised that a transcontinental railway line would be built if British Columbia joined the Confederation. The pledge and an agreement to take over its debt won the colony over, and on 20 July 1871 British Columbia became the sixth province of the Confederation (though the boundaries were not finalised until 1903).

### The railway arrives

It is a measure of the financial and engineering difficulties in fulfilling MacDonald's commitment that 16 years would pass before the first passenger train from Montreal came to a hissing stand beside Burrard Inlet, on 23 May 1887; it had completed what was then the world's longest continuous train journey at 4,655km (2,909 miles).

Being Queen Victoria's Golden Jubilee year, it carried a large picture of the queen on the front and was festooned with garlands. Port Moody had had its "15 minutes of fame" as the temporary terminus for 10 months.

For speculators, there was a pot of gold at the end of the steel rainbow: land prices more than tripled in just over two months in anticipation of the effect the railway would have in

### RUDYARD KIPLING'S VIEW

When the writer Rudyard Kipling first came to Vancouver in 1889, he was 23 and his well-known short story *The Man Who Would Be King* had just been published. He wrote about his visit to the young city in *From Sea to Sea*:

"Vancouver three years ago was swept off by fire in sixteen minutes, and only one house was left standing. To-day it has a population of fourteen thousand people, and builds its houses out of brick with dressed granite fronts. But a great sleepiness lies on Vancouver as compared with an American town: men don't fly up and down the street telling lies, and the spittoons in the delightfully comfortable hotel are unused; the baths are free and their

doors are unlocked... An American bade me notice the absence of bustle, and was alarmed when in a loud and audible voice I thanked God for it . . .

"Vancouver possesses an almost perfect harbour. The town is built all round and about the harbour, and young as it is, its streets are better than those of western America. Moreover, the old flag waves over some of the buildings, and this is cheering to the soul. The place is full of Englishmen who speak the English tongue correctly and with clearness, avoiding more blasphemy than is necessary, and taking a respectable length of time to getting outside their drinks."

spurring the city's growth. For the CPR it was a bonanza, having been given 3,750 hectares (6,000 acres) of land in and around the city as reward for the huge sums it had spent in construction. The CPR has remained a major property player for decades, from the early days when it spent $2 million laying out leafy Shaughnessy before a single house was built to today's interests in waterfront development and the Arbutus right of way through its real-estate arm, Marathon Realty.

The economy of BC has always been based on the extraction of resources from lumber to mining, so completion of the railway was as much of a boost to the broader economy as property: the mining, forestry, agriculture and fishing industries were able to send their products east as well as to the port at Vancouver for shipment. Given the heavy nature of the mining and forestry industries and the perishable products of agriculture and fishing, they could achieve little without the railway. Cattle ranching in the Cariboo and Chilcotin, and fruit growing in the Okanagan became major industries.

## Early immigrants

The reasons for Vancouver's early success are easy to see: its natural deep-water harbour encouraged its choice as terminus of the first trans-Canada railway line; wood, salmon and other plentiful natural resources in the region added to its exports; and its glorious location and equable climate made it an attractive place to live and visit.

The largest group of early "visitors" was Chinese, many of them contracted to help complete the CPR, but once that task was complete they were in competition with European immigrants for each job. Their willingness to work for 75 cents a day when white labourers expected $1.25–$2 led to the first outbreak of job-market-induced violence in 1887 when a Chinese camp at False Creek was attacked.

Measures were taken to limit or stop the immigration of Chinese, but as early as 1907 the *Illustrated London News* was describing Vancouver as "probably the most cosmopolitan city in the world". Many poor Chinese

from Hong Kong and Canton saw working in BC as a temporary measure that would allow them to go back home with enough money to buy land. Many never returned to China, and some who did came back to Vancouver when the communists took over.

## Saloons to opera

The few decades before World War I saw the city in that transitional state between raw frontier town and a city adopting the more sophisticated and cultured mores of the well-to-do. At the same time as Sarah Bernhardt was treading the boards at the CPR's newly built Opera House, Vancouver was topping the

league for alcohol consumption in Canada. This wasn't helped by yet another influx of miners, this time on their way to the Yukon in 1898. Tramcars rattled along the streets among the horse dung, and the first petrol arrived in barrels to fuel the mixed blessing of the motor car.

A second transcontinental railway line, the Grand Trunk Pacific (GTP) through the Yellowhead Pass and Prince George, opened to the coast at Prince Rupert in 1914, and the Canadian Northern (later Canadian National) arrived in Vancouver in 1916, using the lines of the Great Northern from the Fraser river bridge, creating a rival to the CPR for east–west traffic. The financial distress of both the GTP and

**LEFT:** interior of a CPR sleeping car, 1888.
**RIGHT:** Chinese "visitors" in front of a post office.

Canadian Northern prompted the creation of Canadian National in 1922 to take over their operations.

## War and Prohibition

The city's population roughly tripled between 1900 and 1910, helping to make the city's four newspapers immensely profitable as new arrivals scanned the columns for jobs and property. The opening of the Panama Canal a few weeks after war was declared in 1914 dramatically shortened the sea journey between BC and Europe, stimulating trade and particularly grain exports.

The supply of professional soldiers from local regiments as well as volunteers was complemented by fundraising and a greater role for women in replacing men who had left for Europe. It was the newly empowered women who voted in Prohibition during the war to counter the city's reputation for heavy drinking, but pressure from returning veterans enforced a relaxation of controls.

A quick post-war way to riches, providing you weren't caught, was rum-running to the US during the Prohibition era from 1920 to 1933. This illicit trade put serious money into the Vancouver economy. One of the vessels at the Britannia Heritage Shipyard at Steveston (see page 160), MV Fleetwood, was

### HARD TIMES

Although shipbuilding in North Vancouver had grown during World War I, the yards experienced a downturn long before the Wall Street Crash heralded the Great Depression. For other industries the 1920s were buoyant, though contemporary accounts speak of heavily polluted air from the mills, food-processing plants, shoe and clothing factories and breweries. Despite the modest prosperity, many returning soldiers found jobs occupied by immigrants from Europe. Fringe political parties sprang up to articulate their grievances; some later became part of the left-of-centre Co-operative Commonwealth and the right-of-centre Social Credit parties.

built specifically for contraband trade, with a diesel engine and two 450hp aircraft engines that would enable her to outrun government patrol ships.

## The Great Depression

But most had no such option, and Vancouver's streets filled with the unemployed from shut-down factories, mines, lumber camps and canneries. It was preferable to be destitute in Vancouver's mild climate than in the towns of the interior where it was freezing in winter and too hot in summer, so hard-up unemployed men headed west along the tracks of the CPR and Canadian National Railway, earning the city the reputation of being the "hobo capital of Canada". Hobo shanties around the False Creek and Burrard Inlet rail yards became home to thousands. By 1931 Vancouver's unemployment levels were the highest in Canada at 28 percent. Schoolteachers even agreed to work the month of December 1933 without pay to prevent the near-bankrupt authorities closing the schools. Industrial unrest boiled over in April 1935 when 2,000 men marched on City Hall demanding work and wages.

Much more serious was the 1938 occupation of the main post office, Hotel Georgia and the Art Gallery by 1,500 demonstrators demanding a works programme on the lines of

ments of conflict and women returned to the workplace in greater numbers than ever.

Preliminary siting of gun batteries and the creation of recruitment centres were overshadowed by the attack on Pearl Harbour, prompting nightly blackouts and the uprooting and internment of Japanese Canadians in rudimentary camps. Despite their contribution in the previous world war, their property was seized and liquidated, and little of it was ever returned, though compensation has been paid. The 2,450-km (1,520-mile) Alaska Highway between Dawson Creek in BC and Fairbanks was completed in 1943, having been built largely by African-American units of the US Army.

Edgar Hoover's in the US. It was a month before batons and tear gas were used to evict the occupiers, but not before some most un-Canadian scenes of looting and violence. The docks at Vancouver were effectively under martial law for almost three years. Some public works to reduce unemployment were instigated, such as Kitsilano swimming pool and the Burrard Bridge.

World War II brought an end to the Depression, as Vancouver geared up for the require-

## Post-war boom

With the return of peace, many veterans who had trained in BC returned to settle, and immigration resumed in 1947. The Social Credit premier W.A.C. Bennett dominated BC politics for two decades, riding the wave of post-war baby-boomer prosperity with policies that reflected the "frontier ethic of limitless resources". Much of the growth was fuelled by the port, which had its facilities and channels enlarged for bigger ships. The 1954 British Empire and Commonwealth Games in Vancouver made world headlines when Roger Bannister broke the four-minute mile record. Traffic congestion became a chronic problem, compounded by

**LEFT:** Hastings Street, 1939. **ABOVE:** relocating a Japanese Canadian, 1942. **RIGHT:** Roger Bannister breaks the four-minute mile record in 1954.

lack of investment in a transit system that was allowed to contract; as a consequence transit use halved between 1946 and 1964, despite the population doubling to 800,000.

The 1960s saw the beginnings of Whistler as a ski resort and construction of the Grouse Mountain Skyride, but Vancouver's future appeal as a tourist destination unwittingly owes much to the activity of students and hippies during the decade. It was they who began to press for more pedestrian-friendly streets and helped to oppose a number of immensely damaging highway proposals – a freeway through Chinatown and around Coal Harbour to English Bay was among the schemes. In

1971 this concern for the environment was translated into the formation of Greenpeace, when 12 activists sailed to protest against US atomic testing off Alaska.

The long period of Social Credit (Socreds) provincial government under W.A.C. Bennett came to a brief end in 1972 before his son was elected as premier in 1975. This was a period of phenomenal growth in the suburbs at the expense of the central areas, a trend that the city has tried to counter by imaginative regeneration over the last two decades. It was Expo '86 celebrating Vancouver's centenary that marked the turning point in the development of the city. Notionally it had a transportation

### ENVIRONMENTAL CONCERNS

The green movement has targeted the logging of old-growth forest and particularly the destructive clear-cut method of laying waste entire swaths of forest. But raw materials remain a cornerstone of the BC economy, including the mining industry with gross revenues of $4 billion a year and accounting for 56 percent of all railway revenues and 69 percent of port revenues. BC is the fifth-largest silver producer in world. Some of the surviving older mines have become fascinating tourist attractions, though many regret that the huge Sullivan mine at Kimberley was not saved. It closed in 2001 after almost a century of activity.

theme: Skytrain and the Coquihalla Highway between Hope and Merritt were rushed to completion just in time, and the exhibition was a huge success, attracting over 21 million visitors. But it was decisions about the use of the exhibition-site land that were to transform the city (see below).

### The legacy of Expo

In 1989 the great uncertainty over the future of Hong Kong led to a huge influx of capital and residents, pushing up real estate prices. Asian interests now own over 20 percent of downtown Vancouver and finance the majority of new development projects. Because of the constraints on expansion imposed by Vancouver's topography, land is often more valuable than the property on it, leading to frequent demolition of older buildings or pressure for permission to add additional storeys.

The city's invaluable asset of wonderful views over the north-shore mountains led to the approval in 1989 of "View Protection Guidelines", designed to prevent new buildings obscuring them. However, there was criticism that some taller buildings might enhance the visual interest of Vancouver's skyline. There was not the risk, as in London for example, of destroying a treasured skyline by introducing an absurdly out-of-scale

would be considered. Five of the sites have been or are being developed, the tallest being the Shangri-La Hotel and residential tower *(see page 117).*

## Population shifts

Such developments contributed to the biggest change during the 1990s; statistics showed that the decline in the proportion of population in central Vancouver compared to the metropolitan area had been arrested. Between 1981 and 1995, the population of the central area increased by 107,000.

Vancouver's success in securing the 2010 Winter Olympics will be the final opportu-

building that would dwarf the iconic outline of St Paul's Cathedral. Such considerations do not apply in Vancouver, but the mountain views are a different matter.

In 1997 a "Skyline Study" was commissioned which concluded that the city's skyline would benefit from a few buildings exceeding the current limits. Under the General Policy on Higher Buildings, five suitable downtown sites were identified where heights up to 137 metres (450ft) would be acceptable and two where 122 metres (400ft)

**LEFT:** Greenpeace activists. **ABOVE:** Expo '86 changed the face of Vancouver's waterfront.

nity for redevelopment of the land around False Creek, where the Olympic village is being built. Though Whistler will host the majority of skiing events, it is recognised that Vancouver is the logical location for some stadiums that would become white elephants in Whistler once the games ended. For example, skating events will be held in a renovated Pacific Coliseum in Hastings Park, while the events of the very Canadian sport of curling will take place in a new Hillcrest/Nat Bailey Stadium Park facility that will leave an ice-hockey rink and eight sheets of curling ice.

With an estimated 3 billion viewers, Vancouver will be in the global spotlight.   ❏

# Decisive Dates

**1670** Hudson's Bay Company founded in London to wrest the lucrative beaver-pelt trade from the French.
**1757** George Vancouver is born in England (in King's Lynn, Norfolk).
**1779** James Cook explores the west coast of Vancouver Island.
**1783** The North West Company is founded in Montreal.
**1791** Spanish navigator José Maria Narváez explores the Strait of Georgia and sails into what became Burrard Inlet.

**1865** First telegraph message from abroad, announcing assassination of President Lincoln.
**1866** Crown colonies of Vancouver Island and British Columbia united.
**1867** First stagecoach service, between New Westminster and Burrard Inlet. Confederation of Canada consists of four provinces: New Brunswick, Nova Scotia, Ontario and Quebec. Gastown springs up around sawmill and Jack Deighton's saloon.
**1868** The capital is moved from New Westminster to Victoria.
**1869** Hudson's Bay Company surrenders Rupert's Land, part of Canada, to the Crown.
**1870** Gastown is incorporated as Granville.

**1791–5** George Vancouver's exploration of the West Coast.
**1808** Simon Fraser arrives down the river that took his name.
**1827** Original Hudson's Bay Company Fort Langley founded on Fraser river.
**1836** *SS Beaver* arrives from England after a six-month voyage, making her the first steamship to reach the Pacific Ocean.
**1843** Fort Victoria (briefly called Fort Camosun) founded on Vancouver Island.
**1858** Discovery of gold on Fraser river. British Columbia declared official crown colony.
**1861** First newspaper established, New Westminster's *British Columbian*.

**1871** British Columbia joins the Confederation of Canada following promise of a transcontinental railway by the prime minister, John A. MacDonald.
**1883** First local telephone call, from Port Moody to New Westminster.
**1885** Last spike ceremony at Craigellachie on 7 November completes transcontinental railway. Lauchlan Hamilton starts laying out township of Vancouver.
**1886** The name Granville is changed to Vancouver, and city status is conferred by royal assent on 6 April.
**1886** Fire destroys all but a few of Vancouver's buildings on 13 June. The first transcontinental

passenger train arrives at Port Moody on 4 July.
**1887** First passenger train arrives in Vancouver on 23 May. First imported cargo arrives in harbour, of tea and silk from China. First use of electricity in the city.
**1888** Stanley Park formally opened and named.
**1889** First Capilano suspension bridge opened. First Granville Street Bridge opened; its successors opened in 1909 and 1954.
**1890** Tramcar service begins on a rectangular route along Main, Cordova, Granville and Pender streets on 28 June.
**1891** Sarah Bernhardt performs at Opera House. First interurban line opens, between Vancouver and New Westminster.
**1900** Vancouver exceeds Victoria in size.
**c.1907** First petrol station opens in Canada, at the foot of Cambie Street, near Smithe.
**1908** The University of British Columbia (UBC) is inaugurated.
**1909** First export shipment of grain from Vancouver. First skyscraper, the Dominion Trust Building at Hastings and Cambie, opens. Regular ferry service across Burrard Inlet begins. City of New York presents poisoned chalice of eight pairs of grey squirrels.
**1911** World's largest indoor ice rink opens, at 1805 West Georgia, on corner of Denman.
**1913** Sam Kee Building erected.
**1914** Canadian Pacific Railway station on Cordova Street opened.
**1915** UBC receives first students.
**1920** First Polar Bear Swim.
**1922** Driving switches from left to right side of street from 1 January.
**1925** The first Second Narrows Bridge links the city with North Vancouver.
**1928** First traffic light comes into use.
**1929** Wall Street Crash. Marine Building is completed.
**1932** Burrard Street Bridge is opened.
**1936** New City Hall is dedicated at 12th and Cambie.
**1938** Lions Gate Bridge is opened.
**1939** The third Hotel Vancouver is opened.
**1942** Building of the Alaska Highway.
**1949** The second Hotel Vancouver demolished.
**1954** British Empire and Commonwealth Games. Current Granville Bridge opened.

**1956** Re-zoning of West End to allow higher density and high-rise developments.
**1960** Second Narrows Bridge opened (renamed Ironworkers' Memorial Bridge in 1994).
**1971** Greenpeace formed in a Dunbar living room, developed from Don't Make a Wave Committee. Metropolitan population tops 1 million.
**1974** Royal Hudson begins regular steam-hauled trains to Squamish.
**1977** SeaBus services across Burrard Inlet begin. Vancouver Lookout! opened.
**1979** Arthur Erikson's Courthouse and Robson Square complex completed. Granville Island Market opens.
**1983** BC Place Stadium inflates and opened.

**1985** SkyTrain between Vancouver and New Westminster opens.
**1986** Expo '86 marks Vancouver's centenary.
**1988** First Gay Pride Festival, now an annual week-long event.
**1993** Shooting of *X-Files* TV series begins in Vancouver. Closure of the landmark Woodward's department store, following bankruptcy.
**1995** New library and the Centre for the Performing Arts open.
**1997** The Chan Centre for the Performing Arts opens at UBC.
**2001** Millennium line of SkyTrain opens.
**2003** Vancouver is chosen to host the 2010 Winter Olympics. ❏

---

**LEFT:** early settlement of Vancouver.
**RIGHT:** SkyTrain moves over 220,000 people daily.

# LIVING IN VANCOUVER

Blessed with an equable climate, a stunning location and an enviably laid-back lifestyle, it's no wonder that the city is regularly voted one of the world's most desirable places to live

Vancouver is unlike any other North American city. Superficially it may resemble others with its high-rise downtown, busy streets, sprawling suburbs and over-dependence on the car, but the lifestyle of most Vancouverites makes the city an object of desire for many urban Canadians and those of other nationalities.

It's a young city and a city of the young – in spirit if not in age. Walk or cycle the seawall around Stanley Park and you'll see retired people as fit and vigorous as most people twenty years younger. Vancouverites live so much of life outdoors: sailing, canoeing, windsurfing, walking, cycling, swimming, tennis, golf, netball on the beach, kite flying in Vanier Park, eating alfresco. Even in winter, when it can rain for days on end, it's never too cold to get your skates, walking boots or tennis whites on.

Perhaps because of the outdoor nature of society, Vancouver is a casual city. It's not a place to make a living out of selling ties and briefcases, and many businessmen look as though it was dress-down Friday every day. While casual attire is complemented by a relaxed, easygoing manner, it's certainly not at the expense of common courtesy, and many visitors from other cities are struck by the warm politeness that seems a hallmark of social intercourse. Some say this is only skin-deep; a 2006 survey about the deeper friendliness of Canadian cities wasn't quite so complimentary about Vancouver.

**LEFT:** relaxing on the west side.
**RIGHT:** rollerblading in Stanley Park.

## Outward-looking

Right from the beginning, resource-rich Vancouver has been cosmopolitan, always looking overseas for trading opportunities and labour. Its first shipload of lumber was exported to Australia in 1864, and the first ship to dock at its new deep-water port in 1887 came from across the Pacific carrying tea and silk and 80 Chinese "visitors".

It hasn't all been plain sailing, and Vancouver has seen its racial tensions explode into violence, but since World War II the city has developed an ingrained liberalism that overlooks differences. It's clear that for all the vicissitudes of the past, the South Asians feel at home in Vancouver: many have bought bolt-holes in new high-rise apartment buildings around False Creek and invested heavily in property.

## Counter-culture

At the last count, 68 ethnicities were represented in the city. As the founding artistic director of the Vancouver Opera, Irving Guttman, was quoted as saying, "I get the impression that people of the West Coast, regardless of ethnic origins, are able freely to be themselves." This liberalism is reflected in the counter-culture of some of the arts, the fertile ground for co-operative housing schemes, a strong concern for the environment, and in

Vancouver having one of the largest per capita gay and lesbian communities in North America – a San Francisco-based firm that specialises in tourism trends in the US gay and lesbian community reported in 2006 that Vancouver was the most favoured city in a poll of 7,500 people. BC also has the largest population of First Nations in Canada, with 197 bands which play a significant role in the economic, social and artistic life of the province.

Even within Canada, Vancouver acts as a magnet. You're as likely to be served at a bar or restaurant by someone from Montreal, Nova Scotia or New Brunswick as a native of the city.

## The greening of a city

Concern for the environment, too, goes back a long way. Even though the decision of the city fathers to protect Stanley Park has been traduced as a ploy to protect their existing landholdings and rents, it shows an early awareness of the need for green space. About 10 percent of the city area is parkland, dominated by the large Pacific Spirit Regional Park on the University Endowment Lands and Stanley Park. Beyond the city centre are vast protected areas along the mountains of the north shore.

Much of Vancouver is easy on the eye, helped by over 130,000 street trees, though the typical North American feature of electricity poles and cables is an undeniable eyesore. The enormous asset of the sea is exploited by the creation of public space along more than half the city's waterfront, with the longest stretch of 23 km (14 miles) between Crab Park and Kitsilano Beach Park. New developments often incorporate imaginative landscaping and sometimes water features which help to soften the city and provide a pleasing sound amid the hubbub of traffic.

Recycling figures large in the city's policies, with colour-coded bins for household collections. In an effort to minimise their footprint, many of the leading hotels go beyond the self-serving offer to leave your towels for

ing", and it likes to think of itself as an environmentally responsible city. Certainly it has nurtured some notable environmentalists, including some of the founders of Greenpeace and Dr David T. Suzuki, the award-winning scientist and environmentalist who was a professor at UBC. But the success of the regeneration of the downtown area as a place where people would choose to live – in marked contrast to many other North American cities – came about in good measure because of an initial failure of the re-zoning of downtown south, from commercial to mixed use. It was the danger of this developing into a kind of developmental anarchy that provoked a reaction by

another day. A growing number of restaurants are trying to use as much local and organic produce as possible, with menus using ingredients that have been sourced from within a 100-mile radius, and some leading fish restaurants have signed up to Vancouver Aquarium's "Ocean Wise" kitemark to help diners make sustainable choices when choosing their fish.

## Revitalising the centre

It has been Vancouver's proud boast that it offers the world a "model for sustainable liv-

**LEFT:** in a Chinatown grocery; on Kitsilano Beach.
**ABOVE:** downtown Vancouver.

concerned residents. A forum organised by the Community Arts Council convinced the City of the need for the more structured and properly planned approach with which the city's former co-director of planning and mayor, Larry Beasley, became associated.

He is now adept at presenting Vancouver as a showcase for the virtues of high-density living from the Expo '86 site, halting and even reversing the flight from the centre to the suburbs. The philosophy of creating areas with high-density, mixed-income housing with plenty of parks and facilities for families has been a spectacular success, so much so that Beasley has been asked to advise other cities and has now left City Hall to spread the message around the world. It taps into all the requirements of sustainability and concern with climate change to minimise the footprint of housing and transport. Density is more efficient than sprawl, and two-thirds of journeys downtown forsake the car in favour of walking, cycling or public transport. Because there are more people on the streets, either walking or cycling, they are safer.

Vancouver may be a successful model for a new kind of urbanism in North America, but the high demand for housing has had some curious effects. Because of the high turnover of land and quick obsolescence of buildings,

### PROTECTING OLD BUILDINGS

About 59 pre-1896 buildings still stand. The Vancouver Heritage Register lists 2,147 buildings which have been evaluated for their architectural, historical or contextual value, but only about 17 percent are protected through designation. The oldest designated building still on its original site is Brynes Block (1887). Hastings Mill Store is older (1865) but was moved in 1930.

A study has identified 100 post-1940 landmark buildings and historic interiors, of which 24 have been added to the Register. Buildings not previously considered for the Register come to light every year through a public nomination process.

one sees jarring juxtapositions of a swanky new apartment building standing cheek-by-jowl with a run-down hotel whose status is obvious from its unsavoury substitutes for curtains. It has also led to a sharp decline in affordable rental accommodation, as a result of which there are noticeably more people living rough on the streets and begging (euphemistically called "panhandling" in Canada) than even five years ago.

The increase cannot be simply attributed to the preference of the homeless for the mild climate of Vancouver rather than the searing temperatures or bitter cold of the central and eastern provinces. Many social experts see a direct link between the growing homeless problem and recent provincial government changes, making it much more difficult to qualify for welfare; 75 percent of street homeless were ineligible for welfare in 2005 compared with 15 percent in 2001.

This may save money in one budget, but it loses BC millions of dollars in other ways: conference bookings have been cancelled as a result of organisers' perceptions.

## Sustainable transport

SkyTrain has been a success, a new line serving the airport and Richmond is now under construction, and the first new electric trolleybuses to replace the rather tired trolleybuses from 1982–3 entered service in late 2006. Nonetheless, a consequence of discarding in the 1950s the electric trams that carried 100,000 people a day in 1912 is that a quarter of the land area of Vancouver is now given over to roads or parking, and 300,000 cars a day enter and leave the downtown core.

The recent provincial government decision to expand road capacity, partly through the costly addition of extra lanes on the Port Mann Bridge, would seem to threaten Vancouver's credentials as a model of sustainable development. The city is opposed to this expansion of suburban road capacity, which will increase downtown congestion and pollution.

With homes for an additional 15,000 residents under construction around False Creek, a start needs to be made with a light rail system, beginning with the long-proposed extension of the heritage line from Granville Island through Waterfront to Stanley Park.

The Greenways Plan is benefiting walkers and cyclists by linking the city's parks and walkways with greenery, also helping to defray mounting pollution counts from vehicular traffic. Coupled with new bicycle pathways, seawall walkways and restrictive one-way systems, the plan is a key component of much downtown development.

## Economic growth

Vancouver's buoyant economy certainly has a lot to do with the city's sense of well-being. Job creation has kept up with the influx of new residents, and it sometimes looks from adverts in shop windows that every third business is

crew and their pantechnicons of equipment commandeering a section of street.

Pressure for jobs and growth in BC's traditional industries inevitably arouses controversy and sometimes conflict. Long-standing battles with lumber companies over the felling of old-growth forest are ongoing: there are currently plans for a resumption of logging in old-growth valleys on Vancouver Island and for oil and gas exploration in the wildlife-rich habitat of Lancaster Sound.

## Towards the Olympics

In much the same way as Expo '86 acted as a catalyst for regeneration, it is hoped that the

in need of staff. Overwhelmingly the growth has been in service-related industries – finance, insurance, retail, hi-tech and education – though mining and forestry remain cornerstones. Vancouver is Canada's largest port, generating employment in shipping and connecting transport by the two transcontinental railway lines. Tourism has boomed, not only in Vancouver itself but as a gateway to BC and a point of call for the cruise ships heading for Alaska. It's a popular city for conferences and for filmmakers – it's common to encounter a

**LEFT:** the old and the new.
**ABOVE:** on location in Gastown; the heritage line.

Winter Olympics in 2010 will do the same for the last parts of False Creek to be redeveloped. Part of the area will be the athletes' village, and significant investment is being made at Hastings Park and other venues around the city.

Before the event, imaginative action will have to be taken to tackle the drug problem that continues to afflict the east side of the downtown area. Though most visitors will be oblivious to the unpleasant scenes of back-street life in that quarter, the focus of the world's media will be on a city that has a commanding position in the league of "most desirable places to live", and the tendencies of the media are well known. ❑

# Gay Vancouver

In recent years Vancouver has emerged as an international tourist destination for gay and lesbian travellers, particularly Americans who appreciate the city's relaxed, live-and-let-live attitude and highly visible gay presence. The gay community is widely recognised as playing a pivotal role in the city's quality of life and growing cosmopolitanism, and is strongly represented at both the municipal and provincial levels.

That said, Vancouver does not offer the range of exciting nightlife found in Canada's

establishments continue north along Denman Street, which intersects with Davie by the beach at English Bay.

Among the favourite hangouts in this neighbourhood are:

**1181** (1181 Davie Street, tel: 604 687 3991), a slick, trendy gay cocktail lounge that appeals to an upmarket crowd.

**Delilah's** (1789 Comox Street at Denman, tel: 604 687 3424; www.delilahs.ca), with its fabulous postmodern rococo decor, is a local tradition, and with good reason. The upscale restaurant regularly receives rave reviews for its fabulous food, famous martinis and friendly staff.

bigger gay travel destinations, Montreal and Toronto. It is a city that attracts couples and friends travelling together, looking for a relaxing getaway and plenty of outdoor activities, more than singles in search of nightlife.

## Gay neighbourhoods

The downtown **West End** neighbourhood is home to the city's gay village. Gay bars, restaurants and shops stretch west of Burrard Street along Davie Street. Hot pink bus shelters and litter bins and streetlamps festooned with rainbow flags and banners by GLBT (Gay, Lesbian, Bisexual, Transgender) artists line several blocks. A number of gay

**The Fountainhead Pub** (1025 Davie Street), where the reasonably priced drinks and pub food, jovial staff, smoking patio and relaxed ambience attract a diverse, all-ages crowd of men and women.

**Melriches Café** (1244 Davie Street, tel: 604 689 5282) is a favourite hangout with the java and laptop crowd, and a good place to strike up conversations with strangers. Wireless internet connection is pay-per-use by credit card. **Delaney's Coffee House** (1105 Denman St, tel: 604 662 3344) is the same deal, but without wireless.

**Oasis** (1240 Thurlow Street at Davie, tel: 604 685 1724, www.oasisvancouver.com)

is a casually sophisticated, New York-style gay piano lounge featuring live entertainment most nights, a tasty menu, a huge martini list and a pleasant smoking patio. **Pumpjack** (1167 Davie Street, tel: 604 685 3417 www.pumpjackpub.com), a down-to-earth bar, attracts an older, mainly male denim-and-leather crowd.

A few kilometres from downtown, bohemian and multicultural **Commercial Drive** on the city's east side stretches north of Broadway to Hastings Street. It is the main artery of a neighbourhood that is home to a large lesbian community. The centre of Vancouver's Italian community as well, "The Drive" is a favourite hang-out for artists and writers, and is lined with funky shops, cafés and restaurants. The American magazine UTNE Reader lists The Drive as one of North America's "hippest neighbourhoods".

Located across English Bay from the West End, and anchored by 4th Avenue, the hilly, beachside **Kitsilano** neighbourhood was home to a growing counter-culture of gays and lesbians during the burgeoning years of Gay Liberation in the late 1960s and early '70s. Kitsilano was then Vancouver's version of San Francisco's Haight Ashbury, and its ambience was captured in the 1977 novel *The Young in One Another's Arms* by Jane Rule. Today, most of the orginal wood-frame Edwardian houses have been renovated or razed, replaced by million-dollar-plus homes and luxury condos. Kitsilano remains a gay-friendly neighbourhood and home to a large number of affluent gay and lesbian couples.

## Western Canada's largest Pride parade

Vancouver holds an impressive Pride parade in early August. Drawing crowds of 300,000, it is the city's largest annual event. The parade caps a week of related celebrations including Homopalooza, a day-long festival of gay entertainers in an outdoor beer garden at the Plaza of Nations on False Creek's inner city shoreline (tel: 604 687 0955; www.vancouverpride.ca).

---

**LEFT:** walking the dog in the West End.
**ABOVE:** Gay Pride parade through Davie Street.

## Gay weddings

Canada is one of a handful of countries where same-sex couples may legally marry, and Vancouver has become a popular wedding and honeymoon location for a growing number of gay people. To date more gay Americans have been married in Vancouver than gay Canadians. Same-sex wedding planners **Two Dears and a Queer** (tel: 604 306 1340; www.twodearsandaqueer.com) and **Belles and Balls Extraordinary Weddings & Events** (toll free: 1 888 540 7455; www.bellesandballs.com) can plan and arrange every detail in advance for visitors wishing to marry here.

## Information sources

**Xtra West** (www.xtra.ca)
*Xtra West* is Vancouver's bi-weekly gay and lesbian newspaper, and is distributed for free in establishments and newspaper boxes across the city centre.
**Gayvancouver.net** (www.gayvancouver.net)
Comprehensive information on all aspects of gay life in Vancouver.
**Gayvan.com** (www.gayvan.com)
A site especially for gay and lesbian travellers to Vancouver.
*For gay and lesbian nightlife, accommodation and other listings, see the Travel Tips section at the back of the book.* ❑

# THE PERFORMING ARTS

**Vancouver's multicultural heritage has produced a thriving arts scene that's dynamic, diverse and unafraid to experiment. The theatre and dance scenes are particularly active, and there are many great venues for live music. Summer in the city is celebrated with a series of lively festivals**

**V**ancouver exhibited a strong interest in culture and live entertainment at a very young age. Its first theatre, Blair's Hall, was built in the year of the city's incorporation, 1886. This was followed by the Imperial Opera House, and then the de luxe Vancouver Opera House in 1891. The city's population was 8,000 and the theatre was designed to seat 2,000. It was filled to the rafters when the premiere performance of Wagner's *Lohengrin* was given and was again packed when Sarah Bernhardt performed.

A theatre district sprang up in Gastown. The heart of Vancouver from the late 19th century to the early 1900s, this area saw the construction of numerous vaudeville theatres, owned and operated by theatrical entrepreneur Alexander "something for everyone" Pantages. Among them was the Empress Theatre, where Anna Pavlova performed in 1910. Vancouver's oldest surviving theatre is the Pantages on East Hastings Street. A smaller version of the Empress, it is at long last being refurbished.

### Showing an ankle

As Vancouver was on the touring minstrel-show circuit, many variety acts came to town, with great vaudeville names like Charlie Chaplin, Stan Laurel and English Music Hall Queen Marie Lloyd creating quite a stir.

Lloyd, who was known for her somewhat risqué humour, was asked to discontinue performing one of her more colourful numbers, "The Ankle Watch", during which she lifted her skirts to reveal her ankle. The outraged city's licence inspector declared: "It might go all right in London but Vancouver will not stand for it."

### Principal venues

Vancouver's love of the arts has grown with the city. Today's audiences can enjoy performances in many languages, with many different aesthetics and from a wide variety of performing traditions and styles. Commercial Drive, South Granville, Old Strathcona/Gastown and Granville Island are hubs of activity, with galleries, theatres, clubs and cafés. Even the suburban areas of Greater Vancouver have numerous performing and visual arts centres.

The city's largest performance venues are

concentrated in downtown Vancouver: the opulent Orpheum Theatre, home to the Vancouver Symphony Orchestra, and the Commodore Ballroom, with one of the best dance floors in the city. The Centre for the Performing Arts, designed by Moshe Safdie as a companion piece to the Public Library, was originally used for Broadway musicals, but in recent years has become known for producing large-scale musicals based on Asian stories and themes.

Across the street from the library, the Queen Elizabeth Theatre and Playhouse host touring musical theatre productions as well as serving as performance venues for the Vancouver Opera, Ballet BC and the Playhouse

did new Roundhouse Community Centre. Among its many facilities is a performance centre used for theatre and dance, and an exhibition hall. Housed in a 100-year-old fire station in the Old Strathcona/Gastown area, the Firehall Arts Centre produces and presents dance, theatre and interdisciplinary work by some of the city's most exciting new artists.

Granville Island has a number of performance spaces used by many of the city's independent theatre and dance companies, including Performance Works, Festival House and the Waterfront Theatre, as well as outdoor stages where in the summer months dance, theatre and music groups entertain.

Theatre Company. Right next door, General Motors Place sports arena serves as a venue for big-name acts like The Rolling Stones, Van Morrison and The Dixie Chicks.

The Vancouver East Cultural Centre, locally referred to as the "Cultch", is one of a number of small but funky cultural venues dotted around the city. In a converted church with great acoustics, it offers an eclectic programme of contemporary dance, theatre and music from around the world. Set in a converted railway depot in Yaletown is the splendid

**LEFT:** Firehall Arts Centre production of *Urinetown the Musical.* **ABOVE:** outside the Queen Elizabeth Theatre.

The summer months see outdoor performances in many of the city's parks, offering audiences the opportunity to enjoy Vancouver's beautiful surroundings to the sound of music.

## Music

Vancouver's live music scene ranges from classical concerts by the Vancouver Symphony Orchestra to a wide range of rock, pop, folk, jazz and blues bands who perform at festivals, pubs and clubs like the Railway, the Commodore Ball Room, the Yale and Rossini's. Popular artists such as Bryan Adams, Diana Krall, Nelly Furtado and Sarah McLachlan all built their careers in and around Vancouver. For those who like their music loud, live and with an edge, Vancouver's underground music scene is alive and kicking (see www.livemusicvancouver.com for band listings).

The beautiful Chan Centre, in the grounds of the University of British Columbia, has the best acoustics in the city and stages primarily classical and choral music. Vancouver Opera provides a challenging mix of traditional and contemporary interpretations of classics such as their recent aboriginally-themed production of *The Magic Flute*. Look out also for performances by Vancouver-based Japanese drummers Uzume Taiko and SWARM, the extreme percussion orchestra.

## Comedy

Vancouver's comedy scene is going from strength to strength, and there are numerous venues dedicated to stand-up and improv. Comedy clubs such as LaffLines, Yuk Yuks and Vancouver Theatresports League launched the careers of Ryan Stiles (*The Drew Carey Show*, *Whose Line Is It Anyway?*), Colin Mochrie (*This Hour has 22 Minutes*) and Brent Butt (*Corner Gas*).

## Theatre

With more than 60 professional theatre companies, Vancouver's theatre scene is very active. The largest of these, the Arts Club

## FESTIVALS

Vancouver has lively festivals throughout the year, especially in summer. Large-scale events like the Vancouver Jazz Festival, Festival Vancouver, the International Writers and Readers Festival, the Vancouver Fringe Festival, the Vancouver Folk Festival and the Vancouver Film Festival keep city parks and venues full during the summer and fall. Push, Chutzpah and Dancing on the Edge illustrate Vancouver's interest in the alternative. The Vancouver International Children's Festival brings together the best in arts performances for young audiences. The Powell Street Festival celebrates the Japanese Canadian contribution to Vancouver, while the annual Dragon Boat

Festival incorporates cultural activities with dragon-boat racing. Public Dreams Society creates two signature events: Illuminaires, with fire jugglers, stilt walkers and music on the shores of Trout Lake park during the summer solstice, and Parade of Lost Souls at Hallowe'en.

The Chinese New Year's celebration and parade is the second-largest in North America, while the annual Fireworks Festival draws over 200,000 viewers to the beaches of English Bay and Kitsilano to watch pyrotechnic competitors test their skills against the backdrop of the ocean and North Shore Mountains.

● *For a calendar of festivals and events, see page 248.*

Theatre, operates year-round producing a mix of contemporary and classic Canadian, British and American plays along with Broadway musicals at its flagship theatre, the Stanley, and at the Granville Island Stage. The Vancouver Playhouse, the oldest professional theatre company in the city, performs at the Queen Elizabeth Theatre complex in a six-month season.

Smaller companies such as the Firehall Arts Centre theatre company have led the way in producing theatre that reflects the city's pluralism, bringing many First Nations and culturally diverse voices to the stage.

Vancouver is recognised for its physical theatre work, and Axis Theatre's *The No. 14* has been touring internationally since its conception in the early 1990s. Other international hits by Vancouver playwrights include *Billy Bishop Goes to War*, *The Overcoat*, *Vigil* and *Mum's The Word*.

Each summer Vanier Park is taken over by Bard on the Beach, a very successful festival of Shakespearean work that is performed nightly in tents with the cityscape as its backdrop. Across the water in Stanley Park, Boca del Lupo presents two weeks of storytelling amid the Douglas fir and greenery. Further east in the inner city, Leaky Heaven Circus puts together a lively carnival, complete with trapeze artists, clowns and performing dogs.

## Dance

Vancouver's flourishing contemporary dance scene grew out of the work of choreographers Anna Wyman, Judith Marcuse and Paula Ross. The 1980s saw a huge period of growth with the establishment of the EDAM (Experimental Dance and Music), Mascall Dance and Kokoro companies.

Holy Body Tattoo, formed in the early 1990s, continues to create new works that have been performed all over Asia, Europe and the United States. Vancouver choreographer Crystal Pite's new company, Kidd Pivot, is kicking up a storm internationally, while graduates of the Simon Fraser University contemporary dance programme flow into the milieu, mixing contact improvisation, West Coast, Asian and modern aesthetics to create unique dance works.

Under the artistic direction of John Alleyne, Ballet BC has broken new ground in creating original contemporary ballets while also performing in repertoire works of William Forsythe, Twyla Tharpe and James Kadelka.

Places to catch dance include the Scotiabank Dance Centre, the Vancouver East Cultural Centre, the Firehall Arts Centre and the Queen Elizabeth Theatre. Each July, the annual Dancing on the Edge Festival of Contemporary Dance brings together choreographers and dance companies from across Canada and beyond for ten energetic days of dance. ❑

### LISTINGS AND TICKETS

The most useful guide for just about everything is the free weekly publication, the *Georgia Straight*. For live music listings, www.livemusicvancouver.com is also a good source. Advance tickets for major events and performances can be bought through Ticket Master (tel: 604 280 3311; www.ticketmaster.ca) or on the same day from the Tickets Tonight booth in the tourist information centre near Canada Place (Plaza level, 200, Burrard Street; tel: 604 231 7535; www.ticketstonight.ca).

● *For further information and useful websites, see the Activities section, pages 246–9.*

**LEFT:** mainstream jazz joint, Rossini's.
**RIGHT:** dancing in the street during a Sikh festival.

# THE GREAT OUTDOORS

With mountains, beaches, rivers, lakes and ocean all on their doorstep, it's no surprise Vancouverites are passionate about their outdoor pursuits. The possibilities for recreation and adventure are endless

The south coast of British Columbia is a kaleidoscope of eye-popping geography, with the snow-capped Coast Mountain Range, powerful Fraser river, freshwater lakes and towering forests, edged by the sparkling Pacific. Its setting in the midst of all this majestic nature is the single best reason for visiting Vancouver – that and the limitless opportunities for outdoor recreation.

For outdoor enthusiasts, the crowning glory is the weather. The fact that you can ski and sail on the same day is something Vancouverites rub in the noses of less climatically blessed Canadians. Average temperatures in the area are among the highest in Canada. A temperate coastal climate brings a winter requiring little more than a warm jacket. Cold enough, however, to deposit ski-worthy snow on the local North Shore peaks.

## Mixing pleasures

Spring comes early and softly, with a February average temperature of 7°C (44°F). Summer follows quickly, stretching the sunny weather to the end of October, with longer days that are perfect for outdoor pursuits. Vancouverites think nothing of making a beeline from their hiking, biking or golf activity to attend a symphony concert at the Orpheum Theatre, a *grande dame* among the city's entertainment venues. Jeans and fleece jackets are at home beside gowns and tuxes.

Whether you're in the mood for a leisurely sunset stroll along one of the city's eleven beaches or an adrenalin-pumping challenge such as zip-trekking, Vancouver and its environs offer plenty of opportunities for activity. From the gentle to the extreme, the choices are endless: cycling along Vancouver's extensive city-wide bike routes, in-line skating along English Bay, kayaking off Jericho Beach or ocean swimming at Kitsilano Beach.

Further afield, you can go hiking in Mount Seymour Provincial Park, salmon fishing in Horseshoe Bay, mountain biking in Whistler, river rafting on the mighty Thompson river or smaller but equally exciting Chilliwack river. The area also has dozens of golf courses.

**LEFT:** climbing the Grand Wall, Squamish.
**RIGHT:** sailing in the Strait of Georgia.

## Protected parkland

Parks come small, medium and large, and are privately run or under the supervision of the provincial or federal authorities. You don't have to venture far to immerse yourself in nature. In the heart of the city, Stanley Park's marked inner trails lead through a dense forest of conifers interspersed with hardwood species such as maple, birch and alder, to Beaver Lake, where sightings of racoon, rabbit and coyote are possible. Huge Pacific Spirit Regional Park on the University of British Columbia campus offers more rugged but well-marked trails through diverse terrain, with centuries-old western red cedar, Douglas fir, Sitka spruce and western hemlock in an unbroken canopy.

On the North Shore, Lighthouse Park in West Vancouver leads through giant, original stands of Douglas fir with scatterings of red-barked arbutus trees, a tree unique to British Columbia. In North Vancouver, Lynn Canyon Park is a wilderness close to civilisation, with an informative ecology centre and a suspension bridge that swings between the giant firs. It's an equally fascinating alternative to the neighbouring and often crowded Capilano Suspension Bridge – and what's more, it's free.

Outside the city, there are many areas of protected wilderness to explore – some of these

---

### WINTER SPORTS

The peaks of Grouse Mountain, Mount Seymour and Cypress Bowl are lined up on the North Shore across Burrard Inlet. They are all well equipped for winter sports and easily accessible, and each has its own specialities.

**Grouse**, with 22 runs for skiers and boarders, is easy to reach by car or bus across the Lions Gate Bridge. It offers ski and boarding lessons and stupendous views from the summit. Sleigh rides and ice skating are alternative attractions.

**Cypress** is a magnet for cross-country skiers, with the largest vertical downhill drop of the three peaks. It is the future home of the 2010 Olympic and Paralympic Winter Games' snowboarding and freestyle skiing events. For beginners, the ski lessons, snowshoe trails and snow-tubing thrills of Mount Seymour are a great draw.

Canada's number one ski resort, **Whistler**, is 120 km (75 miles) away, and its ski season is a long one, running from the United States' Thanksgiving weekend in November to the end of April and beyond.

Other winter sports practised in and around Vancouver include snowboarding, ice-skating, skiing, tubing and snowshoeing. In Whistler, add dog-sledding, snowmobiling, snowcat tours and sleigh rides to the list *(for more information, see pages 178–9)*.

provincial parks offer the bare minimum in the way of amenities, others have fully equipped campgrounds which can accommodate everything from tents to huge recreational vehicles.

Just beyond Vancouver's urban boundaries is the Cypress Provincial Park, a 3,000-hectare (7,500-acre) protected area with many well-marked trails which make it a popular spot for daytrippers from the city. The further north you go, the more rugged the terrain in this park gets.

Just off Highway 99, between Squamish and Whistler, the Garibaldi Provincial Park has been a favourite since it was established in 1920. An area of 195,000 hectares (480,000 network of clearly signed trails, with numerous campgrounds and recreation sites to welcome visitors. It is also popular with mountaineers and cross-country skiers, and Whistler and Blackcomb Ski Mountains are not far away.

From small parks with swimming lakes such as Alice Lake Provincial Park near Squamish to Golden Ears Provincial Park, at 55,590 hectares (138,250 acres), one of the largest parks in BC, activities in all these well-cared-for environs include exceptional (and inexpensive) camping, fishing, swimming, hiking, birdwatching, canoeing, kayaking, picknicking and other pursuits. For a full list

acres), it is a stunning wilderness of mountains, glaciers, forests, lakes and rivers. It also includes the Garibaldi Volcanic Belt, part of the Pacific Ring of Fire. The last eruption, more than 11,000 years ago, left some remarkable landmarks, such as the Barrier, a 300-metre-high (980-ft) cliff created by a meeting of molten rock and glacier ice. Cinder Cone also resulted from volcanic fires, this time beneath glacial ice. The effect acted like a jelly mould, leaving the amazingly flat-topped, steep-sided cone. The park has an extensive

of provincial parks in the Vancouver area, their facilities and how to reach them, visit www.bcadventure.com.

## Sea kayaking and whitewater rafting

Sea kayaking is one of the most ancient forms of transport in these parts. Centuries ago, First Nations of the Pacific Northwest paddled the ocean in impressive dug-out canoes made of red cedar. Sitting low on the water, kayaks offer the chance to see seals and water birds up close. It is not difficult to master the manoeuvring of these stable craft. The best place to learn is the more urban setting of False Creek.

**LEFT:** cyclists on the trans-Canada trail at Penticton.
**ABOVE:** fly-fishing at dawn.

The Ecomarine Kayak Centre (tel: 604 689 7520; www.ecomarine.com) operates rental outlets and kayaking lessons on Granville Island and at Jericho Beach. On the North Shore, flanked by mountains, the finger-shaped fjord known as Indian Arm is an idyllic setting for kayaking. At the top of the inlet and just a 30-minute bus ride from downtown, Deep Cove offers both kayak and canoe rentals and courses (tel: 604 929 2268; www.deepcovekayak.com).

Whitewater river rafting is offered at various locations on the Fraser, Nahatlatch, Thompson, Green, Elaho, Birkenhead and Lillooet rivers. Strict safety regulations apply, which is reassuring in the face of such notorious rapids as the Chilliwack river's Darth Vader, Gun Barrel and Pinball *(see page 253 for operators)*.

## Fishing

Ten rivers around Whistler guarantee some of the best fishing in Canada. A non-tidal angling licence is required and can be purchased from local hardware stores or gas stations. The best fishing months are March to May for Dolly Varden, rainbow trout, steelhead, Chinook and cutthroat trout, but there is good angling year-round. The Ashlu, Mamquam, Elaho, Cheakamus, Green, Lillooet, Birkenhead, Stawamus, and Squamish are all attractive fishing rivers.

## WHALE-WATCHING

The best place to embark on a whale-watching expedition is from Tofino on the west coast of Victoria Island. Every year in March and April thousands of grey whales swim past en route from the calving lagoons of Baja California to Alaska, returning south from October to December. Sightings of these and other whales including orca (also known as killer whales) are common in this area.

Tours in the Vancouver area leave from various bases in the main harbour and from Steveston village in Richmond, about a half-hour bus ride south of downtown. While not guaranteed, sightings of some combination of orca, seals and Dall's porpoises are likely.

Unfortunately, the famed Cheakamus river was contaminated by a railway accident several years ago. Environmentalists are working hard to return this once-pristine river to its original condition.

Ocean fishing is largely for Chinook along Howe Sound. Horseshoe Bay is one of the most popular areas on the coast for salmon fishing.

For a more luxurious experience, you can charter private and self-skippered boats for fishing trips, with rental locations from English Bay to Horseshoe Bay. Sewell's Marina is a BC institution (tel: 604 921 3474; www.sewells-marina.com). In 1931, ex-Londoner Dan Sewell arrived in Horseshoe Bay and purchased the only waterfront property with a private beach. His fishing lodge soon became popular with local and visiting entertainers, Bing Crosby among them. The marina continues as a family-run business and supplies everything from bait to boats.

## Swimming

With nearly a dozen beaches on their doorstep, sunbathing, ocean swimming and people-watching are favourite pastimes among locals. After a vigorous hike, bike or in-line skate around the 10-km (7-mile) Stanley Park seawall, go for a dip in English Bay or in the outdoor pool at Second Beach.

On the North Shore, Ambleside Beach in West Vancouver is a more refined experience, where you will share the water with some of the richest folk in the Lower Mainland. *For more on Vancouver's beaches see pages 136–7.*

## Diving and windsurfing

Those lucky enough to be able to dive can enjoy more outstanding natural beauty beneath the ocean's surface. The West Coast has some 200 species of marine life, and divers can choose from several convenient locations. Cates Park in Deep Cove, Whytecliff Park near Horseshoe Bay and Porteau Cove Marine Park on Howe Sound are all rec-

It's an easy bus ride from downtown to Kitsilano Beach on the opposite shore of English Bay. It is a hedonistic setting, complete with adjacent, 137-metre (450-ft) Kitsilano Pool overlooking the sandy beach. Following the shoreline west is a series of attractive beaches, including Jericho Beach and Spanish Banks (both on the bus route).

Further west below the cliffs of the University of British Columbia is Wreck Beach, Vancouver's notorious nude beach (where ogling clothed visitors are most unwelcome).

**LEFT:** diving off Vancouver Island.
**ABOVE:** the view from Grouse Mountain.

ommended sites. Further afield, Vancouver Island also offers some great diving. In many of these sites underwater playgrounds have been lovingly created with artificial reefs that have formed on specially sunken ships (log on to www.artificialreef.bc.ca for details). Be warned that the water in these parts is cold and currents can be strong.

Back above water, windsurfing is also popular. Jericho Beach and English Bay are good for the less experienced, and there are opportunities here to rent windsurfs and wetsuits and take lessons *(see page 253)*. The real pros head for the town of Squamish, 64 km (40 miles) north of Vancouver, which offers some of the world's best windsurfing conditions. Cold air funnels down the Cheakamus and Squamish valleys over Howe Sound, averaging 40 knots on the water with gusts as powerful as 70 knots. The nickname for the area, Malibu on the Sound, is apt. The launch site is managed by the Squamish Windsurfing Society (tel: 604 926 9463) which charges a daily fee.

### Birdwatching

Along the Fraser river, a stroll on a level dyke system begins in Steveston, a village now incorporated into the City of Richmond. Keen birdwatchers should head for the walkways of the Fraser river estuary, with 300 hectares

For those up to a challenge, the 30-km (18-mile) Howe Sound Crest Trail is the way to go. Tackling the Grouse Grind, a 2.9-km (1.8-mile) hike almost straight up the gnarly face of Grouse Mountain, is a badge of courage for many Vancouverites, but don't attempt the Grind unless you are fit and prepared.

Further afield, the Highway 99 corridor from Vancouver to Whistler passes through the logging town of Squamish, "the outdoor recreation capital of Canada". The small-town atmosphere of Squamish is a leisurely alternative to the fast pace of Whistler, and preferred by some. Aside from being the country's windsurfing capital, and offering

(850 acres) of protected wetland. More than 200 species of birds frequent the area, including great blue herons, eagles, hawks, Canada geese, ducks, swans and owls.

### Mountain trekking and climbing

At night, the lights of the three local slopes of Grouse Mountain, Cypress Bowl, and Mount Seymour form a twinkling backdrop to the city. Each peak is only 30 minutes away by car. In winter they are transformed into playgrounds for a wide variety of snow sports *(see above)*. In summer you can hike on these same three peaks that are full of trails, some of which are wheelchair- and stroller-accessible.

**GOLF**

Golf's popularity does not abate, and the natural setting of Vancouver's courses, with a backdrop of mountains, sky and water, is hard to beat.

Closest to downtown are the University Golf Club, Langara and Fraserview courses, which are open to non-members. There are also pitch-and-putt courses at Stanley Park and Queen Elizabeth Park.

En route to Whistler, nestling on the mountainside overlooking Howe Sound, the Furry Creek course is the most scenic. In Whistler itself, three 18-hole courses are joined by an additional course in Pemberton to the north *(see page 252)*.

great hiking, mountain biking, fishing and kayaking, Squamish is also one of Canada's top rock-climbing destinations, thanks to the granite monolith known as the Stawamus Chief. Climbers from around the world flock here to tackle one of the 1,000 routes along the 652-metre (2,139-ft) face of one of the world's largest free-standing rocks.

## Adrenalin sports

New adrenalin sports appear with regularity on the West Coast. The latest is surf skiing, a more extreme version of kayaking. The sport began with the invention of special sleek kayaks used by lifeguards to break through

first heli-ski tours in 1965. The audacious sport is now an international phenomenon. Established operators use Bell 212 twin-engine helicopters with skiing from 1,371 to 1,838 metres (4,500 to 6,000 vertical ft).

Soaring and skydiving are spring-to-early-autumn activities. Soaring operates in the Fraser Valley from Hope Airport, which has the longest turf airfield in Canada, and from the Pemberton Soaring Centre.

Skydivers leave from the Pitt Meadows Airport to float above spacious meadows with a view of Vancouver Island and towering white-capped peak of Mount Baker in Washington State to the south. Paragliding is closer to

surf. Manoeuvering the delicately balanced vessels straight into the waves is part of the rush. The vessels are available for hire from the Deep Cove Canoe and Kayak Centre *(see page 48)*.

Heli-skiing, a once-in-a-lifetime dream experience for many advanced skiers, was invented by a British Columbian. Hans Gmoser hailed from Brunau, Austria, arriving in BC in the early 1950s. A daring mountain climber, Gmoser founded the Association of Canadian Mountain Guides in 1963, and introduced the

home at Grouse Mountain, where two-person para-glides catch the high currents.

Zip-trekking and bungee jumping are Whistler-area sports that make the most of the forest settings. Zip-trekking in Whistler is a newer activity. Participants wear custom harnesses to launch themselves along a cable from a tree top deck on Blackcomb Mountain. After soaring 610 metres (2,000 ft), they land on Whistler Mountain. Passing below spectacularly at a speed of 80km/h (50 mph) are the steep Whistler Valley and the whitewaters of Fitzsimmons Creek.

Bungee jumping is offered above the Cheakamus river near Whistler.  ❑

**LEFT:** paraglider taking off from Grouse Mountain.
**ABOVE:** zip-trekking in Whistler.

# FLORA AND FAUNA

Remarkably close to the skyscrapers and busy boulevards of
the city is a vast wilderness of coastal rainforest, Alpine
meadows and glacial mountains. Beneath towering
canopies of red cedars and Douglas firs, black
bears, coyotes and cougars roam

Forests cover almost two-thirds of the
province of British Columbia, and what a
vast area of trees and mountains that is –
and more than 13 million hectares (about 32
million acres) of this is protected. Much of the
Coast Forest Region, which runs from just south
of Vancouver up to the Alaska panhandle, is
uninhabited wilderness. In fact, most of BC's
four million residents are concentrated in and
around the cities of Vancouver and Victoria, in
the province's southwestern corner. Barren
mountain peaks, vast forests, mighty rivers and
fertile valleys cover just about all the rest.

British Columbia has been dubbed the "Wet
Coast". Annual precipitation in the Coast
Mountains averages 2 metres (6½ ft), as storm
winds filled with moisture roll in from the
Pacific, hit the mountains, rise, cool and con-
dense into rain or snow. The resulting rainforests are lush nurseries for Douglas fir,
western hemlock, western red cedar and Sitka
spruce. Arbutus trees, the only broadleafed
evergreen trees in Canada, grow on stony
ridges along the water's edge. The red-brown,
papery peeling bark of the arbutus makes it one
of the easiest coastal trees to identify.

## Gold rushes

Lighthouse Park in West Vancouver is one of
the best places to encounter a variety of these
magnificent coastal trees. The park's old-
growth forest includes giant Douglas firs,
western red cedar, contorted shore pines, hem-

locks and arbutus (*for more about provincial
parks, see page 46*).

Two major gold rushes in the mid-19th century brought thousands of transients to British
Columbia. But it was the primeval forests of
the coast that drew settlers, who honed their
axes and ran their steam donkeys to pull the
massive old-growth forest logs to the ocean
for transport to all corners of the globe.

Vancouver's founders recognised the area's
unique natural beauty even as they exploited its
bountiful forests. On 13 June 1886, the fledgling city burnt down in what is known as the
"Great Fire". Given the rare opportunity to start
over, land surveyor and alderman Lauchlan

**LEFT:** arbutus tree.
**RIGHT:** grey whale tail, seen off the Gulf Islands.

Alexander Hamilton suggested the creation of a large park on the outskirts of the city. Three years later Stanley Park was a reality, located on a peninsula jutting out into Burrard Inlet. Until then, Musqueam and Squamish aboriginal people had lived in the park in Khwaykhway, one of their villages. Park development effectively put an end to their habitation. The park had already been logged, but a few old-growth trees remained. The Hollow Tree, a huge western red cedar tree trunk with a girth of 18 metres (60 ft), is a remnant of its massive rain-forest ancestors. Other old-growth trees, including Douglas firs, hug Beaver Lake in the interior of the 405-hectare (1,000-acre) enclave.

## Garden city

It's ironic that two of Vancouver's most popular public gardens were built with donations from the powerful lumber barons. Queen Elizabeth Park's Bloedel Floral Conservatory was financed by lumber magnate Prentice Bloedel, who had a passion for gardening. The Van-Dusen Botanical Garden was funded by Whitford Julian VanDusen, another lumber tycoon and philanthropist.

Queen Elizabeth Park, built on Little Mountain, the highest point in Vancouver at 167 metres (505 ft) above sea level, offers splendid panoramic views. The basalt hill began life as a quarry for Vancouver's growing road system.

### THE MIGHTY CEDAR

The cedar, both western red and yellow varieties, remains the wood of choice for coastal First Nations people. This giant tree was traditionally used to build huge longhouses for communal families. It was shaped into canoes for whale hunting, travelling and raiding. Everyday objects such as storage boxes were made from cedar, then painted with curved forms to become objects of beauty and refinement. Cedar was also the material of choice for totem poles and masks. Some carved poles tell family history, others commemorate respected individuals. A collection of old and new poles is proudly displayed at Stanley Park's Brockton Oval.

In 1929, the Vancouver Park Board began work on the abandoned 52-hectare (130-acre) site. Over the years, it has been transformed into a lovely sloping park dotted with examples of every native Canadian tree and many international ones. Trails weave through the old quarries past waterfalls and grottoes filled with blooms. At the top of the hill stands the Bloedel Floral Conservatory, opened in 1969. Inside the climate-controlled triodetic glass dome are over 500 varieties of exotic plants and tropical flowers and more than 100 free-flying birds.

The VanDusen Botanical Garden is located on a former golf course built over an early city water reservoir. After the golf course closed in the 1960s and the reservoir was abandoned and sealed in the 1970s, the site was transformed into a world-renowned botanical garden. Its 22 hectares (5 acres) are planted with more than 7,500 varieties of flowers, shrubs and trees. Spring's blossoming trees and flowers including camellias, rhododendrons, magnolias, Pacific dogwood and glorious Japanese cherries (more than 19,000 such trees have been planted throughout the city). Seasonal displays continue through to winter's bursts of shiny green holly dotted with red berries.

Further afield but easily accessible via the limited-stop No. 99 city bus, the University of British Columbia (UBC) on Point Grey com-

turesque Rose Garden features some 300 varieties. Near by is the Nitobe Memorial Garden, designed by outstanding Japanese landscape architect Kannosouke Mori to feature native trees and shrubs. Another prominent area is the UBC Botanical Garden and Centre for Plant Research. This 28-hectare (70-acre) site is home to rare and unusual plants and includes a stunning rhododendron grove.

## The Fraser river

The great Fraser river is the backbone of British Columbia. Originating in Mount Robson Provincial Park, the river meets the sea after a journey of 1,375 km (854 miles) at its estuary

prises a wealth of parks and gardens. British Columbia's oldest university, established in 1915, takes pride in having one of the most beautiful campuses in Canada. The dense forests of UBC's Pacific Spirit Regional Park are criss-crossed with trails that transport you back to a time when forests dominated the West Coast. The park even includes a bog with its own world of wetland wonders such as frogs and bog cranberries.

Many gardens dot the UBC landscape. Overlooking the Pacific Ocean, the pic-

**LEFT:** old-growth forest, Vancouver Island.
**ABOVE:** exotic flora inside the Bloedel Conservatory.

### BEARS AND COYOTES

Over time, urban settlement has forced the black bear population northwards. They inhabit the North Shore's higher elevations, appearing in the yards of those who choose to dwell at these heights in palatial homes. They also appear in numbers on the slopes of Whistler Mountain every summer. Coyotes range on both sides of Burrard Inlet, with the creatures spotted in Stanley Park and even the much-populated West End.

Misguided folk think it kind to leave food out for these wild animals, but it is an offence under the Wildlife Act for a person to feed bears, cougars, coyotes or wolves.

in Vancouver, where it merges with the Pacific Ocean among vast wetlands. The Fraser is the largest salmon river in the world, notable for its sockeye runs. In the late 19th century, Steveston, the town at the mouth of the river, was awash with thriving salmon canneries. Salmon was so plentiful that it was unimaginable that they would ever disappear. Yet they almost did. Coastal salmon are now struggling to recover from the past's greedy harvesting.

Nevertheless, the Fraser's estuary and delta are marvellous resources that continue to nourish the countless animals and plants thriving where fresh water meets salt water. Trails along the river in Vancouver, Richmond and elsewhere provide opportunities to see beaver, muskrat, river otter, deer, black bear, mink, red fox, skunk, coyote, racoon, opossum and squirrels. More than 1 million migratory birds stop over here along the Pacific flyway, resulting in the largest concentration of wintering waterfowl and shorebirds in Canada. Geese, ducks, shore birds and songbirds nest in the tidal flats, marshes and forests along the river banks. Overhead, bald eagles, marsh hawks and other raptors circle their prey.

The river feeds into the Pacific which counts chum, chinook and coho salmon, orca (killer) whales, grey whales, octopus, seals, and sea lions among its treasures. ❑

## FESTIVAL OF EAGLES

Bald eagles are revered by First Nations people, who admire their skills of sight and flight. Nearly half of the world's bald eagles make their home in British Columbia. Few sights are as powerful as these huge birds of prey nesting, roosting or diving for salmon along the Squamish river near Brackendale, 10 km (6 miles) north of Squamish. Bald eagles boast a wingspan that can exceed 2 metres (6½ ft). Their size and distinctive white head and tail feathers make them easy to spot.

Since 1985, volunteers have gathered in Brackendale every January to count the feathered multitudes. The Brackendale Winter Eagle Festival and Count attracts devotees from around the world armed with binoculars and cameras. Hundreds of birds roost in eyries in the cottonwood trees along the river. Snow-capped Mount Garibaldi, at 2,678 metres (8,786 ft), acts as a backdrop, adding to the grandeur of the scene.

Eagle numbers are highest during January and February, but they can be seen in smaller numbers year-round. Guided walks and kayak tours in the Squamish area are a great way to learn about eagles and other flora and fauna. River kayaking reveals seals, herons, cormorants and trumpeter swans. Golden eagles are sometimes seen among the bald eagle congregation.

# Whistler's Wild Animals

T hirty-five years ago the Whistler Valley consisted of a few fly-fishing lodges and isolated homesteads; there was no town, just an unpaved highway cutting beneath the high, glaciated mountains. Today Whistler is a four-season resort with cobbled streets, shops, restaurants and countless hotels, lodges and condominiums.

The vast wilderness in which this top resort is set, however, has remained unchanged. Coastal hemlock and cedar forests share the rugged mountains with Alpine meadows – this is the typical habitat of the black bear. Some 50 bears make their home in the old-growth forests of Whistler and Blackcomb mountains. Between May and July, they are often seen on the slopes, feeding on the grass growing on the open ski runs. They also wander through high-elevation timber-shrub forests foraging for huckleberries, red raspberries and insect larvae. From August to October, bears eat voraciously, fattening up for winter hibernation.

Whistler campaigns to limit bear and human interaction. Sadly, each year several bears must be destroyed when they become too comfortable with human habitats, breaking into homes and even vehicles in their hunt for food. Residents and visitors are warned, "A fed bear is a dead bear."

## Year-round residents

Bears are not alone in the Whistler area. They have a profusion of other birds and animals for company. Some are temporary visitors, others year-round residents. In April, trumpeter swans stop over on their migration north, resting on Green Lake, while hummingbirds return from wintering in South America. Snows melt in May, and mountain goats can be seen on the south face of Wedge Mountain in the Black Tusk Nature Conservancy. In northern areas, moose graze along shorelines.

Birdwatchers are likely to see eagles, hawks, warblers, woodpeckers, osprey and

great blue herons. Grebes, geese and beaver can be spotted along the River of Golden Dreams during a canoe trip.

In the summer months, as well as bears, deer, coyote, bobcats and cougar can often be seen roaming the area. Smaller mammals include minks, weasels, squirrels, ptarmigan, pikas and marmots.

On the Gates and Birkenhead rivers north of Whistler, red Pacific sockeye salmon make their way upriver to spawn. In September, the salmon runs are at their peak. By late November, bald eagles return to Brackendale, south of Whistler, to feast on chum salmon. The Brackendale Winter

Eagle Festival held in January is renowned worldwide for its count of more than 1,600 eagles annually *(see box on opposite page)*.

Protecting nature is important to the region. Environmental and conservation groups play an important role in managing growth and sustainable development along the Sea to Sky Highway 99 corridor to Whistler and beyond.

If you're interested in wildlife tours, Michael Allen has spent two decades studying the black bears of Whistler and leading bear-watching tours. For more information on these and other ecology tours, visit www.whistlerblackcomb.com. ❑

---

**FAR LEFT:** a bald eagle catches a fish.
**LEFT:** coyote pups. **RIGHT:** a black bear.

# FOOD AND WINE

**Vancouver is heaven for food lovers. A happy combination of circumstances makes it home to a tremendous variety of superb cuisine at relatively affordable prices**

There is no standard Canadian food, so people here have embraced what is good from everywhere else, improving it with local ingredients and often imparting a West Coast imprint on the recipes. Vancouver is about variety – even in shopping malls, fast-food choices are far more extensive and exotic than the usual hamburger stall or sandwich place.

British settlers set the tone, bringing their recipes along. But since that first migration well over 100 years ago, countless waves of newcomers have overwritten the food template, easing their own recipes and approaches to food into the mainstream. Italian and Chinese restaurants that have been operating for 30 years or more are now so much a part of the culture that the food is a real fusion of their original "home cooking" and the Canadian palate. Spaghetti Bolognese and chop suey are more Canadian than anything else, but some hint of the old country still shines through.

## Food as lifestyle

The success of these "new immigrant" restaurants has led to a second eruption of restaurants, looking to emulate the best of what is being done today in the old country, while taking advantage of the fresh produce British Columbia has to offer – all this, while aiming to please a discerning public.

Vancouverites are very demanding when it comes to eating. Food is lifestyle, and the West Coast lifestyle translates into time to sit and have coffee with friends *(see box on page 61)*, time to devote a day to cooking a meal. The Canadian organic food movement is deeply

Some people visit Vancouver on the strength of the food alone. Ethnic diversity has spawned a cosmopolitan city where there is room for pretty much every kind of food, and the quality is exceptionally high. During a typical week of eating in Vancouver, it would be easy to travel around the world with tuna tataki (Japan), fettucine alle vongole (Italy), prawn vindaloo (Indian), dim sum (Chinese), lamb souvlaki (Greek), pho (Vietnamese) and quiche Lorraine (French). For the less adventurous, keen on having something "Canadian", a salmon burger or a roasted garlic chicken Caesar salad at one of the upscale chains like Earl's is available.

rooted in this province; food stores with a focus on organic and "green" are a huge success here, with Choices, Capers and Whole Foods all competing for consumer dollars. People here want to know where their food comes from, and many are willing to pay a significant premium for that knowledge.

Strangely enough, although Canada is a bilingual country, there are very few French-speaking inhabitants in Vancouver. Happily, it's one nationality that is over-represented in the restaurant industry. Tradition is important, and restaurant names like Le Crocodile and Le Gavroche may seem familiar to those who follow Michelin stars. From the first, expect excel-

The fine distinction between French, continental and contemporary cuisine is navigated quite comfortably by a number of outstanding upper-end restaurants, with proprietors who focus on the ingredients to produce beautiful and tasty, if sometimes small, plates. While the food may be world-class, the prices aren't – coming from New York or Paris, the value here is undeniable. Whether it is John Bishop's eponymous restaurant along an unprepossessing section of West 4th Avenue in Kitsilano, "C" (focusing on seafood), or the Relais et Châteaux-accredited Lumière, the obsession with quality is apparent. Getting a reservation may be a challenge – if a phone

lent Alsatian fare; from the latter, enjoy one of the continent's best wine cellars, with a selection that includes everything from vintage Bordeaux to New World cult wines, and a lot of good drinking in between. The array of French restaurants (L'Hermitage, Le Mistral, Pastis, Provence, La Régalade, to name but a few) will satisfy any cravings for traditional as well as innovative French cuisine, with some establishments boasting pommes frites good enough to be from Belgium.

call brings a "sorry, no room", it may be worth using the services of the hotel concierge. They often have access to the few tables kept free for emergencies.

## Asian food

It's a phrase that conjures up countless images – in Vancouver, they are jumbled and confusing, as there are so many good choices. Different provinces of China have completely different styles of food (hot and spicy, more or less meat, exquisite use of tofu to create amazing vegetarian dishes), and restaurants range from the ultra-formal Imperial (in a beautiful Art Deco building) to the quick and

**LEFT:** fresh ocean fish, like this panroasted wild BC halibut, is the highlight of many a menu. **ABOVE:** the busy kitchen of Yaletown's popular Blue Water Café.

simple in strip malls all over the city. Other Asian cuisines include Thai, Japanese, Vietnamese, Korean, Malaysian and Philippine.

Chinese dim sum is a bit like tapas – a chance to try many dishes without investing too much in the mysterious. A safe strategy is to choose a restaurant that still brings the food around on rickety trolleys to patrons. That way, even though you don't know what something is called, if it looks appetizing, you can give the small plate of food a try. Sun Sui Wah Seafood (in both Vancouver and Richmond) is one of the restaurants that still displays the food. On this occasion, there is a definite advantage to sitting near the kitchen.

## Fish and seafood

Salmon and other West Coast seafood is the type of food most sought out by tourists. If British Columbia has a speciality, then it is ultra-fresh wild salmon. It can be sublime when properly prepared, and disappointing if overcooked.

This is one type of meal where choosing the restaurant carefully is worthwhile, as it is so easy to produce mediocre salmon. Seek out a restaurant known for its seafood, and try to confirm that the salmon is wild, not farmed. Don't ignore some of the other fabulous offerings from the Pacific Ocean, including halibut, as well as oysters and crab.

## BRITISH COLUMBIA'S BURGEONING WINE INDUSTRY

The provincial government controls the distribution of alcohol in British Columbia, and prices will seem very high to the visitor. The good news is that local wines are excellent and of exceptional value, particularly those bearing the industry stamp of quality ("Vintners' Quality Alliance" or VQA). International acclaim is growing with every vintage. The 2004 Jackson-Triggs Okanagan Estate Proprietors' Grand Reserve Shiraz was chosen as the world's best in the Shiraz/Syrah category at the prestigious International Wine and Spirits Competition in London.

Both red and white wines are produced, with the whites generally offering a good balance of fruit and acidity, a perfect match for food. The spicy Gewürztraminer pairs beautifully with Asian cuisines, while the crisp acidity of the Pinot Gris and Pinot Blanc marries well with the richness of Pacific salmon. Depending on how it is cooked, Salt Spring Island lamb will call out for one of the chewy Bordeaux blends or more delicate Pinot Noirs. To try a few different wines without investing in a heavy night of drinking, Vintropolis and Raincity Grill *(see page 85)* both offer excellent tasting selections (three 2-ounce/60ml glasses), allowing you to get to know these wonderful wines that are generally hard to find outside the province.

Since it is all about choice, it's also worth knowing that odd requests are handled as routine here. For the vegetarian, many restaurants automatically ensure they have three or four meat-free selections. Allergies? Mainstream restaurants and holes-in-the-wall alike are comfortable with enquiries about wheat, dairy, egg, nuts and other common allergens, and chefs go out of their way to offer safe choices. Of course, not every restaurant is compliant, but having special dietary requirements is rarely a problem.

## Neighbourhoods and streets

Wonderful neighbourhoods that are well-suited to wandering, shopping and eating are

duck confit sits beside pâtés of every description, while across the way, Duso's has over a dozen types of fresh pasta.

Along Main Street from Broadway south past King Edward, a full day can be devoted to wandering in and out of vintage clothing stores and antique shops, stopping along the way for coffee, then for a Jamaican lunch at The Reef, and finally at The Main for a Greek dinner and live music.

Yaletown is where the cool people hang out. The concentration of excellent restaurants in this hip district will make choosing a place difficult. Most have good websites, so planning in advance is not a problem. ❑

easily accessible by public transport. There are many, but these four offer a good sampling.

Both sides of Denman Street, in the West End, are jammed with restaurants, from casual places to pick up a bite to take to the beach at nearby English Bay, to more formal places for a full meal. Most stay open late along this strip.

To understand thoroughly the obsession with fresh and local, a visit to Granville Island and its wonderful market will bring it into focus. The speciality stalls offer an amazing selection of foodstuffs – at Oyama Sausage,

**LEFT:** Italian café on Commercial Drive.
**ABOVE:** fish and produce stalls, Granville Market.

### COFFEE CULTURE

Like its American cousin Seattle, Vancouver has embraced coffee in all its forms. The cafés along Commercial Drive still cater to the Italian immigrants who arrived 40 years ago, and similar spots on West Broadway serve as meeting places for their Greek counterparts. But the real eye-opener is the number of coffee shops here. The ubiquitous Starbucks will feed a habit, but small independent operators also abound. One wonders how all these people have so much time to sit and drink their *venti* (extra large) sugar-free vanilla non-fat no-foam extra-hot lattes. But sit and sip they do, and you should join them if you can, and watch the world go by.

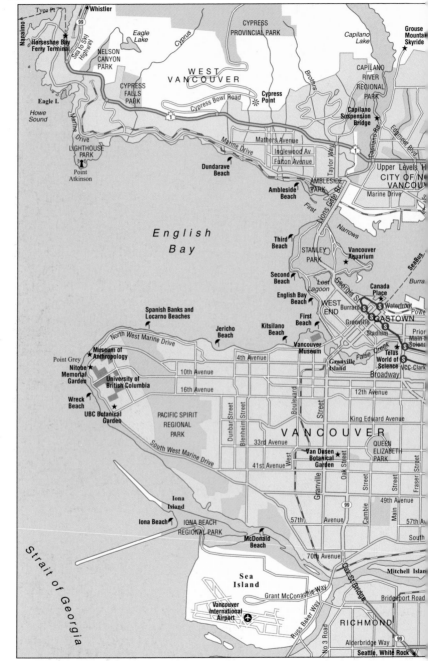

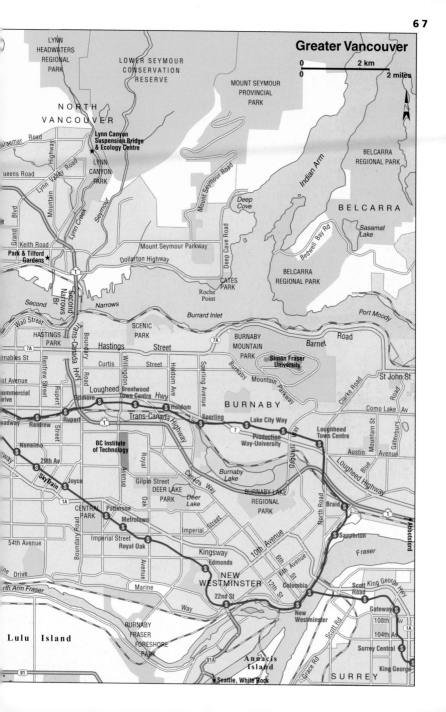

**Greater Vancouver**

# PLACES

A detailed guide to the city with the
principal sites clearly cross-referenced
by number to the maps

T he heart of Vancouver is the peninsula between Stanley Park and the eastern end of False Creek. It encompasses the site of the city's first muddy streets in Gastown and areas of surprisingly different character: the downtown shopping streets of Robson, Howe and Granville, the trendily revived warehouse district of Yaletown, the quiet residential streets of West End, the clusters of tower blocks overlooking the water at both Coal Harbour and False Creek, and the commercial buildings northwest of Georgia.

Because the grid-pattern streets are so long, their character can change dramatically: Nelson Street, for example, starts off as a quiet, tree-lined street and morphs into a hive of retail commerce. Equally their length makes it necessary to know at which point along the street you are, or want to be: the best way to make it obvious you're not from Vancouver is to use 'Street' when you're asking for directions; locals simply refer to Robson, or 21st and Dunbar, which means 21st Avenue off Dunbar Street.

Many of Vancouver's districts still have a strong neighbourhood feel, with residents' and business associations working to foster a sense of community and improve amenities. Some areas owe their origins to waves of immigration, most obviously Chinatown, but also the district now known as Commercial Drive, still referred to as Little Italy. Today it is more cosmopolitan, with Portuguese, Spanish and Latin American shops and restaurants. More recently, the name Punjabi Market has been given to an area populated by a community that has its origins in the Punjab. Other districts still derive their character from decisions taken during the last century, such as the university-centred Point Grey or the jealously guarded position of West Vancouver as an upmarket, almost purely residential area.

Many visitors never venture much beyond Kitsilano or Gastown. It would be absurd to suggest that you would miss the best of Vancouver by not exploring further afield, but there are some jewels that it would be a shame to miss: Steveston for anyone with a love of the sea and boats; New Westminster (briefly BC's capital), Burnaby and Fort Langley for those interested in architecture and social history; North Vancouver's mountain trails for walkers; Delta and Burns Bog for natural historians.    ❏

---

**PRECEDING PAGES:** downtown Vancouver at dusk; Queen Elizabeth Park.
**LEFT:** totem poles in Stanley Park.

# MIDTOWN AND WEST END

Many of Vancouver's main sights are concentrated in
this area, and all are within walking distance of each
other: from the harbour's epicentre, Canada Place, via
the city's premier art gallery, to the appealing West End
neighbourhood and the city's busiest shopping street

The sea and residential density
are the two qualities that distin-
guish Vancouver from Canada's
other cities. Nowhere in downtown
Vancouver is very far from the shoreline, and the gentle hill on which it is
built means that water is often part of
the view. The conscious policy to
foster a much higher density of population close to the central business
district has helped to make Vancouver one of the most attractive and
liveable cities in the world.

The centre does not become a
ghost town once the office and service industry workers have gone
home, because home for at least
some of them is within walking or
cycling distance of work. (Not
enough, some would argue, judging
by the number of cars that still pour
over the Lions Gate and Mann
bridges in the morning rush hour, and
the steep increase in the price of centrally located properties has meant
that many can no longer afford to live
near their place of work.)

This vibrancy is certainly helped
by the location of so many hotels in
the downtown area, which fosters the
city's exceptional restaurant scene.
Burgeoning demand for city-centre
property and the regeneration policies of the city have combined to
enlarge the downtown area eastwards
into the districts of Gastown and
Yaletown. But the office district
remains largely west of Granville,
with a forest of glass-clad towers
where firs and cedars once grew. It's
hard to credit that it is less than 150
years since the land hereabouts was
going for $1–2 an acre.

## Pacific gateway

In 1862 three Englishmen bought a
chunk of land corresponding roughly
to today's West End. One of them, a
potter John Morton from Yorkshire,
tried his hand at making bricks but

Map
on page
72

**LEFT:**
cruise ship docked
at Canada Place.
**BELOW:**
a bustling corner
of Denman Street.

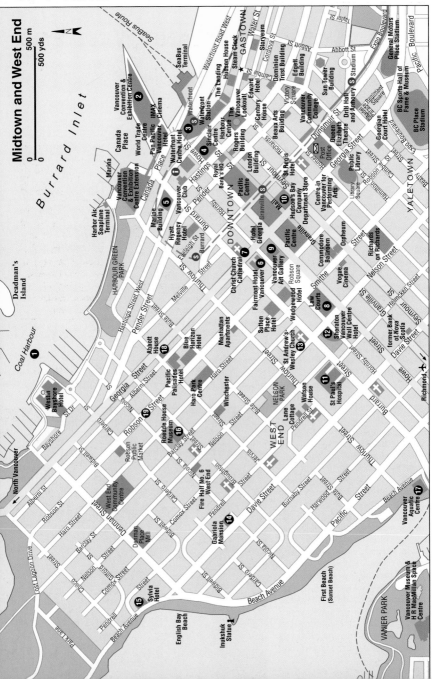

## Midtown and West End

0  500 m
0  500 yds

Burrard Inlet

North Vancouver

Deadman's Island

Coal Harbour ①

HARBOUR GREEN PARK

Westin Bayshore Hotel

SeaBus Route

SeaBus Terminal

Watertown Road West

Vancouver Convention & Exhibition Centre ②

Canada Place

World Trade Centre

Pan Pacific Hotel

IMAX Vancouver Cinema

Harbor Air Seaplane Terminal

Marina

Vancouver Convention & Exhibition Centre Extension

Marine Building

Vancouver Club

Hyatt Regency Hotel

Waterfront Station

Waterfront Centre Hotel ③

Sinclair Centre

Harbour Centre

Rogers Building

London Building

Pacific Centre

Hastings

Pender

DOWNTOWN

Royal Bank's HQ

Bank's HQ

Christ Church Cathedral ⑦

Hotel Georgia ⑥

Fairmont Hotel Vancouver ⑥

Vancouver Art Gallery ⑨

Robson Square

Law Courts ⑧

Steam Clock

GASTOWN

Storyeum

Dominion Trust Building

The Landing

Hobson House

Edgett Building

Edward Hotel

Vancouver Lookout

Century House

Victory Square

Beaux Arts Building

Vancouver Community College

Sun Tower Building

Drill Hall and Armoury

Georgian Court Hotel

BC Sports Hall of Fame & Museum

General Motors Place Stadium

Expo Boulevard

Pacific Boulevard

BC Place Stadium

Post Office

Queen Elizabeth Theatre

Centre in Vancouver for Performing Arts

Public Library

Library Square

Hudson's Bay Company Department Store ⑩

Orpheum

Commodore Ballroom

Pacific Centre

Richards on Richards

Vogue Cinema

Sheraton Vancouver Wall Centre Hotel ⑫

former Bank of Nova Scotia

St Regis Hotel

YALETOWN

Abbott House ⑱

Blue Horizon Hotel

Manhattan Apartments

Sutton Place Hotel

Wedgewood Hotel

St Andrew's-Wesley Church ⑬

Pacific Palisades Hotel

Haro Park Centre

Winchester

Watson House

St Paul's Hospital ⑪

Lane Cottage

Pendrell House

NELSON PARK

WEST END

Barclay Street

Roedde House Museum ⑯

Robson Public Market

Robson Street ⑲

West End Community Centre

Fire Hall No. 6 West End

Deadman Place Mall

Gabriola Mansion ⑭

First Beach (Sunset Beach)

English Bay Beach

Sylvia Hotel ⑮

Inukshuk Statue

Beach Avenue

Vancouver Aquatic Centre ⑰

VANIER PARK

Vancouver Museum & H R MacMillan Space Centre

Lost Lagoon Drive

found he was too distant from the only good market at New Westminster to make a profit. The "three greenhorns", as they were dubbed, talked of creating a city comparable to Liverpool, but for two decades that looked a forlorn hope.

All that changed with the arrival of the Canadian Pacific Railway at Port Moody in 1886, a momentous year in which Vancouver was both incorporated and consumed by fire *(see page 23)*. The CPR's first land commissioner, Lauchlan Hamilton, had the task of laying out the streets in the downtown peninsula, which had been granted to the company in exchange for building the transcontinental railway. The railway opened its terminus on the waterfront at the end of Howe Street on 23 May 1887, and within a week a ship sailed in laden with silks and teas bound for London. It was the harbinger of Vancouver's role as a gateway to Pacific trade.

## Coal Harbour

Looking at the affluent surroundings of **Coal Harbour** ❶ today, with its yacht and rowing clubs and million-

dollar apartments, it is a world away from the image conjured by its name. This was bestowed simply because a thin seam of coal was found here, soon becoming the site of Vancouver's first pier. Its later suitability as a landing place for seaplanes was anticipated in March 1919 when the first international air mail service in North America took off for Seattle. Its pilot was one William E. Boeing, president of the eponymous aircraft company based in neighbouring Washington State. The sight of seaplanes gliding gracefully in and out of the harbour, against a backdrop of shimmering glass towers on one side and mountains and pines on the other, captures the essence of Vancouver's character.

The marina at Coal Harbour echoes False Creek as a favoured mooring for yachts and cabin cruisers, as well as offering a variety of day cruises. As part of the recent redevelopment right along Burrard Inlet as far as Canada Place, a linear park has been created with segregated cycle and footpaths through landscaped areas with places to sit

Map on page 72

*Children playing in a newly laid-out park, part of the Coal Harbour district redevelopment.*

**BELOW:** a floatplane coming in to land at Coal Harbour.

*Seaplanes are a common form of transport in these parts, but for most visitors, a flight in one of these tiny, noisy craft will be a new experience. Harbour Air runs regular floatplane tours and a shuttle service to Victoria. It's worth splashing out on a flight (see page 232).*

**BELOW:** freight trains at Waterfront Station.

and watch the constant activity on the water or to have a drink and an alfresco lunch.

## Canada Place and Waterfront

Built out into Burrard Inlet, Canada Place stands on the site of Pier B-C, which opened in 1927 as the terminal for Canadian Pacific's rapidly growing trade with the Orient. Here millions of dollars of teas, spices and silks were unloaded and transferred to waiting trains *(see below)*.

The present pier was built for the **Vancouver Convention & Exhibition Centre ❷**, which opened in 1986 as a showcase pavilion for Expo '86. Because the building was also designed to become a cruise-ship terminal, it was given a strongly nautical feel with its five brilliant white sails made of Teflon-coated fibreglass and the sense as you walk around it of promenading the deck of a liner. It's a good vantage point from which to watch the busy water- and air-borne traffic.

Cruise ships dock on the eastern flank and just beyond, backing on to

the main station, is the busy SeaBus terminal, where ferries connecting downtown and North Vancouver dock (SeaBuses ply the Burrard Inlet every 15 minutes). The western flank of Canada Place is taken up by the Harbor Air seaplane terminal *(see left)*.

As well as the conference centre, the Canada Place complex contains an **IMAX cinema** (tel: 604 682 2384; www.imax.com/vancouver), the **World Trade Centre** and, rising above it all, the impressive **Pan Pacific Vancouver Hotel** – one of the city's most luxurious (and expensive) hotels, with magnificent views from its rooms.

Other than a yard full of freight trains, the only reminder of the once dominant presence of the railway along the shoreline is **Waterfront Station ❸**, which has become the principal interchange between all SkyTrain lines, the West Coast Express and the afore-mentioned SeaBus. Inside the classical Beaux Arts-style CPR station, which was built in 1914, part of the public area is decorated with 16 paintings of

## The Silk Train

No regular train on the Canadian Pacific Railway had higher priority than the famous silk trains that whistled their way across Canada with only guarded stops for locomotive changes and water stops. Even express passenger trains were held to allow unimpeded passage for these prestigious trains. Then accounting for 40 percent of Japan's exports, silk was a perishable commodity, attracting an insurance rate of up to 6 percent per hour from the time it came off the boat until it reached its destination, usually the National Silk Exchange in New York. The apogee of the silk trains was the 1920s, with the opening of a shorter route via the Niagara Falls Bridge.

landscapes that can be seen from a transcontinental train journey through the Rockies.

Almost opposite Waterfront Station at 750 Cordova Street is the **Sinclair Centre ❹**, an imaginative amalgam of four period buildings into a single retail and office centre. On the southeast corner is the former Beaux Arts post office and clock tower of 1905–10 which was the main post office until 1958. On display in the public area is the bronze bell which used to be on the roof, and the mechanism of the clock – both manufactured in England.

In the southwest corner is the 1908–11 building named after R.V. Winch, who made a fortune in the salmon-canning industry. The **Customs & Excise Building** (1911–13) occupies the northwest corner, and the **Federal Building** (1937) – one of the city's few surviving Art Deco buildings – the northeast corner.

Established in 1889, the elite **Vancouver Club** (tel: 604 685 9321; www.vancouverclub.ca) occupies an elegant 1913 building at 915 West Hastings Street. Its lovely entrance facade is frequently used as a film location.

### Art Deco treasure

Still in the vicinity of Canada Place, the **Marine Building ❺** (355 Burrard Street on Hastings) is an outstanding example of Art Deco and one of Vancouver's treasures. Sir John Betjeman even thought it the best Art Deco office building in the world. Panelled terracotta vignettes of transport – ships, trains and airships – form a band around the building. Step through the seashell-encrusted brass surround of the revolving doors into the entrance lobby and admire the ships' prows forming lights above the lifts, the marble floor incorporating the 12 signs of the zodiac and the mosaic surrounds to the five lifts.

The building was designed to put Vancouver on the map and exploit its growing importance as a port following the opening of the Panama Canal in 1914. Construction began on 14 March 1929, and it was formally opened just 19 months later, on 7 October 1930, by which time

Map on page 72

*Outside the World Trade Centre. An extension to the west of the centre will house the press facilities for the Winter Olympics in 2010 and also create Canada's largest green roof – a 2.4-hectare (6-acre) expanse of grass and wild flowers.*

**BELOW:** Canada Place.

*When it opened in 1930, the Marine Building was the tallest building in the British Empire at 25 storeys and 97.8 metres (321 ft); it was designed by McCarter & Nairne and had the fastest elevators outside New York.*

**BELOW:** the splendid entranceway of the Marine Building.

the world was in recession and only four floors were let. In 1933 it was bought by the Guinness family for $900,000; it had cost $2.3 million. A.J. Taylor was put in charge of the building, and he and his wife lived in the two-storey, three-level penthouse. Unfortunately his wife was afraid of heights and he had to abandon his eyrie, which was subsequently let to a woman who kept a Shetland pony on the balcony.

## West Georgia

One of the grandest and best-loved buildings in the city is **Fairmont Hotel Vancouver** ❻ (900 West Georgia Street, at Burrard Street). Building began in 1928, to replace the Canadian Pacific's second Hotel Vancouver, which it had built in 1916 with several ballrooms and a glassed roof garden. The new hotel was to be 17 storeys high at 111 metres (364 ft). However, construction was suspended when the Depression affected trade and only resumed in expectation of the royal visit of King George VI and Queen Elizabeth in 1939. In common with

CPR's other grand hotels across the country, it was a distinctive pastiche of French and Scottish castles with a steeply pitched copper roof and gabled dormers.

The rush to complete the hotel for the royal visit was needless, as the royal couple did not stay the night, arriving at the CPR station in the morning and embarking for Victoria the same afternoon. Grand as the Royal Suite was with its 90-square-metre (972-square-ft) reception room (since divided), perhaps even more remarkable is the Lieutenant-Governor's Suite; its Art Deco interiors have remained unchanged since 1939. It was Vancouver's tallest building until 1957.

Opposite the hotel is **Christ Church Cathedral** ❼ (tel: 604 682 3848; www.cathedral.vancouver. bc.ca), the oldest church building in Vancouver and the place where the royal family worships when in the city. The Gothic Revival sandstone building with narrow arched windows and hammerbeam truss roof was built in 1889–95. It became a cathedral in 1929 as the seat of the

Anglican diocese of New Westminster. Its atmospheric interior has been greatly enhanced by recent restoration schemes in which the cedar ceiling and Douglas fir floor were renovated. Additional lighting supplements the striking 1930s lanterns installed along the nave and choir.

Among the many stained-glass windows is a depiction of Captain James Cook in remembrance of his role in opening up the West Coast, and there is a wall plaque to Henry John Cambie (1836–1928), who was born in Tipperary and died in Vancouver. A founder of Christ Church, he is remembered as an explorer, surveyor and engineer and "the last and one of the greatest of the pathfinders of the CPR". Cambie Street was named after him. The church hosts frequent concerts.

Just east of the Hotel Vancouver and the cathedral is the Georgian Revival-style **Hotel Georgia** (closed for renovation), which was opened by Edward, Prince of Wales, in 1927. It has played host to such megastars as John Wayne, Elvis Presley and The Rolling Stones.

### Hornby and Howe

The main feature of these streets is the complex formed by the Law Courts and the Vancouver Art Gallery, with Robson Square sandwiched between them. These three city blocks are bounded by Hornby Street to the north and Howe Street to the south.

The seven-storey **Law Courts** ❽ (1979) were designed by award-winning architect Arthur Erickson, the creative force behind many of the city's landmark buildings, who is famous for his love of concrete. The building is distinguished by its vast sloping glass roof, which shelters 35 court rooms. Outside, copious amounts of greenery and waterfalls soften the concrete. Government and university offices also occupy some buildings, and the stepped lower sections are a favourite place for alfresco picnic lunches on weekdays and summertime concerts. Under a domed section of the lower level near the Art Gallery is a recessed floor to provide a skating rink in winter.

The **Vancouver Art Gallery** ❾ (tel: 604 662 4722; www.vanart-

Map
on page
72

*The Law Court building accommodates 35 courtrooms: 13 civil, 11 criminal, 3 appeal, 3 assize, 3 motion and 2 courtrooms specially designed for complex commercial cases.*

**BELOW:** the Fairmont Hotel Vancouver.

### Hotel Vancouver

When the CPR built its first hotel immediately after the great fire of 1886, it chose the highest spot at 43 metres (140 ft) above sea level, thereby helping to move the embryonic city's centre inland. Even there, "on quiet nights, the creak of ships at anchor can be heard". As the grande dame of Vancouver's hotels, the Hotel Vancouver in its three guises has welcomed the well-to-do and famous for over a century, from Mark Twain, Bing Crosby and J. Pierpont Morgan to Winston Churchill and Indira Gandhi. Its rooms have been carefully refurbished to retain the elegant style that remains the hotel's hallmark.

**BELOW:** outside the Vancouver Art Gallery.

gallery.bc.ca) occupies what was the Provincial Courthouse, designed in 1905 by Francis Mawson Rattenbury, and a west wing added in 1912 by Thomas Hooper. The neoclassical building with massive Ionic columns, a central dome and ornately carved stonework has been turned round so that the purpose of the original entrance front, flanked by lions (modelled on those of the New York Public Library), has been lost. It was converted into an art gallery in 1983 by Arthur Erickson.

Founded in 1931, the Art Gallery owns about 7,900 works; they include some 170 paintings by the Canadian Group of Seven, who emulated the Impressionists in preferring to work outside from life, but its most famous collection is its 200 works by Emily Carr, British Columbia's best known painter. She is said to capture the haunting mysticism of the region's First Nations, particularly the Haida.

The gallery specialises in buying contemporary art as well as hosting changing exhibitions of both historical and contemporary art.

## Granville Street

One of the principal entertainment and shopping streets, Granville is awaiting a renaissance from the closure of some sections for excavation work on SkyTrain's Canada Line and the concurrent reconstruction of part of the Pacific Centre. The building-site atmosphere and felling of trees has not done any favours for those blocks. But the arts scene remains vibrant, and elsewhere are some of the best historic corporate buildings.

On the corner of Hastings and Granville is the **Royal Bank**'s imposing BC headquarters (1931), built of Haddington Island sandstone with Romanesque decorations. Its interior layout mimics the nave and aisles of a church, with a magnificent roof created by Italian craftsmen hung with huge brass chandeliers. Square marble columns are matched by counters of Belgian black and gold and Travertine marbles.

Between Pender and Hastings on the east side is the white-glaze-tiled 11-storey **Rogers Building** (1911), designed by Seattle architect Carl F. Gould. The building takes its name

from Jonathan Rogers, who was born near Llangollen in north Wales and arrived in Vancouver on the first transcontinental train, fortified by an aunt's legacy. He used this to buy four plots of forest now in the heart of the downtown area, becoming a builder and developer.

On the west side approaching Georgia is the cream terracotta pile of the **Hudson's Bay Company Department Store** ❿, which dates from 1914. The company's first Vancouver store opened on Cordova Street in Gastown in 1887. Granville Street SkyTrain station can be accessed from the store's lower two floors.

On the east side is the former department store of Holt Renfrew, which opened its new premises in the North Atrium of the Pacific Centre in 2007. Its old premises are being subdivided with a food court at basement level.

Between Robson and Smithe is a cluster of cinemas and theatres: the Granville Cinema, Empire Theatre (now a cinema) and Plaza (three cinemas on west side).

Opposite on the east side at 870 Granville is the red-brick, Art Deco-influenced **Commodore Ballroom**, with curious tiled panels beneath the windows that resemble mosaics and Venetian windows.

On the south corner of Granville and Smithe is the **Vogue Cinema**, built in 1941, and another great product of Art Deco. It has a V-shaped front surmounted by the winged golden figure of the goddess Diana. Built to accommodate both movies and live shows with curved walls and a tiered ceiling, it has superb acoustics and dramatic lighting. It is currently closed and, despite being A-listed, is under threat of redevelopment into a supper club and cabaret that would destroy its interior. Critics say that Vancouver's need for a medium-sized performance venue would be perfectly met by a sensitively restored Vogue.

On the northeast corner of Granville with Davie is the former Bank of Nova Scotia (1929), its façade all that's left to front a glass confection dumped on top of and behind it.

Map on page 72

*In its heyday, the Vogue Theatre, renowned for its state-of-the-art acoustics and elegant decor, played host to some of the biggest names in showbiz.*

**BELOW:** an absorbing game of chess on Denman Street.

## Burrard Street

Three blocks north of Granville, linking Canada Place and Burrard Bridge, Burrard Street is another of the main downtown thoroughfares lined with hotels, shops and office blocks. The first landmark if you're heading to Canada Place from the Burrard Bridge end is the **St Paul's Hospital** ⑪ (1913). This fine red-brick building with decorative bands of beige brick and stone cornicing was built in the shape of a cross to a design by German-born Robert F. Tegen. It was sympathetically extended with two flanking wings in 1931–6. Though A-listed on the Vancouver Heritage Register and a landmark of downtown Vancouver, a question mark hangs over its future, since listing is symbolic and confers no legal protection.

Opposite Century Plaza and fronted by a pleasant green space is **Sheraton Vancouver Wall Centre Hotel** ⑫. Behind the striking design and coloured-glass façade lies a turbulent story, for the building wasn't supposed to look like this. Its developer, Peter Wall, chose a dark silver-blue colour for the glass, but when it began to be installed the city planning authorities got cold feet and insisted a lighter colour had been chosen. Writs flew until a compromise was reached, whereby the dark glass was retained for the lower 30 floors that form the Sheraton Hotel and lighter glass was installed for the luxury condominiums above. Three of these were bought by muscle-bound film star Jean-Claude Van Damme.

A little to the northeast, on the corner with Nelson Street stands the Gothic Revival-style church of **St Andrew's-Wesley** ⑬ (tel: 604 683 4574), opened in 1933. Its congregation is a model of ecumenicalism since the United Church of Canada is the outcome of a merger between four Protestant denominations. It has many stained-glass windows, mostly made in England by Morris & Co., and the organ was donated in memory of Mrs Thomas Bingham "who pioneered Scottish country dancing in Vancouver". Jazz Vespers are held every Sunday at 4pm.

*Burrard Street, Burrard Inlet and Burrard Bridge are named after Admiral Sir Harry Burrard, who served with George Vancouver on HMS* Europe *in the West Indies in 1785. He had a reputation for being one of the most considerate Navy officers of his day and quickly rose through the ranks.*

**BELOW:** car-free zone

## The West End

Northwest of Burrard Street was, and remains, a largely residential district, though condominiums have replaced many a mansion, and it took years for the western side to be developed – as late as 1900 you could pick blackberries near the junction of Thurlow and Davie streets, and there was nothing but tree stumps and scrub as far as Denman Street. Only then did development get under way, with sites close to English Bay used for grander Edwardian mansions prior to the area's gradual eclipse by Shaughnessy *(see page 139)* as the most desirable residential district from 1909.

Until re-zoning in the 1950s, the area remained a genteel and relatively cheap place to live with nothing higher than the eight-storey Sylvia Hotel *(see below)*. Then over a decade of crass redevelopment saw most of the two-storey houses swept away in favour of over 220 high-rise blocks, many so badly configured and designed that most residents had no views of sea or mountains.

That said, there is something very appealing about this inner-city district. Quiet as it seems, it is, in fact one of the city's most densely populated neighbourhoods and home to a vibrant gay community. Its leafy streets, its close proximity to Stanley Park, friendly atmosphere and still reasonable rents are what make it so liveable.

Almost the only surviving indication of what the West End once looked like is the **Gabriola Mansion** ⓮ at the western end of Davie Street. This elegant Queen Anne-style house was built in 1900–1 for B.T. Rogers, founder of the BC Sugar Refining Company. It took its name from the Gulf island that provided the sandstone with which it is faced. Today it is Romano's Macaroni Grill (www.macgrillbc.com).

Another West End landmark is the **Sylvia Hotel** ⓯ overlooking English Bay Beach on the corner of Morton Avenue and Gilford Street. Opened as the Sylvia Court Apartments in 1912, the eight-storey brick-and-terracotta building was converted into a hotel in 1936. It even had a roof garden and an eighth-floor restaurant that advertised "dining in the sky". Sylvia Ablowitz, after whom the hotel was named (by her father who built it), died in 2002 at the age of 102.

## Thurlow, Bute and Jervis

These streets embrace an area with the finest collection of heritage houses in the downtown area. Within Barclay Heritage Square at 1415 Barclay Street is **Roedde House** ⓰ (tel: 604 684 7040; www.roeddehouse.org), Vancouver's only house museum. Built in 1893 in the Queen Anne Revival style, it was almost certainly designed by Francis Rattenbury, who was a friend of Gustav Roedde, the first bookbinder in Vancouver, who had learned his trade at home

Map on page 72

TIP

This part of Vancouver is stuffed with bars and cafés. Just follow your nose or ask any Vancouverite where they go. People here take their coffee-drinking very seriously, and there is a strong trend towards organic, Fair-trade coffee. Most coffee places will also sell snacks and light lunches, and some have downright adventurous menus. For recommendations, *see page 85*.

**BELOW:** one man and his dog.

**TIP**

The stretch of Davie Street west of Burrard Street and the northern end of Denman Street, near the beach at English Bay, form the hub of the West End's gay community. Both streets are interspersed with gay bars, restaurants and shops, and dotted with decorated bus shelters and bus stops *(see pages 38–9)*.

**BELOW:**
a bedroom
in the historic
Roedde House.

in Leipzig. Guided tours take you round the furnished rooms with entertaining anecdotes about the family and their life in the house. The walls of the drawing room are panelled with cedar, and the deep cornice is also of wood. Some ceilings have a special wallpaper to reflect the light from oil lamps, and the main bedroom is downstairs to take advantage of heat from the kitchen stove. There is a delightful small room on the first floor, which must have had lovely views when the house was built; it was used by Matilda Roedde for sewing and reading.

The other nine houses on **Barclay Square** are of a piece with Roedde House and make an attractive ensemble, with landscaped grounds and places to sit beside the footpaths.

Near by, on Nicola Street, is **Fire Hall No. 6 West End** in beige brick with red-brick trimmings and banding and an Italianate tower. Built in 1907, it was claimed to be the first firehall in North America built to accommodate motor vehicles. A little

to the south, at 962 Jervis Street on the corner with Barclay, is **Winchester**, a classic four-storey apartment building with the typical Vancouver sash-windows of glazing bars on the upper sash and none on the lower.

On the corner of Thurlow with Robson is the West End's first apartment block, the **Manhattan Apartments** (1908). The building was used as the main location for the 1993 film *Look Who's Talking Now!* starring a bickering John Travolta and Kirstie Alley.

Between Bute and Thurlow in the block between Comox and Pendrell streets is another collection of wooden clapboard heritage houses with verandas and decorative bargeboards, but some of these are not on their original site. The **Watson House** (1897) was the home of Rev. Cloverdale Watson, minister of the Homer Street Methodist Church; it was donated to the city in 1986 and moved here in 1989. Once the home of a Yaletown plasterer, nearby **Lane Cottage** dates from 1901. An attractive footpath links the two streets.

Near the western end of Thurlow Street off Beach Avenue is the **Vancouver Aquatic Centre**  (tel: 604 665 3424; www.city.vancouver.bc. ca), a 50-metre (164-ft) pool and one of the very few public heated saltwater pools in the world. There's also a diving tank, whirlpool, sauna and fitness centre.

## Georgia and Alberni

By far the most important northwest/southeast street in the downtown area, Georgia Street was developed from 1888 as part of the Canadian Pacific's landholdings. The expensive houses it sold to the fledgling city's affluent gave the section of Georgia Street and adjacent Hastings Street the nickname of "Blueblood Alley". But even during the first decade of the 20th century, apartment buildings were starting to replace the city's first family mansions. Just one remains, the **Abbott House** ⑱ at 720 Jervis Street between Alberni and Georgia. This red-painted house clad in wood lap siding and cedar shingles was built by Harry Abbott, who was the first superintendent of the Pacific Division of the Canadian Pacific Railway and a prominent figure in the city's development. When built in 1900, the house had a great view over Stanley Park and the mountains.

## Robson Street

Last but not least, **Robson Street** ⑲. Vancouver's most famous shopping street used to be known as Robsonstrasse, but it has been many years since its German heritage was palpable. Schnitzel and schapps have become croissants and cappuccino. Shoppers should head for the three-block section between Hornby and Bute where many of the best-known brand names of fashion are to be found, such as Ferragamo, Armani Exchange, Club Monaco, Guess, BoysCo, BeBe, Zara, Laura Ashley, Banana Republic, Nike, Levi's and Gap. The Virgin Megastore occupies the former library building.

It's also easy to find good restaurants such as Zin and CinCin, cheap eateries like Hon's Wun-Tun House, as well as numerous places for a coffee. ❑

Map on page 72

*Nelson Park, afterwork meeting place for dogs and their owners.*

**BELOW:** a coffee and a kiss on Robson Street.

# RESTAURANTS & BARS

## Restaurants

### Aqua Riva
200 Granville St. Tel: 604 683 5599. Open: L Mon–Fri, Sun, D daily. $$$
www.aquariva.com
Overlooking the harbour and the mountains beyond, this huge glass room has one of the most enviable views in Vancouver. Its open-plan grill kitchen specialises in chargrilled meats, game and seafood.

### Bacchus
845 Hornby St. Tel: 604 608 5319. Open: B, L & D daily. $$$
www.wedgewoodhotel.com
Set within the award-winning Wedgewood boutique hotel, this dining room oozes Old World charm – dark wood, comfy soft furnishings and an open fire. The food is modern French with lighter saucing and makes great use of local ingredients. Afternoon tea here is a real treat.

### Bin 941 Tapas Parlour
941 Davie St. Tel: 604 683 1246. Open: D daily. $$
www.bin941.com
This small, lively space has a tapas-only menu, but what tapas! Try to get a seat at the bar overlooking the kitchen so you can watch the cooks prepare a host of fabulous dishes, such as slow-roasted five-spice pork tenderloin and red wine-braised pork belly with cauliflower goat

cheese purée. Good wine list. No reservations. A sister spot, Bin 942 on Broadway, works the same magic.

### "C" Restaurant
2–1600 Howe St. Tel: 604 681 1164. Open: D daily. $$$
www.crestaurant.com
Voted best seafood restaurant by Vancouver Magazine for eight years running, "C" is all about fish and fireworks. Finesse and presentation are high on chef of the year Robert Clark's agenda. Ultra-rare albacore tuna with confit fennel risotto, house-made bacon and salsa verde is one gem. Enthusiastic service, and lots of wines available by the glass, encourage guests to experiment with different wine pairings. Large patio overlooking the harbour.

### Cincin
1154 Robson St. Tel: 604 688 7338. Open: L Mon–Fri, D daily. $$$
www.cincin.net
A lovely room overlooking the street, with tables outside in fine weather. Modern Italian food using local produce is the focus, and the menu changes with the seasons and market availability. Try the grilled squid in a rich tomato sauce with chorizo, capers, garlic, raisins and chilli. The pastas are all house-made, and the wine list formidable.

### Hapa Izakaya
1479 Robson St. Tel: 604 689 4272. Open: D daily.
A loud and lively Japanese restaurant where orders are shouted across the restaurant in traditional style. Beautifully presented sushi and sashimi dishes made with the catch of the day and the Korean hot stone dishes are wonderful. Kick off with a cocktail from the imaginative list. Draws a young crowd.

### Hy's Encore
637 Hornby St. Tel: 604 683 7671. $$$
www.hyssteakhouse.com
Wood panelling, red velvet seating and prints of Old Masters give this dependable place for carnivores a club-like atmosphere. Part of a small chain that prides itself on the quality of its beef and the service it provides.

### Il Giardino di Umberto
1382 Hornby St. Tel: 604 669 2422. Open: L Mon–Fri, D Mon–Sat. $$$
www.umberto.com
Set in a period house with the prettiest courtyard in the city, this Italian restaurant is a Vancouver institution. The food is exceptional – fresh, unpretentious and of the finest quality. The Angus beef carpaccio with Dijon lemon mayonnaise, cannelloni filled with game meats and osso bucco are first-rate. Extremely popular.

### Kirin Mandarin
1166 Alberni St. Tel: 604 682 8833. Open: L & D daily. $$
www.kirinrestaurant.com
Awarding-winning restaurant that specialises in northern Chinese cuisine, particularly in live seafood prepared in both traditional and exotic styles. Dim sum, freshly prepared, is a daily feature and has many fans.

### Le Crocodile
100–909 Burrard St. Tel: 604 669 4298. Open: L Mon–Fri, D Mon–Sat. $$$
www.lecrocodilerestaurant.com
Quintessential French fare is the order of the day in this lovely Alsatian restaurant. Roasted quail farcie with sweetbreads and grilled veal medallions with veal demi-glace and morel mushrooms are representative dishes. What is reported to be the most intelligent wine list in the city is updated weekly by award-winning sommelier Robert Stelmachuk.

### Le Gavroche
1616 Alberni St. Tel: 604 685 3924. Open: L & D daily. $$$
www.legavroche.ca
Set in a pretty Victorian house, Le Gavroche has been serving French cuisine with West Coast flair since 1979. Using the formidable ingredients grown in this part of the world – Salt Spring lamb, Fraser Valley veal, wild Pacific salmon – Le Gavroche creates dishes

of surprising lightness and depth, and its wine cellar is splendid.

### The Mill Marine Bistro

1199 West Cordova St. Tel: 604 687 6455. Open: L & D daily. $

www.millbistro.ca

With the largest patio dining area in Vancouver, this pub/restaurant over-looking Coal Harbour gets very busy in the summertime and only takes reservations in autumn and winter. It produces Pacific North-west staples, and seafood and pizza are specialities. Fun, buzzy and inexpensive.

### Nu

1661 Granville St. Tel: 604 646 4668. $$

Right under Granville Bridge, Nu is a trendy addition to the restaurant scene, serving up eclectic fare in great surroundings. The menu is sensibly divided into small and large plates so that you can chose to suit your appetite. The jazz brunch on Sunday is justifiably popular.

### O'Doul's

1300 Robson St. Tel: 604 661 1400. Open: B, L & D daily. $$

www.odoulsrestaurant.com

Set in the Listel Hotel, O'Doul's is a great place to eat. Eclectic, fresh and reasonably priced, the food ranges over a number of cultures – try the crab-and-prawn cake, frisée-and-pea-shoot salad with toasted pumpkin seeds and lemon aioli. Live jazz every night.

### Raincity Grill

1193 Denman St. Tel: 604 685 7337. Open: L Sat & Sun, D daily. $$/$$$

www.raincitygrill.com

Award-winning Raincity Grill has a sublime 100-mile tasting menu – all ingredients are organic and come from within 100 miles of Vancouver. Each of the courses is paired with a superb local wine. Not only are chef Andrea Carlson and her staff passionate about food and sustainability, the service is friendly and enthusiastic.

### Rare

1355 Hornby St. Tel: 604 669 1256. Open: D Mon–Sat. $$$

www.rarevancouver.com

Hard-to-find ingredients and a seasonally changing menu are features of this smart restaurant – smoked sablefish with red carrots, steelhead roe and vermouth beurre, or a wild rabbit burger with cipollini onions and Saskatoon berries are among the dishes singled out for praise, as are the wine pairings. Excellent for a special occasion.

### Zin

1277 Robson St. Tel: 604 408 1700. Open: B, L & D daily. $$

www.zin-restaurant.com

West Coast ingredients and a global cuisine is what Zin is all about. The room is a mix of dark woods, leather banquette seating and dark orange colour scheme, and the flavours tend towards

Asian and Latino fare, but the ingredients are seasonal, locally sourced and ethically sound.

### Bars and Cafés

Close to the waterfront is **Café Natura** (310 Bute St on the corner with Cordova), serving good tea as well as coffee. There are several downtown branches of **Caffè Artigiano** (1101 West Pender St, 763 Hornby St and 740 West Hastings St), a small family-run chain offering superior coffee, brunch, salads and panini. **Bread Garden** (101–889 West Pender St) sells sandwiches, salads and wraps of every description. **Trees Organic Coffee Co.** (450 Granville St) prides itself on selling 100 percent organic coffee which is shade-grown, bird-

friendly, hand-picked and Fairtrade. All coffee is roasted on the premises in small batches. Fresh pastries, cheese cakes and sandwiches are also served. **Triggiano's Caffe** (402 Davie St) is another good choice for coffee and a snack. **Smiley O'Neals** (911 West Pender St) is a typical Irish pub, with a large selection of whiskeys and beers, and live music on some evenings. **Whineo's** (1017 Granville St) is a wine bar, with good food and nibbles for those who want them.

### PRICE CATEGORIES

Prices for three-course dinner per person with a half-bottle of house wine:
$ = under C$30
$$ = C$30–50
$$$ = C$50–80
$$$$ = more than C$80

# MARITIME VANCOUVER

## Vancouver's history and identity have been forged by its relationship with the sea

The coastline of British Columbia is so indented that it measures 27,200 km (17,000 miles), and its topography has inevitably made for a very close relationship with sea. In the early 19th century, the sailing ships that had explored the coast on behalf of Spain and Britain started to give way to steamships. Commerce with the Orient began in the late 1860s. As volumes grew, the Canadian Pacific Railway built some outstandingly elegant clipper-bowed liners for trade with Japan and China. The first, *Empress of India*, arrived in Vancouver on 28 April 1891, followed by *Empress of Japan* and *Empress of China*. Besides passengers, they carried valuable cargoes such as silk and tea, which were unloaded at Pier B-C. Canada Place now stands on the site of this terminal, where millions of dollars of teas, spices and silks were unloaded and transferred to special trains.

Passenger ships no longer ply the Pacific on scheduled services, but Vancouver remains a major commercial and cruise-ship port.

**LEFT:** the maritime lifeblood of BC is the network of services operated by BC Ferries. Today 35 ships serve 47 ports of call, making it one of the largest and most sophisticated ferry systems in the world. The ferry pictured here is the service from Horseshoe Bay, West Vancouver, to Nanaimo on Vancouver Island. Plans are afoot to upgrade the fleet and facilities at a cost of C$2 billion by 2020.

**BELOW:** the AquaBus ferries that dart between five points around False Creek add colour and atmosphere to the inlet, as well as saving long walks across the bridges to Granville Island.

**ABOVE:** the golden age of travel: two little girls salute the captain of the Canadian Pacific liner *Duchess of Bedford* during a voyage in 1931.
**LEFT:** Hong Kong-bound Canadian Pacific liner, *Empress of France*, 1928.

## BURRARD INLET

Ferries have been running across Burrard Inlet since May 1900, but today's frequent SeaBus catamarans have transformed the short journey between downtown and North Vancouver. The northern shoreline of Burrard Inlet became the site of busy shipbuilding yards. Ships are no longer built here, but some of the surviving slipways and buildings near Lonsdale Quay may become part of a new maritime centre and market on the lines of Granville Market. The inlet remains a busy waterway, dominated by commercial traffic, much of the mineral and timber cargoes delivered to Vancouver by rail from Prince George.

In summer and at weekends, the inlet to the west of Lions Gate Bridge shares the sea with up to 30,000 pleasure craft – yachts, cabin cruisers and kayaks off the beaches around English Bay. Some of them will be taking visitors out in search of killer whales, which sometimes come right into Burrard Inlet, though the west coast of Vancouver Island is a more likely place to see them. The spectacle of huge white cruise liners passing under the Lions Gate Bridge and easing round the corner to berth at Canada Place is worth seeing, if you can time your walk or cycle round the seawall to coincide.

**ABOVE**: container and bulk cargo ships with coal, sulphur, grain, timber and petroleum from the resource-rich western provinces sail mainly to Australia, Japan, the US, Brazil, Korea, China and Taiwan, while the cruise ships sail principally up the Inside Passage to Alaska.

**BELOW**: the province's many maritime museums trace the story of man's use of the sea, from fishing by the First Nations to today's busy trading links of the West Coast ports and the intensive pleasure use off the spectacular coastline. Below is the modified cedarwood canoe *Tilikum* in which Captain John Voss circumnavigated the world from Victoria to Margate in Kent in 1901–4. The vessel was exhibited at Earl's Court in 1905 and then sold. She was discovered in 1929, returned to Victoria and is now in the Maritime Museum of BC.

**BELOW:** salmon remains a major export from BC, though the vast majority is now farmed. From the mid-1990s, salmon catches declined from an annual figure of 60,000 tonnes to less than 20,000 by 2001. New conservation measures have been agreed between the US and Canada to try to avoid a repetition of the destruction of the Newfoundland cod-fishing industry.

# GASTOWN, CHINATOWN AND YALETOWN

**Wander the cobbled streets where it all began, meditate in a Chinese garden, admire Vancouver's first tall buildings, sip Italian coffee on "The Drive", browse the designer shops in uptown Yaletown, then hop on a ferry and take in the cityscape from the water**

The eastern side of downtown Vancouver contains far more contrasts than the West End and midtown. Some areas have been totally transformed – someone who knew False Creek at the end of World War II, for example, would barely recognise the place today. Others are distinctly edgy, with daytime sights down alleyways that will surprise and shock some visitors. Yet they are only a few blocks away from a district of Vancouver on almost every tourist's itinerary, Gastown, for it was here that the fledgling city was established, taking its name from the loquaciousness of its first bartender.

In the saloons of early pioneers like Gassy Jack *(see box page 93)*, prospectors talked up the probability of a quick path to riches in the goldfields of the Kootenays and the Cariboo. In the stores they gathered supplies for the long journey to the goldfields, while traders built warehouses close to the quays of Burrard Inlet. For decades Gastown retained this function, as housing, hotels and offices migrated to surrounding, more fashionable districts.

What all the areas covered by this chapter have in common is a greater wealth of historic buildings than the western downtown areas. This is evident in the number of walking

tours on offer. You can go with a guide or pick up one of the widely available leaflets for self-guided exploration.

Map on page 90

## GASTOWN

A good place to start a tour of Vancouver's oldest district is the point where Alexander and Powell streets merge to become Water Street: here is something unusual in downtown Vancouver – a space approaching a small square. It can also claim to be the centre of old Gastown. On the

**LEFT:** Chinatown.
**BELOW:** one of many Gastown shops selling Cuban cigars.

**TIP**

A small stand outside The Landing at 375 Water Street is the starting place for a 90-minute conducted walking tour of Gastown.

south corner is a **statue of Gassy Jack ❶**, erected on the site of a maple tree to which was pinned the notice of the first civic election in Vancouver, in November 1886. On the corner of Water and Carrall streets is the 1886–7 **Byrnes Building ❷**, built on site of Gassy Jack Deighton's second hotel, which then offered a great view of the harbour. The Byrnes Building has been described as the symbol of Gastown. Decorated with pediments and pilasters, this commercial block was built shortly after the Great Fire of 1886. One of the city's first brick

buildings, it was developed by Victoria developer George Byrnes and housed the relatively opulent Alhambra Hotel, one of the few in town then charging more than a dollar a night. It became one of the first buildings in Gastown to be rehabilitated in the late 1960s, helping to revive the then shabby district.

In the apex of Alexander and Powell streets is Vancouver's flat-iron building, the **Hotel Europe ❸**, which was designed by Parr and Fee in 1908–9 using their trademark glazed brick. Clad in beige brick above marble facing, it was Van-

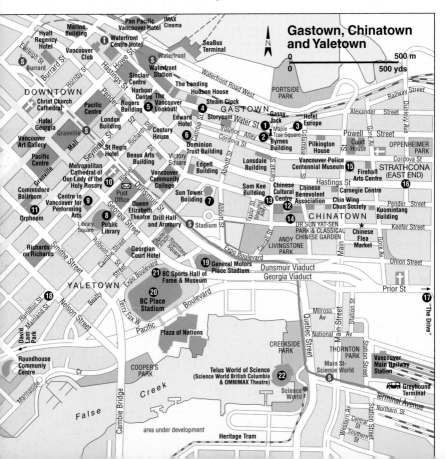

couver's first reinforced-concrete building and has a fine glazed-brick and tiled entrance hall, though it is now a rather seedy hostel. It was built for the Italian-Canadian hotelier Angelo Colari to be the best hotel in Vancouver, with a "sitting parlour" on every floor.

Where Gastown starts to become edgy, on Cordova just before Carrall, is the long **Lonsdale Building** (1889) with two pediments. It was designed for alderman Thomas Dunn and Jonathan Miller, who was the city's first constable and postmaster. Above a hardware store were the city's first synagogue, a reading room and the offices of the tramway company. The area is architecturally very varied, most of the buildings being constructed of stone or red brick between the 1890s and 1920s and often in an Italianate style. A particularly fine example is brick-built **Pilkington House** (120 Powell Street), which was the warehouse and office for the distribution of Pilkington Brothers' glass for the whole of North America. Before the opening of the Panama Canal in 1914, the glass had to be shipped right round the Horn.

Further east, the sections of Cordova and Hastings between Abbott Street and Chinatown form a shabby, drug-infested enclave which cannot be ignored but is best avoided.

## Water Street

The hotels along Water Street were built on the south side, as the north side of the street was often under water until the Canadian Pacific Railway fully reclaimed it in the 1890s. By 1900 Gastown was the headquarters of the city's food and dry goods wholesalers, a role it retained until the 1940s. The Edward Hotel at 300 Water Street, built shortly after a fire in 1899, is a fine stone building with a deep cornice and decorative floral bands.

At 142 Water Street stands the premises in which the once popular history extravaganza *Storyeum* was staged. Popular as it was, the theatrical romp through BC's history went bankrupt and closed in October 2006.

At the crossroads with Cambie is the famous **steam clock** , the first of its kind in the world, though it's actually powered by electricity and dates back to the 1970s (so don't be fooled into thinking it's a slice of Gastown history). It has attracted clusters of tourists waiting for the quarter-hour hissing and whistling. The steam comes from an old underground heating system for buildings, and a plaque explains how the clever device works.

Near the Water Street junction with Cordova is **Hudson House**, the Hudson's Bay Company's main warehouse for fur and liquor; built in 1895 and used until the 1960s, it was converted into offices in 1977.

Map on page 90

*Almost everyone stops to watch the famous steam clock, which hisses and whistles every 15 minutes.*

**BELOW:** Hotel Europe, the city's flat-iron building.

*The Harbour Centre Tower. Take the glass elevator to the lookout tower for great views of the city and beyond.*

## DOWNTOWN

The Harbour Centre Tower on Hastings and Richards is home to **The Vancouver Lookout!** ❺ (May–mid-Oct 8.30am–10.30pm, mid-Oct–Apr 9am–9pm; tel: 604 689 0421; www.vancouverlookout.com) which was formally opened by astronaut Neil Armstrong in 1977 and provides a 360-degree view of the city from the 150-metre (500-ft) high viewing gallery on the 50th storey. It is reached by glass-walled lifts on the outside of the building, giving a spectacular, almost too rapid 50-second ride. The glass of the gallery is sharply angled to deflect the sun's rays and to allow visitors to look vertically down. On a clear day, you can see Mount Baker in the US, 145 km (90 miles) to the south, and the most northerly of 11 volcanoes in the Cascade Mountain Range.

The entrance to the tower is on Seymour Street between Hastings and Cordova, close to Waterfront SkyTrain station, and tickets are valid all day so you can return in the evening to see the city at night.

There is also a separately managed revolving restaurant at the top.

Across West Hastings Street and one block south, turn into Richards Street and look up at no. 432, where you'll see on the pediment a pair of cast-concrete beavers flanking a lighthouse; this was the emblem of the Canada Permanent Mortgage Company which commissioned the building in 1912 from Scottish architect J.S.D. Taylor. It became **Century House** after the Century Insurance Company purchased the building in 1951. Within the solid granite walls is an ornate barrel-vaulted ceiling, original Victorian chandeliers and a marble staircase. This is now the lavish setting for the Century Restaurant & Bar.

## West Hastings and Pender

During the first half of the 20th century, the area around Hastings and Pender at the northeastern end of Cambie Street was the heart of Vancouver's financial district. It was distinguished by a series of tall buildings that laid successive claims to be the tallest in the British Empire. Most

were built between 1907 and 1913, the "golden years" of Vancouver's growth. The first was the idiosyncratic 13-storey **Dominion Trust Building** ➏ (1908–10) at Hastings and Cambie. Its distinctive bands of tan terracotta and brick rise to 53 metres (175 ft) and are surmounted by a three-storey mansard roof reminiscent of late 19th-century Parisian town houses. Its architect, J.S. Helyer, died after falling from a staircase in the building.

This was followed by one of the city's most striking buildings, the six-sided, 17-storey **Sun Tower Building** ➐ on the corner of Pender and Beatty. When completed in 1912 to a design by W.T. Whiteway, the Beaux Arts-style building was known as the World Building and was the tallest in the British Empire at 83 metres (272 ft), but only for two years. It was built by Vancouver's longest-serving mayor, Louis D. Taylor, who had bought *The World* newspaper in 1905 when advertising revenues were booming. His tower was to be a new home for the paper, but the 7,560 square metres (84,000 square ft) of office accommodation were too much for the recession of 1913, and in 1915 he lost the paper and the building.

Steel for the tower's frame was taken from dismantled ships. The lower part of the building is adorned with terracotta panels, arched windows and classical details, but it is the supports to the cornice halfway up the walls that arrest everyone's attention – a row of nine barebreasted maidens in sensuous poses, executed by the sculptor Charles Marega *(see right)*. When unveiled, these sculptures scandalised many of Vancouver's more prudish citizens. An excuse to ogle the maidens was provided in 1918 when Harry Gardiner, the "Human Fly", climbed the building, and again in 1920 when Houdini suspended himself from the top. The dome on the top looks like weathered copper but is in fact painted.

The building was bought in 1937 by the *Vancouver Sun*, which was published there until 1965.

On the east corner of the intersection of Pender and Cambie overlook-

*No sculptor has left a greater mark on the city than Charles Marega (1871–1939), who emigrated to Vancouver from Italy in 1909. He produced a wide range of civic works including the statue of George Vancouver in front of City Hall, the lions that flank Lions Gate Bridge, the busts of Vancouver and Burrard on Burrard Bridge, motifs on the Marine Building, and the 14 statues of figures from BC's past on Victoria's Parliament Building.*

**BELOW:** statue of Gassy Jack.

## John "Gassy Jack" Deighton

It is said that John Deighton was Vancouver's first settler, in 1867. He quit New Westminster and his work as a Fraser river pilot to become a saloonkeeper by – legend has it – offering to reward anyone who would help build the bar with all he could drink once it was up. The makeshift pub was in business within a day, and with it was born a reputation for its owner's garrulousness. Gastown was a world away from the Hull in Yorkshire where Jack was born in 1830: he later wrote that the Globe Saloon was "a lonesome place when I came here first, surrounded by Indians. I cared not to look outdoors after dark. There was a friend of mine about a mile distant found with his head cut in two." He had the eye of a sailor when he presciently forecast that Burrard Inlet's suitability as a harbour would one day make it a great port. By 1870 the tiny settlement of 2.4 hectares (6 acres) around the saloon had been named Granville after the British colonial secretary, Earl Granville. Jack built a better, two-storey establishment on Water Street called the Deighton Hotel, with a veranda shaded by a maple tree where his statue now stands. Jack died in 1875 aged 44, 11 years before his hotel was consumed in the conflagration that destroyed the city.

TIP

Catch a performance at the dynamic Firehall Arts Centre (www.firehallartscentre.ca), which offers a varied programme of avant-garde theatre and contemporary dance, often used to showcase new or emerging talents. The theatre is set in a converted fire station at 280 East Cordova, not far from Chinatown, and has a cosy lounge bar and outdoor courtyard stage for fair-weather performances.

**BELOW:** inside the Moshe Safdie-designed Public Library.

ing Victory Square is the **Edgett Building** (1911). This newspaper building originally housed what was claimed to be the "largest, best and most complete grocery store in the Dominion of Canada". It is now home to the Architectural Institute of BC, which organises six architectural walking tours of the city between early July and the end of August (tel: 604 683 8588; www.aibc.ca).

At 330 West Pender is a splendid Beaux Arts building built in 1907 for the BC Permanent Loan Co. Inside are mosaic tiled floors and a magnificent Tiffany-style stained-glass dome, the second-largest in BC after the Parliament Building in Victoria. In the window glass are the arms of the Yukon, Great Britain and eight provinces. The current occupants now sell jewellery-making materials, but are tolerant of visitors.

At 626 West Pender is the **London Building**, a fine Edwardian commercial building made of Haddington Island stone with elaborate ornamental iron panels and cornice. It has an open staircase with marble treads and cast-iron risers reaching the full height of the building. Now occupied by the Western Town College, visitors are still allowed in to see the staircase.

## Beatty Street

The fortress-like building on Beatty Street between Georgia and Dunsmuir is the **Drill Hall and Armoury** of the British Columbia Regiment (Duke of Connaught's Own). Flanking the two central towers are a Sherman tank which fought in a 14-hour tank battle north of Falaise and a Ram Mk II tank of which 1,949 were built by the Montreal Locomotive Works in Quebec. The building has served as the regimental headquarters since its opening in 1901 by HRH the Duke of Cornwall and York, and its 90-cm (3-ft-thick) walls were built of brick and Gabriola Island sandstone.

## Georgia Street

On the corner of West Georgia and Homer opposite the main post office is Library Square and the Colosseum-like new **Public Library** ❽, clad in pre-cast concrete the colour of rich

African soil. Designed by Moshe Safdie & Associates and opened in 1995, it has a spectacular atrium entrance to the seven levels of stacks housing 1.2 million books as well as shops and government offices.

Across the street is the **Centre in Vancouver for Performing Arts** ❾ (tel: 604 602 0616; www.centrein-vancouver.com), also designed by Moshe Safdie in 1995. The largest performing arts facility in western Canada has a spiral glass cone to its curvilinear marble staircase and an auditorium with 1,800 purple velvet seats and impeccable acoustics.

### Dunsmuir Street

You won't miss the **Metropolitan Cathedral of Our Lady of the Holy Rosary** ❿ on the corner of Dunsmuir and Richards if you're near it on Sunday morning, when the eight large bells in its 66-metre (217-ft) east tower ring long and loud. The Gothic Revival church with steeply pitched roof and pointed windows and doorways was built in 1899, becoming a cathedral in 1916.

At 602 Dunsmuir, the Edwardian-style **St Regis** (1913) is the last of the pre-World War I hotels to survive as a hotel.

### Seymour Street

The best-known building on Seymour Street is the **Orpheum** ⓫ on the corner of Smithe. The fine heritage theatre has first-class acoustics and is home to the Vancouver Symphony Orchestra. When it opened in 1927 it was the largest theatre in Canada and the Pacific northwest, with 2,800 seats. It hosted Chicago-based vaudeville shows and still has its original 1927 Wurlitzer 240 organ, believed to be the only vaudeville organ still in operation in its original setting. The theatre's extravagant decor is Spanish Baroque-inspired, the arches and tiered columns decorated with mouldings in marble, travertine and plaster.

### CHINATOWN

Vancouver's compact Chinatown, dating from 1885, is the biggest in Canada and the third-largest in North America (after San Francisco and

Map on page 90

*Exhibits in the Chinese Cultural Centre's small but informative museum.*

**BELOW:** the lobby of the Orpheum.

*Playing football in the Andy Livingstone Park, not far from Chinatown.*

**BELOW:** Chinatown grocery store.

New York), having defeated freeway proposals in the 1960s that would have destroyed much of the area. It stretches for several blocks east from Main Street, bounded to the north by Hastings Street and the Georgia Street viaduct to the south, and is easily reached from Stadium-Chinatown station on SkyTrain or buses 19, 22 and 50 from downtown.

A good introduction to the quarter's history and the part played by the Chinese in western Canada's history can be gained from the **Chinese Cultural Centre** ⑫ (Tues–Sun 11am–5pm; tel: 604 658 8880; www.cccvan.com) at 555 Columbia Street. The frontispiece of the concrete post-and-beam structure is a traditional gateway, made in China and erected here after having first been installed at Expo '86. The Centre's small museum reveals the background to Chinese immigration: most came from Hong Kong and Guangdong Province in south China, leaving in waves both to escape famine and in the hope of quick riches with the discovery of gold in California, Australia and then

Canada. By 1863 there were 4,000 Chinese working on construction of the Cariboo Wagon Road, and in 1881–5 17,000 Chinese labourers were under contract to finish building the western section of the CPR. On the corner of Columbia and Main streets is a statue commemorating the contribution made by the Chinese to both the construction of the railways and during World War II.

Concern over the levels of immigration prompted the government in 1885 to impose a head tax of $50 on all persons of Chinese origin entering the country. This had little effect, so it was increased in 1900 to $100 and three years later to $500. With many Chinese taking the low-paid jobs, resentment built up, and anti-Asian riots broke out in 1907. In 1923 the Exclusion Act closed the door to Chinese immigrants. Two facts indicate a measure of post-war change: only in 1945 was a bar lifted against the use of the Crystal swimming pool by Chinese, and in 1988 David Lam, an immigrant from Hong Kong, became the first Lt Governor of British Columbia of Chinese origin.

Chinatown has become one of Vancouver's most popular tourist destinations for its won-ton and dim-sum houses, market stalls and exotic shops selling things you won't find anywhere else in the city. From esoteric Chinese herbs and spices to jade and silks, there are numerous specialist shops to fascinate even the most shopping-averse.

The **market section** runs between Main Street and Gore Street and includes East Pender, Keefer and East Georgia streets, while the **merchandise section** runs from Columbia to Main and includes East Pender and Keefer streets. The **Chinese flea market** is on Keefer Street between Gore and Main.

## Chinatown buildings

Because of its appearance in the *Guinness Book of Records* as the narrowest building in the world, the **Sam Kee Building** ⑱ at 8 West Pender Street on Carrall is on many a visitor's itinerary. This curiosity came about when the city expropriated land without compensation on either side of the street to widen it. This left

Chang Toy with a property just 1.5 metres (4 ft 11 in) deep. Rather than sell cheaply to his neighbour, Chang Toy defiantly commissioned a two-storey building with protruding bay windows on the first floor and a cellar under the pavement lit by glass blocks. The latter accommodated a bathhouse used as an escape route from opium dens in nearby Shanghai Alley by means of a connecting tunnel. The building is made entirely of riveted steel.

Further along Pender at No. 108 is the **Chinese Benevolent Association Building** (1909). The CBA had been formed in 1895 to help destitute railway workers after completion of the CPR. This fine example of southern Chinese architectural style with recessed balconies, decorative tiles and ornate ironwork housed its offices and meeting rooms. The fusion of Chinese and Western elements can be seen in the pedimented building of the **Chin Wing Chun Society** at 160 East Pender.

Of historical rather than architectural interest is the Kuomintang Building at 296 East Pender Street.

Map on page 90

**TIP**

A night market is held in Chinatown on Friday, Saturday and Sunday evenings from 6.30–11pm between June and mid-September.

**LEFT:** statue commemorating the Chinese contribution in World War II.
**BELOW:** the famously narrow Sam Kee building.

*Dr Sun Yat-sen (1866–1925) has been described as "the father of modern China", but it was his political philosophy rather than his practical contribution to the revolution that was more influential. He was the first provisional president of China when the republic was founded in 1912.*

**BELOW:**
the sometimes serene
Sun Yat-sen Garden.

This was the western headquarters of the Kuomintang, founded in 1912 by Dr Sun Yat-sen to overthrow the Manchu dynasty.

## A piece of Suzhou

After the bustle and noise of commerce in Chinatown, it's easy to find quiet if not solitude in the **Dr Sun Yat-sen Park and Classical Chinese Garden ⑭** (May–mid-June 10am–6pm, mid-June–Aug 9.30am–7pm, Sept 10am–6pm, Oct–Apr 10am–4.30pm; closed Mon Nov–Apr; tel: 604 662 3207; www.van-couverchinesegarden.com). Located at 578 Carrall Street, it fulfils the original purpose of providing a sanctuary of nature within a bustling city, though the popularity of this garden makes it hard to find tranquillity among its various discrete spaces.

Built in 1985–6 by 52 artisans who came over from China with all the materials and tools they required, the garden claims to be the first full-scale classical Chinese garden built outside China. Its design is based on elements from private Ming-dynasty gardens of the 14th century and relies more on

architectural forms than plants for its effect, with courtyards, pavilions, bridges, covered galleries, sculptured rocks and jade-green areas of water, symbolising tranquillity.

Covering 1 hectare (2½ acres), the garden was designed to create a proper yin and yang from the elements and to achieve the harmony between the man-made and natural worlds that lies behind the design of Chinese gardens.

## North of Chinatown

Close to the principal downtown police station is a museum that will appeal to devotees of P.D. James and Colin Dexter: the **Vancouver Police Centennial Museum ⑮** (Mon–Sat 9am–5pm; tel: 604 665 3346; www.city.vancouver.bc.ca/police/museum) at 240 East Cordova Street is located in the former Coroner's Court built in 1932 for the investigation of unusual deaths. The rooms include displays about unsolved murder cases, police firearms, a gruesome collection of confiscated weapons, the history of the city's force which dates from

1858 and the establishment of Fort Langley, early breathalyser devices such as the "Drunkometer" of 1953, fingerprinting, forgery, drugs, gambling, uniforms and hats, police dogs, the marine squad and even cast models of police cars from around the world. The autopsy room with body drawers comes with a health warning for the squeamish about the various specimens on display. The actor Errol Flynn was almost certainly brought here in 1959 when he died in Vancouver under suspicious circumstances. Children can play with computers storing fake police records.

The imposing columns surmounted by a dome at the corner of Hastings and Main streets announce the entrance to the **Carnegie Centre**, which was the main library between 1903 and 1958. One of 2,509 libraries paid for by Andrew Carnegie in his Bill Gates-style determination to give away most of his fortune, the neo-classical building designed by George Grant can be entered to appreciate its elegant circular staircase and the stained-glass portraits of various writers, from Shakespeare to Scott. Today the building is used as a community centre.

Map on page 90

## East of Chinatown

The area between Chinatown and Clark Drive has been called the East End as well as **Strathcona ⑯**, and has been home to successive waves of immigrants from Italy, Scandinavia, the Ukraine, Japan and China since its establishment in the 1880s. Its eclectic mix can still be seen in the variety of religious buildings, such as the Korean Foursquare Gospel Church and the Holy Trinity Russian Orthodox Church. It has the city's largest concentration of historic houses built before World War I, but little thought was given to their qualities in the 1950s and '60s when the area was regarded as a ghetto. Freeway proposals that would have swept them away were again defeated, and now the charming wooden Victorian and Edwardian houses are gradually being restored with a strong sense of community and pride.

The area is characterised by narrow lots that reflect the pressure on

*The Vancouver Police Centennial Museum will appeal to those with a taste for the macabre. Good for a rainy afternoon.*

**BELOW:**
East Vancouver's bohemian neighbourhood centres on "The Drive" *(see page 100).*

housing when it was laid out, so neighbouring gutters can almost touch in places. Though the houses on many of the streets look superficially similar, there is a wealth of individuality, with frilly bargeboards and decorative gables, balconies and porches. This is partly because each builder and client designed them with the help of a catalogue of proprietary windows and decorative details.

One of the oldest houses in the whole of Vancouver is at 451 East Pender Street, a lovely twin-gabled house dating from about 1889. At 602 Keefer Street is an unusual corner house of about 1902 with a symmetrical composition around a conically topped tower. The oldest remaining school building in the city is further along the street at the 500 block: the red-brick Italianate Lord Strathcona School dates from 1897.

### "The Drive"

If you've more time on your hands another district worth exploring is the bohemian quarter to the east of Gastown. It's a little scruffy round the edges, but this is where you'll find cosmopolitan Vancouver at its most culturally diverse. The northern end of Commercial Drive between Venables Street and Grandview has become one of the city's trendiest areas. Today best known as **"The Drive"** ⑰ but also called Little Italy, this area was scheduled for a huge redevelopment in the early 1980s, but its residents successfully fought off the plans. Besides attracting Italian immigrants, the area was also popular with the Portuguese. With numerous cafés and restaurants and the sort of eclectic shops that sell things you're unlikely to find in anodyne malls, it's a good area to wander round for an afternoon. Specialist chocolates, coffee, ethnic crafts, music, bookshops, antiques and bric-a-brac and furnishings can all be found here, as well as the wackier end with such items as belly-dancing accoutrements.

### YALETOWN

This former warehouse and commercial district has undergone an extraordinary renaissance to become

one of the city's liveliest areas, packed with great restaurants, up-market grocery stores, cafés, upscale boutiques and furnishing stores and galleries, as well as the city's most hip hotel.

Former warehouses have been converted into homes or offices, and the new Yaletown-Roundhouse station on the SkyTrain Canada line will further increase the area's appeal.

The area's name was bestowed in the late 19th century when the Canadian Pacific Railway moved its repair facilities from Yale in the Fraser river canyon *(see page 225)*. The only reminder of the era of whistles and clashing boxcars around the north shore of False Creek is the 1888 locomotive roundhouse which today forms the centrepiece of **Roundhouse Park** (daily; admission free). This was restored as a pavilion for Expo '86 and then turned into a community centre. Inside a glass-walled extension is locomotive No. 374, which hauled the first transcontinental train into Vancouver from Montreal on 23 May 1887, carrying 150 passengers. The locomotive is wheeled out onto the turntable on the anniversary for a day of celebration.

Yaletown was a pretty rowdy place in its early years, encouraging the more respectable residents to move to the more salubrious West End. Many of the warehouses built in the early 20th century have survived to become restaurants on the ground floor, with the loading dock as an open-air terrace, and flats or offices above, benefiting from generous areas of glazing.

The main hub of activity is around **Hamilton** and **Mainland streets** ⓳, which have a concentration of trendy interior design stores, "in" restaurants and an upmarket supermarket.

## False Creek

Along the north shore of False Creek *(see also pages 119–24)* the CPR was enticed into building its yards and repair facilities by a 20-year exemption from local taxes. These and the workforce that manned them were moved from Yale, with whole buildings being loaded onto flat cars. The extensive yards were cleared for the site of Expo '86. Once the fair was

Map on page 90

*For a swan's-eye view of the glistening glass towers, learn to kayak in False Creek (see page 252).*

**BELOW:**
hip Hamilton Street.

*The little bucket ferries are the most efficient and pleasant way of crossing the Creek (see page 234 for details).*

**BELOW:** BC Sports Hall of Fame.

over, it was expected that the land would be developed by a Crown corporation, but the provincial governor of the day had different ideas and sold the entire 84-hectare (208-acre) site to a single top bidder, Hong Kong billionaire Li Ka-shing, who paid $320 million over 15 years. It was not a popular decision: too hasty, too small a sum and not enough transparency were typical accusations. Equally, the high-rise residential towers that have risen along the waterfront are too close to one another for many people's liking, but **David Lam Park** and the seawall path for cyclists and walkers are an unquestionable benefit to the city as a whole.

Near the eastern end of False Creek on the north shore are the city's two principal sporting stadiums: the **General Motors Place Stadium** ⑲ on Griffiths Way, opened in 1995 with seats for 20,000 at the annual 170-odd events. The ferociously competitive game of ice hockey is Canada's national sport, and this is the place to watch the Vancouver Canucks on their home ice. Lacrosse isn't a sport

for retiring flowers either, and the stadium is home turf to the Vancouver Ravens. The stadium also hosts concerts and other shows, with a fine sound system and great acoustics.

Dwarfing GM Place is the nearby **BC Place Stadium** ⑳, completed in 1983 as the biggest air-supported domed stadium in the world, covering 4 hectares (10 acres) and seating 60,000. The fibreglass and Teflon roof is only 0.85mm thick but stronger than steel, kept up solely by 16 electric fans which maintain a higher pressure inside the stadium than outside. It's home to the BC Lions football team as well as another concert venue – David Bowie, The Beach Boys and The Rolling Stones have all played here. Expo '86 was inaugurated here by Queen Elizabeth, and it will host the opening and closing ceremonies of the 2010 Winter Olympics.

Within the enormous structure is the **BC Sports Hall of Fame & Museum** ㉑ (10am–5pm; tel: 604 687 5520; www.bcsportshalloffame.com), which is dedicated to

## Sporting Heroes

Terry Fox was a university student when he discovered in 1977 that he had bone cancer in the right knee. During his Marathon of Hope across Canada, he hobbled 3,339 miles in 144 days before a recurrence of the cancer cut short his run and his life. He had raised C$24 million for cancer charities. Annual Terry Fox runs across Canada continue to raise huge sums.

A car crash left 15-year-old Rick Hansen a paraplegic, but he went on to win 19 wheelchair marathons and three world championships before setting out from Vancouver in 1985 to circumnavigate the world. In two years he wheeled through 34 countries, raising C$24 million for spinal cord research and wheelchair sports.

honouring the province's athletes and teams. There are plenty of touch screens and hands-on displays in the sections which are each devoted to a decade, with more general displays to evoke the spirit of the times. The museum highlights the contribution made by two sporting heroes in particular, Terry Fox and Rick Hansen (see left).

## Science World

One of the landmarks on False Creek is the huge shiny golf ball at its eastern end, built as the main entrance and centre of Expo '86 and adapted to become **Science World British Columbia** ㉒ (Mon–Fri 10am–5pm, Sat–Sun 10am–6pm; tel: 604 443 7440; www.scienceworld.bc.ca). Located at 1455 Quebec Street, close to Main Street-Science World SkyTrain station, the building has a stainless-steel skin held in place by a white-steel geodesic frame. This is interactive heaven for children, with two floors of buttons, levers, wheels, joysticks and mouses to work to develop their knowledge and understanding of scientific principles.

There are supervised workshops building something different each day, a host of machines to test such things as your reactions or ability to relax, and entertaining scientific demonstrations on its centre stage. There is a section with live animals and a crawl-through beaver lodge. The kinetic sculpture outside the entrance is mesmerising. When these possibilities are exhausted, there's a 400-seat **OMNIMAX theatre** (separate admission charge), with a domed screen as opposed to the IMAX rectangular screen. The screen is 27 metres (89 ft) in diameter and has a six-track sound system to match.

To the east of Science World is Vancouver's **main railway station**, the former Canadian Northern/ National terminus on Station Street. Today it is served by VIA and Amtrak trains and the tourist trains operated by Rocky Mountaineer Vacations (see page 233). The imposing station was opened in 1919 to the design of Ralph Pratt, chief architect of the Canadian Northern. The large neon sign along its two wings dates from the 1930s. ❑

Map on page 90

*Pulling into the SkyTrain station outside Science World.*

**BELOW:** the shiny dome of Science World dominates the eastern shore of False Creek.

# RESTAURANTS & BARS

## Restaurants

### Amarcord

104–1168 Hamilton St (Davie and Helmecken). Tel: 604 681 6500. Open: L Mon–Fri, D daily. $$
www.amarcord.ca

This unpretentious trattoria acts as an antidote to the uber-trendiness of many Yaletown restaurants, serving traditional pastas, fish and meat dishes and risottos from the Emilia-Romagna region. Gnocchi alla reggiana with Italian sausage, fresh tomato and basil is simplicity itself but perfect; the linguine with clams was deemed to be the best one customer had ever eaten. Not fantastically chichi but the service is super and the welcome genuinely warm.

### Bluewater Café

1095 Hamilton St. Tel: 604 688 8078. Open: D daily. $$$
www.bluewatercafe.net

A Yaletown star specialising in wild seafood of the utmost freshness, the Bluewater is housed in a brick-and-beam warehouse conversion made elegant by the clever use of lights and wood. The restaurant is overseen by chef Frank Pabst, a classically trained European who has helped make this restaurant an international success. You can have meat if you want, but with such sublime fish and seafood on offer, why would you – Yukon Arctic char, Queen Charlotte halibut, local Dungeness crab. And the oyster menu is laid out like a wine list – a selection from Washington State and the East Coast if you must, but the best of all are the BC oysters, eleven types, each one lovingly described. Really well-informed and friendly service and excellent wine list.

### Capone's Restaurant and Live Jazz Club

1141 Hamilton St. Tel: 604 684 7900. Open: D daily. $$
www.caponesrestaurant.net

This restaurant with terrace in an old industrial building was here before all the Yaletown trendies, and continues to attract a real mix of those who have been coming for years and the super-cool who have discovered a good deal and the great music. Prawn and scallop skewers and beef carpaccio with white truffle oil are on a popular menu that features steak, duck, lamb shank and beef tenderloin. The big attraction here is the live jazz every night of the week from 7.30pm.

### Cassis

420 West Pender St. Tel: 604 605 0420. Open: L & D daily. $$.
www.cassisvancouver.com

Attractive bistro and lounge serving a number of bistro staples (coq au vin, bouillabaisse and a daube of beef are all there) with a West Coast slant. The kind of place you wish you had in your neighbourhood – casual enough for jeans, but smart enough that you feel you are dining out.

### Century

432 Richards St. Tel: 604 633 2700. Open: L Tues–Fri, D Tues–Sat. $$

Set in Century House, a heritage building that was once a bank, this restaurant and bar is graced with some striking features, including barrel-vaulted ceilings, modern stained-glass light fixtures and a stylish bar. Cowboy murals and comfy leather seating make it an inviting setting for the Latin/Spanish/French cuisine which makes ample use of the best West Coast ingredients. Excellent cocktails too.

### Chill Winston

3 Alexander St. Tel: 604 288 9575. Open: L & D Wed–Sun. $$
www.chillwinston.ca

A motto of "Eat, Drink, Chill" says it all about this lounge and restaurant aimed at a hungry, hip crowd that likes meat. Many of the daily dishes focus on beef, but tempura, scallops, organic greens and crab cakes all make a showing. Good wine, good beer, good place to hang out.

### Cioppino's Mediterranean Grill

1133 Hamilton St (Davie and Helmeken). Tel: 604 688 7466. Open: D Mon–Sat. $$$
www.cioppinosyaletown.com.

Award-winning Yaletown Italian with an international reputation, Cioppino's Mediterranean Grill and sister restaurant Enoteca (1129 Hamilton St; tel: 604 685 8462) are owned and run by Giuseppe Posterara. He focuses on fresh ingredients, particularly vegetables, and aims for a lighter cuisine using olive oil rather than animal fats and creams. Local seafood, local beef and veal, game and poultry are all beautifully handled – lobster tortelli naturale with sweet pepper sauce and the organic lemon tart are particularly toothsome.

### Elixir

322 Davie St. Tel: 604 642 6787. Open: B, L & D daily. $$

www.elixirvancouver.ca

Cleverly designed brasserie-style restaurant with four distinct areas to suit your taste and mood. The French bistro-inspired food produced by chef Don Letendre (who has worked in Tokyo and also in Britain for Raymond Blanc and Bruno Loubet at l'Odeon) sets it apart from the crowd.

## Floata
400–182 Keefer St. Tel: 604 602 0368. Open: B, L & D daily. $
www.floata.com
This gargantuan Chinese restaurant in the heart of Chinatown gives mass-dining a whole new meaning – 1,000 seats make this the largest in western Canada. It serves largely Cantonese cuisine, but does a good line in local seafood specialities and dim sum. Needless to say, it is a popular spot for big Chinese weddings and celebrations, and anyone after reasonable and very cheap Chinese food.

## The Mouse and the Bean
207 West Hastings St. Tel: 604 633 1781. Open: L Mon–Sat, D Fri & Sat. $
www.themouseandthebean.com
Now in a new location on the corner of Cambie and West Hastings, this reasonable Mexican place has been cheerfully decorated and its menu expanded. The chicken quesadillas are a big favourite, and you can eat well for under $10.

## Provence Marinaside
1177 Marinaside Crescent. Tel: 604 681 4144. Open: B, L & D daily. $$
www.provencevancouver.com
Another Yaletown stalwart with a Provençal flavour – offering pre-dominantly fish, but with an oyster bar and an antipasti showcase. The seafood platter of lobster or crab, scallops, prawns, mussels, clams and fish with mixed sautéd vegetables is a great bargain, and a fixed-price four-course game menu in the autumn is a treat. A pretty patio and a casual atmosphere make it a great spot for lunch and weekend brunch as well as dinner.

## Shiru-Bay Chopstick Café
1193 Hamilton St. Tel: 604 408 9315. Open: D daily. $$
www.shiru-bay.com
This Yaletown hotspot is set in an old warehouse with outdoor patio, bar seating, communal tables and a few individual tables for those who book. Shiru-Bay is an izakaya-style Japanese eatery serving Tokyo-inspired tapas. It has an open kitchen and bar seating that allows you to watch the food being prepared. Spicy ebi-chili-mayo prawns and asparagus gyoza and the sashimi platter are particularly good. But there are more traditional dishes too – duck breast with duck-leg confit and the like, along with a daily menu. It's a popular place for after-work drinks and dinner, so make reservations or get there early.

## Steamworks Bar and Restaurant
375 Water St. Tel: 604 689 2739. Open: L & D daily. $
www.steamworks.com
In recent years, Canada has been treated to an explosion of small brewing companies, and Vancouver is blessed with several. Steamworks gets its name from the famous Gastown steam line that runs through its premises, which Gastown Brewing Company uses to provide the steam to fire its on-site brewing kettles. The food is straightforward pub fare, but good quality and good value. Needless to say the beer is excellent!

## Top of Vancouver Revolving Restaurant
555 West Hastings St. Tel: 604 669 2220. Open: L & D daily. $$$
www.topofvancouver.com
A glass elevator whisks you to the top of the downtown Harbour tower to the most spectacular view over the city. The restaurant makes a complete revolution every 60 minutes, so that every diner has a panoramic view. Open for brunch,

### PRICE CATEGORIES
Prices for three-course dinner per person with a half-bottle of house wine:
$ = under C$30
$$ = C$30–50
$$$ = C$50–80
$$$$ = more than C$80

**RIGHT:** the Floata dining hall.

# RESTAURANTS & BARS

lunch and dinner, with a fairly straightforward menu of pasta, seafood and meat dishes competently cooked, the restaurant doesn't claim to provide cutting-edge cuisine; the main attraction here is the view.

### Villa Del Lupo
869 Hamilton St. Tel: 604 688 7436. Open: D daily. $$
www.villadellupo.com
This charming Italian is set in a lovely heritage house, with a number of very pretty rooms in which to dine. Period details, open fires and beautiful furnishings enhance the fine-dining experience. Osso bucco is a signature dish, and it makes ample use of the best the West Coast has to offer. Excellent

selection of grappas and a fine wine list, with tons of Italians, and a good selection of New World and other Europeans listed by grape varietal.

### Yaletown Brewing Company
1111 Mainland St. Tel: 604 681 2739. Open: L & D daily. $
Soups, pizza, noodles, burgers, sandwiches and salads are served in Vancouver's original brew pub, which is housed in a converted industrial building with wood-beamed ceiling. (A brew pub produces beer on site and only sells it within the pub. It isn't available anywhere else.) Voted Best Brew Pub in Canada on several occasions, the Yaletown is a very popular

after-work stop for Vancouverites. Try the Red Truck Ale along with Charlie's meatloaf.

### Commercial Drive

### Bukowski's Bar and Bistro
1447 Commercial Drive. Tel: 604 253 4770. Open: D daily. $$
Named after the American writer, this cool place in a cool neighbourhood, lined with black-and-white photographs and books, has live jazz, blues and poetry most nights of the week. The book-lined bar downstairs encourages mingling, eating and drinking in equal measure. Dishes feature unusual combinations such as roast chicken and Thai noodles or sea bass with orange glaze.

### Federico's Supper Club
1728 Commercial Drive. Tel: 604 251 3473. Open: D Wed–Sun. $$
www.federicossupperclub.com
This legacy from the area's Italian community is a great place for old-fashioned Italian food and, believe it or not, dancing – ballroom, smoochy stuff, the hustle and a conga line at the end of the evening. Great fun and good food. As one reviewer put it, "If you ever wanted to beam yourself back to what

night-clubbers considered the peak of classy back in the 1950s, here you go." Wed–Sun 5.30–midnight.

### Havana
1212 Commercial Drive. Tel: 604 253 9119. Open: L & D daily. $$
www.havana-art.com
Trendy Cuban and Latin American-influenced restaurant/bar with lively Latin vibe. The patio outside is great for gawping at the local colour on the street; inside it's lined with photographs of old Havana on the distressed walls. Salads, sandwiches, soups and tapas served all day – yam fries and Baja squid mentioned in dispatches – and it's open for breakfast. A small theatre and an art gallery attached to the restaurant make it a very popular spot.

### Szechuan Chongqing
2808 Commercial Drive (East 12th Ave). Tel: 604 254 7434. Open: B, L & D daily. $
www.szechuanchongqing.com
This Chinese restaurant, along with its sister on Broadway, has pioneered Szechuan cuisine in Vancouver – the hot and sour soup is exceptionally good, as are Szechuan green beans and beef in black bean sauce. Rated one of the top Chinese restaurants in the city (in spite of the plain decor).

**LEFT:** the Luna Café.

## Bars and Cafés

At the western end of Gastown, **Brioche Urban Baking** (401 West Cordova) is a popular place for pastries, panini and coffee. **The Luna Café** (117–131 Water St) offers breakfast, sandwiches on a great choice of breads, and organic coffee. Also holds poetry readings and small concerts in the evening. Among the most characterful cafés in this very touristy part of town. The **Opus Bar** (322 Davie St) in the eponymous hotel has a tapas-inspired menu and innovative cocktails, while its Café O is good for morning papers and a café au lait. Nearby **Boulangerie la Parisienne** (1076 Mainland St), a café and bakery with a pretty all-blue interior, serves the usual pastries and decent coffee and opens up onto the pavement in the summer. **Water Street Café** (300 Water St) has a fairly substantial menu and is a good place for a quick lunch if you find yourself in this neck of the woods. On 177 Davie St is **Urban Fare**, a huge grocery store that also has a café serving breakfast and light lunches, pasta, salads and the like. **Waves** (492 West Hastings St) provides free Wi-Fi along with decent coffee and the usual muffin-pastry-cake scenario.

### Commercial Drive

Commercial Drive is heaving with trendy coffee places, ethnic cafés and bars. The section between Broadway and Venables is particularly lively. It is worth a cruise up and down, looking for somewhere that appeals, although you will be spoilt for choice. Here are some recommendations:

**Juicy Lucy's Juice Bar and Eatery** (1420 Commercial Drive) is a good place for freshly squeezed fruit and vegetable juices, or a quick snack of fresh sandwiches and pastries. **Clove** (2054 Commercial Drive) is a laid-back late-night café with South Asian food. Also has a branch on Denman. **La Casa Gelato** (1033 Venables St) claims to sell the largest selection of ice cream in the world, with 218 flavours on offer from its repertoire of over 500 varieties. There is something for everyone, with non-fat, non-dairy, low fat and sugar-free ice-creams in flavours ranging from the imaginable honeydew melon or chocolate Oreo cookie to off-the-wall ideas such as wild asparagus or pear and gorgonzola. **Prado Café** (1938 Commercial Drive at East 4th Ave) is a minimalist Wi-Fi café open from 6am serving organic Fairtrade coffee, organic juices, smoothies and baked goodies made in-house. **Tony's Deli** (1046 Commercial Drive) specialises in delicious Italian salads, including sun-dried tomato penne, a dozen different panini, muffins, coffee cakes and rich Italian coffee, all served in a homey, authentic setting. **Uprising Breads Bakery** (1697 Venables St) produces organic and wholegrain breads and sells home-made soup, sandwiches, salads, baked goodies and organic Fairtrade coffee. **La Grotta del Formaggio** (1791 Commercial Drive) is a gourmet deli with a sidewalk patio where you can grab a bite and a coffee. **Latin Quarter** (1305 Commercial Drive) serves excellent tapas to a local crowd.

### PRICE CATEGORIES

Prices for three-course dinner per person with a half-bottle of house wine:
$ = under C$30
$$ = C$30–50
$$$ = C$50–80
$$$$ = more than C$80

**RIGHT:** Water Street Café, a good lunch stop in the heart of Gastown.

# STANLEY PARK

This spectacularly located park is Vancouver's playground and exercise yard. Healthy hordes of cyclists, joggers and in-line skaters share the Seawall Promenade with amblers taking in the views at a more leisurely pace

It's hard to imagine Vancouver without Stanley Park. It is one of the attributes that makes it such a spectacular city, and it's all thanks to the threat of US belligerence; when the US occupied the San Juan Islands in 1859, fears rose of a possible US invasion, and the land was set aside in 1863 as a military reserve. This saved it from development until the need for it had passed and far-sighted advocates for its preservation came forward. In 1887, Stanley Park was designated a recreational reserve.

It was named after Lord Stanley, who was the first Governor-General of Canada to visit Vancouver. As an observer recorded, "Lord Stanley threw his arms to the heavens, as though embracing within them the whole of one thousand acres of primeval forest, and dedicated it 'to the use and enjoyment of peoples of all colours, creeds and customs, for all time'."

A village in the park was occupied until the late 19th century by the Squamish band of the Coast Salish Indians, and the army created sports facilities for the soldiers billeted in the eastern side of the park, such as a cricket field, rugby pitch and tennis courts, but all trace of the original facilities has gone. Scout camps were also held here before World War I, when the company of bears was not unknown.

## Seawall Promenade

Today Stanley Park is the green lung of Vancouver and one of the largest parks in any city, covering 404 hectares (998 acres). The 9-km (5½-mile) **Seawall Promenade** for walkers and cyclists follows the sea around the park and is so heavily used that cyclists and in-line skaters are allowed to use it only in an anti-clockwise direction. The seawall

Map on page 110

**LEFT:** cycling the seawall.
**BELOW:** mesmerised by beluga whales in the Aquarium.

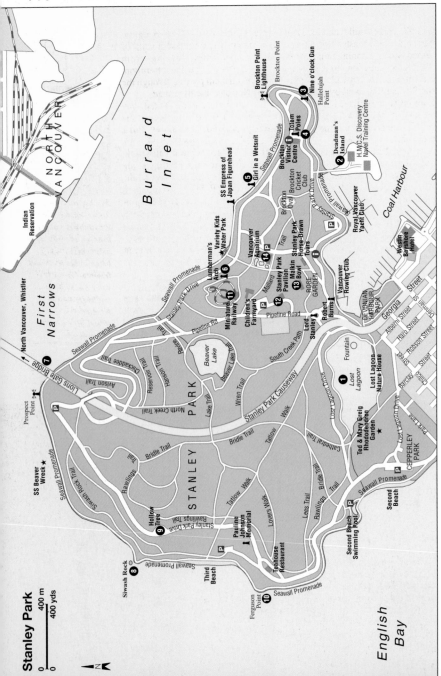

# Stanley Park

0 _____ 400 m
0 _____ 400 yds

N

First Narrows

Burrard Inlet

NORTH VANCOUVER

Indian Reservation

North Vancouver, Whistler

Lions Gate Bridge

Prospect Point

SS Beaver Wreck ★

Siwash Rock ★

Siwash Rock

8

Seawall Promenade

Third Beach

Seawall Trail

Seawall Promenade

Ferguson Point

10

Teahouse Restaurant

Pauline Johnson Memorial

Hollow Tree

9

Stanley Park Drive

Rawlings

Bridle Trail

Lovers Walk

Lees Trail

Tatlow Walk

Tatlow Walk

STANLEY PARK

Rawlings Trail

Bridle Trail

Swishuk Trail

Chickadee Trail

Reservoir Trail

Tatlow Trail

Beaver Lake Trail

Lake Trail

Wren Trail

Beaver Lake

Pipeline Rd

Pipeline Road

North Creek Trail

South Creek Park

Cathedral Trail

Stanley Park Causeway

Stanley Park Causeway Walk

Second Beach

Second Beach Swimming Pool

CEPPERLEY PARK

Ted & Mary Greig Rhododendron Garden ★

Lost Lagoon Drive

Lost Lagoon Drive

Lost Lagoon

1

Fountain

Lost Lagoon Nature House

English Bay

Park Lane

Barclay Street

Chilco Street

Denman Street

Robson Street

Haro Street

Alberni Street

Georgia Street

DEVONIAN HARBOUR PARK

Westin Bayshire Hotel

Coal Harbour

Royal Vancouver Yacht Club

Vancouver Rowing Club

ROSE GARDEN

Robert Burns

Lord Stanley

Malkin Bowl

12

Stanley Park Pavilion

13

Children's Farmyard

Miniature Railway

11

Lumberman's Arch

6

Variety Kids Water Park

Vancouver Aquarium

14

Stanley Park Horse-Drawn Tours

7

Malkin

Mallard Trail

Avison Trail

Squirrel Trail

Stanley Park Drive

Seawall Park Drive

Seawall Promenade

Girl in a Wetsuit

SS Empress of Japan Figurehead

5

Seawall Promenade

Brockton Point

Brockton Visitor Centre

Totem Poles

1

4

Nine o'clock Gun

3

Hallelujah Point

Brockton Point Lighthouse

Brockton Point

Brockton Oval

Brockton Cricket Club

Park Drive

Deadman's Island

2

H.M.C.S. Discovery Naval Training Centre

took 53 years to build, and for 32 of them a Scottish master stonemason named James Cunningham coordinated its construction; his dedication is commemorated by a plaque opposite Siwash Rock and by the James Cunningham Seawall Race run on the last Sunday of October.

Step inland into the forest onto the extensive network of paths partly made out of old logging roads and within minutes you will find relative solitude, even in high summer. After a walk through the quieter parts of the forest, it comes as no surprise to learn that Stanley Park inspired some of Emily Carr's first landscapes, while she was teaching children's art in Vancouver in 1906.

The best way to explore and appreciate the park properly is by bike *(see right)* if you're short of time, or on foot. In summer there is a steady stream of cyclists crossing Georgia Street to pick up the path – it has become one of the most popular activities for visitors, since the views are enough to convince anyone of Vancouver's claim to be one of the most beautifully situated cities in the world. It's also a great way to see the impressive sight of the cruise ships leaving from Canada Place in the late afternoon, and watch them passing through the First Narrows at close range.

Another, albeit more limited, way to see the park is to join one of the tours operated by **Stanley Park Horse-Drawn Tours** (Mar–Oct; tel: 604 681 5115; www.stanleypark. com). The roomy carriages are drawn by Grey Shire, Clydesdale, Percheron or Belgian horses, which meander along the roads with a professional guide to interpret the sites. The hour-long tours leave from a kiosk at Coal Harbour car park adjacent to the information booth. Reservations are not required.

## An anticlockwise tour

The waterfront area between Canada Place and Stanley Park is known as Coal Harbour, after a thin seam of coal first noted by Captain Vancouver. The waters that once teemed with herring and clams are now filled with pleasure craft, behind which soars a glittering row

Map on page 110

*Just before Denman Street reaches Georgia, there is cluster of bike rental shops providing all kinds of bikes, child seats and trailers. Go early if you want to have a relatively unobstructed ride or rollerblade around the seawall.*

**BELOW:** the stunningly located Brockton Oval.

*The thicket of totem poles near Brockton Point represent the traditions of the Coastal First Nations people.*

**BELOW:** an evening stroll along the seawall promenade.

of glass towers, that together form one of the classic vistas seen across the water from Stanley Park. As you enter the park from Georgia Street, the body of water on your left, known as the **Lost Lagoon ❶**, was part of Coal Harbour until the causeway was erected in 1916, turning it into a freshwater lake fed from the city's supply. The rush-fringed lake dotted with small islands is a haven for many varieties of birds, including swans, ducks and Canada geese. Beside the south side of the lake is the **Lost Lagoon Nature House**, operated by the Stanley Park Ecology Society (tel: 604 681 5115; www.stanleyparkecology.ca), which offers natural history information and guided walking tours.

Pipeline Road leads to a cluster of visitor attractions. Near the entrance to the park, directly behind the Rowing Club building, is a **statue of the poet Robert Burns** which was unveiled by Ramsay MacDonald on 25 August 1928, a year before he became British Prime Minister for the second time. Near by is a **statue of Lord Stanley** (1960) by English sculptor Sydney Marsh, which captures Stanley's expansive gesture at the ceremony.

Beyond the Royal Vancouver Yacht Club lies **Deadman's Island ❷**, so named because it was once a native burial ground when bodies were ceremoniously placed in bentwood boxes high in the Douglas firs and red cedars. It became an isolation site and burial ground after smallpox epidemics in 1888 and 1892, but the island has been a regular source of dispute. A 99-year lease of the island by the federal government in 1930 stipulated that it should be used as a park, but it has been a naval reserve, HMCS *Discovery* since 1944.

Every night at 9 o'clock the boom of a cannon issues from Hallelujah Point, so named because it was the frequent meeting point of a small troop of the Salvation Army. The **Nine o'clock Gun ❸** was cast in England in 1816 and has been fired since 1894, initially from a site near the present-day Hudson's Bay Company store. Some say it started as a fishing curfew signal, others that it's just a noisy timepiece. It's fired electronically from the harbourmaster's perch on top of a skyscraper, and is protected by a fence to stop a repetition of its kidnap by UBC students who ransomed the gun for a donation to a children's hospital.

Just off the main path are eight **totem poles ❹** representing the Kwakiutl and Haida nations, and each is explained by interpretive boards at the nearby **Brockton Visitor Centre** (www.city.vancouver.bc.ca). As you round Brockton Point, North Vancouver and the Coast Mountains are spread out in a majestic sweep to the north. The point is marked by a small red-and-white-striped lighthouse built in 1914.

It had been the intention to site beside the next section of the path a replica of Copenhagen's famous waterfront statue of the Little Mermaid, but a licence was refused, so a contemporary version was commissioned from Elek Imredy. The **Girl in a Wetsuit**  complete with goggles was unveiled in 1972.

A slight detour inland, **Lumberman's Arch** ❻ is a replica of the arch built over Pender Street in 1912 to welcome Queen Victoria's son, the Duke of Connaught, while he was Governor General of Canada. The arch was built near the site of a Squamish village of four houses and a lodge until the 1860s, where potlatches attended by thousands of native people were held. Tonnes of seashells from the village midden were used to surface the first roads through the forest.

Just after passing underneath the **Lions Gate Bridge** ❼ *(see below)* is Prospect Point, site of the most famous wreck in Vancouver history when the first steamship on the West Coast, the *Beaver*, went aground in 1888. She sat on the rocks for four years, being steadily stripped by souvenir hunters, until the wake of a passing ship sent her to the bottom.

Many of the salvaged items can be seen in the Vancouver Museum and the Maritime Museum, and she is depicted in a mural in the Marine Building *(see page 75)*.

The offshore 15-metre (49-ft) high column of grey basalt rock is known as **Siwash Rock** ❽, created according to Indian legend when four giants were so impressed by the devotion of a young chief to his newborn son that they turned him to stone, as a monument to probity in fatherhood. This curious notion of a reward was recorded by a half-Mohawk from Ontario, Pauline Johnson (1861–1913), who spent her last four years in Vancouver where she wrote a series of newspaper articles. Her grave inland from Ferguson Point is the only marked grave in Stanley Park.

Just beyond the tarmac road inland from Siwash Rock is the **Hollow Tree** ❾, a huge red cedar. It is probably Canada's most photographed tree, thanks to an early 20th-century photographer who spent years snapping visitors beside this remnant of old-growth forest.

Map on page 110

*Look out for the* Girl in a Wetsuit *just after Brockton Point. The unmistakable bright yellow mounds visible on the north shore beyond are piles of sulphur.*

## Lions Gate Bridge

For most people, the Lions Gate Bridge is the most striking of Vancouver's many bridges, spanning the waters between the forest of Stanley Park and the steeply rising land of the north shore. Astonishingly it was not a city or federal project but constructed for the Guinness family in Ireland, designed both to enhance the development potential of the 1,620 hectares (4,000 acres) of land they had bought along the north shore of Burrard Inlet but also to provide jobs during the Depression. Construction began in March 1937, and it opened to traffic in November 1938, having cost C$5.8 million. It was formally opened by King George VI and Queen Elizabeth in May 1939 during the first visit of a reigning monarch to Canada.

Officially known as the First Narrows Bridge, the suspension bridge has a total length of 1,820 metres (5,890 feet) and a tower height of 111 metres (364 feet). The centre of three lanes is reversed according to the direction of commuter traffic, and heavy trucks are banned. The bridge was sold by the Guinness family to the province in 1955 for C$5.9 million, and in 1963 the tolls were abolished. The lighting that makes the bridge such a spectacular sight at night was given to the city by the Guinness family in 1986.

**TIP**

There's a frequent free shuttle bus service every 15 minutes linking 15 stops around the park, which operates between late June and late September between 10am and 6.30pm. The buses are powered by propane gas and have picture windows.

**BELOW RIGHT:**
the Sequoia Grill.

Past Third Beach is **Ferguson Point** ❿, named after an early member of the Parks Board. Almost on the point is the Sequoia Grill at the Teahouse restaurant, created out of a tearoom that was opened on the site of a World War II gun battery. During the warmer months along the western beaches of the park, an artist in stone creates Inukshuk-style, precariously balanced piles of rocks that attract crowds at weekends. Near Second Beach is a 50-metre (164-ft) summer-only freshwater swimming pool overlooking the sea, tennis courts, miniature golf course and even an outdoor dance floor.

The seawall trail ends near the **Ted and Mary Greig Rhododendron Garden**, which is composed of 4,500 plants. A walk in May along the wood-chip path between the massed blooms of pastel-coloured flowers is not to be missed.

### Attractions within the park

Accessible from the Plaza off Pipeline Road is a **miniature railway** ⓫ winding through the forest, with a diesel-powered replica of steam locomotive No. 374 which pulled the first transcontinental train into Vancouver in 1886. Nearby is a **children's farmyard** (both summer, 11am–4pm) with goats, sheep, cows, ponies and pigs as well as some snakes and exotic birds. To the south of the plaza, **Stanley Park Pavilion** ⓬ was designed to resemble a Swiss chalet, originally housing the Vancouver Park Board offices and a refreshment area. Constructed of stone and wood in 1911 to the design of Otto Moburg, it was grand enough to host a reception given by the Prince of Wales in 1919 for the families of soldiers killed in World War I. The café has a terrace overlooking the garden and serves light meals and drinks.

The open-air theatre and concert area known as the **Malkin Bowl** ⓭ was built in 1934 by the grocery wholesaler and former mayor W.H. Malkin in memory of his wife. The future of its crescent-shaped proscenium arch is uncertain because the Theatre under the Stars company wants to replace the heritage structure with a better facility,

## Flora and Fauna

**M**ost of Stanley Park's red cedar, hemlock and Douglas fir trees are second- and third-growth forest, since it was logged several times in the second half of the 19th century. However, there is a delightful scattering of deciduous trees such as vine maple and red alder, and even some old-growth trees such as the National Geographic Tree – a cedar described by the magazine as one of the oldest and largest trees in the world at about 1,000 years and 5 metres in diameter. It can be found on the path south from the hollow tree to Third Beach. The park is home to large populations of racoons, squirrels, skunks and coyotes. Despite notices urging people not to feed the racoons and squirrels, both have become accustomed to easy handouts. The open water of Beaver Lake and Lost Lagoon attract migratory birds, though many Canada geese, swans and ducks have made their home in the park. You may also spot a blue heron or a wood duck.

The best way to experience all this wonderful nature and wildlife is to venture off the beaten track, away from the seawall, and follow one of the many hiking trails through the tranquil woods.

while conservationists argue that the current structure could be upgraded.

Though the large garden south of the Malkin Bowl is described as a **Rose Garden**, it is actually the thoughtful colour combinations of the massed bedding plants that provide the more impressive displays between April and September. To the east is a memorial to US President Warren Harding, who visited Vancouver in 1923. He was the first US President to visit Canada, and created such a favourable impression that Vancouverites were stunned when he had a heart attack and died in San Francisco seven days after leaving Canada. A competition was held for the design of a monument, won by Charles Marega *(see page 93)*, to be erected on the spot where Harding spoke to the public.

The most popular of the park's attractions is the **Vancouver Aquarium ⑭** (10am–5.30pm, July–Aug 9.30am–7pm; tel: 604 659 3473; www.vanaqua.org). Tanks range from domestic aquariums to open-air pools large enough for beluga whales, with underground viewing

windows to watch the vast, blubbery creatures in motion. The vibrant colours of the tropical corals are spectacular, and children are fascinated by such weird-looking fish as the box-shaped black porcupine fish. An area devoted to Amazonia has a tank of some extraordinary fish found in the river, such as redtailed catfish, tambaqui and the arapaima, – the world's largest freshwater fish, growing up to 4.5 metres (15ft).

A large, and very humid conservatory recreates the atmosphere of the rainforest with free-range birds, butterflies, tortoises, sloths and lizards. The scarlet ibis is the most colourful thanks to its diet of carotine-rich crab and shrimps. Tanks of frogs, snakes and insects are followed by an area for eerily motionless Yacare caimans.

But of all these fascinating sea creatures, those in the outside pools are the biggest crowd-pullers, particularly at feeding times. It's hard not be mesmerised by the sea otters' balletic performance as they spin around excitedly retrieving the fish, then use their tummies for a dining table. ❑

Map on page 110

*Tanks filled with marine life from a variety of habitats fascinate, but the snowy white beluga whales and sea otters steal the show.*

## RESTAURANTS

**The Fish House**
901 Stanley Park Drive. Tel: 604 681 7275. Open: L & D daily. $$
www.fishhousestanleypark.com
Award-winning restaurant in a charming setting overlooking English Bay, specialising in fresh fish and seafood. Signature dishes include tiger prawns sautéed with garlic at your table. Weekend brunch and afternoon tea are also served.

**Prospect Point Café in Stanley Park**
Prospect Point Lookout, Stanley Park Drive. Tel: 604 669 2737. Open: L & D daily in summer, L only in winter. $
www.prospectpoint.ca
Seek out this great viewing point, which nestles on the cliffside overlooking Lions Gate Bridge. The café focuses on West Coast cuisine, with wild BC Salmon as a speciality, along with pastas, burgers and fish and

chips. Save room for their famous home-made ice.

**Sequoia Grill at the Teahouse**
Ferguson Point, Stanley Park Drive. Tel: 604 669 3281. Open: L & D daily. $$
Voted the best place to watch the sun set, Sequoia Grill lives up to expectations. This former teahouse transformed into a restaurant has a conservatory, drawing room, patio tables, and open fires in the winter. The food is straightforward, relying on fresh ingredients, with some platters to share – the

seafood platter is stunning. Venison and halibut are also excellent.

**Stanley Park Pavilion (at the Rose Garden)**
610 Pipeline Road, Stanley Park. Tel: 604 602 3088. $$
www.stanleyparkpavilion.com
High tea is the thing to go for here. The Pavilion is a Swiss-style building with verandas and patios in a fabulous setting in the Rose Garden.

● ● ● ● ● ● ● ● ● ●
*Price includes dinner and a half-bottle of house wine.*
*$ under C$30, $$ C$30–50, $$$ C$50–80, $$$$ C$80+*

# MODERN ARCHITECTURE

**In a generation the skyline of Vancouver has been pierced by a succession of ever taller buildings, reflecting the return of residents to the city centre**

In its short history, Vancouver has developed a reputation for innovative architecture, helped by being the home of some leading 20th-century architects, most famously Arthur Erickson. Like every city, there are plenty of buildings that contribute little or nothing to the city's visual appeal, and equally it would have benefited from a more sparing use of the wrecking ball. But there is much to celebrate from most periods of Vancouver's development.

Until the 1960s the pace of change was slow, and someone who knew the city before World War I would have had no difficulty recognising it half a century later. But since then the appearance of the city has been utterly transformed, giving opportunities for architects to design new, and adapt old, mostly industrial buildings, for residential and office use. Most of the attention goes to the large sites and commissions such as Simon Fraser University and the redevelopments around Coal Harbour and False Creek, but West Vancouver has some exceptional modern houses by such architects as Ron Thom, Peter Thornton and Erickson.

**LEFT:** the interior of the Museum of Anthropology at UBC was designed in 1976 by Arthur Erickson to house the outstanding collection of ethnographic and archaeological objects. The traditional West Coast post-and-beam structures of First Nations peoples was the inspiration for the design. Glass walls 15 metres (49ft) high light the interior.

**ABOVE:** the terraced access levels of Arthur Erickson's Law Courts are wonderfully light, thanks to sloping planes of glass above the plants and sculptures that decorate them.
**LEFT:** the city's Central Library invites comparison with Rome's Colosseum, though architect Moshe Safdie has denied that it inspired his design.

**RIGHT:** at the top of the 177-metre (581ft) Harbour Centre Tower is The Lookout! Perched on top of a conventional office building, the pod designed by Eng and Wright in 1977 contains a viewing platform and a revolving restaurant.

## SHANGRI-LA

In 2008 Shangri-La Hotel will open at 1128 West Georgia Street to become Vancouver's tallest building at 199 metres (652ft). Designed by James K.M. Cheng, the 62-storey triangular building has no levels 4 or 13. The 15-storey hotel will contain 120 rooms, and floors 16–42 will accommodate 227 condominiums. Above them, on floors 43–59, will be "private access residential units", with two penthouses on the top two floors. The upper one has a roof garden and swimming pool for $13 million. At ground level will be retail units and an art gallery.

At the same time as Shangri-La is being built, the last stage of the redevelopment of False Creek is taking place with construction of the Olympic Village. Low and mid-rise accommodation is being built for 2,500 athletes in 1,100 units. After the games are over, the temporary Olympic structures in the vicinity will be dismantled, leaving a model sustainable community with market and affordable housing, parkland, and office and shopping complexes.

Another Olympic venue, the Richmond Oval for speed skating events, is forming the centrepiece of a 13-hectare (32-acre) redevelopment along the banks of the Fraser River with a waterfront plaza and park. The 8,000-seater Oval itself will become a multi-purpose sports and recreation centre.

**ABOVE:** the west side of the Academic Quadrangle at Simon Fraser University. In 1963 a competition held to decide the architect of Simon Fraser University was won by Arthur Erickson and Geoffrey Massey. They rejected multi-storey buildings as inappropriate for the location on Burnaby Mountain, and used the hill towns of Italy as inspiration to integrate the university into its setting.

**BELOW:** the "sails" of Canada Place, overlooking the Inner Harbour, which was designed by Toronto's Zeidler-Roberts Partnership with Downs-Archambault for Expo '86. The building contains a hotel, cruise ship terminal and conference centre.

**BELOW:** at the east end of False Creek is the geodesic dome of 766 triangles designed by Bruno Freschi for Expo '86 and adapted by Boak Alexander into the popular attraction of Science World.

# GRANVILLE ISLAND AND FALSE CREEK

Once the site of sawmills and heavy industry, this patch of land has been transformed into a model of urban living. At its hub, a thriving farmers' market offers fresh regional produce to a health-obsessed clientele. Throw in some great restaurants, a handful of museums and artists' studios, and you have the elements of a perfect day out

If there's one area of Vancouver that almost every visitor goes to, it's Granville Island, lying in the shadow of Granville Bridge on the south shore of False Creek. This model of urban regeneration is packed with theatres, craft workshops and studios, restaurants, cafés, bars and a huge fresh-produce market, making it one of the most vibrant parts of the city. There are still chandlers, boat companies, an engineering workshop and a cement plant to give the area some "grit", and the island is also an appropriate home for the Emily Carr Institute, which offers courses in art, photography and film.

A few people live on the island in attractive houseboats, and there is a hotel and a couple of microbreweries. Two parks and plenty of trees soften the well-adapted industrial buildings, and the views across the water from the perimeter of the island are some of the best in Vancouver. The only blight is the traffic which clogs the narrow streets in the often vain hope of finding somewhere to park.

Salvation may come in the form of a new railway which, once in operation, will allow restrictions to be placed on car access. The island is already at one end of the heritage tram route (*see page 120*), and there

has long been talk of extending the route beyond the end of False Creek to take the tracks along Quebec Street to Columbia and then up Cordova to Waterfront Station and Stanley Park, as part of a wider plan to reintroduce light rail to the city.

The most pleasant way of reaching the island is by the double-ended small ferries operated by AquaBus (which takes bikes) and False Creek Ferries (which does not). *For more information on ferry transport in False Creek see page 234.*

Map on page 120

**LEFT:** Granville Island by night. **BELOW:** the AquaBus ferry.

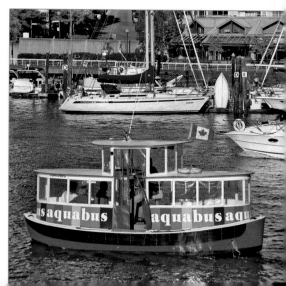

*A halt by Lamey's Mill Road at the entrance to Granville Island is the terminus of the streetcar ride to Science World. (www.trams.ca). The 1905-built cars operate every half-hour from 1–5pm (departing from Science World every half-hour from 12.30–4.30pm) at weekends and holidays from mid-May to early October.*

## History

Until the arrival of Europeans, False Creek had teemed with fish, and its south shore had been a wintering ground of the Squamish nation. False Creek was so named in 1859 when Captain George Richards found a dead end during Royal Navy survey work instead of the expected link to coal deposits that he had found in Burrard Inlet. Mills were erected around the creek to process the immense stands of Douglas fir in the district that became Shaughnessy, and factories making sash windows and doors grew up alongside the mills.

The decision of the Canadian Pacific Railway (CPR) to terminate its transcontinental line at English Bay rather than Port Moody, coupled with construction of the first of three Granville bridges and settlement of the south shore after the 1886 fire, increased the importance of this once peaceful inlet.

Granville Island was created in 1915 when 760,000 cubic metres of sea mud was sucked from the bed of False Creek and poured into wooden shuttering to form the island. It was part of a much larger scheme to reclaim 25 hectares (61 acres) of land for railway yards, which reduced False Creek to one-fifth of its original size. The island was an immediate success, quickly occupied by a range of companies, from ironworks and shipyards to manufacturers of rope and machinery geared to the needs of the mining and forestry industries. Most occupied corrugated-iron factories, and many had barges on one side and rail lines on the other. False Creek echoed with the constant shunting of boxcars and the noise of heavy machinery.

By the end of World War II, the rail-linked lumber yards, sawmills and greasy rat-infested wharves had degenerated into such a state that

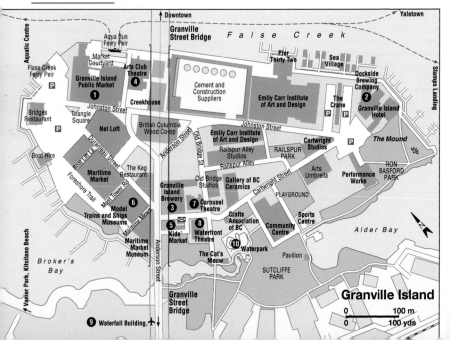

Granville Island

studies were made into completing the job of filling in the entire creek. Thankfully the prohibitive cost forced the development of more imaginative solutions. The city and the CPR agreed a land swap, but having gained control of the creek's south side, the city was split over whether it should continue to be used by industry or whether it should be turned over to housing. Campaigners for the latter won. The waterfront was cleaned up and walled and the popular neighbourhood of False Creek came into being.

## Foodie heaven

The main **Public Market** ❶ is actually five buildings brought together to form a covered market. In sheds that once repaired mining equipment and made wire rope is a farmers' market of astonishingly high quality produce: piles of beautifully arranged fruit and vegetables from the lower mainland and the Okanagan; great counters of ice-cooled seafood; fresh pasta; well-butchered and trimmed meat; over 150 different kinds of cheese; herbs, spices

and breads to meet the needs of the city's cosmopolitan population; and specialist makers of fudge, chocolate and ready meals.

In the northern corner is a Food Court where you can buy healthy hot and cold food of a quality that matches the market. There is an area to eat inside, but unless it's raining most people eat outside overlooking the water and Burrard Bridge and listening to the street musicians.

The small island is home to two microbreweries. **Dockside Brewing Company** ❷ at 1253 Johnston Street has a German brewmaster who's also worked in Bolivia and Nigeria and now produces eight beers which can be sampled in the Dockside Lounge of the Granville Island Hotel (which has special offers on beers on Tuesday and Wednesday).

The **Granville Island Brewery** ❸ (tel: 604 687 2739; www.gib.ca) at 1441 Cartwright Street was Canada's first microbrewery, founded in 1984. It produces five staple and additional seasonal brews, which are on offer in the

Map on page 120

**TIP**

Siegel's Bagels (inside the market) makes authentic Montreal bagels, kettle-boiled and then baked in a 25-ton wood-burning oven, producing a smoky flavour, crunchy on the outside and chewy on the inside.

**BELOW:** mouth-watering displays fill the market.

# BC Microbrews

**Y**ou can't go far in British Columbia without meeting a local microbrew – or craft beer, to use the hop-head vernacular. The province is home to dozens of brewpubs and independent breweries, most of them between Vancouver Island and the Okanagan Valley. You'd need a mighty thirst to sample all of BC's indigenous suds during your stay, but here are a few lagers and ales worth quaffing.

First, the big craft-beer players: Granville Island Brewery, which bills itself as Canada's first microbrewery, and Okanagan Spring Brewery. Both have won many international awards. Like their smaller BC counterparts, they fashion preservative-free beer using just four primary ingredients: barley, hops, yeast and water. Granville Island brews a range of easy-drinking products, from its crisp Cypress Honey Lager to the limited-release GI Bitter. Okanagan Spring's six offerings run to slightly darker. Try the 1516 Bavarian Lager with food, or make a meal of the delicious, stout-like Old English Porter, a hit at 8.5 percent alcohol.

Prefer something small batch? Storm Brewing and R&B Brewing recently won first- and second-best brewery in the inaugural Vancouver Beer Awards, bestowed by the local chapter of CAMRA, the Campaign for Real Ale. The brewmasters at these outfits are passionate about big, flavourful ales, as Storm's Highland Scottish Ale and R&B's Hop Goblin India Pale Ale will attest. Also in the Vancouver area, you'll find several top-notch brewpubs, such as Dix BBQ & Brewery, the Steamworks Brewing Company and the Howe Sound BrewPub, located in the mountains near Whistler. For a taste of a uniquely BC sensibility, try the latter's Mettleman Hemp and Honey Ale, brewed in honour of a nearby mountain-bike race.

Vancouver may have its share of craft breweries, but Victoria is a favourite destination for beer lovers. On the self-guided Ale Trail, visit Spinnakers Gastro Brewpub, the country's oldest such establishment. Don't miss the delightfully hoppy India Pale Ale or, during summer, a sleeve of the clove-scented Hefeweizen, a German-style wheat beer. Spinnakers also makes its own line of malt vinegars. Close by, Swans Brewpub serves a host of national-award-winning beers: standouts include a strong Raspberry Ale and the Buckerfield's Bitter. Another Victoria contender is the Phillips Brewing Company, whose smooth Longboat Double Chocolate Porter lives up to its name.

The wine-producing Okanagan is BC's third microbrew hub. Kelowna-based Tree Brewing rolls four of its products – among them the bittersweet Thirsty Beaver Amber Ale – into a convenient eight-pack. From the Cannery Brewing Company in Penticton there's the punchy Anarchist Amber Ale, whose recipe calls for three kinds of hops. Made in the same town, the Tin Whistle Brewing Company's Killer Bee Dark Honey Ale adds five different barley malts to the mix. Drink it slowly so you don't miss any.

Many of these beers are available for takeaway at their respective breweries and brewpubs, in both bottles and kegs. British Columbia's government liquor stores also carry a wide variety. For prices and availability, see www.bcliquorstores.com or call 1 800 667 9463. ❑

**LEFT:** Granville Island Brewery's award-winning beers are made from 100% natural ingredients.

brewery's taproom. It also offers daily tours of the brewery at noon, 2pm and 4pm followed by tastings.

### Artists and artisans

Granville Island is home to the studios or workshops of 50 creative people who can be found in a free leaflet, "Artists & Artisans of Granville Island". The range of their work is astonishing: jewellery, ceramics, slippers, embroideries, paintings, Shaker oval boxes, paper, silk weaving, letterpress printing, tapestries, baskets, furniture, beadworks, hats, even a designer and maker of handmade eyewear in wood, horn, gold or silver who has made glasses for Elton John.

Most have individual studios, but the Gallery of BC Ceramics at 1359 Cartwright Street is a good place to find useful as well as decorative items by a variety of potters. A few doors along, at No. 1386, the Crafts Association of BC has a wide variety of products. There are also numerous shops selling artists' supplies, postcards, clothes, stationery and native crafts.

Besides ateliers, the barn doors of the **Arts Club Theatre** ❹ are often wide open in summer so that passers-by can watch the scenery makers at work, as are the doors to a company making delicate architectural models.

**The Kids' Market** ❺ sells clothes, toys, books, CDs, magic and party supplies, and has play areas and cafés with "child-friendly" menus.

To see why the island is such a focus of cultural life and activity, visit www.granvilleisland.com.

### Attractions

Claiming to have the world's largest public display of international model and toy trains is the **Model Trains Museum** ❻ (1502 Duranleau Street; 10am–5.30pm, May–Sept daily, Oct–Apr Tues–Sun; tel: 604 683 1939; www.modeltrainsmuseum.ca). The working model train layout is a joy for enthusiasts. It is complemented by an adjacent Model Ships Museum in which the prize exhibit is a 4-metre (13 ft 6-in) model of the ill-fated British Battleship HMS *Hood* (www.modelships museum.ca). The

*Even dogs and cats are not forgotten among Granville Island's food outlets: in Cartwright Street there's a converted caboose selling treats for pampered pooches and moggies.*

**BELOW:** Granville Island Water Park.

Map
on page
120

**TIP**

Chocoholics should not miss Rogers Chocolates at 1571 Johnston Street. Founded in 1885 in the back of a shop by an itinerant greengrocer from Massachusetts named Charles Rogers, the company commemorates its Vancouver Island origins in Victoria Creams and Empress Squares.

**BELOW:**
a wandering minstrel.

museum also contains a collection of sport fishing history and equipment.

Besides the Arts Club, **Carousel** ❼ and **Waterfront** ❽ theatres (*see page 247*), the island is home to Performance Works at 1218 Cartwright Street, set up in a 1920s machine shop to provide a rehearsal and performance space which hosts year-round events and productions.

Though just off the island at 1540 West 2nd Avenue, the **Waterfall Building** ❾ housing the Elliott Louis Gallery should not be missed by admirers of Arthur Erikson's work. Built in 1996, the Waterfall Building – actually five buildings designed for commercial and live/work use around an atrium – is approached past a thin curtain of water falling into a rectangular pond.

### Activities

Children adore racing through the water jets and fountains in the **waterpark** ❿ (daily 10am–6pm from the third weekend of May to the first weekend of September) at Sutcliffe Park, where there is also a playground.

Cycling the traffic-free path along the seawall is one of the most popular ways of appreciating Vancouver's stunning location, and Granville Island is a good starting place, with bike hire available at Reckless Bike Stores at 1810 Fir Street (tel: 604 731 2420; www.reckless.ca). Child seats and trailers are also hired out. Heading west, the path winds past the condominiums and houses that line the creek before reaching Vanier Park and Kitsilano Beach.

### Olympic Village

East of the houses and apartments of False Creek South lie the last remnants of the area's industrial past. This section of land is undergoing huge redevelopment, including the construction of an Olympic Village in preparation for the 2010 Winter Olympics. Housing for 14,000 residents is being built. Consequently the seawall path is subject to re-routing as work progresses, but the priority being given to pedestrians and cyclists in the planning should guarantee the restoration of one of the city's principal attractions. ❏

# RESTAURANTS & BARS

## Restaurants

### Bridges Restaurant and Bistro

1696 Duranleau St. Tel: 604 687 4400. Open: L & D daily. $$ www.bridgesrestaurant.com
The bistro menu is sensibly divided into small, medium and large portions, while upstairs the restaurant has a more limited and expensive menu focusing on fish. Lovely location in sight of Burrard Bridge.

### Dockside Restaurant

1253 Johnston St. Tel: 604 685 7070. Open: B, L & D daily. $$
www.docksidebrewing.com
Part of the Granville Island Hotel, the cooking revolves around the wood-fired grill, rotisseries and pizza oven, and is open for breakfast as well as lunch and dinner. In summer the patio offers a great view over False Creek; in winter eyes are on the giant aquarium.

### The Keg

1499 Anderson St. Tel: 604 685 4735. Open: L & D daily. $$
A chain restaurant specialising in steaks, the Keg can be relied on to provide good-quality steak at a reasonable price.

### Monk McQueens Fresh Seafood & Oyster Bar

601 Stamps Landing. Tel: 604 877 1351. $$
www.monkmcqueens.com

A lovely position overlooking False Creek and Yaletown, Monk's has a downstairs bar with huge patio and a restaurant upstairs. Oysters are served in a variety of ways, and the selection of entrées is enticing – Pacific halibut, Dungeness crab, salmon burger, a ravioli stack and much more. Weekend brunch is popular, and the restaurant upstairs offers a more refined (and more expensive) menu.

### Pacific Institute of Culinary Arts

1505 West Second Ave. Tel: 604 734 4488. Open: L & D Mon–Sat. $
www.picachef.com
Catering students at this institute prepare a three-course set lunch in the marina-view restaurant at the approach to Granville Island. There is also a café and bake shop on the premises with really great pastries.

### Sammy J. Peppers

1517 Anderson St. Tel: 604 696 0739. $
www.sjpeppers.com
Soups and salads, burgers, sandwiches, steaks, pasta, chicken and pizzas are the staples of this local chain eatery.

### Sandbar Seafood Restaurant

1535 Johnston St. Tel: 604 669 9030. Open: L & D daily. $$

Though specialising in seafood with such signature dishes as Wok Squid Chillies, Cioppino Fisherman's Stew and Cedar Plank West Coast Salmon, carnivores are also catered for. Great view over False Creek marina. Pre-theatre menu for those going on to the Arts Club Theatre.

## Bars and Cafés

### Arts Club Back Stage Lounge

(1585 Johnston St). Light lunches, pizza, smoked salmon and bruschetta in a waterfront setting. Good selection of beers. **Blue Parrot** (1689 Johnstone St) serves great organic coffee, strudels, gooey cinnamon buns and grilled focaccia sandwiches.

### Nons Drinks to Go

(1669 Johnston St) sells a variety of hot and cold beverages made from organic ingredients.

### Pedro's Coffee House

(1496 Cartwright St) sells organic coffee, light meals and refreshments.

### Railspur Alley Cafe and Bistro

(1363 Railspur Alley) serves burgers, panini, salads, pizzas and quesadillas, and has live jazz on Thursday evenings.

### PRICE CATEGORIES

Prices for three-course dinner per person with a half-bottle of house wine:
$ = under C$30
$$ = C$30–50
$$$ = C$50–80
$$$$ = more than C$80

**RIGHT:** Bridges riverside bistro.

# WEST SIDE

Take a walk on the West Side: its beaches, mountain
views, elegant tree-lined streets, lofty parks,
and dizzying choice of bistros and restaurants
make it one of the city's most desirable districts

**N**ot to be confused with West
Vancouver or the West End,
the West Side covers the University of British Columbia and the
heart of residential Vancouver that
straddles the upland area known as
the Mackenzie Heights: the sylvan
mansions of western Shaughnessy;
the former hippy enclave of Kitsilano and now one of the city's
favoured areas for young professionals; Kerrisdale, with its expanding shopping area and eclectic
architectural mix; and the leafy
streets of suburban Point Grey and
Mackenzie Heights bordering the
University Endowment Lands – one
of the city's treasured green lungs.

## West Side beaches

The peninsula stretching to Point
Grey along the south shore of English Bay has the city's most popular
beaches, convenient distractions for
university students and residents
alike. On a summer weekend the
city's Punjabis put the reputation of
Aussies in the shade with their elaborate barbecues along the grassy
hinterland of Locarno and Spanish
Banks beaches, rated the best
beaches for swimming. **Jericho Sailing Centre ❶** (tel: 604 224 4168;
www.jsca.bc.ca) beside the eponymous beach offers courses in windsurfing, kayaking and sailing, and the

nearby pier is a fabulously romantic
place to watch the sun set, looking
out to sea with the mountains on the
north shore etched against the orange
sky and the lights of North Vancouver across the water.

The most popular beach is probably Kitsilano, thanks to its proximity to a good range of cafés, bars and
restaurants as well as downtown.
Several basketball games are usually
in progress, and beside the tennis
courts there is a huge heated saltwater
pool; **Kitsilano Pool ❷** is Canada's

Map
on page
128

**LEFT:** family-friendly
Kitsilano Beach.
**BELOW:** Jericho
Sailing Centre.

*Built in 1932, the "Gateway" function of Burrard Bridge is reflected in the medieval-style town gateways, lantern-topped pylons and Art Deco sculptural details. Busts of Captain George Vancouver and Harry Burrard jut out from the bridge's superstructure (a V under Vancouver's bust, a B under Burrard's).*

longest public pool (2305 Cornwall Avenue; tel: 604 731 0011; www.city.vancouver.bc.ca; open mid-May–early June Mon–Fri 12–8.45pm, Sat–Sun 10am–8.45pm, early June–early Sept Mon–Fri 7am–8.45pm, Sat–Sun 10am–8.45pm, early–mid-Sept Mon–Fri 7am–7.15pm, Sat–Sun 10am–7.15pm).

## The bridges

The link between downtown and the south shore of English Bay is **Burrard Bridge ❸**, one of Vancouver's favourite landmarks and tall enough for ships to pass under. However, this classic structure may lose its graceful lines under insensitive plans to cantilever massive outrigger structures to the sides, because the City Council refuses to designate the outer lanes of the bridge for cyclists and buses.

Just off the southern end of the bridge near the Molson brewery is a large Scots baronial building with stepped gables, round towers and thistles. Known as the **Seaforth Armoury**, it is home to the Seaforth Highlanders of Canada and was opened in 1936 by the Governor General, Lord Tweedsmuir, better known as the novelist John Buchan, author of *The Thirty-Nine Steps*. The various upstairs mess rooms with their dark wood and heavy beams provide one of the city's most elegant settings for large functions.

To the southeast of here stands **Granville Street Bridge**, opened in 1954 and the third bridge more or less on the same site. Lacking the architectural finesse of Burrard Bridge, it is none the less an imposing steel structure.

## Kitsilano

This popular residential area parallels the south shore of English Bay, and its proximity to the beaches

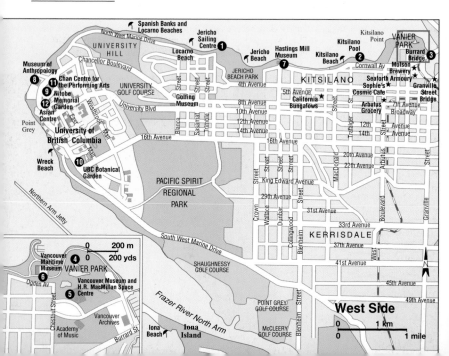

gives the area a relaxed atmosphere, with lots of alfresco cafés and restaurants. It's no coincidence that the largest branch of organic supermarket, Capers, a dog bakery and a multitude of designer baby shops lie on West 4th Avenue, where a huge variety of restaurants, bookshops and specialist shops can be found.

With the arrival of the streetcar line along English Bay in 1905, the Canadian Pacific Railway began development of the forested area on the south shore. They named this newly developed district after Chief Khahtsahlanough, whose grandson lived in the native village of Sun'ahk that had stood near Kitsilano Point until the late 19th century.

Construction continued apace through the first decades of the 20th century and many attractive houses from this period survive, their design influenced by the English Arts and Crafts movement. The eastern part of the neighbourhood, where apartment buildings are now concentrated, has lost many of its original houses, but most Kits residents are keen to preserve the character of the streets further west.

Walking or cycling around Kitsilano, you get a sense of community pride in the well-cared-for gardens and plant-strewn verandas. The best place to find Craftsman-style houses is the area bounded by Macdonald, Stephens, 5th and 6th avenues. A virtually intact row of "California Bungalows" can be seen on the south side of 5th Avenue between Bayswater and Balaclava.

For a quintessential Kits experience, have brunch at **Sophie's Cosmic Café** *(see page 135)*.

## The South Shore museums

Just west of Burrard Bridge is the green promontory of **Vanier Park** ❹ (bus routes 2, 22, 32, 44, 258), created on the site of what was Kitsilano Indian Reserve and named after the first French-Canadian Governor General of Canada, George Vanier. Kites can be seen flying above the park most weekends.

The park is home to three museums, two sharing a 1968 building designed by Gerald Hamilton with a

Map on page 128

**TIP**

A Kitsilano landmark to look out for is the tiny Arbutus Grocery at the corner of 6th Avenue and Arbutus Street. Built in 1907, it is one of the finest old grocery stores in the city. The novelist Alice Munro lived for a year at 1316 Arbutus Street, when newly married in 1952. The city is accurately described in some of her short stories.

**BELOW:** volleyball on Kits Beach.

*In May colourful tents go up in Vanier Park for the Children's Festival and the subsequent Bard on the Beach celebration of Shakespeare.*

**BELOW:** Vanier Park.

distinctive dome that resembles a woven basket made by the Northwest Coast First Nations peoples.

The **Vancouver Museum** ❺ (1100 Chestnut Street; Tues–Sun 10am–5pm; tel: 604 736 4431; www.vanmuseum.bc.ca) tells the fascinating story of the city's history with panache and humour: "Vancouverites, like other Canadians, insist on spelling colour the honourable way, lest we be confused with our neighbours to the south," reads one card. There is an absorbing film shot in 1907 from the front of a streetcar, showing Vancouver's business centre and the West End mansions as they were a century ago. Made by the Seattle filmmaker William H. Harbeck, who went down with the *Titanic* while making a film of its maiden voyage, it reveals just how much ordure horses deposited on the roads and how quiet streets were before the arrival of the car.

There are themed rooms and displays on Chinese immigration, work, trade unions, the Salvation Army, the inter-war boom and bust years, and the Japanese internment camps set up in the interior of BC during World War II. The post-war decades are evocatively portrayed with a reconstructed kitchen and other interiors, and the watershed decade of the 1960s is covered, when protest saved Vancouver from being as severely subordinated to the car as most US cities and whole districts were saved from the wrecker's ball. The Vancouver origins of Greenpeace and its early environmental protests are very well documented. The museum also has Pacific Rim and World Heritage collections.

The contiguous **H.R. MacMillan Space Centre** (Tues–Sun 10am–5pm; tel: 604 738 7827; www.hrmacmillanspacecentre.com) charts the history of space exploration and looks at celestial subjects that affect us more directly, such as light pollution. In a domed theatre similar to the London Planetarium, *Is Anybody Out There?* looks at the evidence for, and likelihood of, other life forms in space. For children there is a Disneyland-style ride on the theme of a mission to prevent an asteroid hitting the earth.

Two minutes' walk away at 1905 Ogden Avenue is the **Vancouver Maritime Museum** ❻ (3rd Mon in May–1st Mon in Sept daily 10am–5pm, 1st Mon in Sept–3rd Mon in May Tues–Sat 10am–5pm, Sun 12–5pm; tel: 604 257 8300; www.vancouvermaritimemuseum.com). The most impressive exhibit is the stout schooner *St Roch*. Built in North Vancouver in 1927 as a supply ship and patrol vessel for the Royal Canadian Mounted Police, it was the first vessel to negotiate the Northwest Passage in both directions and the first to circumnavigate North America using the Panama Canal. After a film about the ship, visitors can go aboard and inspect the cramped cabins and wheelhouse.

In a connected building are some superb ship models. Other sections look at pirates, ships named *Vancouver*, the first container ship, lighthouses, shipwrecks, fishing, diving, Canadian Pacific Railway steamers, old Vancouver and native canoes. There are several educational play areas for children with reconstructed ship decks.

At the eastern end of the large expanse of Jericho Beach Park is Vancouver's oldest surviving building, though it is not on its original site. The **Hastings Mill Museum** ❼ (Sat–Sun 1–4pm; tel: 604 734 1212) at 1575 Alma Street (bus routes 4, 7, 44, 84, 258) occupies the former store that stood beside the Hastings lumber mill on Burrard Inlet; one of less than a dozen buildings to survive the fire of 1886, it was moved to its present site in 1930 and now contains a large collection of Vancouver memorabilia. A cairn on Dunlevy Avenue marks the original site of Hastings Mill and commemorates its first export of lumber, to Australia in July 1867.

## The University of British Columbia (UBC)

BC's principal university is much more than a seat of learning for its 50,000 students: it has some of Vancouver's major tourist attractions and some impressive buildings. Easily reached in 30 minutes by the frequent 99 B-Line bus from downtown, UBC enjoys a wonderful

Map on page 128

*The False Creek ferry stops right outside the Maritime Museum, housed in a distinctive A-frame building.*

**BELOW:** Hastings Mill Museum occupies Vancouver's oldest building.

## Hastings Mill

The mill set up in Gastown flourished because of the Canadian Pacific's decision to terminate on the south shore of Burrard Inlet. In an age when wood was the major component of buildings and ships throughout the world, demand was almost insatiable. But at that time it took a whole day to fell an 800-year-old tree – on one side an axeman worked on a "springboard" notched into the trunk several feet above the ground, while a two-man saw cut away on the other. Within weeks of the mill starting work, as many as four ships at a time were being loaded. The mill miraculously survived the fire of 1886 and retained a key role in the community until it closed in the 1920s.

location on Point Grey, with ocean on three sides and 763 hectares (1,885 acres) of forested parkland to the east, designated the **Pacific Spirit Regional Park**.

Foremost among UBC's attractions is the **Museum of Anthropology** ❽ (mid-May–Sept 10am–5pm, Sept–mid-May Tues–Sun 11am–5pm; tel: 604 822 3825; www.moa.ubc.ca) which houses 35,000 ethnological objects and 500,000 archaeological objects in a stunning building designed by Arthur Erickson *(see page 116)*. Built on a site sacred to the Coast Salish people, Erickson's 1976 building looks north across the water towards Howe Sound and uses a repeated motif of concrete arches to echo the wooden gateways and post-and-beam style of many Pacific cultures.

The huge walls of glass maximise the view of the mountains and sea and are perfectly appropriate for the museum's exceptional collection of Northwest Coast totem poles. In the smaller and more intimate spaces are carved boxes, bowls, feast dishes, ceramics and paintings.

*"What is important is to try to develop insights and wisdom rather than mere knowledge, respect someone's character rather than his learning, and nurture men of character rather than mere talents."*

*– INAZO NITOBE (1862–1933)*

**BELOW:** Nitobe Memorial Garden.

Exhibits are not confined to the West Coast; there are significant collections from East and South Asia, the South Pacific, the Americas, Africa and Europe.

Directly across the road from the museum is the **Nitobe Memorial Garden** ❾ (mid-Mar–mid-Oct 10am–6pm; tel: 604 822 9666; www.nitobe.org), an authentic Japanese garden, complete with ceremonial teahouse. The garden honours the agriculturist, philosopher and writer Inazo Nitobe (1862–1933) who strove "to become a bridge across the Pacific". Each tree, stone and shrub has been deliberately placed to reflect an idealised conception and symbolic representation of nature. The garden is designed to suggest a span of time – a day, a week or a lifetime – with a beginning, choice of paths and ending. Water and its soothing sounds are an important element in the garden. Guided tours help visitors to understand the very different concept of Japanese gardens. Spring is the best time for the tree blossoms, summer for irises and autumn for the maples.

On the southern corner of the campus is the **UBC Botanical Garden** ❿ (mid-Mar–mid-Oct 10am–6pm; tel: 604 822 9666; www.ubcbotanical-garden.org), established in 1916, initially to study the native flora of BC but now a research centre for temperate plants from around the world. The gardens straddle the coast road and are linked by a pedestrian tunnel. Covering 44 hectares (110 acres), it has Alpine, Asian, native, food, physic and winter gardens, with over 8,000 plants. The physic garden was begun with plants from the Chelsea Physic Garden in London, and recreates a 16th-century monastic herb garden. The best months for floral displays of magnolias and rhododendrons (over 400 varieties) are April and May, summer for the Alpine garden and autumn for the food garden.

The botanical garden overlooks the Fraser river estuary and the two unusual spits of land forming a "V" from Iona Island. Part of the Pacific Spirit Regional Park, the coastal strip offers walks that join up with the main area of the park and its upland temperate rain forest, amounting to 50 km (31 miles) of trails.

Some of Vancouver's finest concerts are held in the UBC's **Chan Centre for the Performing Arts** ⓫ (tel: 604 8222 9197; www.chan-centre.com) at 6265 Crescent Road. Opened in 1997, the striking silver cylinder contains a concert hall with superb acoustics, a studio theatre and a cinema, allowing the centre to host a varied programme of opera, classical recitals, jazz and folk concerts, as well as lectures and films.

Another notable building on the campus is the **Asian Centre** ⓬ at 1871 West Mall, designed by Vancouver architect Donald Matsuba, who drew on traditional Asian styles, including the Japanese farmhouse. Reflected in the pool that surrounds it, the clean, uncluttered lines and pyramidal roof lend an air of calm.

## Kerrisdale

This largely residential neighbourhood lies south of 41st Avenue stretching to the Fraser river and bordered by Blenheim Street to the west and Granville to the east. The shopping area stimulated by the railway surrounds the junction of 41st with the East and West boulevards. The Bowser Block of 1912 still stands on the corner of the intersection.

There has been a long tradition of stability in Kerrisdale. Many of its residents have never moved from the district and know the name of everyone on their street. Rising property prices have weakened that cohesion, but the strong sense of community pride survives in the "Beautification Committee", which has made some attractive civic improvements, such as decorative sculptures made out of railway items to recall its early links.

Apart from the district's Gothic Revival churches such as Ryerson United Church of 1927, Kerrisdale's architecture derives from an interesting mixture of Spanish colonial revival, neo-Tudor, Beaux Arts and English Arts and Crafts styles. ❏

Map on page 128

*For those who prefer soaking up the sun in the buff, Wreck Beach has been the place to do it since the 1920s, but it takes a descent of 237 steps from this point to reach the sand below the cliffs.*

**BELOW:** Haida artist Bill Reid's acclaimed sculpture, *The Raven and the First Men.*

# RESTAURANTS & BARS

The West Side is a large area, incorporating several neighbourhoods, including Kitsilano with its fantastic beaches, Point Grey and leafy Kerrisdale, with their own collection of one-off shops, cafés, bars and restaurants of every imaginable ethnic persuasion, and for every purse. When the weather is fine, grab a table on a patio – alfresco dining is a big thing in this city, and many restaurants and cafés boast outdoor eating space.

### Abigail's Party

1685 Yew St (off 1st Ave). Tel: 604 739 4677. Open: B & L Sat, Sun, D Mon–Sat. $$
www.abigailsparty.ca
Named after the Mike Leigh film of the same name, this casual restaurant likes to think of itself as a gastropub. A seasonal menu featuring tapas with the usual West Coast twist and cocktails, along with a lively vibe make it a hot spot in Kits.

### Banana Leaf

3005 West Broadway. Tel: 604 734 3005. Open: L & D daily. $
www.bananaleaf-vancouver.com
This Malaysian restaurant with informal ambience and friendly service has two other branches (820 West Broadway and on Denman in the West

End). All the usual suspects appear, but the big focus is on local fresh seafood with a Malaysian twist. Choose your seafood, then select your favourite sauce – from Singapore chilli to black peppercorn garlic. Good beers by the pitcher.

### Bishop's

2183 West 4th Ave. Tel: 604 738 2025. Open: D daily. $$$
www.bishopsonline.com
Award-winning restaurant for foodies, Bishop's uses the best ingredients the West Coast has to offer, most of them organic. Try the cornmeal-crusted Fanny Bay oysters with grainy mustard mousseline, bison loin with wild mushroom ragout, and plum and peach galette with cream cheese sorbet. Seasonal menus, the freshest ingredients, good service and an extensive wine list keep its loyal customers coming back for more.

### Bistro Pastis

2153 West 4th Ave. Tel: 604 731 5020. Open: L & D Tues–Sun. $$
www.bistropastis.com
French bourgeois cooking at its best in this quiet, smartly furnished room with good service and a fine wine list, much of it French.

### Enigma

4397 West 10th Ave. Tel: 604 222 6881. Open: L & D daily. $

www.enigmavancouver.com
Up near the university on a stretch of eclectic shops and restaurants, Enigma serves contemporary West Coast staples – Caesar salads, home-made soups and delicious burgers – along with comfort food and daily specials like Guinness and beef stew. Brunch at the weekend and a giant screen to watch sporting events.

### Fish Café

2053 West 41st Ave. Tel: 604 267 3474. Open: L Sun–Fri, D daily. $
This simply furnished restaurant serves the freshest fish and seafood the Pacific has to offer at very reasonable prices. Brilliant crab cakes and salmon burgers served with fries or rice are great, and the specials board changes every day. Everything is home-made, service is fast and friendly and the locals love it. A slightly trendier version has opened on 4th Ave in Kits.

### The Galley Patio & Grill

1300 Discovery St, Jericho Park. Tel: 604 222 1331. Open: B, L & D daily (weekends only in winter). $
www.thegalley.ca
Located on the upper level of Jericho Sailing Centre with great views over English Bay, this is a good place to break a bike tour of the beaches. Signature dishes include

Huevos Scramblaros (eggs scrambled with turkey sausage, roasted corn and black-bean salsa) and Classic nachos.

### Hell's Kitchen

2041 West 4th Ave. Tel: 604 736 4355. Open: L & D daily. $ www.hells-kitchen.ca
Soups, salads, burgers and pasta on offer, but famed for its pizzas, voted best in Vancouver in 2005. Brunch at the weekend.

### Lumière

2551 West Broadway. Tel: 604 739 8185. Open: D Tues–Sun. $$$$
www.lumiere.ca
Award-winning French restaurant Lumière is a fantastic gastronomic experience. A beautiful minimalist room, expert service and lovely wine list accompany the menu. Three set menus, with a minimum of eight small but perfectly formed courses, are hard to choose from, but the squab breast, pan-seared foie gras and pistachio-crusted confit leg with truffled gnocchi are outstanding. Two other establishments within the same stable – Feenie's and the Tasting Bar – are less expensive and allow you to sample the work of the maestro.

### Maria's Taverna

2324 West 4th Ave. Tel: 604 731 4722. Open: L & D daily. $$ www.mariastaverna.com

Greek restaurants are plentiful along this stretch of 4th Avenue and this simple whitewashed room is among the best. An appetizer platter of tzatziki, hummus, olives, taramasalata, olives and pitta is enough for three, and the kleftiko tender and delicious.

### Naam

2724 West 4th Ave. Tel: 604 738 7151. Open: B, L & D daily. $

www.thenaam.com

A venerable institution, the Naam is the oldest vegetarian restaurant in Vancouver, dating back to the 1970s when Kits was hippy heaven. The food is good and the atmosphere funky – wooden tables and chairs, an open fire, live music every night, and it's open 24/7.

### Le Petit Genève

2106 West 41st Ave. Tel: 604 266 9611. $$

At this popular neighbourhood restaurant you'll find French staples such as crab and crème fraîche Napoleon and grilled duck breast with cherry sauce.

### Sophie's Cosmic Café

2095 West 4th Ave. Tel: 604 732 6810. Open: B, L & D daily. $

www.sophiescosmiccafe.com

A Kitsilano institution since it opened in 1988, Sophie's is a great place for breakfast, brunch or lunch. Decorated in diner style with red leatherette booths and a fantastic collection of memorabilia,

Sophie's is renowned for its breakfasts, salads and wonderful array of burgers including wild salmon, chicken and oyster. Patio dining in good weather if you can nab a table, but expect queues at the weekend.

### Watermark Café on Kits Beach

1305 Arbutus Street. Tel: 604 738 5487. Open: L & D daily. $$

www.watermarkrestaurant.ca

You'll need sunglasses if you stop for a drink or a meal at this glass-walled restaurant overlooking Kits Beach. The food is imaginative, and the stunning views over English Bay, glam waiters and a very trendy vibe make this a place to see and be seen.

### Yuji's Japanese Tapas

2059 West 4th Ave. Tel: 604 734 4990. $

Sushi is another Vancouver obsession; everyone has a favourite place, and there are lots to choose from. This 4th Avenue spot is a favourite with 20-somethings on a budget.

### Bimini's Tap House

(2010 West 4th Ave) is another well-known Kits institution, with restaurant, bar and a games room with darts and pool. Although it serves food, the focus is the pub atmosphere – lots of big screens for watching

sporting events. **Capers** (2285 West 4th Ave) is an organic supermarket but also a great place for a sit down and a quick coffee or a light lunch from its take-away counter. Fantastic cakes, salads and filling pasta dishes. **Kitsilano Coffee Company** (2198 West 4th Ave) has a big patio, lots of tables and newspapers to go along with the cinnamon buns and coffee on a Sunday morning. **Pane Formaggio** (4532 West 10th Ave) is a bakery, Italian deli and fab place to have coffee near the university while you browse the shops on 10th Ave. **Red Onion** (2028 41st Ave West, on West Boulevard) is a very traditional burger and milkshake joint that also serves soups, and you can have a beer with

your burger. **Secret Garden Tea Company** (5559 West Boulevard) has a wonderfully period atmosphere for afternoon tea, with a wide selection of teas and pastries. Also does breakfast and light lunches. **Terra Breads** (2380 West 4th Ave) has been repeatedly voted the best in Vancouver for its artisan breads baked in a stone-hearth oven and for its sandwiches, but its café also serves cakes, soup and organic salads. A branch on Granville Island.

### PRICE CATEGORIES

Prices for three-course dinner per person with a half-bottle of house wine:
$ = under C$30
$$ = C$30–50
$$$ = C$50–80
$$$$ = more than C$80

**RIGHT:** award-winning gourmet restaurant, Bishop's.

# VANCOUVER'S BEACHES

**Few big cities can boast 11 beaches fit for swimming, nor the variety and quality of water sports that are available so close to the city centre**

Life in Vancouver is more bound up with the sea than in most cities. For much of the year a good part of people's leisure time is spent on the beach. The city is blessed with some golden stretches of sand in surroundings that belie their proximity to a large urban centre. Moreover, despite the presence of commercial shipping in English Bay, the water is remarkably free from pollution, and many swim off the beaches.

One of the closest to downtown and therefore one of the most popular is Kitsilano Beach, invariably referred to as "Kits". Games of volleyball are often in progress, and the safe swimming makes it popular with families from the neighbourhood.

Further west, Jericho and Locarno beaches have a large hinterland and are popular with families who need the space for army catering-scale barbecues. A bike route weaves among the trees along the front to Spanish Banks. Around the headland on which UBC stands is Wreck Beach, for decades the beach where you can bare all. It's not remotely voyeuristic, and the fine sweep of sand is cared for by its own society.

**ABOVE:** the fascinating waterfront at Steveston is more suited to walking than swimming, but there are plenty of places to sit beside the sea in Garry Point Park.

**RIGHT:** the beach at Ambleside Park is one of the most popular in North Vancouver, with a long sandy beach and placid water. A playground and duck pond in the park makes it great for children. It's also a good place to watch the coming and going of cruise and cargo ships into Burrard Inlet. North Vancouver also has smaller beaches in Pilot Cove, Sandy Cove and Dundarave.

**RIGHT:** between Tofino and Ucluelet on the west coast of Vancouver Island there is a series of glorious beaches with wide expanses of sand. They are often covered with drift logs washed up by the tempestuous seas that are common along this coast. The waves at Long Beach attract surfers from all over the world.

**ABOVE:** close to Kits Beach is a heated saltwater swimming pool. Lifeguards are on duty for most of its opening times, and there is a gentle slope to the pool for younger children. Beside the pool there are grassy areas with swings and climbing frame.

**RIGHT:** Wreck Beach is Vancouver's nudist beach, and it's immensely popular: over 14,000 people can line the 8-km (5-mile) strip of sand on a warm summer day. Beach huts sell organic juices and *empanadas*.

Clothing is optional at beach ahead.

## WATER SPORTS

The popularity of water sports in Vancouver is obvious on any summer weekend, as English Bay fills with sailing boats, kayaks and skimboards dodging the power boats.

False Creek is a good place to learn to kayak or canoe, as it's sheltered, sailing is forbidden and boats are limited to 5 knots. Alternatively, courses and guided tours for experienced paddlers are available from Jericho Beach. One of the best places for the sport is the tranquil Indian Arm, an 18-km (11-mile) finger of water from Deep Cove in North Vancouver.

Sailing takes place mainly from Jericho Beach, where lessons are available from the Jericho Sailing Centre. Skimboarding, a cross between surfing and skateboarding, is becoming popular. Surfing lessons are available, but there is little around Vancouver to attract the serious surfers who make for the big rollers on the west coast of Vancouver Island.

For the proficient, the finest area for sailing is among the Gulf Islands and along the Inside Passage, where the scenery and tranquil coves seem a world away from city life.

Windsurfing is possible off Jericho Beach and the beaches of English Bay, but Squamish is regarded as the best place close to Vancouver. *(See page 253 for details of water sports providers.)*

**ABOVE:** Jericho Beach is the place to head to for water sports: its eastern end is set aside for windsurfing, kayaking and sailing under the auspices of the Jericho Sailing Association. Swimmers occupy the western end. There is also fishing off Jericho Pier, and Vancouver Youth Hostel is situated near by.

**LEFT:** there are two main beaches around Stanley Park: Second and Third beaches which both overlook English Bay. Second Beach has a heated outdoor pool with adjacent playground, and the beach is often decorated with Inukshuk-style towers of precariously balanced rocks. Further south and closest to downtown is the long expanse of English Bay Beach and Sunset Beach, which almost reaches Burrard Bridge. Both are bordered by parkland, which provides a good screen.

# CENTRAL VANCOUVER

**At first glance, this amorphous area may appear to
have little to offer, but there are two fabulous
gardens worth crossing the water for, while the
genteel neighbourhood of Shaughnessy and vibrant
Punjabi Market show another side to the city**

This chapter spans the area south of False Creek, from the shopping district around Granville Street, through genteel Shaughnessy down to Vancouver's Indo-Canadian community around Punjabi Market. Besides the shops, galleries, restaurants and cafés likely to appeal to those who prefer individuality to chains, the great attractions for visitors and residents are the two outstanding gardens.

## Shaughnessy

The Canadian Pacific Railway had been granted the land on which this old-money area of Vancouver was built, and the astute company spent over $1 million on the infrastructure and landscaping before selling a single lot. The district took its name from Milwaukee-born Thomas Shaughnessy, who was president of the CPR from 1899 to 1918.

Beginning in 1907, generous lots and curving streets named after CPR directors were laid out to lure the city's elite from the West End. Some of the larger houses were built of stone from the quarry that forms the focus of Queen Elizabeth Park. Exclusivity was guaranteed by stipulating that all houses should cost at least $6,000, and the provincial government later reinforced this by restricting development to single-

family dwellings and prohibiting subdivision of lots. By 1914, there were 243 houses in Shaughnessy.

Houses were designed by the city's leading architects using such styles as English Arts and Crafts, neo-Tudor, Georgian and American Gothic. By the 1920s the social scene revolved around costumed balls, croquet and tennis matches. The grandest residence was Hycroft at 1489 McRae Avenue, now the home of the University Women's Club. Built in 1909 for BC industrialist A.D.

Map
on page
140

**LEFT:** the beautifully landscaped Queen Elizabeth Park.
**BELOW:** grand Shaughnessy residence.

*Award-winning restaurant West is a gastronomic temple. Native Vancouverite chef David Hawksworth has worked with Marco Pierre White and Raymond Blanc, and was head chef at l'Escargot in London, retaining its Michelin star. He draws on the best the West Coast has to offer (see page 145).*

McRae, Hycroft was the place to be on New Year's Eve for the McRaes' costume ball. The ballroom floor was laid over seaweed to give better spring, and the house had three large gardens, an enormous greenhouse, riding stables, tennis courts, guest house, mirrored bar and a solarium.

One of the most unusual mansions is Glen Brae at 1690 Matthews Street, built for sawmill owner William Tait. This supposedly Scottish baronial-style home has bulbous twin towers with domed roofs flanking the entrance. It, too, has a sprung dance floor, fine stained glass and tiling and an ornate wrought-iron fence imported from Glasgow. The house is now home to Canuck Place, a hospice for children.

Other important survivors include the Nichol House at 1402 McRae Avenue, the Frederick Kelly House at 1398 Crescent, the MacDonald House at 1388 Crescent and the Fleck House at 1296 Crescent.

The number of repossessions by CPR during the Depression gave the area the nickname "Mortgage Heights" and led to some illegal conversion to multiple dwellings. Glen Brae, for example, was valued at $75,000 in 1920 but sold for $7,500 in 1939. Despite some relaxation of the restrictions on internal and plot subdivision, the district's character remains distinctive, and the area is one of the city's most valuable heritage landscapes. Anyone interested in architecture will find a leisurely tour of Shaughnessy on foot or bike rewarding.

## Granville Street

North and south of the intersection with Broadway lies Granville Street's **shopping district** with a mix of galleries squeezed out of the downtown area by rising rents, fashion shops, home furnishings, delicatessens and restaurants (most notably West, *see left*). Sandwiched

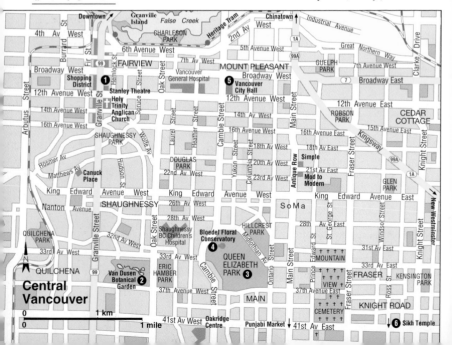

between the shops is the heritage **Stanley Theatre ❶**. Designed by H.H. Simmonds, this 1,200-seat Moorish-style Art Deco cinema was built in 1931 and screened films until 1991. It reopened as a theatre in 1998 and is the only one of four Vancouver neighbourhood cinemas designed by Simmonds to survive.

Some of the well-to-do of Shaughnessy worshipped in the Chalmers Presbyterian Church, now the **Holy Trinity Anglican Church**, at 12th and Hemlock Street. This impressive neoclassical church, noted for its extensive stained glass and fine brickwork, was built in 1911 in response to the rapid expansion of area.

## Van Dusen Botanical Garden

To the south of Shaughnessy lie two of BC's finest gardens. The **Van Dusen Botanical Garden ❷** (daily Mar–Apr 10am–5pm, May 10am–8pm, June–Aug 10am–9pm, Sept 10am–7pm, Oct 10am–5pm, Nov–Feb 10am–4pm; tel: 604 878 9274; www.city.vancouver.bc.ca) is at 5251 Oak Street on bus routes 17, 488 and 492. Unusually, the land was a golf club until 1960, when the club moved to a new site near UBC; local residents persuaded the city and provincial governments that a botanical garden would be preferable to more houses, and the result is an outstanding garden that ranks in the top ten of North American gardens. Named after the leading donor, it is the kind of garden that appeals to everyone, whether or not they are gardeners. Its miles of path through the 22 hectares (55 acres) take you beside lakes, across ponds and through woodland to visit 40 small specialised gardens within the framework of the main landscaped setting. Cleverly devised vistas look out over the city or to the mountains to the north.

Thanks to Vancouver's mild climate, the garden contains more than 7,500 different plants grouped by botanical relationship or geographical origin, though the main focus here is on plants that are native to BC. Redwoods are among the trees most associated with the West Coast,

Map on page 140

### TIP

The Arts Club Theatre is Vancouver's largest professional theatre company and stages a mixture of contemporary and classical plays and Broadway musicals at its flagship theatre, the Stanley (2750 Granville Street; box office: 604 687 1644, www.artsclub .com) and at its larger sister venue, the Granville Island Stage (1585 Johnston Street, web address and box office as above).

**BELOW:** Meinhardt, a gourmet's delight on Granville Street.

*Dotted around the grounds of the Van Dusen Botanical Garden are some intriguing modern sculptures by internationally renowned artists, made with either stone from Iran or travertine from Turkey.*

**BELOW:** the Elizabethan hedge maze in the Van Dusen garden.

giant Sequoias growing for up to 3,800 years and Coast redwoods for over 2,000. Some specimens remind us how vital the work of botanical gardens is when habitat destruction threatens the extinction of many plant species. A Dawn redwood grows near the Cypress Pond thanks to the discovery of a Chinese forester, T. Kan, while travelling in eastern Sichuan province in 1941. He found three specimens and took cuttings from which all subsequent trees derive.

Children love the multicursal maze, made up of 2–3,000 pyramidal cedars. One of the more unusual areas is the Canadian Heritage Garden, which has areas of commercial crops such as barley, wheat, flax, oats, amaranth and sunflowers, planted in a setting that feels convincingly rural. In spring, the highlight are the 220 varieties of hybrid rhododendron which provide an avenue of colour along the Rhododendron Walk. In summer attention turns to the rose, fragrance and perennial gardens, and in the autumn maples and heathers provide splashes

of red and purple. Even in winter there is something to enjoy, with witch hazel, winter-flowering shrubs and 140 kinds of holly.

## Queen Elizabeth Park

To the east of the Van Dusen Garden is **Queen Elizabeth Park ❸** (tel: 604 257 8570; www.city.vancouver.bc.ca) on bus route 15, created around an extinct volcano known as "Little Mountain" at the highest point of the city, 153 metres (501 ft) above sea level. The land covered by the park was set aside as a reserve as long ago as 1912, having served as a source of stone for the city's first roads. However, it was not until after the dedication of the area by the late Queen Mother during her visit with King George VI in 1939 that work began in earnest.

At the heart of this 52-hectare (130-acre) park are two former quarries which have been developed into beautiful ornamental flower gardens, producing a riot of colour in summer and making them a favoured location for wedding photographs. Even during dry periods in the summer,

the grass in these areas is luxuriantly green. The North Quarry Garden has an oriental note and specialises in plants that prefer drier conditions. It was created to commemorate the 75th anniversary of Vancouver's incorporation, in 1961.

The park's gentle northern slope is an arboretum of Canada's indi–genous trees and shrubs.

The Little Mountain Drinking Water Reservoir on top of the hill has been covered over and a new plaza built on top with a water fea-ture, arbours, tree, shrub and lawn areas. The summit offers panoramic views over the city, and the Seasons Hill restaurant *(see page 145)*, where Presidents Clinton and Yeltsin dined in 1993, was built to take advantage of them.

Near the highest point is the **Bloedel Floral Conservatory** ❹ (10am–5pm; tel: 604 257 8570; www.city.vancouver.bc.ca), which is the second-largest domed conserva-tory in the world (the largest is in St Louis, Missouri). Inside the dome are over 500 varieties of trees and plants living beside the path that wanders

through three climate zones: lush tropical rainforest, subtropic and desert. Flying free are over 60 species of tropical birds and parrots obtained from captive breeding sources, and the knowledgeable staff are happy to help with identification.

## Civic centre

North of the gardens, just before Cambie Street meets Broadway is **Vancouver City Hall** ❺ at 453 West 12th Avenue. Designed by the city's leading practice, Townley and Matheson, in 1935–6, the curious location of the building was intended to symbolise the recent absorption of the municipalities of South Vancou-ver and Point Grey by erecting the new City Hall near their common boundary. Or so one story goes. Another cites a downtown demon-stration by 2,000 unemployed work-ers demanding accommodation and food; the riot act had to be read, and a location less susceptible to such protests was deemed advisable. It's now a rather anomalous location, and its hard edges and lumpen mass, albeit relieved by some Art Deco zig

Map on page 140

**TIP**

If you would like to grow some of the flowers you've admired at the Van Dusen Botanical Garden back home, seed packets can be bought from the shop.

**BELOW:** the giant Bloedel Conservatory dome.

## Vancouver Foundation

The principal benefactor of the Van Dusen Botanical Garden was the Vancouver Foundation, which began in the 1940s with $1,000 saved by a secretary named Alice G. MacKay. She wanted to do something special for Vancouver, particularly for homeless women trapped in a cycle of poverty. The industrialist and philanthropist W.J. Van Dusen developed the foun-dation with the support of nine other prominent Vancouverites who each contributed $10,000. From its original fund of $101,000, it now has a capi-tal fund of over $650 million, making it the largest community fund in Canada. It gives away about $35 million each year in eight defined areas of public endeavour.

Map
on page
140

*The largest street tree in Vancouver is thought to be the Giant sequoia on the Cambie Street median near King Edward, which has a trunk circumference of 5.5 metres (18 ft).*

**BELOW:** Indian sweet shop, Punjabi Market.

zag decoration, evoke totalitarian architecture. Near by is the vast Vancouver General Hospital, the largest in BC.

## SoMa

Short for South Main, this is one of Vancouver's newest shopping destinations, focused around 21st Avenue but stretching from Broadway to 33rd Avenue, with fashion and home furnishings to the fore. A series of shops known as Antique Row is located between 20th and 23rd avenues. Collectables and memorabilia from the 1950s and '60s can be found at Mod to Modern (3712 Main Street), while Simple (3638 Main Street) is a great place for unusual gifts.

## Punjabi Market

This district between Main and Knight streets south of 41st Avenue is the epicentre of Vancouver's community of 60,000 Indians, mostly from the Punjab. Known too by its more official name of Sunset, the area has also been home to the Mennonite community since the 1930s,

clustered around 49th Avenue and Fraser Street.

The name "Punjabi Market" applies to the district as well as the shopping area on Main Street between 49th and 51st avenues, which is denoted by special street signs and has the largest concentration of jewellers in Canada. Haggling is expected. It's worth visiting the area just to see the beautiful silk fabrics sold at bargain prices in many of the shops and enjoy the pungent aromas from the spices and vegetables which are sure to tempt you into sampling one of the restaurants. Just wander round and soak up the atmosphere of this lively corner of India.

On the short stub of Ross Street between Marine Drive and Kent Avenue stands the **Sikh Temple ➏** designed by Arthur Erikson in 1969–70. A simple white block is capped by a series of stepped, diagonally interlocked square sections, and crowned by an open steel onion-shaped dome. Those who knew it before the additions to the east regret its loss of isolation.   ❑

## A Muliticultural City

From its very foundation, Vancouver has been a multicultural city, much as the province of British Columbia has been as a whole. The opportunities offered by the embryonic province and city have attracted Cambodians, Chinese, Filipinos, Greeks, Indians, Indonesians, Italians, Jews, Laotians, Russians, Scandinavians, Thais, Ukrainians and Vietnamese as well as a large number of people from Britain – Scotland in particular. The Chinese are the largest community, forming the third-largest Chinatown in North America (after San Francisco and New York), though it was not until the 1947 repeal of laws limiting immigration that the numbers swelled.

# RESTAURANTS

## All India Sweets & Restaurant
6507 Main St. Tel: 604 327 0891. $ www.allindiasweets restaurant.com
Very cheap Indian food at the city's largest Indian restaurant – the vegetarian buffet is $6.95. There is a large à la carte menu as well, but the big draw here is the vast array of Indian sweets.

## Ashiana Tandoori
1440 Kingsway. Tel: 604 874 5060. $
www.ashianatandoori.com
Decorated with Indian antiques and art, this restaurant has a loyal following for its clay oven-cooked dishes using fresh spices and herbs prepared each day. Authentic.

## Aurora Bistro
2420 Main St. Tel: 604 873-9944. Open: D daily. $$
www.aurorabistro.ca
Another award-winning and popular bistro with its own take on West Coast cuisine. Chef Jeff Van Geest allows the best ingredients to speak for themselves, and has cultivated close relationships with local organic farmers, fish-mongers, cheese makers and mushroom foragers. Kurtis Kolt, the sommelier, has selected the best from BC's thriving wineries. Fantastic service and a lively atmosphere in a vibrant part of town.

## Memphis Blues Barbeque House
1465 Broadway West (off Granville). Tel: 604 738 6806. Open: L & D daily. $$ 1342 Commercial Drive (near Charles Street). Tel: 604 215 2599. Open: L & D daily. $$
www.memphisbluesbbq.com
Voted best barbecue and best place for carnivores in Vancouver, with slabs of ribs, pork or Cornish game hen (signature item). If you're really hungry, order an Elvis Platter, and if that's not enough the Priscilla throws in fish as well. No reservations.

## Nyala Ethiopian Restaurant
4148 Main St. Tel: 604 876 9919. Open: D Tues–Sun. $
A complete one-off, Nyala has a spicy, individual take on African food. Dishes like merguez kebabs, vegetable pakoras and spicy goat stews are served on a common platter and eaten with injera, an unleavened flat bread, or chickpea flour cakes. Cheap and unusual, the restaurant also has live music some nights.

## Paul's Place Omelettery
2211 Granville St. Tel: 604 73 72857. Open: B & L daily. $
A fabulous place for brunch by any standards, so be prepared to queue. It is particularly busy at the weekend but you can window-shop up and down Granville Street while you wait for

your table. It's worth the wait for the best Eggs Benny and wonderful omelettes – try the wild game chorizo with mushroom and feta. Everything is made on the premises of this cheery, slightly ramshackle café, using the best and freshest ingredients.

## Seasons Hill Top Bistro
Queen Elizabeth Park. Tel: 604 874 8008. Open: L Mon–Fri, D daily. $$$
Elegant dining with fine views over the city. Imaginatively interpreted West Coast cuisine fit for presidents – Clinton and Yeltsin dined here in 1993. The restaurant is also open for brunch on Saturday (11.30am) and Sunday (10.30am).

## Shaughnessy Restaurant
Van Dusen Botanical Garden, 5251 Oak St. Tel: 604 261 0011. Open: B Sat & Sun, L Mon–Fri, D daily. $$
www.shaughnessyrestaurant.com
The location of this smart restaurant makes it a great favourite for weddings and events, but it also serves breakfast, lunches, teas and dinner. Weekend brunch is particularly popular in fine weather. Lots of salads and great seafood.

## Vij's
1480 West 11th Ave (between Granville and Hemlock). Tel: 604 736 6664. Open: D daily. $$
www.vijs.ca

Widely regarded as the best Indian in Vancouver, this popular restaurant doesn't take reservations, so be prepared to wait for this treat. Using sublimely fresh West Coast ingredients, Vij's produces an inventive take on modern Indian, fusing various regional styles. Vancouverites queue without complaint for their favourite dishes, including marinated lamb Popsicles with fenugreek cream curry.

## West
2881 Granville St. Tel: 604 738 8938. $$$
Serious food for serious foodies. The seafood, game and local produce are transformed into intense, complex creations. Everything about this elegant dining room has been considered, from the leather chairs to the wall of wine accessible by library steps, and the kitchen screened with bevelled glass. Well-informed service and a proper pacing of courses make an evening at West a celebration. World class.

### PRICE CATEGORIES

Prices for three-course dinner per person with a half-bottle of house wine:
$ = under C$30
$$ = C$30–50
$$$ = C$50–80
$$$$ = more than C$80

# EAST VANCOUVER

Beyond Chinatown, East Vancouver is largely residential, but the suburbs of New Westminster, Burnaby and Port Moody all offer attractions that make the short SkyTrain journey worthwhile. Unearth Vancouver's early history, take a paddle-steamer cruise, go fishing in the Fraser or shop in one of Canada's biggest malls

Maps
Area 148
City 150

**LEFT:** blacksmiths' demonstration at the Burnaby Village Museum. **BELOW:** Rocky Point pier, Port Moody.

**R**elatively few visitors to Vancouver visit the eastern districts of Vancouver except to pass through them on their way to the interior by either Trans-Canada Highway 1 or the Lougheed Highway 7. These districts may lack the visual appeal of neighbourhoods around the city's waterfront, but they still have plenty to interest the visitor. Both New Westminster and Burnaby can be explored by using SkyTrain, and if you have only half a day a **SkyTour** (*see page 234*) will provide a pleasurable and relaxing introduction to the area.

## Fur trappers and gold diggers

Though Gastown may be the key to an appreciation of Vancouver's settlement, to understand what led up to it you need to go east. For it was the rivers of central and western Canada that carried the commodity that led to the first European settlements – furs. Most of the early explorers were travelling east to west, following rivers to discover where they met the sea; once a course had been mapped, their successors were able to make the less arduous journey by sea, almost invariably arriving by ship up the Fraser river.

However, it was gold rather than furs that prompted the British gov-ernment to send the first detachment of troops in the form of Royal Engineers, responding to concerns that the discovery of gold along the Fraser and Thompson rivers in 1857 could lead to a breakdown of civil order. The soldiers arrived from Britain via Victoria on the separate crown colony of Vancouver Island early in 1859, two months after the colony of British Columbia had been proclaimed. In charge was Colonel Richard Moody, who had been given the task of selecting a

*The caricatured figure of a Royal Engineer on the waterfront has the dubious distinction of being the tallest tin figure in the world at 10 metres (32 ft) tall.*

site for the capital of BC. He rejected the area around Fort Langley *(see page 217)* set up by the Hudson's Bay Company, and chose a sloping site on the north bank of the Fraser river which Queen Victoria named New Westminster.

Early photographs of the Royal Engineers' camp between 1859 and 1863 show a higgledy-piggledy collection of wooden houses and shacks, but Moody and his sappers transformed the area in their four years: 300 lots were soon surveyed and auctioned off, and by 1864 Government House had a ballroom capable of holding "with ease" over 200 dancers. In 1865 a cricket match was held between New Westminster and Victoria. Though New Westminster continued to grow, despite losing its capital status with the decision to move it to Victoria in 1868, in 1898 a fire broke out in a pile of hay on a sternwheeler and quickly spread. All but a handful of

buildings in the city were destroyed; even the church bells were reduced to a heap of contorted metal.

### Exploring New Westminster

Approaching **New Westminster ❶** by SkyTrain from the north, you can see the 1878 Penitentiary where the notorious train robber Billy Miner was incarcerated *(see page 224)*. From the SkyTrain station, turn right to reach the river, passing the restored Canadian Pacific Railway station of 1899 designed in a French château style. This handsome brick building with stone facings was one of the first buildings to go up after the fire of 1898, and has been restored as a restaurant.

Across the tracks is the modern **Westminster Quay Public Market ❷**, which has a good variety of shops, galleries and places to eat. Some overlook the Fraser river which was once teeming with sternwheel steamboats calling in on their

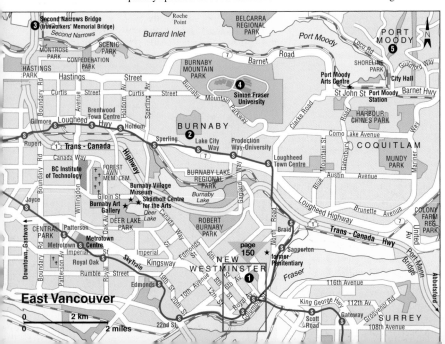

East Vancouver

way between Victoria and Yale *(see page 225)*.

The presentation of information in the **Fraser River Discovery Centre**  (Tues–Sat 10am–4pm; tel: 604 521 8401; www.fraser-riverdiscovery.org) is uninspired; it's better to rely on the information boards dotted along the attractive boardwalk, which extends for a mile westwards. Dominating the riverfront is the huge sternwheeler *Royal City Star* ◉ (10am–3am; tel: 604 519 3660; www.royalcitystar.bc.ca), built in New Orleans as the *Queen of New Orleans* in 1994 as a floating casino. She still performs this role, offering various table games and 350 slot machines as well as a restaurant.

A plinthed bust of a rather jowly Simon Fraser reminds passers-by of the role the explorer played in opening up western Canada to trade. The continuing importance of the river named after him is obvious from the Surrey Docks on the south bank opposite New Westminster. Ships sail 28 km (18 miles) up river to unload containers and cars and leave with lumber and general cargoes. Huge rectangular barges piled with sawdust as tall as a small house ruffle the waters with astonishing frequency.

The waterway has to be kept open by constant maintenance, and one of the ships that carried out this work is preserved near the public market: *Samson V* ◉ (noon–5pm May–June Sat–Sun, July–Labour Day daily, Labour Day–mid-Oct Sat–Sun; www.nwpl.ca) was built at New Westminster in 1937 as a steam-powered sternwheeler to keep the river clear of snags and deadheads (tree trunks and branches) and to repair navigation lights and buoys. Retired in 1980, she has been restored to open the engine room, bridge, workshop, mess room and most of her cabins for visitors. There are also displays on the history of the river's ships and their colourful captains.

Trees and flower beds line the boardwalk as far as the former railway swingbridge that took the railway across the North Arm of the river. The Fraser Delta starts just

> *New Westminster's most famous son was the actor Raymond Burr (1917–93). He broke into films in 1946, appearing in 90 over the next decade, most notably in Hitchcock's 1954 masterpiece* Rear Window. *He is best remembered for his television roles as Perry Mason and Ironside. He gave away huge sums to charity, at one time sponsoring 27 foster children. He is buried in the Fraser Cemetery in New Westminster.*

**Map on page 150**

**BELOW:** the *Royal City Star* sternwheeler.

west of New Westminster, and was created by the 20 million tonnes of sand and silt brought down the river past New Westminster every year.

## Columbia Street and downtown

By 1898 New Westminster was the mercantile centre of the Fraser Valley, and its main street, Columbia, was lined with impressive brick stores and offices. For a time it was renowned as the "Miracle Mile", with the highest sales per square foot in the entire province. The legacy of those years can still be seen in the historic buildings that survive, and a guide to them is available from the museum *(see page 151)*. Many are still awaiting the kind of sensitive restoration done to the city's first "skyscraper" erected in 1912, the **Westminster Trust Building E** at 709–713 Columbia Street, but work is in hand on another of the city's landmarks, the historic **Columbia**

*The site on which New Westminster City Hall now stands was originally intended as the location for the British Columbia Parliament Buildings when the city was briefly the provincial capital.*

**BELOW:** shopping mall, Westminster Quay.

Theatre **F** at 530 Columbia Street.

Renamed the Raymond Burr Centre for the Performing Arts after the famous actor *(see page 149)*, the theatre was opened as a combined vaudeville theatre and cinema in 1927. It has an outstanding interior, decorated in a fantasy style depicting a Moorish garden in a walled city, with wisteria and wild roses winding round pillars and twinkling stars above. This tour de force was painted over but is now being restored.

## Irving House

The arrival of the railway in 1886 quickly extinguished river-borne passenger traffic, but in the preceding decades a few people became exceedingly rich from the profits of boat services. One of them was Scottish Captain William Irving, "King of the Fraser River"; his house is a 15-minute walk from New Westminster station, and it's

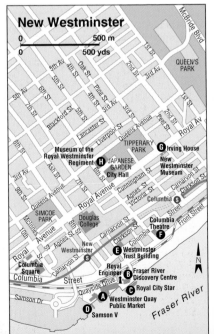

worth the SkyTrain journey just to see it. **Irving House ⓖ** (summer Wed–Sun 12.30–5pm, winter Sat–Sun noon–4pm; tel: 604 527 4640), at 302 Royal Avenue, cost $10,000 to build and was described as "the finest, the best and most home-like house of which BC can yet boast" when completed in 1865.

William died of pneumonia in 1872 at the age of 56, but his descendants continued to live in the house until 1950, when it was purchased by the city as a historic centre. Volunteers take visitors round the 14 rooms, which give an unrivalled insight into the life and times of a BC family over a century. You learn of the 1942 subscription concerts held in the house to raise funds to build a Spitfire, of the clock originally owned by the Southampton-born Rev. Isaac Watts (1674–1748), who wrote the hymn "Joy to the World", and of the important collection of Coast Salish baskets created by the last two sisters to live in the house. Many of the unusually large and tall-ceilinged rooms have their original wallpaper, carpets and furniture.

Within the attractive grounds is **New Westminster Museum** (Wed–Sun noon–4pm, summer noon–5pm; tel: 604 527 4640; www.newwestminster.ca), which has a large collection of local memorabilia, from old radios and televisions, cages of birds, cameras, toys, music and sewing machines to woodworking equipment. It has the coach built in 1876 in San Francisco specially for the visit of Lord and Lady Dufferin on their trip to the Cariboo goldfields in 1876; Lord Dufferin was the first Governor General of Canada to visit BC.

Further up the hill at 530 Queens Avenue is the **Museum of the Royal Westminster Regiment ⓗ** (Tues 1–3pm, 7–9pm, Thur 1–3pm; tel: 604 526 5116). Housed in the old gun room of the historic Armoury building, the museum traces the story of the regiment back to the Royal Engineers who laid out New Westminster, as well as its overseas roles during the two world wars.

At the eastern end of Queens Avenue is the large expanse of Queen's Park and the historic resi-

For antiques and memorabilia, visit Front Street in New Westminster, where a cluster of shops offer better prices than downtown Vancouver, or the Antique Mall at 659 Columbia Street, home to 45 dealers.

**BELOW:** fishing in the Fraser river.

## Fraser River Fish

**B**esides being a major artery, the Fraser river has been a bountiful source of fish for centuries, with more salmon returning to the river system than any other in the world. By the end of the 19th century there were 49 salmon canneries along the south arm of the river, and in 1905 they packed a record 85.6 million cans of sockeye salmon. It is also one of the last rivers with white sturgeon, which can reach 630 kg (1,387 lb), grow to 6 metres (20 ft) and live to 130 years old. Descendants of shark-like fish, they lurk along the river bottoms waiting for anything edible to sink to the bottom. Fished almost to extinction, there is now a ban on fishing them.

dential district of **Queen's Park** straddling the principal shopping street of 6th Avenue.

## Burnaby

Called after the lake which Colonel Moody *(see page 154)* named in honour of his aide, Robert Burnaby, the city of **Burnaby ❷** evolved around the trails hacked through the forest by Moody's Royal Engineers, who also laid out lots for sale. The community was given a municipal charter in 1892, a year after the opening of the interurban between Vancouver and New Westminster, which spurred development beside the tracks. But its real growth came after World War II, with new shopping centres, Simon Fraser University, a hospital and various civic amenities.

Deer Lake is an attractive, well-wooded area in which some exclusive houses were built before World War I, such as Hart House, now a restaurant *(see page 155)*. One of the largest is a magnificent Arts and Crafts-inspired mansion named Fairacres, which now houses the **Burnaby Art Gallery** ( 6344 Deer Lake Avenue; Tues–Fri 10am–4.30pm, Sat–Sun noon–5pm; tel: 604 205 7332; www.city.burnaby. bc.ca). Despite being occupied by the Benedictine monks from Oregon who went on to found Westminster Abbey *(see page 227)*, a bogus religious organisation followed by squatters, it has survived the vicissitudes remarkably well and retains its fireplaces with tiled panels, brass beading and hood, the original bathroom fittings and a remarkable gabled inglenook fireplace in the former billiard room. Bought by the Municipality of Burnaby in 1966, it hosts changing exhibitions of mostly contemporary artists.

Below the terrace are the winding paths and colourful beds of Century Gardens that flow seamlessly towards the **Shadbolt Centre for the Arts** (tel: 604 205 3000; www. city.burnaby.bc.ca), with a busy events programme at its theatre and recital hall. The centre is enlivened by rehearsal rooms, pottery studios, an art shop and a café.

A few minutes' walk from the centre is **Burnaby Village Museum**

**TIP**

Take a lunch or dinner cruise aboard a modern sternwheeler from New Westminster up the Fraser river to historic Fort Langley *(see page 217)*.

**BELOW:** the Pacific National Exhibition fairground.

## Hastings Park

**C**lose to the Ironworkers' Memorial Bridge, Hastings Park has long been home to two institutions: the horse racetrack and the Pacific National Exhibition. The PNE started life as agricultural event, but it has expanded to encompass dog and horse shows, a fairground, motocross championships, live bands, beer garden and charity events. It now attracts over 1 million visitors during the 17-day event from mid-August.

Large areas of the park are being restored to municipal parkland after decades of ad hoc building. So far a landscaped sanctuary, a skateboard park, two soccer pitches, a running track and children's playground have been completed.

(early May–early Sept 11am–4.30pm, late Nov–early Jan noon–5.30pm; tel: 604 293 6501; www.city.burnaby.bc.ca), which recreates a typical Burnaby tram-stop community *c*.1925 on its 4-hectare (10-acre) site. The grounds are big enough and sufficiently well wooded to harbour the odd coyote – as a notice on the door may warn.

Only one of over 30 buildings is on its original site; the rest have been dismantled and relocated. The functions of the rescued buildings include a general store, bakery, post office, blacksmith, music shop, garage, Chinese herbalist, optometrist, print shop, barber and bank. A photographic studio has been cleverly adapted for changing exhibitions about different aspects of local history. Interpreters in period costume are on hand to tell you about a building's history and stories of former occupants.

The building on its original site is Elworth, a cedar shingle-covered house with full-width Tuscan-columned porch built in 1922 by a Canadian Pacific Railway employee.

Map on page 148

Children are enthralled by the hand-carved carousel built in Kansas in 1912 which has 36 horses, 4 ponies, a chariot and a wheelchair, while music from a 1925 Wurlitzer military band organ fills the air. Light lunches and snacks can be bought in the ice-cream parlour.

Beside the SkyTrain line and Metrotown Station is the vast **Metrotown Centre**, Canada's second-largest shopping centre.

Almost a quarter of Burnaby is parkland, with over 100 different parks; one of the largest, **Central Park**, is a forest of huge Douglas firs, hemlock and maple, which can be reached from the adjacent Patterson SkyTrain station.

### Ironworkers' Memorial Bridge

Directly north of Burnaby, the **Ironworkers' Memorial Bridge ❸** is the second bridge on this site across the Second Narrows of Burrard Inlet. The poorly designed first bridge of 1925 was hit by shipping so many times that a replacement with much greater capacity was

*Simon Fraser University, designed by Arthur Erickson, opened in 1965. It has 25,000 students spread across three campuses.*

**BELOW:** Burnaby Village Museum.

**BELOW:** summer market outside Port Moody's old station building.

imperative. Construction of the steel truss cantilever bridge began in 1957, but faulty calculations over the required strength of the footings led to the collapse of a crane and much of the bridge, causing the death of 18 ironworkers. Finally opened in 1960, the bridge is 1,292 metres (4,239 ft) long, with a centre span for shipping, and forms part of the Trans-Canada Highway (Highway 1). The bridge was given its name in 1994 to honour the 27 workers that died during its construction. The old Second Narrows bridge was adapted as a rail-only bridge and stands to the east of the new bridge.

### Simon Fraser University

Curiously located on an isolated campus on Burnaby Mountain and surrounded by a wooded conservation area, **Simon Fraser University** ❹ received its first students in 1965 in buildings designed by Arthur Erickson *(see page 117)*. Covering 174 hectares (430 acres) and now home to 25,000 students, the university is built in the form of ter-

races beside a linear walkway along a ridge, and its homogeneous concrete buildings have provided the set for many a film. As one of Erickson's first and largest commissions, the university is accustomed to visits by those interested in modern architecture.

### Port Moody

This city at the eastern end of Burrard Inlet might have been Vancouver, so to speak, had the Canadian Pacific Railway not reversed its decision to make **Port Moody** ❺ the western terminus of the transcontinental railway, preferring instead to push on to what is now Waterfront near Coal Harbour. Its strategic location as another means of supplying the proposed capital of New Westminster, should that be attacked from the Fraser river, prompted the construction through the forest of a trail later known as the North Road.

From this beginning and bearing the name of the commander of the Royal Engineers who built the road, Port Moody experienced a real estate boom and bust with the CPR's

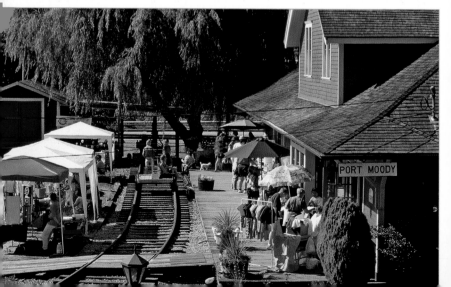

choice and then rejection of the embryonic town as a suitable terminus. The first train from the east arrived on 8 November 1885 with transcontinental passenger services starting the following year. But in 1887, Port Moody was sidelined when the line on to Vancouver was opened. Though sawmills were developed beside the waterfront, the population remained static at 250 for over 20 years. Eventually the pressure of development from Vancouver affected Port Moody, oil refineries were built in the 1900s and it became a city in 1913.

Port Moody can be reached by West Coast Express from Waterfront Station by Canada Place. Though today largely a quiet suburb of Vancouver, the city retains many historic buildings, especially along Clarke Street, and its **station building** (1905) at 2734 Murray Street is a museum with restored telegraph office and station agent's kitchen (Victoria Day–Labour Day 10am–5pm, Labour Day–Victoria Day noon–4pm). In another heritage building at 2425 St Johns Street is the **Port Moody Arts Centre**. In the grounds is a stone cairn with brass plaque commemorating the arrival of the first transcontinental train.

Between the Old City Hall and waterfront is **Shoreline Park**, which attracts birdwatchers for the 125 species recorded in its 40 hectares (99 acres), including loons, cormorants, herons, eagles, geese and warblers. A trail runs through the park in which coyotes, foxes, raccoons and black-tailed deer cannot be spotted. ❑

*The Port Moody Arts Centre is housed in the Arts and Crafts-style Old City Hall, built in 1914, which incorporated the firehall and police station.*

# RESTAURANTS

### Burnaby

**Hart House**
6664 Deer Lake Ave,
Tel: 604 298 4278. Open:
L Tues–Fri, Sun, D Tues–
Sun. $$
www.harthouserestaurant.com
Serving West Coast cuisine with an Asian twist, the restaurant is set in a lovely period house, with a huge fireplace in the hall and white-painted wood panelling in the three dining rooms. Very pretty spot. Worth the expedition. Reservation is advisable.

### Langley

**Bacchus Bistro**
1064, 216 Street (south of intersection with 16th Ave).

Tel: 604 530 9694. Open: L Wed–Sun, D Fri & Sat. $$
www.domainedechaberton.com
This restaurant overlooking the vineyards of Domaine de Chaberton Winery is an undiscovered gem. The menu is French with the advantage of West Coast produce, and the food is as excellent as the service. Terrine maison, mussels, crêpes, sole *à la grenobloise*, rillette, a tarte du jour and a chocolate mousse, the stuff of bourgeois French cooking at its best makes for a divine summer lunch on the patio which overlooks the vines. Be sure to sample the local wine.

### New Westminster

**The Boathouse**
900 Quayside Drive. Tel: 604 525 3474. Open: B, L & D daily. $$$
www.boathouserestaurants.ca
A casual-smart seafood restaurant set right on the shore. Open for all meals, including brunch at the weekend.

**Hon's Wun-Tun House**
408 6th St. Tel: 604 520 6661. $
This unassuming Chinese has won a host of awards – best cheap eats, best Chinese, best casual Chinese – and once you've eaten here you will know why. But be prepared to wait for a table, as there is often a queue. The dim sum is great and the potstickers, noodles and barbecue have all been highly praised.

**The Keg Steakhouse**
800 Columbia St. Tel: 604 524 1381. Open: D daily. $$$
www.kegsteakhouse.com
This chain steakhouse is situated in the old railway station and serves the usual steaks, chicken and seafood. Open for dinner from 4pm.

**Laguna Blu**
Unit 200, 810 Quayside Drive. Tel: 604 771 7252. Open: L & D daily. $$
www.lagunablu.ca
Good Italian restaurant with splendid view of the Fraser River and the constant barge traffic.

● ● ● ● ● ● ● ● ● ● ● ● ●
*Prices for three-course dinner per person with a half-bottle of house wine.*
*$ under C$30, $$ C$30–50, $$$ C$50–80, $$$$ C$80+*

# SOUTH VANCOUVER

There are many good reasons, other than the airport, to visit this delta region. One is Steveston, a historic fishing village with bags of atmosphere. Another is the amazing variety of bird life that comes to nest and feed around the mouth of the Fraser. Recreational trails cater for cyclists and walkers

**M**uch of southern Vancouver is made up of islands within the Fraser Delta. The former fishing and sailing community of Richmond is a group of islands contained within the northern and southern arms of the Fraser river. Even the airport – the reason most visitors head south – is located on Sea Island, so named because it was difficult to tell where sea ended and land began.

Besides this delta region's ever-expanding role as a dormitory of Vancouver, fishing, farming and trade have long been its economic mainstays, although local sources of employment in the high-tech computer and software industries have recently grown.

## Sea Island

Apart from the airport, the only other reason to visit Sea Island is to reach **Iona Island**  for its bird life and an unusual bike ride or walk. Though the shoreline forms Iona Beach Regional Park, the island is also home to a sewage treatment plant, but it is neither a visual nor olfactory intrusion once you are into the sand dunes of the park where over 300 species of birds feed and rest. Besides eagles, osprey and heron, numerous rare birds have been spotted, including white pelican, long-

tailed jaeger, ruff and yellow-headed blackbirds. The southern arm of the peculiar V-shape of the western end of the island stretches for 4 km (2½ miles) out into Georgia Strait; this narrow tarmac-covered jetty covers the outfall pipe and provides an unusual experience for cyclists and walkers. It's known as a good place to watch the stars away from the light pollution of Vancouver. Note that car access to Iona Beach Regional Park is forbidden after dusk, so stargazers need to park outside the gates.

Map
on page
158

**LEFT:** Garry Point Park.
**BELOW:** the delta region attracts many seabirds, both rare and familiar.

*Richmond's beautiful Buddhist Temple, set in landscaped gardens, is a place of sanctuary. It is open for public viewing from 10am–5pm and has a meditation centre where you can take classes (9160 Steveston Highway; tel: 604 274 2822).*

## Lulu Island and Richmond

Steveston and most of the much larger **Richmond** ❷ are located on this island formed by the alluvial sand and silt brought down the Fraser river and flanked by its north and south arms. Without the dykes, large areas of Lulu Island would be under water at extreme high tide. It was given its name in 1863 by Colonel Richard Moody, after a popular entertainer from San Francisco, Lulu Sweet, his travel companion from New Westminster to Victoria. The first white settlers arrived in 1866, and by 1879 Richmond had been incorporated as a township.

Although the area was developed as Vancouver's market garden, it is under huge pressure for development, and the centre of what became the city of Richmond in 1990 is now full of high-rise towers and back-to-back shopping malls – the Lansdowne Park and Richmond centres are the largest.

Nonetheless, 4,800 hectares (11,861 acres) of land within Richmond are protected as agricultural land – the fertile delta soil and absence of trees made it ideal for cultivation, with cranberries emerging as the dominant crop during the 1990s. Landowners no longer have to maintain the dykes, and with their adoption by local and provincial government, they have been adapted to incorporate Richmond's recreational trails for cyclists and walkers.

Richmond was the first Canadian city to declare itself multicultural, and it is indicative of the population's varied ethnicity that it has an Asia Centre shopping mall featuring Asian-made products – predominantly Chinese. That background is also reflected in the impressive **Buddhist Temple** *(see opposite)* and **Cultural Centre** (7700 Minoru Gate; Mon–Fri 9am–9.30pm, Sat–Sun 10am–5pm; tel: 604 231 6457; www.richmond.ca), which houses

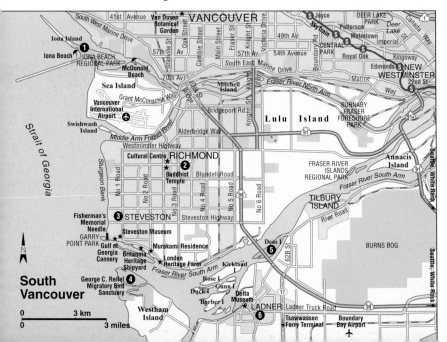

an art gallery, museum, arts centre and archive as well as the main library.

## Steveston

This community at the southwestern corner of Lulu Island has a very different atmosphere from anywhere else around Vancouver, with the coming and going of fishing boats, the tang of fish, seaweed and ozone, and the welcome feeling of a working maritime community. The main street even feels like a village, though the wall-to-wall restaurants along the seafront boardwalk speak of a growing dependence on visitors.

Named after its first permanent settler, Manoah Steves, a native of New Brunswick who arrived in 1877, **Steveston** ❸ was initially a farming community. But it was only 12 years later that the Hudson's Bay Company tea clipper *Titania* carried the first direct shipment of canned salmon from Britannia cannery in Steveston to London, a trip around Cape Horn that took 104 days. Along 2 miles of foreshore known as "Cannery Row", 15 canneries

were set up, one of which was the biggest in the British Empire. Bunkhouses, bars, brothels and opium dens catered for the 10,000 seasonal workers.

By 1895 Steveston canneries were producing around 200,000 cases of salmon a year, and it was not uncommon to have more than a dozen windjammers waiting near Steveston for appropriate tides and westerly winds to dock. Rocks brought in as ballast were unloaded and used to build roads and dykes in the area, and the holds were filled with lumber and canned salmon. Many of the fishermen, boatbuilders and workers were Japanese, until the decision in 1942 to intern them inland.

Steveston is still Canada's biggest commercial fishing harbour even if it is no longer holds the title of "salmon capital of the world". It is surviving buildings from its heyday, coupled with its attractive setting, that makes Steveston so popular with visitors. It is easy to reach, taking the 98 B-Line bus from downtown Vancouver to Richmond and changing to a 401, 402, 407, 410 or 492 bus.

Map on page 158

*The Fraser river is the longest river in BC at 1,375 km (859 miles), rising in the Yellowhead Pass on the continental divide and draining an area the size of Britain.*

**BELOW:**
Steveston waterfront.

### Steveston Waterfront Greenway

The best way to explore the water-front is by hiring a bike *(see left)* and cycling the 5-km (3-mile) long greenway that runs alongside Can-nery Channel. Workers from can-nery days would not recognise the landscaped waterfront, where the restaurant-lined boardwalk and con-dominiums have replaced their places of work.

Panels along the waterfront pro-vide information about the area, including the marvellous complex of preserved wooden buildings around **Britannia Heritage Ship-yard** (5180 Westwater Drive; May–Sept Tues–Sun 10am– 6pm, Oct–Apr Sat 10am–4pm, Sun noon–4pm; tel: 604 718 8050; www.britannia-hss.ca). Built on piles over the water like most of the old buildings along the waterfront, the covered slipways are still being used to restore boats brought out of the water on cradles. Now a National Historic Site, the building had been a cannery, but was con-verted to shipyard; a number of

**TIP**

For bike hire in Steve-ston, visit Kaymaran Adventure Tours (tel: 604 946 7507) on the waterfront at 4860 Chisholm Street or Steveston Seabreeze Adventures (tel: 604 272 7200) at the south end of No. 1 Road/6th Avenue.

canneries closed with the disastrous downturn in salmon stocks on the Fraser river in 1918–19.

Near by is a Seine net loft and the **Murakami Residence**, which is thought to have been built in the 1880s as a traditional Japanese home and bathhouse. The family owned one of the eight Japanese boatworks. It was originally also built on piles, so it has new foundations on its original footprint. In a garden along the front is a commemorative statue to the generations of Japanese fisher-men who worked here.

To the east of London's Landing is **London Heritage Farm** (Mar–June, Sept–Dec Sat–Sun 10am–4pm, July–Aug daily 10am–4pm; tel: 604 271 5220; www.londonheritage farm.ca), which has been restored to portray life *c.*1900. Aged 16 and 17 Charles Edwin London and his brother William came out to Steve-ston from London, Ontario, when their parents died and bought 80 hectares (200 acres) of land. They built the farm in the mid-1880s and also owned the general store and post office. Apart from the piano, none of the furniture is original, but it does not detract from the overall presenta-tion of the house. Volunteers serve excellent tea in period china with home-baked scones.

### Gulf of Georgia Cannery

The importance of salmon and the canning industry to the coastal region of BC has been recognised by the protection given to the **Gulf of Georgia Cannery** (early May– 31 May Thur–Mon 10am–5pm, June–early Sept daily 10am–5pm, early Sept–early Oct Mon–Sat 10am–5pm, Sun 11am–5pm; tel: 604 664 9009; www.pc.gc.ca), built in 1894 and the largest in BC until 1902. After switching to herring reduction following World War II, the cannery finally closed in 1979 but continued in use as a net storage

**BELOW:** fresh Sockeye salmon for sale.

facility while its fate was decided. The Federal government bought the cannery and transferred it to Parks Canada, which organises separate guided tours of the salmon packing and herring reduction sections of the plant, following a film that evokes the way of life that went with the pungent canneries.

Beyond the cannery is **Garry Point Park**, an area of reclaimed intertidal salt marsh. Created as recently as 1989, the park's terrain is mostly sand, with gaillardia growing wild among the sea grass in summer. It's a good place to find a quiet spot to soak up the sun, and the bike trail and footpath continue all the way around the coast almost to the Moray Bridge linking the mainland and Sea Island.

Close to the shore is the **Fisherman's Memorial Needle**, which commemorates the many boats and crews lost at sea over the years.

### Steveston village

The blocks between Moncton Street and the shore at Bayview Street are full of small independent shops, cafés and restaurants. Salmon, crab and prawns can be bought directly from the boats, and fish-and-chip shops and restaurants are legion.

At 3811 Moncton Street is the incongruously sited **Steveston Museum** (Mon–Sat 9.30am–1pm, 1.30–5pm; tel: 604 271 6868; www.richmond.ca), reached by passing through the post office. The 1906 building was originally the Northern Bank; the manager lived on the premises, and at the rear is the kitchen, while upstairs is a bedroom and display of local history in photographs.

If the briny calls, two Steveston companies offer tours. **Kaymaran Adventure Tours** (tel: 604 946 7507; www.kaymarantours.com), at 4860 Chisholm Street along the Waterfront near Britannia Shipyard, offers ecotours ranging from a two-hour cruise around the estuary and kayak tours to a six-hour tour of the Fraser river with buffet lunch. Popular with twitchers are tours to the Reifel Island Bird Sanctuary on Westham Island *(see page 162)*. **Steveston Seabreeze Adventures**

Map on page 158

*There were once 49 canneries on the lower Fraser river, with 14 on the Cannery Channel at Steveston. The last plant closed in 1992. The Gulf of Georgia Cannery (above) traces the history of fishing and canning in the region.*

**BELOW:** cycling the Steveston greenway.

---

## Burns Bog

This vast expanse between Ladner, North Delta and Surrey is the largest area of park in the Lower Mainland. Covering about 2,800 hectares (6,919 acres), the raised peat bog forms the largest undeveloped urban area in Canada. Its sheer size enables it to act as a valuable natural air and water filtration system, as well as being home to many beautiful and rare plants, animals and insects. Though the Annacis Highway slices through the separately protected Delta Nature Reserve in the northeastern corner of Burns Bog, the rest of the reserve is closed to traffic. It has three loops of boardwalks and trails with beaver dam and cedar grove en route.

Map on page 158

### TIP

Just three minutes from the ferry terminal at Tsawwassen, Splashdown Park (Jun–early Sep 10am–4/5/6/7/8pm; tel: 604 943 2251; www.splashdown-park.ca), has 13 slides of various sizes, configurations and degrees of scariness (one is black), volleyball, badminton and basketball.

**BELOW:** sunset fishing trip off Westham Island.

(tel: 604 272 7200; www.seabreeze adventures.ca), at the southern end of No. 1 Road/6th Avenue, offers whale-watching and fishing tours.

## Westham Island

Wine, flowers, herbs, fruit and vegetables are produced and sold from roadside stalls on this large but awkward-to-reach island in the mouth of the south arm of the Fraser river. The principal reason for visiting the island is the **George C. Reifel Migratory Bird Sanctuary ➍** (daily 9am–4pm; tel: 604 946 6980; www.reifelbirdsanctuary.com). The 344-hectare (850-acre) sanctuary is threaded by 3 km (2 miles) of hiking trails from which to see some of the 268 species of birds recorded here, and there are hides and a three-storey observation platform.

The autumn highlight is the arrival of flocks of Lesser snow geese, numbering up to 80,000 and turning the sky white. In winter you may be lucky enough to see the tiny Saw-whet owl roosting in overhead branches. Spring brings cormorants, hawks, eagles, ospreys and other fish-eating wildlife. Many bird species are resident year-round, but among the rare sightings are uncommon species such as Black-crowned night heron and gyrfalcon.

## Deas Island

Further up the south arm lies **Deas Island ➎**, covering 70 hectares (173 acres), named after the first settler, a freed black slave named John Sullivan Deas, who arrived in 1873. He founded an unsuccessful cannery, but others followed until World War I. The rest of the small community was made up of a few farmers and fishermen, but by the 1950s the island was deserted. Created a park in 1981, the island has three old buildings, the most significant being **Burrvilla**, a Queen Anne-style house once owned by an ancestor of actor Raymond Burr *(see page 149)*. Among the furnishings is an 11-leaved dining-table that seats 28.

There are a number of easy, level trails through the cottonwood and alder trees, such as the Island Tip Trail and the Dyke Loop. The western side is the more natural and has been likened to the Mississippi Delta.

## Ladner

A wharf to dispatch agricultural produce to Victoria and New Westminster was the beginning of **Ladner ➏**, a village on the delta of the south arm, founded by and named after two brothers from Cornwall who had come out in the goldrush. The historic and attractive part of the town is Ladner village, with wide, tree-lined pavements and small shops and cafés. The **Delta Museum** (4858 Delta Street, Tues–Sat 10am–3.30pm), housed in a 1912 neo-Tudor building, features a reconstructed prison cell among its exhibits of local history.

The Tsawwassen ferry terminal is near by, for ferries to the capital on Victoria Island. ❏

# RESTAURANTS

## Garry Point Park

### Pajo's

Chatham St. Tel: 604 204 0767. $

A small chain (four locations) of fish-and-chip shops, operating seasonally (spring, summer, and a bit of the autumn), serving fantastically fresh fish: Pacific halibut, cod, chum salmon and yellowfin tuna, all of it wild. You can have burgers, chicken and other fast foods, but the fish is the thing here, and the queues are a testament to the quality.

## Ladner

### La Belle Auberge

4856, 48th Ave. Tel: 604 946 7717. Open: D Tues–Sat. $$$$

www.labelleauberge.com

Situated in the old village of Ladner in a very pretty Victorian house, this fine restaurant is spread over two levels and five small dining rooms. You will find seriously good food here – award-winning chef Bruno Marti's establishment is reckoned to be one of the best restaurants in Canada. Game features quite prominently – butter-poached pheasant with vanilla sauce and bison loin with braised short rib are two delicious entrées. Lobster bisque and pumpkin soup are brilliant

starters. Worth the expedition if you are interested in serious food.

## Richmond

### Sun Sui Wah Seafood Restaurant

102, 4940 No. 3 Road. Tel: 604 273 8208. Open: L & D daily. $$ www.sunsuiwah.com

The area bordered by Sea Island Way, No. 3 Road, Lansdowne Road and Garden City Road, is the heart of the city's Asian population and has been dubbed "Golden Village". There are hundreds of Asian restaurants to choose from. This Cantonese restaurant is famous for its dim sum served in the time-honoured way from trolleys which trundle around the room waiting for you to take your pick. Roasted squab is one of its signature dishes, as is Alaska king crab steamed with minced garlic.

### Thai House Restaurant

129, 4940 No. 3 Road. Tel: 604 278 7373. $–$$

Vancouver-area chain of award-winning Thai restaurants. This popular Richmond branch in the Golden Village offers very good Thai food at extremely good prices.

## Steveston

### Alegria Cafe & Giftware

12151 1st Avenue. Tel: 604 274 1215. $

Serves home-made food using wholefood and organic ingredients. Good place for a light lunch after a browse in the giftshop.

### Cannery Café

3711 Moncton St. Tel: 604 272 1222. Open: L Mon–Fri, D daily. $

www.canneryseafood.com

Located in one of Steveston's oldest buildings, the café has been a cannery cookhouse, an electronics shop and a radio outlet store, and now serves brunches and wholesome lunchtime chowders and chillis to visitors and locals.

### Steveston Seafood House

3951 Moncton St. Tel: 604 271 5252. Open: L Sat & Sun, D daily. $–$$

www.stevestonseafoodhouse.com

The chef at this highstreet restaurant has been here for over 20 years and has won many accolades for her cooking. Every entrée is accompanied by a serving of rice and vegetables, and the desserts come on a trolley. It's like stepping back in time. Brunch is served on Sat and Sun from 11.30am.

### PRICE CATEGORIES

Prices for three-course dinner per person with a half-bottle of house wine:
$ = under C$30
$$ = C$30–50
$$$ = C$50–80
$$$$ = more than C$80

**RIGHT:** Cannery Cafe, a Steveston favourite.

# NORTH AND WEST VANCOUVER

**The north shore is the exclusive domain of prosperous Vancouverites whose mansions command fabulous views, but the real attraction is the wilderness beyond. Grouse Mountain and Capilano Canyon are an easy bus ride from Lonsdale Quay, but if you've time for deeper exploration Lynn Canyon, Mount Seymour and Cypress Park are all outstanding**

I t is the mountains that range along the north shore of English Bay and Burrard Inlet that give Vancouver such a stunning setting. The view from Kitsilano and Point Grey without the sawtooth of peaks along the opposite shore is unimaginable. Both North and West Vancouver are predominantly dormitories, West being the more upmarket, though both have much to offer the visitor. With an abundance of provincial, regional and municipal parks, this area offers the best hiking and biking close to the city.

## Early development

The topography that residents and visitors admire was both the stimulus to the area's development and the reason for southern districts to eclipse the early promise of North Vancouver. Huge stands of cedars and firs encouraged the establishment of the first sawmill on the north shore, in 1862, and two years later international trade out of Burrard Inlet began with the first consignment of timber, to Adelaide. But the absence of a bridge across the inlet and the distance from the local markets of New Westminster and Victoria made it difficult for the pioneers to compete. Even the Methodist minister who preached the first sermon on the inlet had to

arrive by canoe, in 1865. Equally the mountains would constrain eventual development.

Even when North Vancouver became a formal district in 1891, stretching from Horseshoe Bay to Deep Cove, the population was still only a few hundred. Many of the early users of the ferry service established in 1900 were hikers, skiers for Grouse Mountain or visitors to the Capilano Suspension Bridge. The City of North Vancouver was carved out of the area and independently

**Map on pages 166–7**

**LEFT:** Grouse Mountain Skyride.
**BELOW:** Horseshoe Bay harbour.

*Lonsdale Quay is
a pleasant place
for relaxing and
shopping.*

governed from 1907, followed in
1912 by the municipality of West
Vancouver.

The opening of the Second Narrows Bridge for rail and road traffic
in 1925 gave a huge fillip to the
north shore and North Vancouver in
particular. The Depression hit North
Vancouver so hard that about 75
percent of landowners saw their
property revert to the municipality
for unpaid taxes. World War II and
a revival of shipbuilding relieved
unemployment and revived population growth.

### North Vancouver

Most visitors to North Vancouver
arrive by SeaBus at **Lonsdale Quay**
❶, where the bus station and shopping centre are located directly
ahead. Lonsdale Quay is North Vancouver's equivalent of Granville
Market, a former collection of warehouses that was adapted in 1986 to
become a collection of interesting

individual shops. East of Lonsdale
Quay, following the water's edge, is
the former Pacific Great Eastern
Railway station of 1913, which now
serves as a tourist information centre.

Beyond are the remains of the
shipbuilding slips that produced 379
vessels between 1906 and 1992,
including tugs and barges, supply
ships in two world wars, ferries and
icebreakers. Versatile Pacific Shipyard (formerly Wallace Shipyards)
was the largest company, run by
three generations of the Wallace
family after Andrew Wallace established the yard in 1894, but one
company remains active: C.H. Cates
& Sons is one of Vancouver's oldest
companies, having been founded in
1886, and is still carrying out repairs
to its fleet of tugs.

It is hoped to establish a National
Maritime Centre around four of the
slipways and their buildings, with
another Granville Island-style market to provide financial support.

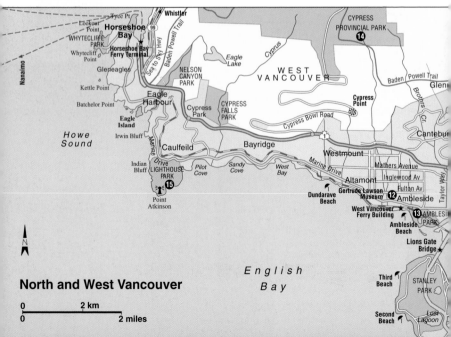

**North and West Vancouver**

The streets north of Lonsdale Quay, known as lower Lonsdale, contain the few heritage buildings left, including two from 1910 – the former Bank of Hamilton at 92 Lonsdale and the Aberdeen block at 84 Lonsdale, in which one of the district's oldest shops, Paines Hardware, is still located.

## Capilano Suspension Bridge

The most popular tourist attraction on the north shore is the pedestrian **Capilano Suspension Bridge ❷** (8.30am–dusk in summer; 9am–5pm in winter; tel: 604 985 7474; www.capbridge.com). The bridges across the thickly forested defile of the Capilano canyon have been attracting visitors since 1889, and the current 137-metre (450-ft) span bridge swaying 70 metres (230 ft) above the river has become a "must see" for visitors. The bridge is served by the frequent 236 bus service from Lonsdale Quay.

Once across the bridge, there are boardwalks through the forest, with a high-level tree walk 30 metres (100 ft) above the floor linking eight Douglas firs ranging from 60–76 metres (200–250 ft) tall. Information boards give an insight into the importance of preserving what temperate rainforest survives: though tropical rainforest has more varieties of plants and animals, temperate rainforest wins hands down for quantity, with up to 2,000 tons of living matter per acre of forest. There is also a large collection of totem poles near the bridge, the earliest ones carved in the 1930s by Danish immigrants.

## Capilano River Regional Park

North of the bridge the **Capilano River Regional Park ❸** (summer 8am–9pm, from Labour Day to the start of summer time 8am–dusk but never before 5pm; tel: 604 224 5739;

Map below

*As the southern terminus of the railway from Prince George and northern BC, North Vancouver receives large quantities of raw materials and agricultural products, such as potash, canola, wheat, barley and flax. Bright-yellow mounds of sulphur are a distinctive feature of the shoreline.*

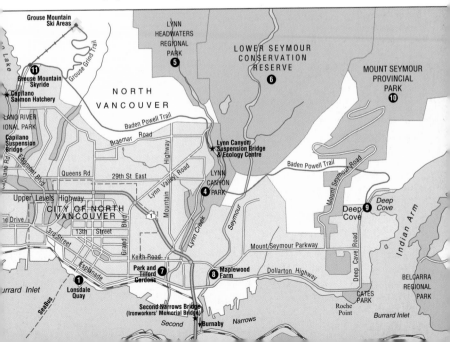

*The Capilano Salmon Hatchery was built to offset damage caused by Cleveland Dam.*

**BELOW:** Capilano Suspension Bridge; totems in the park.

www.gvrd.bc.ca) stretches to the immense concrete wall of Cleveland Dam, which holds back Capilano Lake, the source of 40 percent of Vancouver's drinking water. There are about 26 km (16 miles) of trails in the park; the longest is the Capilano Pacific Trail at 8 km (5 miles), popular with dog-walking and jogging locals. Many walk up the trail along the river from the shoreline **Ambleside Park** (246 bus from Lonsdale Quay, *see page 166*). It's mostly close to the river, except for a short section signed "Town Trail" through a residential neighbourhood at Park Royal and a stretch near the Trans Canada Highway.

For a river-bed view of the canyon, take the path down to Ranger Pool; there are some striking viewpoints along the way. Alternative paths through the forest include one following the gently graded trackbed of the Capilano Timber Company railway, with good views of the Lions (the twin peaks visible from downtown Vancouver).

On the east side of the river, which can be reached by crossing the Cleveland Dam, is the **Capilano Salmon Hatchery** (May, Sept 8am–7pm, June–Aug 8am–8pm, Apr, Oct 8am–4.45pm, Nov–Mar 8am–4pm; tel: 604 666 1790; www-heb.pac.dfo-mpo.gc.ca). The 236 bus from Lonsdale Quay passes close to the hatchery and the dam.

The construction of the dam in 1954 blocked the route of coho and steelhead travelling up the Capilano river to spawn, so the weir and ladder were built to help the fish navigate upriver. The hatchery was opened in 1971 to release salmon below the dam and offset the high losses of young fish travelling downstream over the dam. There's always something to see at the hatchery; best of all is spawning season (Nov–Dec), when you'll see salmon jumping over the fish ladders.

## Lynn Canyon Park

A free alternative to the Capilano bridge is provided in the 250-hectare (617-acre) **Lynn Canyon Park ❹**, which was opened in 1912; it can be reached by bus services 228/9 from Lonsdale Quay.

Near the entrance is an **Ecology Centre** (June–Sept daily 10am–5pm, Oct–May Mon–Fri 10am–5pm, Sat–Sun noon–4pm; tel: 604 981 3103; www.dnv.org), which has well-presented displays on plants, animals, trees and ecosystems, with lots of buttons to press and flaps to open for children. Though not as long as the Capilano bridge, the Lynn Canyon suspension bridge spans a spectacular sheer-walled canyon just above a waterfall of rock, and it has enough wobble to delight children without being too scary for faint-hearted grown-ups.

Once across the bridge, you can do a circular walk by turning south and following a path, partly boardwalk, through the forest and down steep steps to reach Two Falls Bridge, which spans the river above some crystal-clear pools and a double fall in the river. Equally steep steps take you back to the café near the Ecology Centre, which serves light lunches. En route are many stumps of the Douglas firs and Western red cedar which were felled in the late 19th century.

The bridge is on the 41-km (26-mile) Baden-Powell Trail between Horseshoe Bay in West Vancouver and Deep Cove on the west bank of the Indian Arm inlet (see page 171).

## Lynn Headwaters Regional Park

Further north still and also on the 229 bus route is the **Lynn Headwaters Regional Park** ⑤ (summer 8am–9pm, from Labour Day to the start of summer time 8am–dusk but never before 5pm; tel: 604 224 5739; www.gvrd.bc.ca), a wilderness area with 75 km (47 miles) of hiking trails in which the city seems very far away. It offers some spectacular views, and such curious sights as trees growing through an abandoned truck from logging days. An information area on the east side of Lynn Creek near the entrance has details of the park trails, and visitors are asked to self-register.

There are trails of varying lengths and levels of difficulty. The Lynn Loop Trail and Cedar Mill Trail will take less than an hour and require only minimal fitness. The creekside

Map on pages 166–7

**TIP**

In March one of the world's most bizarre charity races takes place when 30,000 yellow rubber ducks are purchased ahead of time by the public, then dropped on to the Capilano river. The first owners to retrieve their ducks at the mouth of the river win prizes.

**BELOW:** Lynn Canyon Park; Lynn Canyon suspension bridge.

15.5-km (9½-mile) Headwaters Trail is a gentle walk that takes you to Norvan Creek, and takes about half a day. More challenging is the aptly named Switchback Trail with the option at the top of heading back along the Lynn Loop or pressing on north to the headwaters. Water levels in Lynn Creek have to be low to be able to tackle the Lynn Lake Route for experienced walkers.

### Lower Seymour Conservation Reserve

Sandwiched between Lynn Headwaters Regional Park and Mount Seymour Provincial Park, the **Lower Seymour Conservation Reserve** ❻ (dawn–dusk; tel: 604 432 6200; www.gvrd.bc.ca) is a 5,668-hectare (14,006-acre) reserve comprising approximately one-third of the 18,000-hectare (44,489-acre) Seymour Watershed, which supplies Vancouver with water. It contains some of the most spectacular and diverse landscapes in the Greater Vancouver area, with beautiful Alpine meadows, forested slopes and river flood plains.

The 25 km (15 miles) of fairly easy hiking trails head off in all directions from the car-park gatehouse. The most challenging ones are the Homestead, Twin Bridges and Fisherman's trails, which lead down into the Seymour Valley and follow the Seymour river. Maps and an interpretive brochure are available at the gatehouse.

### Around the Ironworkers Memorial Bridge

Just west of the Ironworkers' Memorial Bridge *(see page 153)* is **Park and Tilford Gardens** ❼ (daily dawn–dusk; tel: 604 984 8200; www.parkandtilford.ca) at 333 Brooksbank Avenue on bus routes 228 and 239 from Lonsdale Quay. Created in 1969 by a distillery company, the gardens cover 1.2 hectares (3 acres) and are divided into eight themed areas: oriental with plants pruned in bonsai style; white; rock pool with waterfall; native; herb; flower garden with 27 circular beds of colourful annuals replacing spring-flowering bulbs; colonnade with a long pergola; and bog garden.

**TIP**

Heavy rain can cause watercourses to rise so rapidly that paths can become difficult or impossible to follow. This should be borne in mind when planning a hiking route for a day of changeable weather. The best time for walking in the north shore parks is late April to mid-October.

**BELOW:** there are hiking trails to suit all abilities and ages.

### Mountain Hiking

The mountainous backcountry of Mount Seymour National Park and Lynn Headwaters Regional Park is extremely rugged, and hiking in these areas should be attempted only by experienced and properly equipped walkers. Heavy rain and thick fog can quickly change the landscape from beautiful to dangerous. The mountain weather can change very quickly, so be prepared by taking appropriate gear and informing a responsible person of your intentions. If mist and fog should close in and you become lost, stay where you are until the weather clears or you are found. Hiking alone is inadvisable, and you should know what to do if you encounter a bear. Never leave the trail.

To the east of the bridge lies **Maplewood Farm** ❽ (Apr–mid-Sept daily 10am–4pm, mid-Sept–Mar Tues–Sun 10am–4pm; tel: 604 929 5610; www.maplewoodfarm. bc.ca), a great place to take children to see over 200 domestic animals and birds on a 2-hectare (5-acre) farm beside the Seymour river. It is now the last remaining farm on the north shore and offers pony rides (in summer), milking demonstrations and animals to hold or pat. A particularly popular time to visit is spring, when baby animals are born. Located at 405 Seymour River Place, it can be reached by taking bus 239 from Lonsdale Quay and changing to the C-15 shuttle bus at Phibbs Exchange.

### Deep Cove

The small settlement of **Deep Cove** ❾ on Indian Arm is right on the edge of North Vancouver, almost bordering Mount Seymour National Park. It's renowned as one of the loveliest parts of the region, but take rain gear if you go there as it's also the wettest place in the Lower Mainland. It has a vibrant community with plenty of individual shops, pubs and restaurants, and even has a 130-seat air-conditioned theatre and art gallery within the Cultural Centre. Take the bus from Lonsdale Quay to Phibbs Exchange from where the 211/212 go to Deep Cove.

Bikes can be hired at **Deep Cove Bike Shop** (tel: 604 929 1918), which introduced Vancouver to mountain biking when it brought the first bikes to the area during the early 1980s. Indian Arm is a paradise for paddlers – an 18-km (11-mile) fjord of calm, clear, jade-green water flanked by forested slopes. Deep Cove Canoe & Kayak Centre (tel: 604 929 2268) rents boats out for as little as an hour. The best time of year is between April and October unless you're a duck.

It was in a squatter's cabin at Dollarton in Cates Park, south of Deep Cove, that Cheshire-born Malcolm Lowry wrote between 1940 and 1954 the most famous novel written in BC, twice. In 1944 his shack burnt down and with it went the first manuscript of *Under the Volcano*. In 1954

Map on pages 166–7

*The oriental garden, one of eight themed gardens in Tilford Park, is designed to be a place of rest and relaxation.*

**BELOW:** Maplewood Farm is ideal for kids.

*For a true bird's eye view, try parascending off Grouse Mountain.*

Lowry was evicted and the cabin torn down. Its site at the eastern end of Cates Park (bus 232 from Lonsdale Quay and then 212) is marked by a plaque commemorating the events that took place at his "little lonely hermitage", devoid of electricity or plumbing. "Although there was no questioning its hardship, at least in winter," he wrote, "how beautiful it could be then, with the snow-covered cabins, the isolation, the driftwood like burnished silver – the wonderful excruciating absurd shouting ecstasy of swimming in freezing weather." The novel written in this austere setting won the Governor General's award for fiction.

## Mount Seymour Provincial Park

Covering 3,508 hectares (8,669 acres), **Mount Seymour Provincial Park ⑩** (tel: 604 986 2261; www. env.gov.bc.ca) was established in 1936 and named after an early governor of BC, Frederick Seymour. There are trails for hikers and mountain bikers, some offering magnificent views over Indian Arm and the

**BELOW:** orphan bears on Grouse Mountain.

city. In winter people ski and snow-shoe around Mount Seymour.

As one climbs towards the 1,000-metre (3,280 ft) mark, old-growth Douglas fir and Western red cedar interspersed with second-growth coniferous and deciduous trees give way to Amabilis fir, Yellow cedar and Mountain hemlock. Some of the higher meadows are cloaked with sub-alpine flowers, providing colourful early summer displays. Bears, bobcats, cougars and pine marten inhabit the backcountry, while deer, coyote and Douglas squirrel are commonly seen. BC's official bird, the Steller's jay, can be seen besides chickadee, kinglet, sapsucker, grouse and siskin. During their annual autumn migration, several species of hawks may be spotted.

## Grouse Mountain

It's worth heading up Grouse Mountain for the stunning views over Vancouver and English Bay from the summit at 1,250 metres (4,100 ft). There are two ways of getting to the top; the **Grouse Grind** is an extremely arduous climb, largely up wooden steps, gaining around 1000 metres (2,800 ft) in 3 km (1.8 miles). The climb is open May–October, but closes in poor weather. Boots and water are recommended; allow around an hour and a half for the ascent, although the record for men is 24 minutes 22 seconds (32 minutes 54 seconds for women).

The other, more relaxing way to the top is the **Grouse Mountain Skyride ⑪** (9am–10pm; tel: 604 984 0661; www.grousemountain. com), at 6400 Nancy Greene Way (bus route 236 from Lonsdale Quay), a 100-passenger cable car which will whisk you to the upper station in eight minutes. Besides a café and a very good restaurant *(see page 177)*, there are a variety of year-round attractions on Grouse Mountain. The Theatre in the Sky

(10am–9pm on the hour) shows a breathtaking documentary about BC's mountains, and the Refuge for Endangered Wildlife looks after orphaned grizzly bear cubs and grey wolves in a sizeable enclosure. In summer there are hikes with views to Washington State and Mount Baker, and the 45-minute Lumberjack Show (May–mid-Oct at noon, 2.30pm and 4.30pm) entertains the audience with demonstrations of axe-throwing, how to climb 20 metres (66 ft) up a tree, and the indispensable skill of log rolling.

In winter the mountain receives an average snowfall of 305cm (102 inches), so this is the place to ski if you haven't the time to go to Whistler. There are 25 day runs, mostly blue, and 13 night runs, supported by two high-speed quad chair lifts, two tow ropes and one magic carpet. There's also an ice-skating rink with skates for rental, and at Christmas a grotto for Santa.

## West Vancouver

The western side of the north shore is quite different in character from the eastern end, since it has always been an emphatically residential area with a prohibition on anything much more commercial than a shop. At one time it was even necessary to hold a British passport to be able to buy property on the 4,000 acres (1,620 hectares) of land in West Vancouver controlled by the Guinness family. It was to access this property and increase its value that the family company, British Pacific Properties, built the Lions Gate Bridge, which was opened on 11 November 1938 as a toll bridge at a cost of nearly C$6 million.

West Van, as the locals call it, stretches for 28 km (17½ miles) along English Bay with some of the best views in all Vancouver. Until 1909, when the first frequent ferry service started, it was regarded as a summer holiday area, with fresher air than downtown offered at the time. The first white resident was a Welsh deserter from the Royal Navy, Jack Thomas, who married an Indian chief's daughter; their house at 1768 Argyle Avenue in Ambleside, close to Navvy Jack Park, still

Map on pages 166–7

*Lumberjacks put on a daredevil show at Grouse Mountain.*

**BELOW:** restaurant at the top of Grouse Mountain.

*The SeaBus plies between downtown Vancouver (Water-front Station) and North Vancouver (Lonsdale Quay). It's hard to believe that back in the 1860s Burrard Inlet was so quiet that you could shout across the water for Navvy Jack to come and ferry you across.*

**BELOW:** view of downtown Vancouver from the residential heights of West Vancouver.

stands, the oldest surviving building in West Vancouver (*c.*1873).

West Vancouver became an incorporated district in 1912, and has grown into Vancouver's most prestigious residential district, although modest summer cottages still punctuate the multi-million dollar houses.

Per capita income here is the highest in Canada. This concentration of wealth is reflected in the many modern houses commissioned from such award-winning designers and architects as Arthur Erickson, Ron Thom, John Porter and Fred Hollingsworth.

The area is celebrated for its collection of West Coast-style homes inspired by the natural landscape. Among the most highly praised are Erickson's Helmut Eppich House, Smith House and Hugo Eppich House, and two winners of Massey Medals – John Porter's own home at 1560 Ottawa Avenue and Hollingsworth's Maltby House.

This well-heeled and well-connected population was less than thrilled when the Pacific Great Eastern Railway was finally completed

in 1958 with the construction of the coastal section running beside Howe Sound between Horseshoe Bay and Squamish, leading to heavy freight trains rumbling round the tortuous curves along the waterfront.

Today the line also carries the daily Whistler Mountaineer train, operated by Rocky Mountaineer Vacations *(see page 233)*, which leaves from a small station just inside the boundary of North Vancouver.

## Museums and historic buildings

Just off Marine Drive at 680 17th Street is the **Gertrude Lawson Museum** ⓬ (mid-June–Labour Day Tues–Sun 11am–5pm, Labour Day–mid-June Tues–Sat noon–4.30pm; tel: 604 925 7295). This museum of local history occupies an unusual 1939-built house designed by the teacher and artist Gertrude Lawson, supposedly to evoke the Scottish castles she had seen while travelling. Granite blocks thought to have been carried as ballast in sailing ships from New Zealand were used to create a house that was to be a place

where her friends could gather and even live. It has changing exhibitions of local history and a gift shop.

Along the attractively landscaped waterfront at Ambleside, at 101 14th Street, is the clapboard **West Vancouver Ferry Building**, designed by Thompson & Campbell in 1913. The ferry service gave up competing with the Lions Gate Bridge in 1947, and after a period as a bus depot the building was converted into an art gallery.

## West Vancouver parks and trails

Like North Vancouver, West Van has some of the best opportunities for hiking on forest and coastal trails. **Ambleside Park** ⑱, just west of the Lions Gate Bridge, links the walk along the Capilano river with a series of linear parks all the way along the north shore as far west as Dundarave Park (paralleled by buses 250 and 255 from Park Royal interchange).

The 3,012-hectare (7,443-acre) **Cypress Provincial Park** ⑭ (tel: 604 926 5612; www.env.gov.bc.ca/bcparks) is reached via Cypress

Bowl Road, off the Upper Levels Highway (No. 1), which comes to a dead-end at 900 metres (2,950 ft). There are miles of hiking paths up here that become cross-country ski trails when it snows. It's sufficiently popular in winter for the 1920s Hollyburn Lodge to provide sustenance for skiers.

A quick taster of what the park has to offer once the snow has gone is the mile-long Yew Lake Trail from the skiing area, which winds through sub-alpine meadows and old-growth trees. For a spectacular view of the almost impenetrable mountains that recede to the northern horizon, a steep path leads up to Hollyburn Peak at 1,325 metres (4,347 ft), and there's even a lift for mountain bikers. A five-hour intermediate-level walk, the Eagle Bluff Trail, leads hikers up Black Mountain through forest and past small lakes to a rocky bluff with fantastic views over Howe Sound.

To see a giant Douglas fir known to be 1,100 years old and referred to as the Hollyburn fir, take the 5-km (3-mile) Lawson Creek Forestry

Map on pages 166–7

**TIP**

The Cypress Bowl and its lifts (www.cypressmountain.com) are scheduled to host snowboarding and freestyle skiing events in the 2010 Winter Olympics.

**BELOW:** the shores of Lighthouse Park.

Heritage Walk, which begins in Pinecrest Drive (buses 239 or 246 from Lonsdale Quay to Park Royal and then 254).

If you are after a good long walk, Horseshoe Bay at the western end of the north shore might be a good place to start. Here, at the perimeter of the suburban area, is the start of the 44-km (27½-mile) west–east **Baden Powell Trail** which ends up at Deep Cove *(see page 171)*.

From Lonsdale Quay take bus route 239 or 246 to Park Royal and then catch a 257 to the Eagleridge Exit of Highway 1. At the top of the exit ramp, turn right into a cul-de-sac and the trail starts at its end by the sign.

The trail is well marked with bright orange triangular tags attached to trees along the path, and regular signposts indicate directions and provide distance measurements. Because it cuts across various river valleys that flow south, there are a lot of taxing gradients, so you need to start early and be fit to complete it in a day. Experienced hikers should allow 14 hours.

*Fishing at sunset off the shore of West Vancouver.*

However, there are several points at which you can cut the hike short and take a bus back to Lonsdale Quay, such as the base of Grouse Mountain and Lynn Valley. Those who complete it are rewarded with a spectacular view over Indian Arm.

## Lighthouse Park

Located at the entrance to Burrard Inlet, **Lighthouse Park** ⓮ comprises 75 hectares (185 acres) of temperate rainforest with some of the largest Western red cedars and Douglas firs in Vancouver – the longest-standing trees here are thought to be around 500 years old.

Among the trails that thread through the park is a 5-km (3-mile) circuit that leads to the lighthouse at Point Atkinson, built in 1912. Unusually, this hexagonal reinforced-concrete lighthouse has six buttresses and is still staffed, and its two-tone foghorn is a familiar sound to local residents. With lots of coves and big, rounded rocks to clamber on (take care, they are very slippery), this park is a great favourite with children. ❑

# RESTAURANTS & BARS

### North Vancouver

**Arms Reach Bistro**
107C, 4390 Gallant Ave, Deep Cove. Tel: 604 929 7442. Open: L & D daily. $
Fabulous view, a large patio and West Coast cuisine at reasonable prices make this a return destination for many happy customers.

**The Bakehouse**
1050 West Queens Rd, Edgemont Village. Tel: 604 980 5554. Open: Mon–Sat 7am–6pm, Sun 10am–4pm. $

Serves up home-made everything – bread and pastries, but also shepherd's pie and stews.

**Black Bear Neighbourhood Pub**
1177, Lynn Valley Rd. Tel: 604 990 8880. Open: L & D daily. $
Says it all really: friendly atmosphere, with good beer and pub food.

**Brazza Gelato & Coffee**
1846 Lonsdale Ave. Tel: 604 904 2333. Open: daily. $
Terrific lattes and very

good ice cream, including a choice for those who are lactose-intolerant.

**Browns Restaurant and Bar**
1764 Lonsdale Ave. Tel: 604 929 5401. Open: L & D daily. $$
www.brownsrestaurantbar.com
Serving fusion/Pacific Northwest food in a very relaxed atmosphere. Spicy fire-wok squid and Ahi tuna are among their most popular dishes. Also serves brunch. Branch in Yaletown.

**Hamaei**
601 Westview Drive No. 620. Tel: 604 987 0080.

Open: L Tues–Fri, D Tues–Sun. $
Reasonable Japanese serving sushi and hot dishes like teriyaki, noodles and tempura.

**High Boat Café Marina**
Ft Forbes St. Tel: 604 904 3832. Open: B & L daily. $
A dockside diner serving breakfast, burgers and a good eggs benedict, along with great coffee, all at reasonable prices.

**Le Bistro Chez Michel**
224 West Esplanade. Tel: 604 924 4913. Open: L & D Mon–Sat. $$
www.chezmichelvancouver.com
French bistro which is in

fact an offshoot of Chez Michel in West Vancouver, but with a simpler and cheaper menu – mussels, steaks, duck confit and crêpes.

### Moustache Café

1265 Marine Drive. Tel: 604 987 8461. Open: L Tues–Fri, Sun, D Tues–Sun. $$
www.moustachecafe.ca

Set in a 1920s Arts and Crafts-style house serving French and Mediterranean-style food, this charming spot is a real find. Beef carpaccio with truffle oil and Cornish game hen with mash were among the offerings.

### Mythos

1811 Lonsdale Ave. Tel: 604 984 7411. Open: L & D daily. $   A very busy Greek with excellent service and friendly atmosphere. Book ahead.

### The Observatory

1600 Nancy Greene Way. Tel: 604 980 9311. Open: D daily. $$$
www.grousemountain.com

It's worth the journey via cable car up the mountain for the food – even without the view. Grilled squid stuffed with lobster and merguez sausage is a tasty starter; seared scallops with risotto, basil froth and asparagus is a well-judged main.

### Tomahawk Restaurant

1550 Philip Ave. Tel: 604 988 2612. Open: B, L & D daily. $
www.tomahawkrestaurant.com

A family-run burger, chicken and barbecue place with a difference –

it's been around since 1926 and seems to know what it's doing. The rooms are filled with Native American artefacts collected by the owners over the years, and the food is good.

### West Vancouver

### Beach House at Dundarave Pier

150 25th St. Tel: 604 922 1414. Open: L & D daily. $$
Waterfront restaurant with great views set in an old beach house; the cosy dining room and patio are the backdrop to a casual menu that finds favour with families and local regulars.

### Café Trafiq

1860 Marine Drive. Tel: 604 925 2503. Open: daily. $
This café in Ambleside has great coffee, pastries, paninis and ice-creams. Tapas nights Wed to Sat.

### La Regalade

103, 2232 Marine Drive. Tel: 604 921 2228. Open: L Tues–Fri, D Tues–Sat. $$
www.laregalade.com

A French family-run bistro serving a traditional menu – frisée salad, terrine, beef bourguignon and roast duck might be chalked up on the board. Simple bistro style and good service make this the kind of place you wish you had in your neighbourhood.

### Salmon House on the Hill

2229 Folkstone Way. Tel:

604 926-3212. Open: L & D daily. $$$
www.salmonhouse.com

The Salmon House has been open since 1976, and from its perch above Vancouver, has gained a solid reputation. Native American art on the walls and the view help create a cosy atmosphere, and the food is pretty spectacular as well, much of it smoked and grilled. Brunch too.

### Saltaire

Upper level, 235 15th St. Tel: 604 913 8439. Open: L & D daily. $$   www.saltaire.ca
West Coast contemporary with some Asian influences thrown in defines the food here. Large salads, good seafood and meats and a range of pizzas from their forno are a big draw.

### Red Lion Bar and Grill

2427 Marine Drive. Tel: 604 926 8838. Open: L & D daily. $   With cosy fires, a pool table and a friendly atmosphere to go with the good value pub food should you want it.

### True Confections

100 Park Royal. Tel: 604 921 1885. Open: Tue–Thur 2–10pm, Fri–Sat 1–11pm, Sun 1–10pm. $
*The* place to go for dessert. Fantastic cakes and ice creams, cheesecakes and pies. Branches elsewhere.

### Vera's Burger Shack

Dundarave Pier. Tel: 604 603 8372. Open: May–Sept B, L & D daily. $

www.verasburgershack.com

The flagship of a chain of four burger places, Vera's has won many awards for its sublime burgers. Expect to wait.

### Zen Japanese Restaurant

2232 Marine Drive. Tel: 604 925 0667.Open: D daily. $$
www.zensushi.ca

Japanese food with a West Coast air. In a contemporary, understated room, Zen produces Japanese dishes along with interesting twists on Western dishes. Imaginative and good.

---

### PRICE CATEGORIES

Prices for three-course dinner per person with a half-bottle of house wine:
$ = under C$30
$$ = C$30–50
$$$ = C$50–80
$$$$ = more than C$80

---

**RIGHT:** fresh, locally sourced and beautifully presented ingredients – the hallmarks of Vancouver's best restaurants.

# WINTER SPORTS

## In an area surrounded by tall mountains, the opportunities for snow sports are endless

Snow and ice play a big part in Canada's weather and in the Canadian psyche. Visit an ice-hockey game when the local Canucks team is playing during the season from October to mid-April and you can feel how high passions run. When the Canucks lost the Stanley Cup in the final game of the 1994 season, the police had to contend with riots.

It's an unusual Canadian who can't ice-skate, and in winter downtown rinks are set up at Robson Square and at the West End Community Centre at 870 Denman Street, while pros head for the Canlan Ice Sports – Burnaby 8-rinks.

Vancouverites don't have to go to Whistler for a spot of skiing: on the doorstep are the three resorts of Grouse Mountain, Mount Seymour and Cypress Bowl, all on the north shore. Seymour is the highest, and Cypress offers the nearest cross-country skiing as well as downhill and snowboarding. But none can match the extent and variety of Whistler's pistes.

**LEFT:** for many Canadians a snowmobile is a form of transport that has replaced a team of huskies. In Whistler it's a source of thrills, though not everyone welcomes the noise and pollution it introduces.

**ABOVE:** the finest skiing in BC if not Canada is on Whistler and Blackcomb mountains. There are over 200 beginner, intermediate and advanced runs, served by 33 lifts and 17 mountain restaurants. There's plenty for non-skiers too, from sleigh rides to snowshoeing.

**ABOVE:** the clarity of light on a sunny winter's day can be as breathtaking as the cold. Many of the parks around Vancouver offer great opportunities for hiking or snowshoeing, as here on Black Mountain in Cypress Provincial Park in West Vancouver.

## 2010 WINTER OLYMPICS

The delight on the faces of Canadian athletes Catriona Le May Doan and Charmaine Crooks *(left)* when they heard that Vancouver had won the bid to host the Olympics was shared by many.

For 17 days, from 12–28 February 2010, the eyes of the sporting world will be on Vancouver and Whistler; the Paralympic Games in Vancouver follow from 12–21 March. About 5,000 athletes from 80 countries are expected to take part, watched by 10,000 media representatives for whom a new Press Centre has been built near Canada Place. The cost of the facilities is expected to be $1.3 billion, and 1.8 million tickets will be on offer.

Vancouver will stage the ice hockey, ice sledge hockey, curling, figure and speed skating, freestyle skating and snowboarding, while Whistler will host the Alpine skiing, cross-country skiing, Biathlon, Nordic Combined, ski jumping, bobsleigh, luge and skeleton.

Efforts are being made to minimise the environmental impact of the games: buildings are being designed to minimise power requirements and use renewable energy wherever possible; there will be no spectator parking at any of the venues; provision of public transport will be increased, and vehicles will be hybrid and/or use biodiesel; people will be encouraged to walk or cycle.

This is the second time that Canada has hosted the Winter Olympics; the previous venue was Calgary, in 1988.

**RIGHT:** a snowboarder on Mount Seymour, which has produced some world-class boarders and is regarded as the best of the mountains close to Vancouver. Eleven of its runs are lit at night, as is Mount Cypress's Solo Power terrain park. Grouse Mountain has cruising runs suitable for beginners as well as more challenging slopes. At Whistler it's still possible to snowboard in August, on Blackcomb's Hortsman Glacier.

**BELOW:** snow tubing in Mount Seymour Provincial Park. Snow tubes should be used only on designated courses because, being circular, they are extremely difficult to steer or slow down. Putting out a hand merely makes them spin. Tows drag the tubes and riders uphill.

**RIGHT:** a family of four dog-sledding on Whistler Mountain. Sledding expeditions are offered from Whistler in the Soo Valley and are a great way to see the backcountry away from the crowded pistes. The dogs are Alaskan racing huskies, a cross-breed of husky and greyhound. A dog-sled camp on Cougar Mountain gives courses in dog sledding.

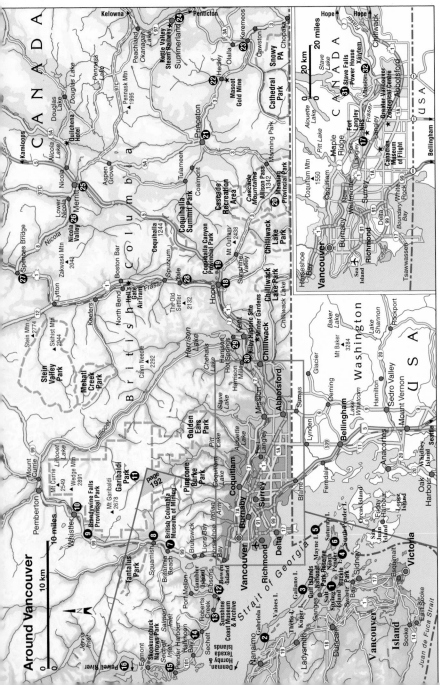

Around Vancouver

# EXCURSIONS

"When people say they love Vancouver, I suspect it's
not so much the city they love but the setting"
— Arthur Erickson

I t's almost a paradox that the residents of a city consistently rated number one in the world for quality of life should be so eager to get out of it. Not permanently, of course, but the pull of all that natural beauty that spreads out in three directions from Vancouver is strong.

British Columbia remains a stunningly beautiful part of Canada with a wide variety of landscapes, and is a paradise for outdoor activities. It is the sheer scale that astonishes many first-time visitors from Europe, and getting to grips with the knowledge that Vancouver Island alone is the size of a small European country.

There can be few lovelier waters in which to sail than the Strait of Georgia between the mainland and the Gulf and Vancouver islands, whether by yacht or one of the many ferries that link them up. All around are mountains and islands in a confusion of land and sea that still claims vessels despite their sophisticated navigational aids. The provincial capital of Victoria is a delightful contrast to Vancouver, with fewer if any no-go areas and a gentler pace.

The island itself has so much to offer that it is deserving of an entire book. Its largely unspoilt wild west coast is in complete contrast to the more developed eastern seaboard, at least as far north as Nanaimo, the most northerly point reached by the excursion in this book.

Whistler is a mecca for its many winter and summer activities, and certain to consolidate its position as Canada's premier ski resort with the 2010 Winter Olympics. A drive along the Sunshine Coast, another worthy weekend destination, would take you as far as Lund, from where there is little but wilderness coastline for hundreds of miles to Prince Edward.

Wine lovers head east to the vineyards of the Okanagan, a journey punctuated in season by fruit stalls selling the irresistible products of the neighbouring fields. It is easy to devise a circular route taking in the many natural sights such as the gorge of Hell's Gate or Lake Okanagan. But to get a feel for what the founders of this country saw in the second half of the 19th century, you need to take off into the back country on horseback, by bike or on foot. It's a hugely rewarding experience. ❏

# VICTORIA AND VANCOUVER ISLAND

**Victoria is the first port of call, but there's more to the island than BC's garden-filled capital. To the west are craggy, storm-battered coastlines with deep fjords and wild beaches, and on the east coast, peaceful country inns and sheltered bays**

British Columbia

Vancouver

Victoria

**V**oted top North American island for seven consecutive years by *Condé Nast Traveller*, Vancouver Island is a beguiling place of snow-capped mountains, verdant forests, gentle farmland and sun-drenched ocean beaches. Lying off BC's West Coast, it stretches for 450 km (281 miles) in length (about a third the length of the province), spanning from 48 to 80 km (30 to 50 miles) across. The island is substantial and, if you want to explore beyond Victoria, best tackled by car, bus or train. The train passes mostly through forested areas, while hiring a car or even an RV in Victoria gives access to the entire island, including isolated western and northern coasts.

## Whale-watching

**Victoria ❶**, BC's capital, is at the southeastern corner of the island, with Duncan, Nanaimo, Courtenay and Campbell river on the east coast the only other sizeable towns, except for Port Alberni to the west of Nanaimo. The small West Coast communities of Ucluelet and Tofino are popular getaway destinations: apart from the Pacific Rim Highway (a spectacularly scenic road), the western coastline remains largely unspoilt and offers some of the best opportunities in BC for whale-watching. Many hotels remain open

in winter thanks to the popularity of watching the spectacular storms and seas that roll in across the Pacific, unhindered all the way from Japan.

There is a regular ferry service from Horseshoe Bay to Nanaimo, but most visitors to the island take the ferry from the mainland terminal at Tsawwassen to Swartz Bay. It is about a 45-minute drive from here to Victoria. Alternatively, coaches provide an efficient and comfortable service to the heart of Victoria, which is easily explored on foot.

**Maps:**
**City 184**
**Area 192**

**LEFT:** Nanaimo docks.
**BELOW:** pretzels and sizzling smokies.

## Colonial capital

Built in 1843 beside the water, Fort
Victoria replaced Fort Vancouver in
Oregon as the Hudson's Bay Company's Pacific headquarters. Initially,
settlement was not encouraged by
the Hudson's Bay Company's governor, James Douglas, who saw the
island as a source of wealth through
its natural resources of timber, fish,
coal and otter pelts (the sea otters
here were so thoughtlessly exploited
that they were wiped out). Douglas
imported labour as necessary to har-
vest the resources. Following the
discovery of coal at Nanaimo in
1850, for example, he recruited 24
miners and their families from the
mining communities of Staffordshire
in England.

The situation changed in 1858
with the discovery of gold in the
Cariboo, because Victoria became
a place of passage en route to the
gold-fields from California. The
population swelled from 500 in 1857
to 5,000 the following year. Though
the numbers subsequently declined
for a while, Victoria's equable climate and pleasant position attracted
many permanent residents among
those who had struck lucky in the
Cariboo, and some of the houses
they built can still be seen along the
city's residential streets. The genteel
aspects of Victoria's character were
reinforced by the decision in 1868
to make the city the capital of the
colony of British Columbia. As the
seat of power and influence, Victoria
attracted such entrepreneurs as the
wealthy Dunsmuirs to build substantial mansions that are now among the
city's attractions.

The survival of so many 19th- and
early 20th-century buildings made of
stone and red brick is Victoria's
greatest asset. The Old England gim-
micks, with Union Jacks and tea
shops on every corner, may not
appeal to everyone, but beyond the
tourist traps is a very charming city.

*The sailing ships that had explored the coast on behalf of Spain and Britain started to give way to steam with the arrival of SS Beaver at Fort Vancouver in 1836. For 50 years this steamship was a floating fur-trading post and a survey ship for the Royal Navy. She helped to establish Fort Victoria on Vancouver Island and carried the official party to set up Fort Langley where the establishment of the Crown Colony of BC was formally announced.*

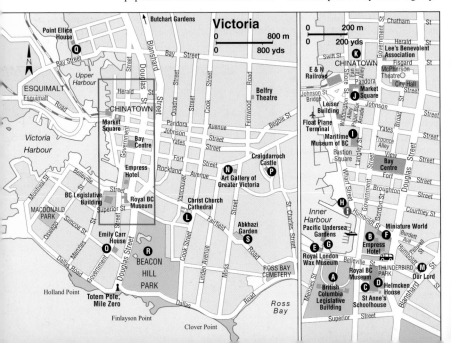

## Exploring Victoria

Victoria is even more compact than Vancouver, so exploring it on foot is easy. It's sunnier here than in Vancouver, too, with nearly a third less rain. The lovely natural harbour is the heart and pulse of the city, and there's always a bustle of activity on the water, from leisure craft, whale-watching and sightseeing boats to ferries and floatplanes. On fine days the throngs of visitors and street performers create a real buzz, though at the height of the summer it can get unpleasantly overcrowded.

Lending a stately grandeur to the scene are two of the city's finest buildings: the British Columbia Legislative Assembly Building, with its 168-metre (500-ft) façade and the huge Empress Hotel – both overlook the Inner Harbour and Fisherman's Wharf, forming the focal point of Victoria.

## On the waterfont

The flamboyant **British Columbia Legislative Building** Ⓐ was designed by young architect Francis Rattenbury and completed in 1897.

The domed building is made of local stone with slate from Jervis Inlet on the mainland. Marble for the Assembly Hall came from Italy, that in the rotunda from Tennessee. After dark, its outline is lit up by over 3,300 lights. Free 45-minute tours of the Parliament buildings are regularly conducted (mid-May–mid-Sept daily 8.30am–5pm, mid-Sept–mid-May Mon–Fri 8.30am–5pm).

Named after Queen Victoria, the Empress of India, the château-style **Empress Hotel** Ⓑ, another Rattenbury design, was opened in 1908. Today, this well-restored monument to colonial grandeur is one of Victoria's top tourist attractions. Afternoon tea remains an institution in Victoria, though for tourists rather than residents, and a reservation is advisable (tel: 250 389 2727). A special blend of tea is served in a pattern of china made by the Booths factory in England in 1914; a set was presented to King George V and first used at the Empress in 1939 during the visit of King George VI. It is now produced exclusively for the Empress by Royal Doulton.

Map on page 184

*Ninety-minute tours of the grand Empress Hotel are conducted at 10am from mid-May to early October.*

**BELOW:** the grand parliament buildings are beautifully lit at night.

**TIP**

Chocoholics and sweet tooths make a beeline for **Roger's Chocolates** (913 Government Street), a Victorian sweet-making institution for over one hundred years. **Munro's Books** across the street (no. 1108) is one of Canada's finest bookstores. **Murchie's** (no. 1110) has been blending tea and supplying coffee in BC since 1894. This is the largest of its tea-rooms.

**BELOW:** the BC flag flies in front of the Legislative Building.

The hotel's 470 rooms are all different, and many have period features – those on the seventh floor retain their original furniture. The corridors in the original wing were sufficiently wide for ladies in hooped skirts to pass without touching. Another interesting feature is the Cutler of Montreal mailing chute, which allowed guests to post a letter from any floor. The most opulent part of the hotel is the Crystal Lounge, its centrepiece an elaborate Tiffany glass dome.

In the apex between the hotel and parliament is the **largest carillon in Canada** with 62 bells in a 27-metre (90-ft) tower given by the Dutch community of BC. It is played every Sunday at 3pm and on Friday at 7pm in July and August.

## Around the Royal BC Museum

In many ways the **Royal BC Museum** ● (9am–5pm; tel: 250 356 7226; www.royalbcmuseum.bc.ca) at 675 Belleville Street is the best introduction to BC, both for the range and the quality of its presentations. It

has excellent dioramas of wildlife and habitats and large sections on the First Nations with a reconstruction of a pithouse, Tsimshian masks used in dramatic performances, pipes, poles, tableware, plates and *haida* figures carved out of argillite. Later displays include reconstructed streets, and rooms devoted to fishing, farming, logging and maritime trades.

At the back of the BC Museum is the **St Anne's Schoolhouse**, built in the French Canadian style with square logs. Begun in the 1840s and completed in 1858, it is one of the oldest buildings in western Canada.

Close by is **Helmcken House** ● (opening times vary; enquire at the tourist office), built in 1852 of squared logs and cedar shingles for Dr J.S. Helmcken. It is thought to be the oldest house in western Canada still on its original site. Dr Helmcken (1824–1920) was a pioneer surgeon and legislator who arrived in 1850 to work for the Hudson's Bay Company. Born in London, he trained at Guy's Hospital and married the elder daughter of Governor Sir James Douglas. He helped

## Rattenbury's legacy

Soon after arriving in Victoria, British-born architect, Francis Mawson Rattenbury won the competition to build the new British Columbia Legislative Building which opened in 1898. Many commissions followed, including the Empress Hotel for the Canadian Pacific Railway. Rattenbury had a habit of falling out with clients, and his lack of professional training was felt when the popularity of his style waned. Shunned for the callous treatment of his wife after he left her for a younger woman, he was forced to leave Victoria. Back in England, financial problems soured his second marriage. His wife began an affair with the chauffeur, who murdered Rattenbury with a croquet mallet in 1935.

to negotiate the union of BC with Canada in 1870. The house has reconstructed interiors with some original furniture and a collection of medical equipment that belonged to the "good doctor".

Clustered together in adjacent **Thunderbird Park** is a collection of Northwest Coast totem poles.

### Children's attractions

There are a number of attractions around the Inner Harbour geared towards children. The Victoria branch of Madame Tussauds in London, the **Royal London Wax Museum E** (470 Belleville Street; daily 9.30am–5pm; tel: 250 388 4461; www.waxmuseum.bc.ca), displays over 300 famous figures and has its own grisly Chamber of Horrors. At the north side of the Empress Hotel is **Miniature World F** (649 Humboldt Street; 8.30am–9.30pm, winter 10am–5pm; tel: 250 385 9731; www.miniatureworld.com), a collection of tiny tableaux including scenes from the Old West, Dickensian England, enchanted castles and a three-ring circus. The highlight is the

large model railway layout, which depicts the story of Canada's great railway-building epoch.

More family adventures are offered in the **Pacific Undersea Gardens G** (490 Belleville Street; daily winter 10am–5pm, summer 9am–8pm; tel: 250 382 5717; www.pacificunderseagardens.com) a vast underwater aquarium where divers perform alongside various creatures of the deep.

### The old town

Leading north from James Bay is Government Street, Victoria's main thoroughfare. Many of its buildings have plaques summarising their history, and grey blocks inset into the brick pavements delineate the boundary of Fort Victoria.

The best way to explore the old town is to follow the downtown walk in the free leaflet of six one-hour walks provided by the Downtown Victoria Business Association. Starting at the **Visitor Information Centre H** on Wharf Street by the harbour, it takes you through Bastion Square, where many of the main

Map on page 184

*The little green-and-yellow sightseeing ferries operate a hop-on hop-off service around the harbour (tel: 250 708 0201; www.harbourferry. com).*

**BELOW:** view of the Inner Harbour from the Information Centre.

**TIP**

Victoria has the highest number of cyclists per capita in the country, thanks to the excellent network of cycling routes. The Seaside Cycling Route does what it says, while the 55-km (34-mile) Galloping Goose Trail uses the trackbed of an old railway to link Victoria with Sooke. In the opposite direction to the north, it joins the Lochside Trail, part of the Saanich peninsula network through farmland and along the coast up to Swartz Bay.

**BELOW:**
Chinatown's "Gate of Harmonious Interest".

municipal buildings were constructed, including the Board of Trade (1892) and the Law Courts (1889), which today house the **Maritime Museum of British Columbia** ⓘ (mid-June–mid-Sept 9.30am–5pm, mid-Sept–mid-June 9.30am–4.30pm; tel: 250 385 4222; www.mmbc. bc.ca). The museum celebrates the close relationship between the sea and the province's history, with sections on exploration, shipbuilding, fur traders, harbours, ships, wrecks, whaling, CPR steamships and the navy. Among the maritime artefacts is a collection of marvellous models.

Yates Street has many turn-of-the-century buildings, such as the **Leiser Building** (1896), which housed a wholesale grocer with a central elevator and tracks radiating from it on each floor to move goods around.

On Waddington Alley is the **Grand Pacific Hotel** (1883) and **Paper Box Arcade**, a beautifully restored alley with a profusion of plants. Attractive **Market Square** ⓙ spans what was a ravine, and has two tiers of arcaded shops specialising in all manner of things from quilts and old furniture to beads, toys, fudge and "intuitive urban art".

## Chinatown

Canada's oldest **Chinatown** ⓚ, dating from 1858, was built north of the ravine and is reached through the mix of shops and houses in tiny **Fan Tan Alley**. By 1881, around 3,000 Chinese had established themselves here. Along the narrowest of streets, they built factories, shops and back-to-back houses around tiny courtyards, and of course the brothels and opium and gambling dens for which the area became infamous. The architecture is adapted from standard forms with flared temple-style roofs, inset and projecting wrought-iron balconies, interior courtyards and brightly coloured roof tiles with pronounced overhangs.

**Fisgard Street** has some fine Chinese buildings, especially Lee's Benevolent Association building at no. 614. Further east is the Chinese Public School, with upturned corners to the eaves.

## Churches

Among Victoria's most notable churches is the neo-Gothic **Christ Church Cathedral ❶** at 930 Burdett Avenue, built between 1896 and 1991 with a cross donated from Tewkesbury Abbey in Gloucestershire and a pulpit made of Sussex oak. It is the episcopal seat of British Columbia's Anglican Church.

On the corner of Humboldt and Blanshard streets is the reformed episcopal **Church of Our Lord ⓜ** (Mon 6pm, Wed 2pm), which is said to be the finest expression of the Gothic Revival in wood in Canada. It was built in 1875 to a design by John Teague with board and batten siding, rose window and a Gothic hammerbeam roof.

## Art and artists

Not far east of Downtown, en route to Craigdarroch Castle (see page 190), the **Art Gallery of Greater Victoria ⓝ** (1040 Moss Street; Mon–Sat 10am–5pm, Thur until 9pm; tel: 250 384 4101; www.aggv.bc.ca) has seven gallery spaces hosting permanent and temporary exhibitions, some drawn from permanent collections. It has a large Asian collection, including a wooden Shinto shrine that was found abandoned in Japan. The house that forms the nucleus of the gallery was built in 1889 as the residence of a banker, A.A. Green. In 1951 it was donated to the city to become the first part of a permanent art gallery, and a few rooms are left to show how the house once looked – including the heavily wood-panelled and ceilinged hall. The Drury Gallery features the work of Emily Carr, Canada's best-known artist and a native of Victoria (see below).

Back in the centre of town, **The Emily Carr House ⓞ** (207 Government Street; May and Sept Tues–Sat 11am–4pm, June–Aug daily 11am–4pm; tel: 250 383 5843; www.emilycarr.com) was where the artist spent her rebellious childhood. All the paintings here are copies and few of the furnishings are original, but the house, built in 1864, does give a good idea of what the home of a middle class Victoria family would have looked like.

**Map on page 184**

**TIP**

For period buildings, the southern end of Government Street has many early houses from the 1860s, some of them attractive B&Bs, and other roads worth visiting are Rockland Avenue, St Charles Street and Linden Avenue.

**BELOW:** the Emily Carr collection in the Victoria Art Gallery.

## Emily Carr

Recognition of Emily Carr's talents as an artist came late in her life. She was born in Victoria in 1871 and studied art in San Francisco, England and Paris. She went on several trips to northern BC and Alaska, living in villages and painting cultural scenes, but her work attracted little approval, and she was forced to make ends meet by breeding dogs, growing vegetables and making pottery. She even gave up painting, but a meeting with the Group of Seven in 1927 proved a turning point. They encouraged her to resume her work depicting vanishing native culture and the west coast landscape. Carr spent the latter part of her life writing about her experiences. She died in 1945, aged 73.

*Craigdarroch Castle was built by Scots-born millionaire Robert Dunsmuir to fulfil a promise made to his wife, who expressed a dislike of her new country. He died before it was completed.*

## Craigdarroch

Admirers of Scots baronial architecture will want to visit the house built for one of Vancouver Island's richest entrepreneurs, Robert Dunsmuir, who was born in 1825 near Kilmarnock in Ayrshire to a family of coal masters. He transferred the skills to BC in developing the rich coal seams around Nanaimo and also built the Esquimalt & Nanaimo Railway, a contract which came with huge land grants: in exchange for building 75 miles of railway, he received $750,000 plus 2 million acres – almost one-third of the land mass of Vancouver Island. With the profits he built the rather ungainly pile of **Craigdarroch** ⓟ (daily 10am–4.30pm, mid-June–Labour Day 9am–7pm; tel: 250 592 5323; www.thecastle.ca). The house has few original contents, except for paintings, but it has been furnished with appropriate pieces and fabrics. It has an opulent atmosphere with wood panelling everywhere and a hand-painted ceiling in the drawing room. The stunning views from the castle tower stretch across Victoria and the Strait of San Juan de Fuca to the Olympic Mountains in Washington State.

## Point Ellice House

Those interested in historic buildings should not miss **Point Ellice House** ⓠ (2616 Pleasant Street; May–Sept 10am–4pm; tel: 250 380 6506; www.pointellicehouse.ca), easily reached by the Harbour Ferry from the pier in front of the Empress Hotel. Built in 1861 and acquired in 1867 by gold-rush magnate Peter O'Reilly, it has the finest collection of Victoriana in western Canada in its original setting. Most of the contents and even wallpapers are original, thanks to the O'Reilly family's occupation for over 100 years. Robert Falcon Scott once dined here. Visitors are provided with an unusual recorded commentary on the house and family history from the perspective of a Japanese servant. Tea on the lawn overlooking the Gorge Waterway is served by waitresses in period costume between 11am and 4pm (reservations recommended).

## Parks and gardens

Known as the City of Gardens, one of the reasons for Victoria's popularity with visitors is the number of beautifully cultivated green spaces in and around the city centre. Just south east of the Inner Harbour lies **Beacon Hill Park** ⓡ, 62 hectares (154 acres) of parkland and garden set aside by Governor James Douglas in 1858. It was named because of its use for two beacons to guide mariners past the treacherous Brotchie Ledge. The sprawling park, which borders the sea at its southern end, features duck ponds, colourful flower gardens, elegant trees, stone bridges, mini-lakes, a children's paddling pool and a petting zoo. A plinthed dial on the hill points to Bentinck Island 10 miles away as a former leper colony, and

on a really clear day it is possible to see the 4,392-metre (14,408-ft) peak of Mt Rainier in Washington state. The world's fourth-tallest totem pole, carved in 1956, rises 38.9 metres (127 ft 7in) above a grassy field. At the corner of Douglas Street and Dallas Road is the Mile "0" milestone, marking the beginning of the Trans-Canada Highway.

At 1964 Fairfield Road, a short journey from central Victoria, is the unique **Abkhazi Garden** ❺ (Mar–Sept 11am–5pm; tel: 250 598 8096; www.conservancy.bc.ca), begun in 1946 by the Georgian Prince and Princess Abkhazi, the year they married and settled in Victoria.

They spent their lives developing the garden, the landscaping strongly influenced by the Chinese gardens which Peggy Abkhazi had known in Shanghai, with Japanese maples, weeping conifers and century-old specimens of rhododendrons. After their deaths the garden was taken over by the The Land Conservancy which saved it from development. It has a tea-room and shop.

To the west of Victoria lies **Hatley**

**Park National Historic Site** ❷ (daily 10am–4pm; tel: 250 391 2666; www.hatleypark.ca), a 229-hectare (565-acre) estate surrounding the castle built in 1908 by BC premier James Dunsmuir, super-rich son of mining magnate, Robert Dunsmuir. Besides daily tours of the house, the extensive Japanese, rose and Italian gardens and woodland walks are complemented by a museum about the house and the history of the rich and powerful Dunsmuir family.

Last but not least, a bit of a jaunt away but a must-see, are the much vaunted **Butchart Gardens** about 14 miles (22 km) north of Vancouver, in Saanich *(see page 192)*.

## Esquimalt

This district lies on the west side of Victoria Harbour and was home to the Royal Navy Pacific Squadron from 1865 to 1902. Within the Canadian Forces Base at Naden is the **Esquimalt Naval & Military Museum** (Mon–Fri 10am–3.30pm; tel: 250 363 4312; www.navaland militarymuseum.org; no access

**Maps:**
**City 184**
**Area 192**

*With the mildest climate in Canada, Victoria benefits from the Japanese current bringing warm moist air which rises and cools when it hits the mountains. It receives only 63 cm (25 inches) of rain. Over a billion blooms have been counted in February, giving Victoria the title of "the garden city".*

**BELOW:**
Butchart Gardens.

*The main focus of the BC Forest Discovery Park is on forestry and conservation.*

without photo ID) which has a World War II minesweeper and displays about West Coast naval and military history. There is a bus from downtown to the base gate.

Overlooking Victoria Harbour from the western bank of the estuary is the **National Historic Site of Fort Rodd Hill and Fisgard Lighthouse** ❸ (Mar–Oct 10am–5.30pm, Nov–Feb 9am–4.30pm; tel: 250 478 5849; www.fortroddhill.com). The coastal artillery fort was built in the 1890s, and visitors can see the original gun batteries, underground magazines, barracks, camouflaged searchlight emplacements and command post. Dating from 1860, the lighthouse is the oldest on the West Coast.

## Saanich peninsula

This area between Victoria and Swartz Bay is rich in visitor attractions, besides many century-old vernacular buildings. Gardeners will not want to miss the spectacular

**Butchart Gardens** ❹ (daily from 9am, closing times change seasonally; tel: 250 652 5256; www. butchartgardens.com), a 22-hectare (55-acre) garden which was begun in 1912 and tended by 55 gardeners. It has rose, sunken, Japanese and Italian gardens of such quality that it has the very rare distinction for a privately owned attraction of being designated a Historic Site. Evening concerts and firework displays are staged in a natural amphitheatre, and there is an exceptionally good restaurant serving lunch, dinner and an afternoon tea on a par with the Empress Hotel.

Run by volunteers, **Heritage Acres** ❺ (7321 Lochside Drive, Saanichton; daily 9.30am–noon, until 4pm in June–Aug; tel: 250 652 5522; www.shas.ca) is a group of display buildings designed to evoke rural village life in bygone times. It includes a two-room schoolhouse, small church, log cabin, black-

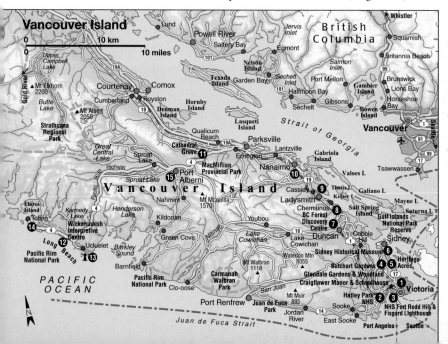

smith's shop, sawmill and dozens of tractors and other artefacts – domestic, agricultural and industrial. On special days, some of the old equipment is put to use, such as horse-drawn ploughs in spring and steam threshers in the autumn.

**Craigflower Manor and Schoolhouse** (May–Sept Wed–Sun 1–5pm; tel: 250 383 4627; www.conservancy. bc.ca) on the corner of Admirals Road and Craigflower Road celebrate the spirit of the early settlers. The oldest schoolroom in western Canada was built in 1855 by workers on Craigflower Farm for their children. The manor, completed in 1856, was the home of the farm's bailiff, Kenneth McKenzie, and his wife and eight children.

Also in Saanich are the **Glendale Gardens & Woodland** (505 Quayle Road; Apr–Sept Mon–Fri 8am–8pm, Sat–Sun 8am–6pm, Oct–Mar 9am–4pm; tel: 250 479 6162; www.hcp.bc.ca), a 3-hectare (8-acre) garden set in 42 hectares (103 acres) of woodland. It contains some impressive rhododendron and heather gardens, a winter garden, and over 10,000 varieties of plants.

An introduction to the early lives of Sidney and North Saanich pioneers is given by **Sidney Historical Museum** ❻ (2423 Beacon Avenue; Jan–Oct 10am–4pm, Nov–Dec 11am–3pm; tel: 250 655 6355; www .sidneymuseum.ca). The town is noted for its bookshops and galleries.

## Up Island

The busy Trans-Canada Highway (Highway 1) parallels the east coast from Victoria to Nanaimo, and there are numerous reasons to break the journey. The **BC Forest Discovery Centre** ❼ (2892 Drinkwater Road; Apr–Oct daily 10am–4pm, mid-May–Aug –5pm; tel: 250 715 1113; www.bcforestmuseum.com) just north of Duncan is one. Here a steam train chugs through the 40-hectare (100-acre) site, viewing a turn-of-the-century working sawmill and logging camp.

A little further north, **Chemainus** ❽ revels in its role as Canada's mural capital. Throughout the town, huge murals decorate any suitable walls, depicting historical subjects

Map on page 192

### TIP

VIA's E&N Dayliner, "The Malahat", is a daily service that runs along the Pacific coast between Esquimalt and Courtenay, 225 km (141 miles) north of Victoria, calling at various stations in between. It goes out and back in a day, so if time is short, this pleasant journey provides the opportunity to gain a sense of the island's topography (tel: 1 888 842 7245; www.viarail.ca)

**BELOW:**
the Malahat Dayliner; mural in Chemainus.

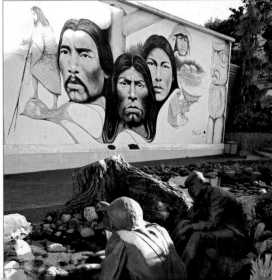

*The Douglas Fir takes its name from the Scottish botanist David Douglas (1799–1834) who undertook three expeditions to Canada, including journeys along the Okanagan and Fraser rivers and the Columbia River to Hudson Bay. He identified over 200 new plant species in North America and introduced over 240 to Britain – more than any other botanist of his time.*

**BELOW:** Douglas firs and young hemlocks.

such as the arrival of HMS *Reindeer* at Chemainus in 1869 or a Shay locomotive on the Mount Sicker Railway. The painting programme was begun in 1982 to revitalise a town whose sawmill had closed down. Now the town has 36 murals and 13 sculptures. Heritage Square, dominated by the First Peoples mural, is lined with small shops and teahouses.

The town of **Ladysmith** ❾ was created by James Dunsmuir to house miners, and was named after the town in Natal where the Boer War siege was lifted in March 1900. Its main street is remarkably unspoilt, but little remains of the port from which coal was shipped.

The principal focus of coal mining was **Nanaimo** ❿ , from which the first coal was shipped in 1852. The most notable building in the island's second city is the 1853 three-storey bastion (June–Aug daily 10am–4pm), built to house offices, an arsenal and space for the town's inhabitants should it be attacked. It's the only remaining original Hudson's Bay Company bastion left in North America. The **Nanaimo**

**District Museum** (100 Cameron Road; May–Labour Day daily 10am–5pm, Labour Day–Apr Tues–Sat 10am–5pm; tel: 250 753 1821; www .nanaimomuseum.ca) tells the story of the coal-mining industry with reconstructed tunnel, blacksmith's shop and miner's cottage, as well as the Nanaimo First Nations people and the city's Chinatown.

### The West Coast

A million people a year cross the island via the **Pacific Rim Highway** from Parksville, a few miles north of Nanaimo, over Sutton Pass to visit the West Coast. The road beyond Port Alberni was not opened until 1959, and even then it was gravel. The drive gives the illusion that this is untouched wilderness because there are so many trees, but everything has been extensively logged for the last 150 years, and there is little old growth left apart from **Cathedral Grove** ⓫ in Macmillan Provincial Park. Trails on both sides of the Highway lead to this large stand of old-growth Douglas firs; the largest trees are 800

### West Coast Trail

The 75km (47-mile) West Coast Trail is one of the most challenging, but rewarding hiking routes in BC. The trek passes sandstone cliffs, huge waterfalls, caves, sea arches, sea stacks and beaches. Facilities on the trail are basic but include boardwalks, ladders, bridges, cableways and outhouses at the most commonly used camping areas. There are no huts for hikers, and because of the severity of winter conditions the WCT is open only between May and September. A charge is levied and reservations, no more than 90 days ahead, are recommended (tel: 250 387 1642; www.westcoast-trailbc.com)

years old, but most sprouted when fire swept through the forest 300 years ago.

The mountains along the West Coast are the first obstruction to moisture-laden clouds rolling in from the Pacific, creating coastal temperate rainforest and forming a boundary between two very different weather systems – rain and fog in the west and sunshine and drier conditions to the east. The wettest place in the whole of Canada is Henderson Lake, just inland from Barkley Sound's northern shoreline where over 8 metres (26 ft) of rain fall in a year.

The best place to gain an overview of the area is the **Wickaninnish Interpretive Centre** ⓬ (mid-Mar–mid-Oct; tel: 250 726 7721 – ring for opening times; www.pc.gc.ca) at the south end of Long Beach, which shows films on the hour and has displays about the Pacific Rim National Park. It also has a restaurant and offers an all-terrain wheelchair for use in the park. If you stop anywhere in the park, you need a pass, which covers admission to the centre. A weekly ticket is available.

## Watching for whales, bears and storms

A great attraction of the two small West Coast towns of Tofino and Ucluelet is the chance to take boat trips to watch the grey whales which stop to feed throughout the summer on the way from their breeding grounds off Mexico to Alaska. Guides also take visitors to watch black bears in May and June when they emerge from winter dens to gorge on salmonberries. In winter, visitors come to the Long Beach peninsula between the towns to watch the storms and 10–15-metre (30–50-ft) ocean swells which toss giant driftwood logs around like toothpicks. In less fierce weather, it is a paradise for surfers, and lessons and guides are available from companies in Tofino.

## Ucluelet and Tofino

An urban-planning award was given to the attractive town of **Ucluelet** ⓭, its harbour dominated by a former hydrographic ship which has been converted into accommodation and a restaurant as part of the Canadian

Map on page 192

*Nanaimo is renowned for diving. Three large ships have been sunk offshore to create artificial reefs (see page 49).*

**BELOW:** grey whale in Clayoquot Sound.

**Map
on page
192**

*A scenic flight in a
floatplane over
Tofino and the sur-
rounding coast is an
unforgettable experi-
ence. The views are
stunning, and while
whale sightings are
not guaranteed they
are common (toll-free
tel: 1 866 486 3247;
www.tofinoair.com).*

**BELOW:** Tofino harbour.

Princess Resort. The dramatically located lighthouse on Amphitrite Point was built in 1914, replacing a 1906-built wooden structure swept away by a tidal wave.

More whale- and seal-watching boats operate out of **Tofino** ⓮, which has had a distinctive culture since it became a favoured bolt-hole for those eluding the Vietnam War draft. It has also been a focal point of protest against indiscriminate logging, sometimes attracting tens of thousands of people from across Canada. The **Saturday market** (May–Sept, 10am–2pm) selling food and crafts is a good place to absorb the atmosphere of the community.

## Port Alberni

The only town between East and West Coast on the Pacific Rim Highway is **Port Alberni** ⓯, which became a European settlement in 1860 when Captain Edward Stamp, an English sea captain, selected it as the site of an export sawmill. Despite being so inland, it was hit by a tidal wave in 1964 caused by an earthquake in Alaska. The town's principal attraction is the **National Historic Site of McClean Mill** (mid-June–Labour Day [early Sept] 10am–5pm; tel: 250 723 1376; www.alberniheritage.com) at 5633 Smith Road, Canada's only operating steam-powered sawmill typical of mills that flourished from the 1880s. It occupies a large forested site and includes such ancillary buildings as cookhouse, bunkhouse, office and all the engineering support services required for a mill.

The best way to reach the mill is by a 35-minute ride on the **Alberni Pacific Railway** (mid-June–Labour Day Thur–Mon, twice a day; tel: 250 723 1376; www.alberniheritage. com). This steam-hauled train leaves from a 1912 Canadian Pacific Railway station and winds through the town before heading into the forest to a station beside McLean Mill.

The **Alberni Valley Museum** (May–Sept daily 10am–5pm, Oct–Apr Mon–Sat; tel: 250 723 1376; www.alberniheritage.com) has a display of First Nations culture, industrial history and folk art with many historic photographs. ❑

# RESTAURANTS

## Victoria

### Blue Carrot Café
18B Bastion Square. Tel: 250 381 8722. Open: B & L Mon–Sat. $
Serves organic coffee, soups, sandwiches, wraps and lots of home-made baked goodies.

### Café Brio
944 Fort St. Tel: 250 383 0009. Open: daily, D only. $$
www.cafe-brio.com
Fresh local seasonal ingredients, much of it organic, and a terrific wine list at reasonable prices along with a warm welcome make for a winning combination here. Confit of pork with Savoy cabbage and roasted apple purée is terrific.

### Camille's
45 Bastion Square. Tel: 250 381 3433. Open: D only Tues–Sat. $$$
www.camillesrestaurant.com
A romantic setting in a turn-of-the-century building, fine food and wine and superb service have made Camille's a popular choice with locals wanting to celebrate a special occasion.

### Empress Room
The Fairmont Empress, 721 Government St. Tel: 250 389 2727. $$$
Afternoon tea at the Empress is an institution that draws tourists and locals in their hundreds. Needless to say, they know how to do tea – finger sandwiches, scones, tarts, cakes, pastries of

the highest quality and tea specially blended for the hotel. Have a drink before dinner in the Bengal Lounge if tea isn't your thing.

### Garrick's Head Pub
69 Bastion Square. Tel: 250 384 6835. Open: daily. $
A neighbourhood pub with 19 different beers on tap. Good pub food and local beers.

### J & J Wonton Noodle House
1012 Fort St. Tel: 250 383 0680. L & D Tues–Sat. $
www.jjnoodlehouse.com
Cheap, cheerful, no-frills restaurant offering excellent Chinese food – some Victorians claim it's the best in the city. Try their special Wor Wonton or the Hot and Sour soup; the rice and noodle dishes are fresh, filling and cheap. Be prepared to queue.

### Rebar Modern Food
50 Bastion Square. Tel: 250 361 9223. Open B, L & D daily, Br weekend. $
www.rebarmodernfood.com
Essentially a vegetarian restaurant with some fish thrown in, Rebar offers imaginative daily menus with an emphasis on local, organic, seasonal and healthy… and it's open for breakfast, lunch, tea and dinner. The pot-stickers are legendary. Excellent stir-fries, wonderful brunch menu and fabulous goodies for teatime.

### Zambri's
110–911 Yates St. Tel: 250 360 1171. Open: L & D Tues–Sat. $$
Italian trattoria serving simple, unpretentious food that has won it many fans in Victoria, in spite of its location in a downtown strip mall. A daily changing menu, a reliance on fresh ingredients, and attention to the Italian tradition of Slow Food and of simple dishes done beautifully.

## Malahat

### Aerie Resort Dining Room
600 Ebedora Lane (Spectacle Lake turn-off). Tel: 250 743 7115. Open: D daily. $$$
www.aerie.bc.ca
The resort overlooks the Cowichan Valley and some of the most spectacular scenery is to be found anywhere. The cusine is modern West Coast and relies on the exemplary produce from the valley below. A romantic, special occasions kind of place.

## Tofino

### Pointe Restaurant
The Wickaninnish Inn, 500 Osprey Lane. Tel: 250 725 31 06. Open: B, L & D daily. $$$
www.wickinn.com
The food here is fantastic, as is the ocean view. Storm-watching from your table is fantastic, and the food matches the drama of the land-

scape – the best West Coast ingredients play their part in an inventive and ever-changing menu.

### Sobo
1028 Pacific Rim Hwy. Tel: 250 725 2341. Open: 11am–6pm Tues–Sun. $
www.sobo.ca
Originally a purple van serving good simple food, Sobo has moved into the Tofino Botanical Gardens. Offerings include tacos stuffed with local fish, fresh or cornmeal crusted oysters, smoked salmon and surf clam chowder.

## Sooke

### Sooke Harbour House
1528 Whiffen Spit Rd (Hwy 14). Tel: 250 642 3421. Open: daily. $$$$
www.sookeharbourhouse.com
Another paradise for foodies – this restaurant grows all its own salads and herbs and sources everything else locally. Organic rabbit, veal, poultry, locally caught game, fish and seafood appear along with locally gathered wild mushrooms and berries on a daily changing menu. Worth a detour for dinner.

---

### PRICE CATEGORIES

Prices for three-course dinner per person with a half-bottle of house wine:
$ = under C$30
$$ = C$30–50
$$$ = C$50–80
$$$$ = more than C$80

# THE GULF ISLANDS

Southwest of the city and sheltered from Pacific storms by Vancouver Island, this string of beautiful, well-wooded islands offer refuge from the urbanity of Vancouver life. Served by frequent ferries and peppered with B&Bs, any of these intimate islands make for a perfect getaway

British Columbia

Vancouver

Strewn across the Strait of Georgia between the mainland and Vancouver Island are hundreds of islands and islets, most of which are uninhabited. Known collectively as the Gulf Islands, this is in fact a misnomer; George Vancouver thought he was sailing up a gulf rather than a strait, but though his error in naming it the Gulf of Georgia was corrected to the Strait of Georgia in 1865, his name for the archipelago remained.

Most of the Gulf Islands are well wooded, with sandy beaches, rocky outcrops and abundant marine life. The beautiful scenery is complemented by the drier, milder climate. The few inhabited islands offer a great contrast to BC's urban centres, with a slower pace of life, small but vibrant communities and a totally different atmosphere. They are famous for the quality of the arts and crafts practised on them, reflecting the appeal of the laid-back lifestyle.

## The island groups

The archipelago is divided into the northern and southern islands, the line roughly formed by the city of Nanaimo, half way up Vancouver Island's east coast. The principal southern Gulf Islands are Gabriola, Galiano, Mayne, North and South Pender, Salt Spring and Saturna,

while the main northern islands are Denman, Hornby and Texada. Cortes and Quadra are often included in lists of Gulf Islands, but as they are not in the Strait of Georgia, they are more accurately part of the Discovery Islands.

The larger islands have golf courses and offer great walking, kayaking and sailing, scuba diving and fishing. Cycling is a popular way of exploring the islands, with the benefit of avoiding the inevitable queues for summer ferries, though

Map on page 180

**LEFT:** house on Mayne Island. **BELOW:** BC ferry en route from Galiano Island.

**BELOW:**
parade of old boats in Ganges Harbour, Salt Spring Island.

care is needed on the narrow and twisting roads. Hotels are few, but there are plenty of high-quality bed and breakfasts. BC Ferries link the principal inhabited islands, and Salt Spring has a minibus shuttle service between Ganges and some ferry sailings. On the few islands that have them, taxis can be expensive.

The value of the islands' ecology was emphasised in 2003 with the creation of the Gulf Islands National Park Reserve, primarily to protect the Garry oak meadows, which are richer in plant species than any other terrestrial system in coastal BC and severely at risk. Delicate wild lilies and orca whales also come within the park's protection. Unfortunately, the Gulf Islands' beauty and mild climate are also attracting the super-rich, some of whom are buying choice sites for luxurious and out-of-scale holiday homes that lie empty or care-takered for most of the year. The population of the islands often doubles or even trebles in the summer.

Set up in 1974, the unique Islands Trust (www.islandstrust.bc.ca) acts as a land use and planning agency on the Gulf Islands with a mandate to preserve and protect the trust area and its unique amenities and environment for the benefit of its residents and of the province generally. It faces the dilemma typical of many spectacularly beautiful areas within reach of urban centres – how to retain sustainable and vibrant communities that are not priced out of their own areas by affluent urbanites in search of a rural retreat – as well as the challenge of water conservation.

## Salt Spring Island

The largest and most populous of the Gulf Islands, **Salt Spring Island** ❶ is reached by two ferries from Vancouver Island – Schwarz Bay to Fulford Harbour and Crofton to Vesuvius Bay – and three ferries into Long Harbour from Mayne and Pender islands, and from Tsawwassen on the mainland. Float planes also link the harbour of the island's capital, Ganges, with Vancouver.

Among the early settlers were Portuguese, freed black slaves from the US in the 1850s and '60s, and Kanakas from Hawaii who came to

BC around 1850 as labourers for the Hudson's Bay Company. Others settled on Salt Spring after the 1858 gold rush where they farmed, fished and logged and married native women.

Threats to log valued forest on Salt Spring Island have been countered by successful fundraising campaigns to halt the felling and buy land, one of which featured a calendar of nude photographs depicting 35 of the island's women. Salt Spring Island Conservancy has bought 40 hectares (100 acres) on the top of Mount Erskine, which, combined with adjacent, already-protected properties, provides permanent protection to an undeveloped area of up to 240 hectares (600 acres).

### The main attractions

One of the island's jewels is **Ruckle Provincial Park**, with rocky headlands and coves along the shore. The surrounding waters are rich in marine life, and if you're lucky you can spot sea lions and whales from the shore. It's a popular spot with divers. The park was named after Henry Ruckle, who came here from Ireland in 1872.

Part of the farm, still in the Ruckle family, is now an 81-hectare (200-acre) organic heritage farm which offers tours (tel: 250 653 4071) to see Highland cattle and sheep herding, and learn about the orchards and pasture rotation.

Today there are 225 working farms on the island, which has become renowned as a centre of organic food production, especially its lamb and cheese. Many of the island's organic food producers open their premises to visitors. A free map is available showing their location, but a good way to see a sample of them and learn about the island is to take an Island Gourmet Safari with Wendy Hartnett (tel: 250 537 4118). Alternatively, the famous **Saturday market** (Apr–mid-Oct 8am–4pm) in Centennial Park at Ganges attracts many of the producers.

Salt Spring is also noted for the number of **studios** open to visitors: 42 artists in wood, paint, glass, textiles, hemp and clay welcome callers.

**Ganges** on the east coast is the island's main village. It was named after the flagship of the Royal Navy's

*Accommodation on Salt Spring Island ranges from the expensive but highly recommended Hastings House (above) to campsites in Ruckle Provincial Park.*

**BELOW:** vintage cars on display at the Salt Spring Island Fall Fair.

*The Gulf Islands attract ornithologists for sightings of ospreys, bald eagles, cormorants, tanagers, juncos, bluebirds and flycatchers.*

**BELOW:** freighter in the Strait of Georgia.

Pacific Station between 1857 and 1860 and the last sailing warship to be commissioned for duty in foreign waters, in 1821. Clustered round its harbour, Ganges has some quirky public sculpture, including a fountain made out of a ship's propellor.

Among its landmarks is Mouat's Store, founded by Shetlanders in 1914, and still supplying all manner of goods to the islanders. The 1904-built Mahon Hall has a large collection of arts and crafts for those who visit between June and September, and the Art Spring community hall hosts an exceptionally good programme of concerts and plays.

Salt Spring has some of the best walking on the Gulf Islands, with the substantial mountains of Maxwell, Erskine, Sullivan and Tuam offering panoramic views over the surrounding islands and the strait. Other attractions include the introduction to the island's history and culture offered by the **Akerman Museum** (tel: 250 537 9977 to arrange visit) in Fulford Valley. The best beaches are on the east coast at Beddis and Ruckle Park.

Every third week in September, Salt Spring Island holds a country fair with sheepdog trials, livestock shows, vintage machinery and plenty of food stalls selling hot buttered corn, home-made pies, barbecued lamb and other wholesome goodies.

## Gabriola Island

The second-most populous Gulf Island, **Gabriola ❷**, is known as the Queen of the Gulf Islands, and is famous for its honeycombed sandstone grottoes such as the cave-like Malaspina Galleries near sandy Taylor Bay. Sandstone quarried on the island went into many a Victoria building and provided grindstones for pulp mills. Accesssible from Nanaimo by a 20-minute ferry ride, Gabriola has a 45-km (28-mile) shoreline and is particularly favoured by cyclists for the 30-km (19-mile) island loop. Five small parks protect various features and habitats, including Garry oak ecosystems and some petroglyphs near Degnen Bay whose origins remain a mystery.

Like Salt Spring, Gabriola has attracted many artists and artisans

Map
on page
180

whose work can be seen at their studios or galleries. In October over 80 studios open their doors for the self-guided Thanksgiving Gallery Tour.

## Galiano Island

Long and thin, **Galiano**  has the lowest rainfall in the region and some fine mature forests of Garry oak, hairy manzanita, maple, cedar and Douglas fir, though they were badly scarred by fire in 2006. Regarded as one of the most attractive of the Gulf Islands, Galiano is rich in bird-life, with over 130 different species recorded.

Ferries from the mainland serve Sturdies Bay at the southeast end of the island, where there is an information booth. Near Sturdies Bay is Bellhouse Park, where seals and sea lions are a common sight, and it is also close to the starting point for the hike up to the 342-metre (1,122-ft) summit of Mount Galiano, a popular walk for the spectacular views.

## North and South Pender

Linked by a single-track bridge, **North and South Pender islands** offer plenty of coves and beaches as well as good services, mostly on the North Island where the ferry terminal at Otter Bay is located to receive ferries from Swartz Bay and Tsawwassen. The islands are particularly appealing to walkers, with 69 different trails including an ascent of Mount Norman at 244 metres (801 ft) on the South Island. There are 37 beaches to choose from, Hamilton on the North Island and Mortimer Spit on the South being among the favourites.

The subdivision of part of North Pender, where 90 percent of the islands' inhabitants live, was one of the catalysts for the formation of Islands Trust, to prevent the character of the islands being destroyed by inappropriate development.

## Mayne Island

Named after a lieutenant on HMS *Plumper* (many of the islands were named after senior crew members of the ship that surveyed the archipelago in 1857), **Mayne Island** ❺ seems anything but "the little hell" it was once called because of the

**TIP**

BC Ferry tickets to the islands cover the return journey, so you are free to choose an alternative route. For example, visitors to Salt Spring Island can arrive at Fulford Harbour and leave from Vesuvius Bay.

**BELOW:** Georgina Point Lighthouse, Mayne.

drunken behaviour of the gold prospectors on their way from Fort Victoria to the Fraser river. Mayne's facilities are clustered around Miners Bay and Village Bay, where the ferry from the mainland docks. At nearby Dinner Bay is the **Japanese Garden** created by the community to commemorate the island's early Japanese Canadian settlers.

**Georgina Point Lighthouse** was built in 1885 and is probably the most photographed lighthouse in BC. On the edge of Active Pass, the most direct but also the most dangerous passage between the islands, it can be visited between 1–3pm. The two cells and main room of the Plumper Pass Lockup of 1896 now house the island's museum. Even older is the 1890 Collinson farmhouse and now Springwater Lodge. There is a lovely beach for swimming on the east side of the island at **Campbell Bay**, where there are also sandstone caves to explore.

## Saturna Island

With a population of little over 300, **Saturna ⑥** offers exceptional peace where the passage of a car seems an intrusion. This is an island where exploring by bike or on foot seems like good manners. Named after the *Saturnina* in which José Maria Narváez explored the Strait of Georgia, the island is so little changed that he would probably still recognise most of it.

Thanks to almost half the island being protected as part of the National Park Reserve, there is a good chance that it will stay one of the jewels of the Gulf Islands. Its tall mountain, Mount Warburton Pike at 497 metres (1,631 ft), offers exceptional views over the islands and the coastal mainland chain. Bird life includes eagles, falcons and vultures.

The most southerly of the islands, it's served by a daily ferry from Swartz Bay and Tsawwassen via Mayne, arriving at the deep inlet of Lyall Harbour. With several B&Bs, a pub, bakery and restaurant, it's easy to stay for a few days to absorb an atmosphere that is rare in North America. The highlight in the social calendar is the Canada Day Lamb Barbecue (1 July) at Winter Cove

*Hornby Island has the largest per capita concentration of artists in Canada, so there are many opportunities to visit studios and galleries.*

**BELOW:** the sheltered waters around Hornby Island are good for gentle water sports.

Marine Park, when over a thousand people, many from visiting boats, enjoy Argentinian-style meat cooked on upright iron crosses.

## Denman Island

**Denman** is often seen as a stepping stone to the more popular Hornby Island, but it has some of the best agricultural land in the Gulf Islands. The 2-km (1¼-mile) ferry ride from Buckley Bay on Vancouver Island arrives at Denman Village, which has a wide range of facilities to cater for the population of over 1,000.

The shops include a co-operative outlet for the island's artisans, and there are over a dozen B&Bs.

## Hornby Island

**Hornby** has a permanent population of around 1,000, but this increases tenfold in summer thanks to its lovely beaches and coves and varied topography. Consequently it has excellent amenities, including many galleries displaying the creations of the island's large artistic community. Typical of the impressive community action on the islands, the residents of

Hornby raised money to help create a 182-hectare (450-acre) provincial park on Mount Geoffrey. The Co-op store is as much for socialising as shopping, with the Ringside Market next door.

The island is reached by a 15-minute ferry ride across the Lambert Channel that separates Hornby from Denman Island. Sheltered Tribune Bay has some of the warmest sea water in BC as well as a fine white-sand beach, with tidal pools to explore. Scuba divers come to the island to experience swimming with the rare six-gill sharks, one of the few places where they can be easily seen.

## Texada Island

This is the most developed of the islands, with a significant proportion of the population of 1,100 occupied in the three huge limestone quarries and logging. Reached by ferries from Powell River or Horseshoe Bay into Blubber Bay, **Texada** is a good place for birdwatchers, with a record of 265 species, including harlequins, scooters and Anna's and Rufous hummingbirds.                    ❑

Map on page 180

**TIP**

Kayaks, boats and bikes can be hired on most of the islands, and on some, like Hornby, scuba-diving equipment is available.

**BELOW:**
Saturna Island jetty.

# RESTAURANTS & BARS

### Restaurants

*Gabriola Island*

**Raspberry's Jazz Café**
Folklife Village, 575 North Rd. Tel: 250 247 9959. Open: L daily, D Thur–Sat. $
Open during the day for homemade soups, sandwiches and good coffee, the café is transformed into a jazz venue in the evening, often featuring the Jazzberrys, the island's favourite jazz ensemble.

**Suzy's Restaurant & Deli**
Folklife Village, 560 North Rd. Tel: 250 247 2010. Open: B, L & D daily. $
Excellent spot for brunch and light lunches. Also a good place to pick up the ingredients for a great picnic since Suzy's sells local cheeses, meats and artisan breads.

**Surf Pub**
885 Berry Point Road. Tel: 250 247 9231. Open: L & D daily. $
www.surflodge.com
Pop in to the Surf Pub, part of the Surf Island Lodge, for a drink and a bite to eat while you watch the sun set from the outside deck.

*Galiano Island*

**Woodstone Country Inn**
743 Georgeson Bay Rd. Tel: 250 539 2022. Open: D daily. $$
www.woodstoneinn.com
The restaurant of this inn, nestled in a quiet valley, has a pretty dining-room and offers a contemporary menu which makes the most of local ingredients and produce from their own garden.

**La Berengerie**
Montague Rd. Tel: 250 539 5392. Open: D daily. $$
www.galiano.gulfislands.com/laberengerie
This welcoming B&B near Montague Harbour serves French cuisine with a southeast Asian twist using local produce.

*Mayne Island*

**Oceanwood Country Inn**
630 Dinner Bay Road. Tel: 250 539 5074. Open: D daily. $$$
www.oceanwood.com
A daily-changing menu to reflect the seasons and what is freshly available is a feature of the award-winning dining-room at this country inn. The five-course fixed menu is fantastically delicious and good value.

**Sunny Mayne Bakery Café**
Mayne St Mall. Open: B & L daily. $
www.sunnymaynebakery.com
A good place for breakfast, lunch or a quick morning coffee. Lots of home-made goodies and great coffee.

*Pender Islands*

**Poet's Cove Aurora Restaurant**
9801 Spalding Rd, South Pender Island. Tel: 250 629 2115. Open: B, L & D daily. $$$
www.poetscove.com
Part of the Poet's Cove Resort and Spa, the restaurant specialises in contemporary local cuisine – fresh seafood, local lamb – in a stunning setting. Spectacular sunsets are free.

**Islanders Restaurant**
1325 MacKinnon Rd, North Pender Island. Tel: 250 629 3929. Open: D Wed–Mon. $$
www.islandersrestaurant.com
Lots of salmon, oysters, mussels and pasta dishes and great setting. A short walk from the Otter Bay ferry terminal.

*Salt Spring Island*

**Hastings House Country Estate**
160 Upper Ganges Road. Tel: 250 537 2362. Open: D daily, mid-Mar–mid-Nov. $$$$
www.hastingshouse.com
Hastings House is a wonder and deserves its rank among the top ten inn dining-rooms in North America. The food is accomplished and imaginative without being pretentious, allowing the quality and freshness of the ingredients to sing out. Grilled rack and loin of Salt Spring lamb, rosemary polenta, braised red cabbage and honey-mustard jus is perfection. And the six-course chef's menu at $100 seems like a steal. The

**LEFT:** Hastings House terrace overlooking the harbour.

wine list is extensive and features good local wines. The service is informed and unfussy. All this and the pretty setting make a meal here a wonderful treat.

### Oystercatcher Seafood Bar & Grill
Harbour Building, Ganges. Tel: 250 537 5041. Open: L & D daily. $$

Fabulous food in a spectacular setting overlooking the harbour. Lunch-time specials include BBQ Fanny Bay oysters with fresh asparagus and Dungeness crab, and shrimp cakes, cranberry corn relish and asparagus. The best crab cakes ever and the local beers – Saltspring Golden Ale and their own Oystercatcher Pale Ale – are excellent. Great puds too.

### Restaurant House Piccolo
108 Hereford Ave. Tel: 250 537 1844. Open: D Tues–Sat. $$
www.housepiccolo.com
Bistro-style cooking using local produce in a tiny heritage house overlooking Ganges. Ring for reservations since there are only eight tables.

### Saturna Island

### Saturna Café
101 Narvaez Bay Rd. Tel: 250 539 2936. Open: B, L & D Wed–Sat, B & L Sun. $$
Local, healthy and fresh are the keynotes here. Try to time your visit with the weekly crab night – a

whole steamed crab and a pair of claw crackers.

### The Restaurant at Saturna Lodge
Tel: 250 539 2254. Open: D daily, Sun brunch. $$$
www.saturna.ca
Organic produce, fresh local seafood, locally reared meats and local wines are a big draw at the restaurant of this very pretty country inn.

### Cafés & Bars

#### Denman Island
A tiny island, but try the **Denman Island Guesthouse Bistro** (Denman village), the **Denman Island Bakery & Pizzeria** (Denman Road), or **Rawganique**, a vegan-vegetarian restaurant (Denman village).

#### Hornby Island
Another small island with few restaurants: visit **Jan's Café** (5875 Central Rd); or the **Thatch Pub** (4305 Shingle Spit Rd) for West Coast specialities, burgers and salads; the **Cardboard House** for pizza, coffees etc; and **VOR1ZO Espresso Bar** for great coffee and homemade goodies.

#### Galiano Island
Try **Max & Moritz**, a mobile takeaway situated at the Sturdies ferry terminal, serving breakfast, German and Indonesian food, hamburgers and stuffed pittas. Or the **Humming-**

**bird Pub** at Sturdies Bay. **The Harbour Grill** at Montague Harbour serves breakfast, lunch and dinner and is very popular with yachties as they can moor nearby.

#### Salt Spring Island
Stop for a morning coffee and a pastry at **Auntie Pesto's Café & Deli** (Grace Point Square) or any of the other bakery/cafés in Ganges after a visit to the Saturday Market. **Barb's Buns Bakery** (121 McPhillips Ave) is considered the best place for breakfast and for local gossip. Everything is fresh and homemade. For a pint of the local brew or other beers, try **Shipstone's English Pub** (Ganges Harbour front) or **Moby's Marine Pub** (Salt Spring Marina). The **Vesuvius Inn** at Vesuvius Bay – although it

claims to be a simple neighbourhood pub – serves excellent food, capitalising on the wonderful local fresh fish and seafood.

#### Texada Island
There are only a few places on Texada to grab a bite or a coffee: **Café Casita** in the Holtenwood Gallery (112 Blubber Bay Rd); **Murphy's Restaurant & Convenience Store** (Gillies Bay, 3110 Balsam Ave); **Texada Island Inn** (Van Anda); or the **Tree Frog Bistro** (Gillies Bay).

### PRICE CATEGORIES

Prices for three-course dinner per person with a half-bottle of house wine:
$ = under C$30
$$ = C$30–50
$$$ = C$50–80
$$$$ = more than C$80

**RIGHT:** a beautifully presented B&B brunch.

# NORTH TO WHISTLER

**The Sea-to-Sky Highway is a scenic fjord drive that leads to one of the best sports resorts in North America. You can also get active along the Sunshine Coast Trail, which offers equally spectacular coastal scenery**

British Columbia

Whistler

Vancouver

T he most popular excursion destination outside Vancouver is the year-round recreational mountain area, Whistler. In winter, it draws crowds for skiing or snowboarding, but this is a four-season resort. Once the snow has melted, hikers and bikers keep the ski lifts rolling, and the winter slopes turn into summer trails.

The other great attraction north of the city is Highway 101 along the coast, which links a series of enchanting small resorts. Whichever route you choose, they both offer stunning scenery and lots of opportunities for outdoor activities en route, from the gentle to the extreme.

## Whistler Mountaineer

Unquestionably the best way to enjoy the scenery between Vancouver and Whistler is to take the **Whistler Mountaineer**, operated by Rocky Mountaineer Vacations *(see page 233)*. Besides enabling you to relax and enjoy the landscapes, the train affords much better views than the road of Howe Sound.

Trains leave from a small station in North Vancouver and pass the Lions Gate Bridge before easing past the Beverley Hills of Vancouver, where some of the city's most valuable houses are located. For much of the way, the sinuous line hugs the

coast, initially looking across to Stanley Park, Kitsilano and the wooded peninsula on which UBC is built. Breakfast is served as the train veers north, offering views out over the dark water of the Sound, broken by a few islands and the heads of curious seals, to snow-dusted mountains bristling with conifers.

The Cheakamus Canyon is a half-mile-long cauldron of olive-green water with sheer rocks above and below the line which curves through the gorge. The train slows to walk-

Map on page 180

**LEFT:** skiing on Whistler Mountain. **BELOW:** arbutus trees at Gospel Rock, Gibsons.

*The guided tour of the old Britannia Mine involves an underground ride in a narrow-gauge train along 400 metres (1,400 ft) of a tunnel bored in 1912, a tiny fraction of the 240 km (150 miles) of tunnels and shafts in the mine.*

**BELOW:** Squamish.

ing pace and allows you time to take absorb the sight of this extraordinary feature, with trees growing out of the most inhospitable planes of rock.

## The Sea-to-Sky Highway

The alternative to the train is to drive Highway 99 – the Sea-to-Sky Highway – controversially widened at a cost of $600 million to cope with traffic for the Winter Olympics. For much of the way, the views are limited, but it does allow visits to places en route. Near the ferry terminal at Horseshoe Bay the road swings north for Lions Bay and Squamish.

One of the most fascinating museums in the province is the **British Columbia Museum of Mining** ❼ (9am–4.30pm; tel: 604 896 2233; www.bcmuseumofmining. org), at Britannia Beach. This BC Historic Landmark was once the most productive copper mine in the British Empire: Britannia Mine closed in 1974 after 70 years' output, having produced 650,000 tonnes of copper as well as lead, zinc, cadmium, silver, gold and iron. It reopened as a mining museum the following year,

and is such an atmospheric location that it has featured in dozens of films. The site is dominated by the vast tiered mill building erected against the hillside; it housed the concentrator which removed valuable minerals from the 55 million tonnes of ore the mine processed. The corrugated-iron building has 14,400 panes of glass, which are gradually being replaced.

Other buildings house displays of equipment and portraits of life at the mine. Underground tours are available *(see left)*. There is no café at the mine itself, but there is a roadside café with home-made cakes a few minutes' walk away.

## Squamish

The only town between Vancouver and Whistler, **Squamish** ❽ (meaning "birthplace to the winds") is overlooked by the towering cliff faces of the mountain named **Stawamus Chief**, and the **Shannon Falls**, at their most impressive in spring. The 650-metre (2,140-ft) granite monolith, geologically comparable to the Rock of Gibraltar, is a great attraction for climbers. Most days when it's not raining colourful ropes can be seen trailing down route lines. A good place to begin a visit is the **Adventure Centre** (summer 8am–8pm, winter 9am–6pm; tel: 604 815 4994; www.adventurecentre.ca), which has visitor information, a theatre, café and exhibition. Aside from rock climbing, there are plenty of other recreational activities on offer: kayaking, whitewater rafting, kiteboarding, hiking, mountain biking, scuba diving, golf, fishing and windsurfing – the windblown town's second-most popular activity.

Many people converge on the area between mid-November and February to witness the gathering of some 3,000 **Bald eagles** drawn to the river by the seasonal salmon run. The main viewing point is Brackendale, a few kilometres upriver.

Until the lumber mill at the head of the Sound closed in early 2006 Squamish had been reliant on lumber and pulp, but closure of the mill is allowing the waterfront to be redeveloped with a view to creating a "Granville Island on Howe Sound".

## Brandywine Falls

The last big attraction before Whistler, 47 km (30 miles) north of Squamish, is **Brandywine Falls Provincial Park** , where a short walking trail leads from the car park to an observation platform at the top of the 70-metre (230-ft) falls. Cross the bridge over Brandywine Creek and follow the path to the right, which brings you to a clearing beside the falls. From this viewpoint, Daisy Lake spreads out beneath the monolith of Black Tusk.

## Whistler

Once known as Alta Lake, **Whistler** ⑩ has become famous around the world as a leading ski resort; *Skiing* magazine has ranked it number one in North America for nine consecutive years, and its facilities and reputation doubtless helped it win the privilege of hosting the 2010 Winter Olympics. The village itself nestles between Whistler and Blackcomb mountains, and even though the resort depends on road access, the streets have at least been designed to discourage car use in

Map on page 180

**TIP**

You don't need to be a rail buff to appreciate the West Coast Railway Heritage Park (10am–5pm; tel: 604 898 9336; www.wcra. org) just northwest of Squamish. It has a huge collection of locomotives, sleeping and mail carriages, cabooses and other rolling stock. The highlight is the magnificent Royal Hudson locomotive, recently overhauled and taken out for special journeys.

**BELOW:** whitewater rafting on the Cheakamus river.

*Brandywine Falls, the favourite stopping place between Squamish and Whistler.*

**BELOW:** the Whistler cable cars operate throughout the year.

favour of walking and cycling. Like some Alpine resorts, Whistler has the unreal feeling of a transient community almost wholly dependent on tourism, with its agglomeration of hotels, designer-label shops, restaurants and condominiums in manicured surroundings.

Whistler is making an effort to develop into a mountain resort that will "become a beacon of hope to the global community to show that sustainability is possible", though it sees no contradiction in promoting heli-skiing and hummer tours.

The additional facilities being built for the Olympics, such as the Nordic and Sliding centres, will add to Whistler's appeal, and the Olympic village for 2,000 people will significantly increase the accommodation available.

The skiing area is now the largest in North America, covering 3,036 hectares (8,171 acres) of terrain serviced by 33 lifts, as is the vertical descent at 1,609 metres (5,280ft). The longest run is 11 km (7 miles). Whistler also benefits from a long ski season, between November and August. There's plenty to do for those who don't wish to ski: snowshoeing, sleigh rides, glacier tours and dog sledding.

In summer there is just about every outdoor activity imaginable. Zip-trekking is particularly popular *(see page 214)*. Ten ziplines cross the Fitzsimmons Creek Valley in the old coastal temperate rainforest, and a tour includes an introduction to the ecology of this increasingly scarce habitat. The longest ride is 610 metres (2,000 ft).

Many of the winter ski lifts offer quick and easy access to hiking trails during the summer. Some of the best hiking routes are in **Garibaldi Park** ⓫ which offers easy walks through alpine meadows, as well as more challenging hikes such as the ascent of the volcanic plug of Black Tusk.

## The southern Sunshine Coast

Highway 101 is one of the great BC drives, hugging the coastline pierced by inlets from Port Mellon on Howe Sound to Lund at the northern end of the Sunshine Coast. Coming from

Vancouver, most join it at Langdale where the BC Ferry from Horseshoe Bay docks after a 40-minute journey. The area is popular for hiking along the Sunshine Coast Trail, cycling, kayaking, fishing and diving as well as sailing.

At 716 Winn Road in **Gibsons**  the **Sunshine Coast Museum and Archive** (Tue–Sat 10.30am– 4.30pm; tel: 604 886 8232; www.sunshine coastmuseum.ca) provides a good introduction to the history of this area and of the Coast Salish nation. A first-floor maritime section has full-sized boats as well as models. In the summer Gibsons hosts an international outrigger canoe race.

The road continues past **Mount Elphinstone**, a coastal rainforest with imposing old-growth cedar, hemlock and maple laced with trails for biking and hiking. **Roberts Creek** has an "alternative" feel to it, a retreat for those who lament the passing of the 1960s counter-culture, with such contemporary manifestations as organic restaurants and cosmic-energy public artworks.

There's a great sandy beach at **Davis Bay**, where the skill of sand-castle building is celebrated by an annual competition.

The "capital" of the Sunshine Coast is **Sechelt**, which has the-atres and galleries as well as the usual tourist amenities. Rockwood Lodge was built as a Union Steam-ship boarding house in 1935 and has been preserved as a centre for com-munity activities. Surrounded by delightful gardens, it now hosts Sechelt's Festival of the Written Arts in August. Totem poles flank the First Nations **Tems Swiya Museum** (Mon–Sat 9am–5pm; tel: 604 885 8991), which displays the art and carvings of the Shishalh people.

From **Sargeant Bay Provincial Park**, north of Smugglers Cove, you can walk to a particularly attractive cove and visit a salmon ladder.

**Pender Harbour** is known as the "Venice of the North" for the waterways that thread the town. There are boat tours up Jervis and sheer-walled Princess Louisa inlets to the magnificently situated 40-metre (131 ft) Chatterbox Falls. The

Map on page 180

**TIP**

Just a 20-minute ferry ride from Horseshoe Bay, **Bowen Island** is popular with Vancou-verites seeking a quick escape from the city. Restaurants and shops are focused on the ferry terminal of Snug Cove. It's a short walk from there to the beaches, but there are good walking trails in the undeveloped centre of the island. The visitor information centre supplies maps and information.

**BELOW:** mountain biking in Whistler.

## Sunshine Coast Trail

This 180-km (112-mile) trail was built in response to the diminish-ing amounts of old-growth forest that had survived the depredations of logging and development. Its southerly point is Saltery Bay and it ends at Sarah Point, north of Lund, on Desolation Sound. En route you should see salmon and otter on the river and lakeside stretches, and numerous waterfalls are passed. A leisurely pace would take about ten days, and there are strategically located B&Bs and a restaurant on or close to the path to allow hikers to plan overnight stops. A complete panorama can be enjoyed from the top of Tin Hat Mountain.

Map on page 180

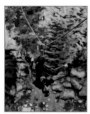

*For a novel adrenalin rush, try ziptrekking with Ziptrek Ecotours (tel: 604 935 0001; www.ziptrek .com). Suspended in a safety harness, you slide along a wire rope between platforms built high up in stout trees. You can even hang upside down, and whizz along with your hands free.*

**BELOW:** Sechelt.

latter inlet has about 60 waterfalls during the summer.

Experienced kayakers head for the Skookumchuck Rapids in **Skookumchuck Narrows Provincial Park** for the tidal rapids created by billions of litres of water being forced through a narrow channel. The park is at Egmont, due east of Earls Cove, from where the ferry departs for the northern section of the Sunshine Coast.

### The upper Sunshine Coast

A 50-minute ferry ride links **Earls Cove** and **Saltery Bay**, where killer whales, sea lions and seals can be seen. The bay takes its name from the fish saltery that was established here in the early 20th century.

The **Powell river** ⓰ has the distinction of being the world's second shortest river – its harbour is protected by 10 World War II cement hulks which form the world's largest floating breakwater. The town itself is a major attraction and one of the few National Historic Districts in all Canada. It was an early example of a planned community on the lines of

a garden city, with 400 attractively designed West Coast Craftsman-style houses set in spacious landscaped grounds. If you're staying in town, don't miss taking in a film at the superbly renovated 1928 Patricia Theatre.

The **Powell River Historical Museum** (4798 Marine Avenue, Mon–Fri 9am–4.30pm; tel: 604 485 2222; www.powellrivermuseum.ca) traces the history of the area between Jervis Inlet and Desolation Sound, including the offshore islands, from the Coast Salish people at Sliammon village to the present.

In early July Powell river hosts one of the world's largest choral festivals, the **Kathaumixw** (pronounced Ka-thou-mew), held bi-annually in even-numbered years. It features over 30 choirs and conductors from all over the world and celebrates music's ability to bring peace to the planet.

At the end of Highway 101 is **Lund**, a fishing village founded by a Swedish family in 1889, an ancestry which is still reflected in the Lund Hotel. ❑

# RESTAURANTS & BARS

Whistler has a plethora of good restaurants, coffee bars, deli-cafés and bars, many serving excellent food at reasonable prices. Here is a selection:

## Restaurants

### Araxi Restaurant and Lounge
4222 Village Square (Whistler Way). Tel: 604 932 4540. Open: D only, daily. $$$
www.araxi.com
West Coast cuisine in a mountain setting. A very smart place, and the food lives up to the decor. An oyster bar is the latest addition, and the patio in summer is a must.

### Caramba Restaurant
12-4314 Main St. Tel: 604 938 1879. Open: L & D daily. $$
A buzzy atmosphere and good pastas, wood-fired pizzas and salads make this a popular place. Their Caramba chicken salad is terrific and great value for diners on a budget.

### Fifty Two 80 Bistro
Four Seasons Resort, 4591 Blackcomb Way (Lorimer Rd). Tel: 604 935 3400. Open: B, L & D daily $$$
www.fourseasons,com/whistler
Seafood is the speciality at this sophisticated dining room, although spit-roasts and prime Canadian beef are also on the menu.

### Keg Steakhouse & Bar
Whistler Village Inn, 4429 Sundial Place. Tel: 604 932 5151. Open: D only, daily $$
www.kegsteakhouse.com
If you are after a straight-forward carnivorous chow-down at a reasonable price, the Keg is a good bet. Steak of every cut and kind is available, along with prime ribs of beef, chicken and fish, plus a good choice of salads and pasta dishes. A good family place.

### Kypriaki Norte
4122 Village Green. Tel: 604 932 0600. Open: D only, daily. $$   www.kypriaki.net
Another local favourite for traditional Greek and Mediterranean food at reasonable prices, Kypriaki also has a bar and patio with terrific views for alfresco eating.

### Il Caminetto di Umberto
4242 Village Stroll (Whistler Village Square). Tel: 604 932 4442. Open: D only, daily $$$
www.umberto.com
Another restaurant in the Umberto Menghi stable of fine Italian eateries, Il Caminetto focuses on fabulous Tuscan food using the best local ingredients. Great home-made pasta dishes and an extensive wine list, with Italy playing a leading role. Try his other Whistler establishment, Trattoria di Umberto, at 4417 Sundial Place, if you can't get in here.

### La Rua Restaurant
4557 Blackcomb Way. Tel: 604 932 5011. Open: D only, daily $$$
www.larua-restaurante.com
Award-winning restaurant within Le Chamois hotel renowned for its inter-national take on seafood, steak and game, with such creative dishes as West Coast bouilla-baisse, Arctic caribou in ruby plum and port sauce and cassoulet.

### Rimrock Café and Oyster Bar
2117 Whistler Rd (Hwy 99). Tel: 604 932 5565. Open: D only, daily. $$$
www.rimrockwhistler.com
One of Whistler's top restaurants, with a repu-tation for outstanding seafood and game and a terrific wine list. Arctic caribou and venison chop feature along with a won-derful array of fish and shellfish. Worth a detour.

### Splitz Grill
104-4369 Main St. Tel: 604 938 9300. Open: L & D daily. $
A must for a quick meal on the run, this burger joint serves the usual and not so usual – salmon, chicken and spicy – with every con-ceivable topping and condiment possible. Very popular and very cheap.

### Sushi Village
4272 Mountain Square (Whistler Village Square). Tel: 604 932 3330. Open: L & D daily. $$
www.sushivillage.com
Trendy hang-out for a younger crowd offering exemplary sushi, salads, Teriyaki dishes and hot pots. Be prepared to wait.

### Sushi-Ya
230-4370 Lorimer Rd (Whistler Village North) Tel: 604 905 0155. Open: D daily, L & D Sat–Sun. $$
Another sushi place to try, with memorably fresh fish and great tempura.

## Bars & cafés

Try the buzzy **Whistler Brewhouse** (north end of the Village Stroll), which has a wood-fired pizza oven and rotisserie. For the best all-day breakfast, try **Auntie Em's Kitchen** (Village North Market-place) which also serves excellent vegetarian sand-wiches, soups and baked goodies. **Gone Bakery & Soup Co.** (off the main Vil-lage Square) has daily specials to eat in or take away. A locals' favourite is the **Cinnamon Bear Bar** (near the Hilton), serving the usual burgers, pizzas and salads. **Black's Pub & Restaurant** (4270 Mountain Square) has more than 90 different beers, a great patio and good pub food.

### PRICE CATEGORIES

Prices for three-course dinner per person with a half-bottle of house wine:
$ = under C$30
$$ = C$30–50
$$$ = C$50–80
$$$$ = more than C$80

# THE OKANAGAN

East of Greater Vancouver the sprawl of industrial plants and strip malls eventually gives way to grassland plateaux, lakes and high Alpine mountains. Known as "Canada's fruit bowl", sunny Okanagan is also a major wine-producing region of increasing renown

British Columbia

Vancouver · Merritt

Compared to the well-publicised areas north of the city and the islands to the west, the area east of Vancouver gets relatively little coverage, something of an injustice as there is plenty to see and do. Don't be put off by the less than scenic beginning to your journey.

Whether you leave Vancouver by Highway 1 or Route 99 to gain access to the Trans-Canada Highway via Route 10, it's easy to be disheartened, either by the industrial plants that site themselves along Highway 1 or the unspeakable ugliness of the strip malls that seem to line long stretches of Route 99.

Even when the malls give way to acres of glasshouses and the shrinking market gardens of Vancouver, the land is flat, largely reclaimed from the Fraser Delta.

Once past Chilliwack, however, development recedes and the coastal range rises up majestically, marking the beginning of the mountains that continue without interruption almost to Calgary. During the summer the roads are punctuated by stalls selling the fresh fruit for which the region is famous.

## Fort Langley

To place both Vancouver and the founding of British Columbia in context, it's worth breaking the jour-ney at the birthplace of the colony, **Fort Langley** , just north of Highway 1. It was here, beside the Fraser river, that the Hudson's Bay Company trading post was founded.

The first fort was built in 1827, but propensity to flooding prompted a move in 1839 to the hilltop site on which the fort has been reconstructed around the one surviving original building, the 1840s storehouse. A 5-km (3-mile) riverside trail links the two sites. Costumed staff at the **Fort Langley National Historic Site**

Map on page 180

**LEFT:** aerial view of the Okanagan vineyards.
**BELOW:** Fort Langley.

**TIP**

In the vicinity of Fort Langley, just 500 metres south of the Trans-Canada Highway (exit # 73) the **Greater Vancouver Zoological Centre** (5048 264th Street, Aldergrove; daily 9am–dusk; tel: 604 856 6825; www. gvzoo.com) has bears, lions, tigers, elephants, and giraffes among the 800 animals roaming its 49 hectares (120 acres).

**BELOW:** cooper's shop, Fort Langley.

(mid-Mar–Oct daily 10am–5pm; Nov–mid-Mar Tues–Sat 10am–4pm; tel: 604 513 4777; www.pc.gc.ca/ fortlangley) help to interpret the eight buildings within the wood-stockaded fort and explain the trading activities, mainly in beaver pelts, that went on with the aboriginal people. It was here that British Columbia was proclaimed a crown colony, at a ceremony in the "Big House" on 19 November 1858.

The town of Fort Langley is beautifully kept and landscaped with several rows of old shops, including a huge antiques emporium. The **Langley Centennial Museum** (9135 King Street; Mon–Sat 10am–4.45pm, Sun 1–4.45pm; tel: 604 888 3922; www.langleymuseum.org) has a reconstruction of an early 20th-century store and post office and a gallery of watercolours of vernacular buildings.

Next door is the **Farm Machinery Museum** (daily 10am–4.30pm; tel: 604 888 2273; www.bcfma.com), with a huge variety of farm equipment, including a crop-spraying Tiger Moth biplane. On the opposite side

of Fort Langley's main street, Glover Road, is the restored former **Canadian National Fort Langley Station** building (summer and autumn weekends 12–4pm), erected in 1915.

Just outside the town, on the other side of Highway 1 adjacent to Langley Municipal Airport is the **Canadian Museum of Flight** (daily 10am–4pm; tel: 604 532 0035; www.canadianflight.org). Its collection of 25 aircraft includes a Tiger Moth and the only Handley Page Hampden RAF bomber plane on public display.

## Hope

To get a feel for the character of small-town BC, turn off Highway 1 to visit the chainsaw-carving capital of **Hope** ⓲, a township situated in the fork of the Fraser and Coquihalla rivers. The Hudson's Bay Company built a fort at Hope in 1848–9 as the terminus of the Coquihalla route from the interior. In 1858 the gold rush began, when four Americans who had heard rumours of gold nuggets being found by native Indians at Spences

Bridge passed through Hope, stopped on a sandbar 16 km (10 miles) north of the town and found gold. By the summer of that year, about 30,000 men and women had arrived from all around the world, many aboard the first steam stern-wheelers. A good introduction to the area's history is provided by the **Visitor Centre** (daily) and **Museum** (mid-May– mid-Sept daily) at 919 Water Street (tel: 604 869 2021).

The streets are punctuated with imposing wood sculptures *(see right)*, and a self-guided art walk round the town takes in the carvings and the town's art galleries.

Dating from 1861, **Christ Church** is the oldest church in continuous use on its original site in mainland BC. It is made of clapboard construction with wood shingles and surrounded by cedar trees.

## Around Hope

The country around Hope is wild and rugged. One of the most dramatic canyons can be walked by taking the easy and popular trail on the abandoned trackbed of the **Kettle Valley Railway** through the deep, dark Othello Quintette Tunnels in **Coquihalla Canyon Provincial Park** , northeast of Hope. To reach the walk-through tunnels (open May–15 Nov), take the Kawkawa Lake Road out of Hope, then join the Othello Road. Sheer walls of rock rise above the route of the line, which crosses the river several times between largely unlined tunnels. The stations on the line were named after Shakespearean characters because the railway's engineer, Andrew McCulloch, loved Shakespeare and would sit round the campfire at night reading sonnets to the construction crew. It was the most difficult railway in Canada to build and operate: one mile cost C$300,000 in 1914, and during the first seven winters the line was closed more than it was open due to mud and snow slides, which finally smothered the line in 1959.

## Manning Park

Most of the mountain highways are subject to landslides, avalanches and flooding. Taking the Crowsnest

Map on page 180

*Chainsaw carving in Hope, a tradition started in 1990 by local carver Pete Ryan, when he fashioned some trees condemned with root rot into animals found in the surrounding forests.*

**BELOW:** cycling along the Kettle Valley Railway, Myra Canyon.

*The Mascot Gold Mine offers dizzying views over the Similkameen Valley from its 1,462-metre (4,800-ft) perch. If you intend to visit, take warm clothes as the temperature drops considerably once inside the mine.*

**BELOW:** on the Othello Quintette Tunnels trail.

Highway, No. 3 southeast from Hope, the road passes the site of the **Hope Slide**; in 1965 Johnson Peak collapsed, engulfing four passing motorists. The colossal amount of debris is a dramatic illustration of the power of nature.

The road soon enters **Manning Provincial Park ㉑**, which offers a fabulous diversity of landscapes with rainforests, grassland slopes, wild rivers, lakes and Alpine meadows. Sumallo Grove is a good place to appreciate the beauty of old-growth forest – the biggest trees here are almost 500 years old – and is home to pine marten, black bear, spotted owls, Northern flying squirrels, bats and black-tailed deer. Above **Manning Park Resort** (the only place to stay in the park, *see page 245*) the Cascade Lookout, reached by a gravel switchback road, offers majestic views of the Cascade Mountains. You would be unlucky not to see a yellow pine chipmunk.

There's a visitor centre just east of the resort, which has maps of suggested walks and details of the imaginative programme of guided walks and events for children. Some of the walks start from an upper parking area 7 km (4½ miles) beyond the lookout, reached by a good dirt road, where there is an Alpine meadow with flowers right into late July. Canoes can be hired at **Lightning Lake**, a few miles from the resort, where it is also safe to swim, and in winter there is downhill and cross-country skiing.

## Underground in Hedley

It's worth pausing in the former mining town of **Princeton ㉑** to visit the **Museum and Archives** (Apr–Oct daily 10am–5pm, until 7pm July–Aug; tel: 250 295 7588; www.princetonmuseum.com). It has one of the most extensive mineral and fossil collections in British Columbia, besides a huge collection of old photographs, and displays on the nearby ghost towns of Allenby, Copper Mountain and Granite Creek.

Further east along Highway 3 is the small settlement of **Hedley ㉒**, where the information centre in the renovated schoolhouse is the starting point for the 4½-hour tour of the

**Mascot Gold Mine** (May–Oct; tel: 250 292 8733; www.mascotmine. com). Gold was first discovered here in 1904, and during its working life 2.5 million ounces of gold were extracted with an equivalent value of C$1.4 billion. In the early days, miners would make the 2½-hour trek up the mountain, work for 10 hours and then walk down again.

Today's visitors are taken up a tortuous mountain road in the school bus. The route passes two isolated Catholic churches (1850 and 1914) before reaching the mine at 1,462 metres (4,800 ft). Armed with a hard hat and torchlight, you can explore a small section of the 58 km (36 miles) of tunnels and chambers. Restoration of the buildings began in the 1980s, and the remains of the 1,433-metre (4,700-ft) long cableway which carried the ore down for crushing and grinding can be seen.

## Keremeos

Known as "the fruit stand capital of Canada", **Keremeos** ㉓ is a welcoming village in the fertile Similkameen Valley, one of the most productive fruit-, vegetable- and wine-growing areas in North America. To the west of the town, surrounded by orchards, is the **South Similkameen Museum** (604 6th Avenue; July–Aug daily 9am–5pm; www.keremeos.ca), housed in a small white property that was built in 1907 as a police station, law court and jail.

To the east of the town, beside Keremeos Creek stands the old **Grist Mill** (1 Upper Bench Road; daily 9.30am–5pm; tel: 250 499 2888; www.heritage.gov.bc.ca). The water-powered mill was built in 1877 to grind flour and is the last pioneer mill in the province that has kept its original operating machinery and building more or less intact. Restoration has included the reconstruction of an operating water-wheel and flume, and staff have planted wheat behind the mill which is ground on the premises. You can enjoy fresh-baked goodies made from the mill's flour in the tearoom.

## Okanagan: Penticton and Summerland

The Okanagan is the name given to the 240-km (150-mile) long slit in the hills that stretches from the US border at Osoyoos north through Penticton, Summerland and Kelowna to Sicamous. Thanks to water from upland lakes, the fertile area has become the fruit bowl of western Canada – from a single boxcar of apples in 1903 production exploded to 17,000 cars of fruit by 1950.

This picturesque region is now also well known for its wine, and a tour of vineyards might begin in Penticton's **Wine Country Visitor Centre** (553 Railway Street on the corner with Eckhardt Avenue; tel: 250 493 4055; www.penticton.ca). Besides racks of wine from local growers, it has copious amounts of tourist information. *(For more on BC wines and a list of recommended vineyards see page 230.)*

Map on page 180

**TIP**

Just west of Keremeos is the so-called Red Bridge. Built in 1911, it is one of Canada's few remaining covered bridges.

**BELOW:** Kettle Valley steam railway.

In Penticton, at the southern end of Lake Okanagan, sits the largest remaining steel-hulled stern-wheeler in Canada, SS *Sicamous* (daily Mar–mid-June 9am–6pm, mid-June–Aug 9am–9pm; Mon–Fri 10am–4pm Nov–mid-Dec, mid-Jan–Feb; tel: 250 492 0403; www.sssicamous.com). Built in 1914 for the Canadian Pacific Railway (CPR), she combined luxury and utility, carrying passengers, freight and mail on Okanagan Lake until 1936.

**BELOW:** Summerhill Estate Winery, on Lake Okanagan.

**Penticton** is one of the region's larger cities, and it straddles two lakes – small Skaha Lake at the southern end of town and the 135-km (84-mile) long Lake Okanagan at the northern end. It's a popular, amusement-filled family resort, where water sports and golf take centre stage.

On the western shore of Lake Okanagan lies the smaller, more restrained and attractive resort of **Summerland ㉔**. It has some lovely beaches and plenty of opportunities for outdoor activities. One of its best-known attractions is the **Kettle Valley Steam Railway** (two trips a day at 10.30am and 1.30pm, Sat–Mon May–June, Sept–Oct and Thur–Mon July–Aug; tel: 250 494 8422; www.kettlevalleyrail.org), which lies to the west of the town. This 10-km (6-mile) stretch is the only working remnant of what was once one of the world's great railway journeys. The scenic journey takes 1 hour 45 minutes, but the train only runs twice a day a few days a week, so reservations are advisable. Much of the Kettle Valley Railway

has been converted into a 600-km (375-mile) **cycling trail**. Even steep railway gradients are easy on a bike, but it is nonetheless a challenging ride, with some trestles clinging to the sides of Myra Canyon.

The other big attraction is **Summerland Ornamental Gardens** (4200 Highway 97; daily 8am–sunset; tel: 250 494 6385; www.summerlandornamentalgardens.org) just south of the town. The gardens were laid out in 1916 by Agriculture Canada around its two-year-old research station. The provincial government had decided that some horticulture was needed to help smooth the rough edges of the new frontier towns – trees to line the streets, public parks and gardening information for new homeowners. The outdoor laboratory provided a garden demonstration area, with trees, shrubs and flowers, which developed into an English-style garden. Today, this relaxing 6-hectare (15-acre) garden features tree-lined walkways, well-tended lawns and a xeriscape demonstration garden, designed to promote water-conserving landscaping.

## Merritt and the Nicola Valley

Opened as recently as 1991, the Okanagan Connector (97C) links the west bank of Okanagan Lake with Highway 5 and the town of **Merritt ㉕**, self-appointed country-music capital of Canada and host of the July Merritt Mountain Music Festival. This event attracts big names in Country and Western music, whose handprints and signatures are proudly displayed in Merritt's version of Hollywood's Walk of Stars. Headline performers such as Kenny Rogers, Johnny Cash and the Dixie Chicks have become the subject of murals decorating the façades of otherwise bland buildings.

Merritt used to have five coal mines, but the last closed in 1946, giving way to copper mining. **Highland Valley Copper** (tours Mon–Fri; tel: 250 523 3307) offers 2½-hour mine tours around one of the world's largest mining operations. (Children under 12 are excluded on safety grounds.) It's worth calling in for a drink at the restored bar of the 1908 Coldwater Hotel (corner of Quilchena Avenue and Voght Street), with its distinctive four-storey tower and copper dome.

The oldest house in Merritt has been restored and furnished to portray life in the early 20th century. Known as the **Baillie Property** (irregular opening times; tel: 250 370 0349; www.bailliehouse.com), it was built by one Cosom Bigney, who sent to England for a mail-order bride, but on the ship over she met and married someone else, and the disappointed Bigney remained a bachelor. Teas are held on the lawn in the summer months.

The **Nicola Valley Museum** (2202 Jackson Avenue; Mon–Fri 10am–3pm, extended hours in summer; tel: 250 378 4145) traces the development of the Nicola Valley, with displays on mining, ranching, logging, transport, war, religion and medicine, focusing on the terrible 1918 Spanish influenza epidemic.

### The Nicola Valley

One of the loveliest areas near Merritt is the **Nicola Valley ㉖**, reached by Highway 5A. The valley takes its

Map on page 180

*The Okanagan was once home to camels brought in during the gold rush in the hope they would ease the chronic transport problems that beset the goldfields. The animals were still around in the early 20th century.*

**BELOW:** mural in Merritt, country-music capital of Canada.

*It took 30,000 work-
ers 4¹/₂ years to build
the section of railway
between Port Moody
and Kamloops, with
27 tunnels, 600
trestles and bridges at
an average cost per
mile of C$185,000.*

name from an Indian chief named Nicolas Hwistesmetxegen, who had 17 wives. By the road in Upper Nicola is the picturesque white **Murray United Church** (1876), named after the Scottish-born Rev. George Murray, who came out to take over the new parish after graduating from Glasgow University.

Halfway along Nicola Lake is the historic **Quilchena Hotel** (www.quilchena.com), a destination in its own right. Built by Joseph Guichon in 1908 in expectation of a railway that never materialised, the hotel is today run by Guy Rose, the grandson of the founder, and his German wife, Hilde. The three-storey timber building is sheltered by trees and has a traditional general store near by. The hotel has tremendous character with an exceptional restaurant, and offers guided horse-riding over the huge ranch that covers the hills to the south east. (*See also page 245.*)

It is a delightful drive through the meandering valley of the Nicola river to **Spences Bridge** ㉗, where the road meets the Trans-Canada Highway. Along this valley run both the Canadian Pacific and the Canadian National railways, the lines paralleling one another through the Thompson river canyon between Spences Bridge and Lytton, where the Thompson and Fraser rivers converge. It is easy to see why the young New York-born engineer Andrew Onderdonk received so much acclaim for driving the railway through such a narrow and steep-sided defile.

The 40-km (25-mile) canyon is also popular for river-rafting expeditions (*see page 253*), though Simon Fraser saw nothing appealing in this stretch of river, describing it as "the gates of hell…a land where no human being should venture".

The **Yale Airtram** (tel: 604 869 8466; www.hellsgateairtram.com) is a Swiss-made 153-metre (502-ft) cable car linking the upper Cascade Mountains station with the lower station in the Coastal Range. From the cable car you can see the salmon run designed in 1913 to help the fish in their battle upriver to spawn, following a rock slide that obstructed

**BELOW:**
"Hell's gate" air-tram.

## Canada's First Great Train Robbery

At 10pm on an extremely rainy Saturday night, 10 September 1904, at Ruskin, just west of Mission, a CPR train was held up by the notorious Bill Miner gang. They had climbed onto the tender of the locomotive during the stop at Mission City and crawled over the coal to hold up the driver and fireman. They unhooked the train, robbed the safe of a shipment of gold dust valued at C$6,000 and C$914 in cash, and proceeded on the locomotive 5 km (3 miles) further west to Whonnock, where they jumped off, ran down the bank to a hidden boat and rowed across the Fraser river, making good their escape. A week after another train robbery at Kamloops in May 1906, the gang was surrounded near Douglas Lake in the Nicola Valley about 48 km (30 miles) south of Kamloops by a patrol of Mounties. Miner was given life imprisonment but escaped from New Westminster penitentiary after serving one year of his sentence. Rearrested in Georgia following the hold-up of a Southern Railway train in 1911, he again escaped from prison but was recaptured and died in Milledgeville State Prison, Georgia, in 1913 at the age of 70.

Map
on page
180

the channel. At the lower station is a restaurant and exhibition about the life cycle of salmon in one of the world's foremost salmon rivers.

From the Alexandra Bridge pull-over, you can walk down to the old wooden bridge across the turbulent water. The original was completed in 1863 and named after Alexandra, Princess of Wales. The current bridge, dating from 1926, was built using the original abutments.

## Yale

Walking among the few embowered houses of **Yale** ㉘, it is hard to credit that this was once the largest town west of Chicago and north of San Francisco; its tranquil streets belie its former reputation as "the busiest and the worst town in the colony". But during the gold rush of 1858 it was a feverish interchange point between the sternwheelers coming up the Fraser river from the coast, and the pack trains of the Cariboo Wagon Road to the north. The road through the Fraser river canyon was largely wiped out by the construction of the main line of the CPR, which goes

along Yale's main street, and there is a memorial to the 6,000 Chinese who helped build the railway in the grounds of the museum. Yale was the centre of operations for CPR's railway engineer, Andrew Onderdonk *(see page 224),* who set up his machine shops here.

The wood-panelled rooms of the **Yale Museum** (3179 Douglas Street; June–Sept daily 10am–5pm; tel: 604 863 2324) have displays on the town's turbulent history – the gold rush, construction of the CPR and the Chinese community.

Just upriver from Yale and approached by a minor road beside the railway sits **Lady Franklin's Rock**, named after the wife of the Arctic explorer Sir John Franklin, who stopped in Yale in 1861 on his world tour. It was thanks to this enormous lump of rock that Yale flourished during the gold rush years, since it prevented stern-wheelers going further upstream.

## Harrison Hot Springs

Taking Highway 7 south from Hope, the short Highway 9 terminates at

*St John the Divine church in Yale was built with the help of the Royal Engineers in 1862–3 and remained in regular use until 1986.*

**BELOW:**
Quilchena ranch.

**TIP**

The Harrison Hot Springs Resort & Spa has extremely popular weekend dinner dances, making it one of the few places in western BC where ballroom dancers can trip the light fantastic, so booking is strongly advisable at weekends.

**BELOW:**
Minter Gardens.

the major resort of **Harrison Hot Springs** ㉙. Despite being only (15 metres) 50 ft above sea level, the town has an almost Alpine setting, with mountains flanking the waters. Harrison offers fishing, boating, cycling, walking and camping on and around its 64-km (40-mile) lake. Waves can reach 1–1.5 metres (3–5 ft), so care is needed if kayaking.

The area was first settled in the 1850s, after three miners returning from the Cariboo goldfields by canoe stumbled upon the hot springs. In 1873 Joseph Armstrong built a health spa here, but his 1886 bath-house was destroyed by fire in 1905 and never rebuilt. Its remains are close to the vast **Harrison Hot Springs Resort & Spa** *(see page 245)* in a lovely position overlooking the lake.

South from Harrison Hot Springs and just to the north of the Trans-Canada Highway are the manicured **Minter Gardens** (Apr–mid-Oct daily varying hours; tel: 604 794 7191; www.mintergardens.com), 13 hectares (32 acres) of colour and immaculate lawns divided into 11 themed gardens, with an emphasis on roses, rhododendrons, ferns, annuals and floral topiary.

### Kilby Historic Site

Just off Highway 7 is **Kilby Historic Site** ㉚ (11am–5pm early Apr–mid-May, early Sept–early Oct Thur–Mon, mid-May–early Sept daily; tel: 604 796 9576; www.kilby.ca), one of the most attractive of BC's many rural museums. Englishman Thomas Kilby was born in 1868 and emigrated to Canada when he was 16, building the store in 1904.

Its construction is distinctive, with walkways on stilts so that you could visit neighbours without getting your feet wet when the nearby confluence of the Harrison and Fraser rivers caused flooding. The general store was in use until the mid-1970s, when the premises became a museum with the Kilbys staying on as the first curators. It is portrayed as it would have appeared in the 1920s, with every shelf crammed with goods and samples hanging from the ceiling: plumbing and electrical fittings, tools, clothes, china, toys, batteries,

food and even a lending library as well as a post office.

Outside on the farm are cows, pigs, chickens, turkeys, rabbits, goats and sheep. The museum restaurant serves delicious "gently grown" food from local family farms.

At nearby **Kilby Provincial Park**, on the shores of the Fraser river is a lovely sheltered beach, popular with water-skiers and anglers (but too cold for all but hardened swimmers).

## Around Mission

The region between Chilliwack and Agassiz is corn-growing country, and stalls of fresh cobs dot the main roads. North of the Lougheed Highway near Mission the **Stave Falls Power House** ③ (mid-Mar–Oct daily 10am–5pm; tel: 604 462 1222; www.bchydro.com/stavefalls) is another National Historic Site worth visiting. You can see the massive turbines and generators of the hydro-electric dam built in 1912. There are plenty of hands-on exhibits and interactive displays for children to learn how electricity is generated.

Off the Loughheed Highway (Route 7), 3 km (2 miles) east of Mission, **Xá:ytem** ㉜ (Sept–June Mon–Sat 9am–4pm, July–Aug daily 9am–4.30pm; tel: 604 820 9725; www.xaytem.ca) is the site of a large 9,000-year-old village, the oldest known dwelling site in BC, once inhabited by ancestors of today's Stó:lo people. Xá:ytem (pronounced "HAY-tum") covers the remains of this village. The focus is a huge rock considered to have great spiritual power. The Longhouse Museum tells the story behind the thousands of artefacts found here and the people who used them, with an introduction to Salish weaving, cedar bark processing and the properties of plants.

In the hills above Mission lies **Westminster Abbey**, home to a community of Benedictine monks. The concrete structure was completed in 1982 after 28 years' work and has strikingly graduated stained glass in its 64 coloured windows. On a clear day, it's worth taking the gravel path to a viewpoint over the Fraser river towards the south and Mount Baker. ❑

Map on page 180

 **TIP**

Highway 7, also known as the Lougheed Highway, follows the northern bank of the Fraser river all the way back to Vancouver from Hope, via Kent, Mission, Maple Ridge and Coquitlam. It's a more scenic alternative to the four-lane Highway 1, which follows the Fraser river on its south bank.

**BELOW:**
Westminster Abbey.

# RESTAURANTS

## Fort Langley

**Fort Pub & Grill**

Fort Langley Riverside Centre, 9273 Glover Road. Tel: 604 888 6166. Open: B, L & D. $

www.fortpub.com

Overlooking the Fraser tributary, serves pub fare.

**Wendel's Café and Bookshop**

103-9233 Glover Road. Tel: 604 513 2238. Open: B & L. $

www.wendelsonline.com

Serves good home-made soup, salads and pastries within the book store.

## Harrison Hot Springs

**Copper Room**

Harrison Hot Springs Resort. Tel: 800 663 2266. Open: daily D only. $$$

www.harrisonresort.com

For a trip into a bygone era, you could do no better than an evening at the Copper Room, the elegant restaurant at this historic resort. The food is excellent – West Coast contemporary – and the setting is amazing. But best of all is the fabulous dancing and the live orchestra playing danceable tunes. People come from all over the Pacific Northwest to dance here – strictly ballroom – but all of them amateur enthusiasts who know that this is a particularly fine venue to strut their stuff. Fun to participate but seriously fun to watch as well. Dress code applies.

## Harrison River Restaurant

Kilby Historic Site, 215 Kilby Road, Harrison Mills. Tel: 604 796 9576. Open: daily L only. $

www.kilby.ca

An impressive little café/restaurant attached to the museum, done in a 1920s style, featuring home-style cooking, with ingredients sourced from local farms and producers. Everything is good, from the simple sandwiches and quiches to the beef stew, all of it made on the day. Even the lemonade is freshly made and served in an icy jug. Lovely pies and pastries for afternoon tea and friendly service. So good it is worth a detour to have lunch there.

## Hedley

**The Hitching Post Restaurant**

916 Scott Ave. Tel: 250 292 8413. Open: B, L & D Wed–Mon. $

Do not leave Hedley without visiting The Hitching Post for at least a coffee and a pastry. You might feel inclined towards the brunch menu – French toast, eggs Benedict, steak and eggs, and a good selection of pasta dishes, steaks and seafood, provide a reasonable choice for lunch and dinner. Don't go on Tuesdays – they are off playing golf!

## Hope

**Blue Moose Deli and Coffee Bar**

322 Wallace St. Tel: 604 869 0729. Open: B, L & D daily. $

www.bluemoosecafe.com

A great place for a quick lunch with terrific coffee and brilliant sandwiches and soups, the Blue Moose is also a music venue in the evenings, with surprising acts – blues, folk, jazz and traditional music featuring prominently.

**PapAndreas Greek Taverna**

904 Old Hope-Princeton Hwy. Tel: 604 869 7218. $

Greek food in a traditional taverna setting.

**Skinny's Grille and Blues Bar**

63810 Flood Hope Rd. Tel: 604 869 5713. Open: L & D daily. $

www.skinnysgrille.com

Another music venue with food – ribs, steaks, pastas – all of it homemade.

## Manning Park

**Pinewoods Dining Room**

Manning Park Resort, 7500 Hwy 3. Tel: 250 840 8822. Open: B, L & D daily. $$

manningpark.fraservalley.com

Busy both summer and winter, this resort is the only business within the park. The restaurant offers a range of food to satisfy its family-oriented clientele. Large salads, a very nice pork loin and a vast amount of ribs are

tasty choices, and the beer – Okanogan Pale Ale and Sleamann's on draft – is excellent. There are steaks, burgers, mussels and salmon on offer, along with pizzas and sandwiches. You may be lucky enough to see tiny hummingbirds visit the feeders outside – a real treat!

## Merritt and the Nicola Valley

**Coldwater Hotel**

1901 Voght St, Merritt. Tel: 250 378 5711. Open: B, L & D daily. $

www.coldwaterhotel.com

Don't bother about the food in here, simply order a beer at the bar and soak up the atmosphere. Built in 1908, the building looks like something out of a Western movie – you can imagine dusty cowboys rolling into the bar to quench their thirst and raise a little hell.

**Quilchena Hotel and Resort**

Hwy 5A (20 km/12 miles north of Merritt). Tel: 250 378 2611. Open: L & D daily. $$

www.quilchena.com

You are in for a pleasant surprise at the Quilchena. The building remains largely unchanged since its 1908 opening and is surrounded by rolling hills and endless sky. The European-inspired food is prepared by a Swiss chef who uses the best local ingredients to the greatest effect. The beef is superb, as one would expect, given that the Rose family who own this gem also have a very large cattle ranch. The Nicola Valley venison is divine – grilled medallions with a cognac demi-glaze, garnished with candied apple and cranberries. Guy and Hilde Rose champion local wines, and the Burrowing Owl Pinot Noir is impressive. To finish, try the pannacotta with Saskatoon berries, a real treat for those who have never tried this western Canadian berry.

### Smokin' Barrel Steak House

2350 Voght St, Merritt. Tel: 250 378 2256. Open: B, L & D daily. $$

www.smokinbarrelsteakhouse.com

Just as the name suggests, this is a steak house, but it does have a fairly extensive menu aside from steaks. Very friendly service and during the Merritt Country Music Festival, the Smokin' Barrel provides a stage for some top-flight country musicians.

### *Okanagan: Penticton and Summerland*

Penticton actually has over 100 restaurants, although most fall into the category of fast-food, pizza-burger-chicken-type places. Five that seem to have floated to the top of most reviewers' lists are:

### Cellar Door Bistro

17403 Hwy 97, Summerland. Tel: 250 494 0451. Open: L & D, Apr–Oct daily, Nov–Dec, Mar Tues–Sat. $$

www.sumacridge.com

The eating arm of Sumac Ridge Winery, this bistro pairs many of its dishes with the wines produced here, so it's a good way to sample some of their wines before buying. Needless to say, the produce is locally sourced and the cooking accomplished. The estate-made pâté sampler is terrific.

### Granny Bogners

302 Eckhardt Ave West, Penticton. Tel: 250 493 2711. Open: L & D daily. $$

www.grannybogners.com

An eccentric little restaurant with bags of charm and mittel-European cooking, Granny Bogners has an international following. Set in a heritage house with open fires and wooden beams, it is a popular place for special occasions but also attracts a regular clientele drawn by its easy-going atmosphere. It offers what might be thought of as an old-fashioned menu – but in a good way. Granny's beef rouladen with spaetzle and red cabbage, Bavarian schnitzel in mushroom sauce, poached pears and apple fritters are all lovingly and expertly prepared.

### Theo's Restaurant

687 Main St, Penticton. Tel: 250 492 4019. Open: L & D Mon–Sat, D only Sun. $$

www.eatsquid.com

Sit in Theo's courtyard on a hot summer's day and you would swear you were in Greece… and the food is authentic Greek with a New World freshness about it. The chicken livers are a recommended house special, as are the moussaka and lamb shoulder. Good wines.

### Villa Rossa

795 Westminster Ave West, Penticton. Tel: 250 490 9595. Open: L Mon–Fri, D daily. $$

www.thevillarossa.com

A good restaurant with many Italian staples – pastas, risottos, veal – Villa Rossa is also a pretty place to eat, especially in the summer. It makes a virtue of the local wineries and teams up with a number to host autumn wine-festival dinners, pairing the wines of a particular winery with a multi-course dinner.

### Zias Stonehouse Restaurant

14015 Rosedale Ave., Summerland. Tel: 250 494 1105. Open: L & D daily. $$

www.ziasstonehouse.com

Italian-inspired but with a few Pan-Asian touches, this quirky restaurant also boasts an enviable wine cellar – 75 different local wines are on offer, as well as a good selection of European and New World wines.

### PRICE CATEGORIES

Prices for three-course dinner per person with a half-bottle of house wine:
$ = under C$30
$$ = C$30–50
$$$ = C$50–80
$$$$ = more than C$80

**RIGHT:** many of the restaurants in the area champion local wines.

# Wines of British Columbia

It may come as a surprise to some that British Columbia produces world-class wine. Compared to other areas like California, Washington, even Ontario in eastern Canada, production is small, and as much as 90 percent of the province's wine is enthusiastically consumed at home. But BC wines – especially those of the Okanagan Valley – are receiving accolades in the most distinguished circles. A breakthrough came in 1994 when a Chardonnay from the Okanagan Valley's Mission Hill Estate Winery captured the Avery's Trophy for Best Chardonnay at the UK's prestigious International Wine and Spirit Competition.

The real turning point for BC wines took place earlier still. It was prompted by the 1988 Free Trade Agreement, stripping away the protected status enjoyed by Canada's largely moribund wine industry. By 1990, barely 560 hectares (1,400 acres) of vines, primarily premium white varieties, were left in BC after the government paid to have two-thirds of them pulled out. The BC wine industry has reinvented itself over the past 10–15 years. It has happened through steps like the launching of many small-estate wineries,

an influx of talented winemakers, large investments in planting premium varieties, selection of suitable clones and updating equipment and facilities. The Vintners Quality Alliance (VQA) appellation system was established in 1990 to ensure origin and quality of BC-produced wines.

Ninety-five percent of BC's wine is produced in the Okanagan Valley, a region of distinct microclimates and diverse soil types, stretching over 160 km (100 miles) from north of Lake Okanagan to the US border. Nestled between mountain and lakes, the region now has more than 2,000 hectares (5,000 acres) dedicated to grape growing, and is undergoing rapid expansion. There are now over 80 wineries in the Okanagan Valley compared to 13 before Free Trade, and 125 in BC. They range from exclusive boutique wineries to large-scale operations, and offer a range of fine wines – with Merlot and Chardonnay leading the pack.

How can a region so far north produce such great wines? Start with near-desert conditions, more so in the south. Add hot, dry summers with long hours of sunlight, and lengthy hang time in the autumn. Of course, the moderating influence of the lake and the protection of the mountains help. Pick a suitable location, a cliff or a hillside, irrigate sufficiently, and healthy grapes are certain.

Touring the Okanagan Valley from the hot, arid south to the wetter, cooler north:

**Osoyoos**: Nk'Mip Cellars, North America's first aboriginal winery, produces superlative Merlot, Chardonnay and Icewine.

**Oliver**: In this area, reds and whites are produced with bright, intense fruit flavours. Much-awarded Tinhorn Creek Winery offers outstanding Merlot. Inniskillin Okanagan Vineyards is a small-scale winery which produces big reds (Zinfandel, Malbec, Cabernet Sauvignon). Chardonnay and Pinot Noir are stars at Golden Mile Cellars. At Burrowing Owl Estate Winery, succulent fruit is the hallmark of their Syrah, Merlot and Chardonnay.

**Okanagan Falls**: Blue Mountain Vineyard & Cellars is an impeccable producer of Pinot Noir and sparkling wine. Hawthorne Mountain Vineyards, at 536 metres (1,760 ft), is the highest elevation winery in the South Okanagan.

**Naramata Bench**: Over 20 wineries dot winding roads and picturesque rural countryside. Begin at larger Red Rooster and artisanal La Frenz, close to Penticton, and finish at Syrah specialist Nichol Vineyard and cliff-hugging Kettle Valley.

**Summerland**: Sumac Ridge offers superb wines and stellar dining.

**Westside**: Two must-see wineries are on the slopes of Mount Boucherie. Unveiled in 2003, Mission Hill's grand mission style winery with a 12-storey bell tower sits dramatically above Lake Okanagan. Quails' Gate, a highly regarded medium-sized winery surrounded by sweeping vineyards, features the elegant Old Vines Patio & Restaurant.

**Kelowna**: The first vines in the Okanagan Valley were planted in Kelowna by Father Pandosy, who established a mission in 1859. BC's oldest continuously operating winery, Calona Vineyards, produces premium wines under the "Sandhill Vineyard" label. One of Okanagan's most acclaimed wineries, Cedar Creek offers brilliantly crafted wines. A champion of organic grape growing, Summerhill Pyramid Winery practises what it preaches both in the winery and at the Summerhill Sunset Bistro with innovative organic cuisine.

**North Okanagan**: Gray Monk produces exceptional Odyssey wines. Larch Hills grows such early-ripening varieties as Ortega, Siegerebe and Madeleine Angevine.

**Similkameen Valley**: West of the Okanagan Valley, this narrow stretch of lowland is lined with tall mountains on both sides. Crowsnest Vineyards features intensely fresh, fruity whites and good reds, a traditional Bavarian-style restaurant, and a soon-to-open inn. Herder Winery & Vineyards turns heads with its awesome Merlot and Chardonnay. Recently opened Orofino Vineyards produces impressive wines, including a sumptuous Pinot Noir, from mature vines.

**Vancouver**: Next door to the bustling West Coast city, the fertile, flat Fraser valley is generally cool and humid. The largest winery, Domaine de Charton, produces Germanic whites, Chardonnay and Pinot Noir from home-grown grapes and classic reds from Okanagan fruit. The winery's Bacchus Bistro specialises in farm-fresh ingredients.

**The Gulf Islands**: Peppering the Strait of Georgia, these pastoral islands are an exciting new region for viticulture. At Garry Oaks Vineyard on Salt Spring Island, estate-grown Pinot Gris and Pinot Noir are highlights. Island-grown Pinot Gris and Okanagan-supplied Merlot are the flagship wines at recently opened Salt Spring Vineyards.

**Vancouver Island**: Most wineries are in the Cowichan Valley, close to Duncan. Venturi-Shulze is one of BC's most celebrated boutique wineries. Blue Grouse features precision-crafted wines from Bacchus, Pinot Gris and Black Muscat grapes. Alderlea makes distinctive wines from Bacchus, Auxerrois, Pinot Noir and Maréchal Foch.

Wine festivals take place in BC throughout the year, one of the most famous being the **Okanagan Fall Wine Festival**, which takes place all through the Valley in early autumn.

## Useful websites:

www.winesnw.com
www.winesofcanada.com
www.winegrowers.bc.ca
www.winesofbc.ca
www.bcwine.ca

---

**LEFT:** Quail's Gate Vineyard, Okanagan Lake.
**RIGHT:** Merlot and Chardonnay lead the pack.

# **T**RANSPORT

## **GETTING THERE AND GETTING AROUND**

### **GETTING THERE**

Unless you are already in North America, the only way to get to Vancouver is to fly there, although some visitors from Europe fly to Toronto and take the train across Canada *(see below)*, which is an experience in itself.

### **By air**

Vancouver International Airport (tel: 604 207 7077; www.yvr.ca) is extremely well served by international and national flights, partly because it is a long way from even the nearest Canadian city of comparable size. Flying time from London is 9 hours, New York 5 hours 15 minutes, Sydney 18 hours and Cape Town 21 hours via London. The airport is 22 km (14 miles) south of the city centre and well linked by frequent buses and (from late 2009) SkyTrain. The most expensive times of year to fly are over Christmas and during the peak holiday season from late June to early September. Apart from the national airlines, a number of smaller airlines operate services from Britain.

Some UK specialist tour operators offer extremely competitive prices on flights and holidays. Canadian Affair, the UK's largest tour operator to Canada, has a range of fares lower than those offered by the national carriers, with flights from London Gatwick, Manchester and Glasgow through its own airline, Air Transat. It also offers remarkably good deals on Club Class. Low-cost airline Zoom flies to Vancouver from London Gatwick, Cardiff, Manchester, Glasgow and Belfast.

### **Internal flights**

In addition to Air Canada, West-Jet offers low-cost flights between Vancouver and Edmonton, Calgary, Winnipeg, Montreal and Toronto. Though it is a pity to miss the lovely ferry journeys between Tsawwassen and Vancouver Island or the Gulf Islands, there are floatplane flights from Vancouver Seaplane Terminal on Coal Harbour to Victoria and Nanaimo, and air services along the coast.

### **By train**

By far the most attractive way to reach Vancouver is by train from Toronto (with the added bonus of reducing your carbon footprint by minimising air travel). Operated by **VIA** (www.viarail.com), *The Canadian* takes three days to cross the continent, leaving Toronto on Tuesday, Thursday and Saturday and returning from Vancouver on Friday, Sunday and Tuesday. It has various classes of sleeping accommodation, dining, dome and observation cars, and some of the station stops are long enough to allow a leisurely walk along the platform while the train is restocked and the windows

### **AIRLINES AND TOUR OPERATORS**

**Air Canada**, tel: 0871 220 1111; www.aircanada.com
**Air Transat**, tel: 0800 2838 7673; www.airtransat.co.uk
**British Airways**, tel: 0870 850 9850; www.ba.com
**Canadian Affair**, tel: 020 7616 9999 or 0141 248 6777; www.canadianaffair.com
**Harbour Air Seaplanes**, tel: 1 800 665 0212

(from North America only); www.harbourair.ca
**Pacific Coastal Airlines**, tel: 1 800 663 2872 (from North America only); www.pacificcoastal.com
**WestJet**, tel: 1 888 937 8538 (from North America only); www.westjet.com
**Zoom**, tel: 0870 240 0055; www.flyzoom.co.uk

cleaned. The train even slows past scenic attractions such as waterfalls. Bookings can be made in the UK through: **Ffestiniog Travel** (tel: 01766 512400; www.festtravel.co.uk), **Great Rail Journeys Ltd** (tel: 01904 521900; www.greatrail.com) and the **Railway Touring Company** (tel: 01553 661500; www.railwaytouring.co.uk). *The Canadian* arrives at Pacific Central station (shared with Rocky Mountaineer Vacations), a fine building but not in a part of the city that could be described as fashionable. Main Street Science World SkyTrain station is a few minutes' walk across a formal garden, and there are always taxis to meet trains.

If you are travelling from the US, the railway between Seattle and Vancouver is a particularly scenic way of arriving. The line runs for over 80 km (50 miles) along Puget Sound, with cliffs above in places, crossing rivers by a series of swing- and drawbridges. The daily *American Cascades* train from Seattle is operated by **Amtrak** (tel: 1 800 872 7245 from North America only; www.amtrak.com). Bookings from the UK can be made through Ffestiniog Travel *(see above)*.

## By coach

The south side of Pacific Central railway station at 200-1150 Station Street is the coach terminal for mainland and island services. Services from Seattle are operated by **Greyhound (US)** (tel: 1 800 231 2222; www.greyhound.com), a different company from Greyhound Canada *(see page 234)*.

# GETTING AROUND

## The airport

**The Airporter** (tel: 604 946 8866; www.yvrairporter.com) bus runs every half-hour from 7.55am to 9.55pm and serves the downdown area, stopping off

at 23 pick-up/set-down points at or near principal hotels. There is also a direct bus direct to Whistler *(see page 234)*.

## By train

The most popular trains out of Vancouver are the double-deck dome car trains run by **Rocky Mountaineer Vacations** (tel: 01622 832244; www.rockymountaineer.com), which operates over three principal routes with numerous permutations. The Yellowhead and Kicking Horse routes both entail a two-day journey from Vancouver with a night in a hotel in Kamloops in the Rockies; the former takes the Canadian National route to Jasper while the latter uses the more southerly Canadian Pacific line to Banff and Calgary in Alberta.

Introduced in 2006, the Fraser Discovery Route provides an end-on link with the daily **Whistler Mountaineer** (tel: 604 606 8460; www.whistlermountaineer.com) between North Vancouver and Whistler, for a two-day journey north through the Cariboo region to Prince George, overnighting in Quesnel. It then turns southeast along North America's longest valley, the Rocky Mountain Trench, and past Mount Robson, the highest peak in the Canadian Rockies at 3,954 metres (12,972 ft), to Jasper. All three routes offer different landscapes but a uniformly high standard of comfort and cuisine, with accommodation in GoldLeaf, offering dome cars and dining room below, or RedLeaf with picture windows and at-seat service. Rocky Mountaineer trains operate from April to mid-October, with some special trains over the Christmas period. The Fraser Discovery Route allows a circular tour through the best of the Rockies, taking in the Columbia Icefield between Jasper and Banff, returning to Vancouver via Kamloops.

From Monday to Friday during commuter hours the **West Coast Express** (tel: 604 488 8906; www.westcoastexpress.com) links

downtown Waterfront station in Vancouver with Port Moody, Coquitlam Central, Port Coquitlam, Pitt Meadows, Maple Meadows, Port Haney and Mission.

## Public transport – TransLink

Public transport in Vancouver is the responsibility of **TransLink** (tel: 604 953 3333; www.translink.bc.ca), which also looks after the road network and facilities for cyclists. It operates SkyTrain, SeaBus and the buses, and tickets are integrated across modes and valid for 90 minutes. The city is divided into three zones for the purposes of fares, and single tickets can be bought for one-, two- or three-zone travel. Maps are displayed at bus stops and on a free leaflet, "Getting Around", which gives advice on all TransLink services. Buy tickets only from vending machines or on the bus, and beware of anyone not in uniform offering to help you buy a ticket. If you buy on the bus, you need to have the exact fare, as no change is given. It is much easier and cheaper to buy books of tickets, or day passes covering all zones, from Fare-Dealer outlets; these include Safeways, 7-Elevens, Mac's, Shoppers Drug Marts, some London Drugs, and some newsstands and convenience stores.

## SeaBus

These double-ended catamarans seating 400 passengers ply between Waterfront and Lonsdale Quay in North Vancouver, taking 12 minutes. The two SeaBuses (tel: 604 986 1501; www.translink.bc.ca) each make the crossing more than 40,000 times a year. For most of the day on weekdays and Saturdays they operate every 15 minutes until between 6–7pm, when it becomes every 30 minutes, as on Sundays. From Waterfront, the first service on Mon–Sat is 6.16am, on Sun 8.16am; the last on Mon–Sat is 12.46am, on

**TRANSPORT**

**ACCOMMODATION**

**ACTIVITIES**

**A – Z**

**LANGUAGE**

Sun 11.16pm. From Lonsdale Quay, the first service on Mon–Sat is 6.02am, on Sun 8.02am; the last on Mon–Sat is 12.32am, on Sun 11.02pm.

## False Creek ferries

Two companies operate small electric ferryboats which scuttle like water-boatmen around a series of piers in False Creek and nearby English Bay, linking up various tourist attractions. They behave like buses, so no reservations are necessary. **AquaBus** (tel: 604 689 5858; www.aquabus.bc.ca) has nine ferries, and its Cyquabuses accept bi-cycles. **False Creek Ferries** (tel: 604 684 7781; www.granvilleisland ferries.bc.ca) has ten vessels serving seven points, including Vanier Park for its three museums, and also operates tours.

## SkyTrain

**SkyTrain** (tel: 604 953 3333; www.translink.bc.ca) is the metro network which pioneered driverless technology. There are currently two SkyTrain lines: the 28-km (18-mile) Expo line which runs from Waterfront to King George in 39 minutes, and the 19-km (12-mile) Millennium line from Commercial Drive station to Columbia, which takes 25 minutes. A third from Waterfront to the airport and to Richmond is due to open in November 2009, and the Evergreen line from Lougheed Town Centre to

Douglas College is due to open in 2011. SkyTrain carries over 70 million people a year, and some of the stations have won design awards. The newer trains have a seat right at the front, where a driver would normally sit, for which kids (and not a few adults) make a beeline.

**SkyTours** (tel: 604 331 0617; www.skytour.ca) offers an audio tour of SkyTrain using commentary, dramatised dialogue, music and sound effects. It's a good way to learn a lot about Vancouver and BC in a short time. The headsets are available from a desk at Waterfront station (May–Aug Mon–Fri 9am–7pm, Sat 9am–8pm, Sun 9am–6pm, Sept–Apr daily 9am–4pm).

## Coaches

**Greyhound Lines** (tel: 604 482 8746 or 1 800 661 8747; www.greyhound.ca) operates services between Vancouver and many cities and towns in Canada. **Pacific Coach Lines** (tel: 604 662 7575; www.pacificcoach.com) operates scheduled services between Vancouver (downtown and airport) and Victoria. The **Whistler Express Bus** (tel: 604 266 5386; www.perimeterbus.com) runs about seven buses a day; some are an express service from the airport, others serve specified downtown hotels. As its name implies, **Island Link Shuttle Bus** (tel: 250 726 7790; www.longbeachlink.com) links east Vancouver Island communities with the Pacific Rim.

Pick-up and drop-off charters, tours and bus services are available. To reach the west coast of Vancouver Island, the **Tofino Bus Company** (tel: 250 725 2871; www.tofinobus.com) offers regular shuttles between Victoria and Tofino from May to October. They leave Victoria in the morning, drive to Tofino, and drive back to Victoria in the same day.

## Sightseeing buses

The **Vancouver Trolley Company** (tel: 604 801 5515; www.vancouver trolley.com) offers various tours aboard its trolleys, which are designed to look like Vancouver's old streetcars. Tours run daily from mid-March to the end of October every 30 minutes, and every 60 minutes the remainder of the year, from 15 stops around Vancouver, including halts at some of the major downtown hotels. No reservations are required. After visiting one attraction, you can hop on again to another stop. **Grey Line** (tel: 1 800 667 0882 from North America only; www.greyline.com) operates a double-decker bus on a 21-stop, two-hour circuit with full driver commentary between mid-April and September.

## Horse-drawn tours

**Stanley Park Horse-Drawn Tours** (tel: 604 681 5115; www.stanley park.com/shuttlebus) operates one-hour tours, with commentary, in covered vehicles between March and October. A variety of elegant horse-drawn carriages is also available for private hire.

Carriage tours lasting for 15–90 minutes around Victoria are available from **Victoria Carriage Tours** (tel: 250 383 2207; www.victoriacarriage.com).

## Cycling

Both Vancouver and Victoria are great cities for exploring by bike, though the capital has more segregated bike routes than Vancouver, if you ignore the seawall. Vancouver produces a free Bicycle Route Map (available at bike shops) showing bike paths and the streets recommended as cycle routes. Bikes are carried free of charge on SkyTrain, SeaBus and those buses that have a front-mounted rack capable of holding two bikes. Bikes are not allowed on SkyTrains until 9am, nor between 4–6pm. Helmets are mandatory in BC. A **City by Cycle** (tel: 604 730 1032; www.citybycycle.com) tour within the competence of anyone remotely fit takes you on a guided tour of Vancouver packed with history, points of interest and some of the most popular attractions. Riders meet at 9am or 2pm each day and set off for a four-hour tour that takes in the seawall, Stanley Park, English Bay, Granville Island by water taxi, Yaletown, Chinatown and Gastown. **Go Time** (tel: 1 800 599 6800 from North America only; www.gotimeevents.com) also runs custom group cycle tours of the Seymour Demonstration Forest, the University of British Columbia and Pacific Spirit Park, and Steveston fishing village.

## By car

Public transport outside the city is limited, so if you want to explore some of the remoter or smaller places in BC, many visitors have

little choice but to hire a car. The principal car-hire companies are represented at Vancouver airport, but it's unwise to pitch up without reserving a car. You can also get better deals online. For example, **Budget** (0844 581 9999; www.budget.com) offers car hire from Vancouver International Airport with unlimited mileage when pre-paid online. Some companies, such as **Discount Car Rental** (tel: 604 207 8180; www.discountcar.com), offer hybrid vehicles to reduce carbon emissions. Remember to return the car with a full tank or face a hefty premium per litre; there is a petrol station on the airport approach road on the left-hand side.

Seatbelts must be worn by drivers and passengers, and children under five must use an approved safety seat. Speed signs are posted in kilometres per hour. You may turn right at a red light after making a full stop, unless signs indicate otherwise. Parking is, as you would expect for a city centre, expensive and at times hard to find. Expect to pay $6–16 per day for parking in a multi-storey (parkade). Parking meters are in effect daily 9am–8pm. Many of the streets become no-parking zones during rush hour. Signposting in Canada leaves much to be desired, so care is needed. Tourist sights are usually indicated by a blue sign.

## Ferries

**BC Ferries** (tel: 250 386 3431; www.bcferries.com) operates 35 vessels serving 47 ports of call along the BC coastline, probably one of the most consistently beautiful in the world. Reservations can be made for ferries between the mainland and Vancouver Island, the Gulf Islands and Queen Charlotte Island and are strongly recommended (essential for some routes) in high season and at weekends to avoid the risk of long waits. Where reservations cannot be made, arrival at the ferry terminal at least 30 minutes before departure is advised during busy periods.

## River Boats

You can retrace the steps of BC's pioneers by taking a replica sternwheeler along the Fraser river from New Westminster Quay, on either day cruises upriver to Fort Langley or downstream to the mouth of the river at Steveston. Evening dinner and dance, lunch and BBQ cruises are also operated. **Paddlewheeler Riverboat Tours** is at 810 Quayside Drive (tel: 604 525 4465; www.vancouverpaddlewheeler.com).

One of the most remarkable boat journeys in BC is the service operated from Port Alberni to places in Barkley Sound by **Lady Rose Marine Services** (tel: 250 723 8313; www.ladyrosemarine.com). Passengers can visit the wheelhouse and engine room when in open water, and the 11-hour round journey gives plenty of time to absorb the beauty and atmosphere of this remote part of BC.

## BIKE RENTALS

**Cambie Cycle**, 3317 Cambie Street. Tel: 604 874 3616; www.cambiecycle.com
**J.V. Bikes Sales & Rentals**, 1387 Richards Street. Tel: 604 694 2453; www.jvbike.com
**Reckless Bike Stores**, 1810 Fir Street. Tel: 604 731 2420; www.reckless.ca. The closest rental to Granville Market and the bike path around Vanier Park and Kitsilano.
**Simon's Bike Shop**, 608 Robson Street. Tel: 604 602 1181; www.simonsbikeshop.com

**Spokes**, 1798 West Georgia Street. Tel: 604 688 5141; www.vancouverbikerental.com. Stanley Park rentals.

### Victoria

**Bicycle Rentals**, 800 Tyee Road. Tel: 250 383 1466; www.switchbridgetours.com. Also offer bike tours of Cowichan wineries and the Galloping Goose Trail.
**Cycle Treks**, 450 Swift Street. Tel: 250 386 2277; www.cycletreks.com. Day or longer guided tours around Victoria.

## Boat rentals

Power boats can be hired to explore Burrard Inlet from **Coal Harbour Boat Rentals** (tel: 604 682 6257), just east of the Cardero restaurant and Westin Bayshore Hotel. No licence is required, and instruction is given for the boats' simple operation.

# **A**CCOMMODATION

## WHERE TO STAY

### HOTELS

Vancouver and BC are generously provided with hotels to suit all pockets, but inevitably there are relatively few hotels that derive their character from the building itself; the young age of so many buildings means that they rely on imaginative interior design to strike an individual note. The overwhelming majority of Vancouver hotels are in the downtown core and have a large number of rooms; there are few boutique- or loft-style hotels, but that is beginning to change with the obvious success and appeal of the Opus Hotel. Few establishments are quintessentially Canadian or even North American, having adopted the global hotel look.

It can get pretty hot in the summer so air conditioning is welcome. It is unusual to find a good hotel or B&B that allows smoking in more than a handful of rooms, if at all, and hefty room cleaning charges are often levied if you ignore the ban.

In terms of location, there is little point in staying in North Vancouver unless you are going to do a lot of walking on the many North Shore trails or take to a kayak on Indian Arm. Traffic over the Lions Gate Bridge is chronically congested in the rush hours, but the SeaCat crossing is short and delivers you downtown.

### Timing and booking

Winter weather in Vancouver is notoriously suited to ducks, so room rates in many hotels are substantially lower during these months, though the number of people staying en route to the slopes of Whistler is growing. From Easter onwards, tourism in the city builds to the busiest months of July and August when it would be unwise to arrive without a reservation. However, if you do, the Tourist Infocentre (tel: 604 683 2000; www.tourismvancouver.com) offers a free accommodation reservation service and on-line listings.

### Cost and quality

The listings given here are subdivided into the following categories, for a standard double room per night: Luxury: over C$250 per night; Expensive: C$175–250; Moderate: C$100–175 and Budget: under C$100. These can only be an approximate guide because many hotels have half a dozen or more categories of room and very few hotels do not discount their room rates, according either to the time of year or the day of the week. Discounts are also sometimes offered for stays of a week and longer.

Bed and breakfasts are not necessarily a cheap option but they can obviously provide a much more individual experience and many are of a very high standard, with rooms on a par with four- and five-star hotels. Reservation services include: Canada-West Accommodations (tel: 604 990 6730); Old English B&B Registry (tel: 604 986 5069; www.bandbinn.com); and, on Vancouver Island, AA-Accommodations West (tel: 250 479 1986).

If you're after cheap accommodation, bear in mind that the quality of some of the hostels is so high that they may be preferable to the cheaper hotel. There are hostels offering accommodation for as little as $20 a night. The more expensive the hotel, the less likely you are to have breakfast included in the price.

Tourist accommodation is subject to an 8 percent provincial hotel and motel room tax and a General Sales Tax (GST) of 6 percent. An additional 2 percent tourist tax may be levied where it has been approved. Campgrounds and houseboats are exempt.

## A PLACE OF YOUR OWN

One of the largest collections of serviced suites is the **Landis** (tel: 604 681 3555; www.landissuitesvancouver.com), at 1200 Hornby Street, which offers two-bedroom suites with living-room and kitchen in a modern tower. Three sizes are available: 74 square metres (800 square feet); 93 square metres (1,000 square feet); and the 143-square-metre (1,450-square-feet) penthouse suite. Bathrooms and kitchens are top of the range, and there is a fitness centre, indoor swimming pool and Jacuzzi. With very similar style and facilities, the **Rosedale on Robson** (tel: 604 689 8033; www.rosedaleonrobson. com), at 838 Hamilton Street, offers the city's newest all-suite apartments and is closer to Yaletown. At 1361 Robson Street, **Tropicana Suite Hotel** (tel: 604 687 6631; www.tropicana.ivancouver. com) has 74 one-bedroom suites. The small ads in the *Vancouver Sun* contain rooms and apartments for rent, though usually for longer stays.

In Victoria there are some balconied waterside suites on the Gorge waterway, close to downtown, operated by **Comfort Inn & Suites** (tel: 250 388 7861; www.comfortinnvictoria.com), which has a large outdoor heated pool. The **Royal Scot Suite Hotel** (tel: 250 388 5463; www.royalscot.com) has 176 rooms and suites close to the Inner Harbour at 425 Quebec Street; it has an exercise room, billiard room and indoor pool as well as restaurant.

## HOSTELS

**Hostelling International** (www.hihostels.ca) maintains high standards in its Canada-wide hostels and has three in Vancouver, with private rooms and four-bed dorms, some in bunks and with en suite facilities, TV and air conditioning. There's a backpackers' bar, kitchen, free internet access and coin-operated laundry; linen is provided, guests have a secure locker and there is bike storage and hire. The Downtown hostel is at 1114 Burnaby Street (tel: 604 684 4565); the Central is also very close to the heart of the city at 1025 Granville Street (tel: 604 685 5335); and for those more interested in being a beach bum, there's one right by Jericho Beach at 1515 Discovery Street (tel: 604 224 3208). The air-conditioned **YMCA Hotel** (tel: 604 895 5830; www.ymcahotel.com) at 733 Beatty Street was built in 1995 and has a choice of room standards in this well-located, safe high rise with indoor pool, gym, sauna and whirlpool. From early May to late August, UBC opens up student accommodation at the **Vanier Hostel** (tel: 604 822 1000; www.conferences.ubc.ca). While it's a long way from the city centre, it is safe, clean and quiet accommodation and confers access to the university's tennis courts, fitness facilities and indoor and outdoor pools. There are frequent buses, as well as several nearby beaches.

Avoid the district between Gastown and Chinatown; the cheap "hotels" in this area are largely inhabited by permanent "residents" of an unsavoury character.

There's also a HI hostel in Whistler at 5678 Alta Lake Road (tel: 604 932 5492), which even has a sauna and kayak rentals.

On Vancouver Island, Hostelling International operates a converted heritage building close to the waterfront (516 Yates Street; tel: 250 385 4511). Further up the island is the **Nanaimo International Hostel** (65 Nicol Street; tel: 250 753 1188).

## CAMPSITES

There is a complete dearth of campsites in or near the city centre, and crashing out in one of the parks is not an option, as you would soon learn from the police. However, in BC there are some spectacularly sited campsites, many in the provincial parks, in which about 3 million people camp each year. They are at their busiest in July and August, when reservations are vital at the most popular. The best way to access the park list and their details is through the parks' website (www.bcparks.ca) which links to a booking system.

For non-provincial sites, www.camping.bc.ca is a well-constructed site which provides a database, searchable by area and type, giving opening dates and a rate guide with a link to the campsite wherever possible. Less user-friendly is www.bc-camping.com which devotes large amounts of space to extraneous information.

The Gulf Islands have some of the most scenic campsites, such as Ruckle Provincial Park on Salt Spring, but it and some others do not accept bookings, so it is advisable to get there early and have a Plan B if you find it full, particularly on the quieter islands where the last ferry of the day may leave little time for alternatives.

**BELOW:** the Pan Pacific Hotel offers spectacular uninterrupted views.

# GASTOWN, CHINATOWN AND YALETOWN

### Luxury

**Westin Grand**
433 Robson Street
Tel: 604 602 1999
www.westingrandvancouver.com
The management at this centrally located boutique apartment hotel boasts about the superior quality of its beds and bathrooms, and that it "provides a suite for the price of a room". It has an outdoor pool and the Aria restaurant.

### Expensive

**Moda**
900 Seymour Street
Tel: 604 683 4251
www.modahotel.ca
The recently rebuilt 1908 Dufferin Hotel combines traditional style with contemporary design. Each of the 57 elegant rooms is provided with luxurious beds and linen, flat-screen TVs and high-speed internet access.

**Opus Hotel**
322 Davie Street
Tel: 604 642 6787
Toll Free: 1 866 642 6787
www.opushotel.com
Called one of Vancouver's coolest hangouts by *Wallpaper* magazine and voted one of the world's top 100 hotels by *Condé Nast Traveler*, the very gay-friendly Opus Hotel is the city's hippest boutique hotel. Situated in Yaletown, the hotel's bar and Elixir French bistro are popular with an international crowd and celebrities.

### Moderate

**St Regis Hotel**
602 Dunsmuir Street
Tel: 604 681 1135
www.stregishotel.com
One of the city's heritage hotels, St Regis was built in 1916 but there's nothing very historic about the interior. The area developed around the hotel and

it's no longer the best part of town, though it's not intimidating. Suites are air conditioned and booking a room confers free use of an off-site fitness centre.

**Kingston Hotel**
757 Richard Street
Tel: 604 684 9024
www.kingstonhotelvancouver.com
Describing itself as "Vancouver's first and finest European-style bed and breakfast hotel", this place has a warm atmosphere and is well located for downtown. Only some of the 55 small rooms are en suite. There's a sauna (unusual in hotels in this price category), and continental breakfast is included.

### Inexpensive

**Urban Hideway**
581 Richards Street
www.urban-hideaway.com
This rare downtown guesthouse was built in 1896 for travellers

heading for the wilderness. It's still a popular backpackers haunt, drawing a young clientele who enjoy the quirkiness and don't mind communal facilities. Bikes are loaned free of charge.

**Victorian Hotel**
514 Homer Street
Tel: 604 681 6369
www.victorian-hotel.com
This is unique downtown: an historic 1898 bay-windowed building constructed as a guest house, which has been sensitively restored to create a most attractive family-run hotel with hardwood floors, decorative mouldings and high ceilings. Not all the bedrooms have en suite bathrooms.

# GRANVILLE ISLAND AND WEST SIDE

### Expensive

**Granville Island**
1253 Johnston Street
Tel: 604 683 7373
www.granvilleislandhotel.com

### PRICE CATEGORIES

Guide prices for a standard double room in high season:
**Luxury:** more than C$250
**Expensive:** C$175–250
**Moderate:** C$100–175
**Inexpensive:** under C$100

In a lovely, quiet position overlooking False Creek, the luxurious boutique hotel has its own garden and terrace beside the water. Rooms with generous glazing are furnished with reproduction antique furniture, and oriental rugs in some rooms. Small spa and complimentary high-speed internet. It even has its own microbrewery.

### Moderate

**Maple House B&B**
1533 Maple Street
Tel: 604 739 5833
www.maplehouse.com
Rooms with en suite and shared bathrooms are available in this blue-shingled heritage house close to Kits Beach and Vanier Park.

**Mickey's Kits Beach Chalet**
2142 First Avenue West at Yew
Tel: 604 739 3342

www.mickeysbandb.com
Three pretty rooms are available in this quiet house just two blocks from the beach. Friendly and good value.

TRANSPORT

# EAST VANCOUVER

### Expensive

**Hilton Vancouver Metrotown**
6083 McKay Avenue, Burnaby
Tel: 604 438 1200
www.hiltonvancouver.com
Shopaholics may wish to rest up in this 283-roomed luxurious hotel at the vast shopping centre, which is a 15-minute SkyTrain ride to downtown.

**Inn at Westminster Quay**
900 Quayside Drive
New Westminster
Tel: 604 520 1776
www.innatthequay.com
Strikingly designed hotel standing on pillars over the quay and river. Free internet. Fitness centre, whirlpool and sauna.

### Moderate

**Best Western Coquitlam Inn**
319 North Road, Coquitlam
Tel: 604 931 9011
www.bestwesterncoqinn.com
feature wood floors, tall

Close to the SkyTrain station, this 106-roomed hotel has two restaurants, indoor pool, Jacuzzi, sauna and an indoor tropical garden. Free high-speed internet. Good value.

### Inexpensive

**The Met**
411 Columbia Street
New Westminster
Tel: 604 520 3815
www.themethotel.com
Built in 1892 by the

ancestors of the actor Raymond Burr, this renovated 26-room hotel has high ceilings and basic amenities. Close to SkyTrain. It's on a busy street so ask for a quiet room.

# SOUTH VANCOUVER

### Moderate

**Abercrombie House Bed & Breakfast**
13333 Princess Street
Richmond
Tel: 604 272 1184
www.abercrombiehouse.ca
This Craftsman-style house is peacefully situated on the South Dyke overlooking the Fraser river near Steveston. The three guest rooms

ceilings, original decorative mouldings and private bathrooms with heated tile floors. There is a yoga/meditation room, and high-speed internet is available.

**The Coast Tsawwassen Inn**
1665 56th Street, Delta
Tel: 604 943 8221
www.tsawwasseninn.com
Close to the ferry

terminal, this hotel with 90 suites and large rooms, has a heated indoor pool, hot tub and sauna.

### Inexpensive

**Days Inn Vancouver Airport**
2840 Sexsmith Road
Richmond
Tel: 604 207 8000
www.daysinn.ca

Ideal place for early flights, with complimentary shuttle to airport and breakfast. Close to Tsawwassen ferries.

# NORTH AND WEST VANCOUVER

### Expensive

**Lonsdale Quay**
123 Carrie Cates Court
Tel: 604 986 6111
www.lonsdalequayhotel.com
The views over Burrard Inlet to downtown Vancouver are what sell this water-side, modern hotel, which is accessed by escalators from Lonsdale Market. Good sized rooms.

### Moderate

**Park Royal**
540 Clyde Avenue
Tel: 604 926 5511
www.parkroyalhotel.com
Situated on the Capilano River (but also close to a huge shopping centre), this ivy-covered faux timber-framed hotel with 30 rooms has an English-style pub and restaurant.

### Inexpensive

**Lynn Canyon B&B**
3333 Robinson Road
Tel: 604 986 4741
www.vancouverinn.com
This bed-and-breakfast is an ideal base for walking in lovely Lynn Canyon Park nearby. With a timber frame and in a wooded setting, the house has two en suite bedrooms

with hot tubs and open fires. Outside is a pool and hot tub surrounded by cedar forest. Good value.

# VICTORIA AND VANCOUVER ISLAND

## Luxury

### The Fairmont Empress
721 Government Street
Victoria
Tel: 250 384 8111
www.fairmont.com
This stately hotel is an iconic landmark in the city. The late Victorian building occupies a prime spot overlooking the Inner Harbour and Parliament buildings. Its public rooms retain a colonial atmosphere and its 476 bedrooms (all of which are different) offer every comfort. Indian cuisine is served in the atmospheric Bengal Lounge, and Sunday brunch among the Lloyd Loom chairs at Kipling's has become popular, but it is afternoon tea in the vast "tea lobby" that has been an institution for the better part of a century. Today, however, the clientele is almost entirely tourist. The C$6 million spa, open 8am–9pm, has 12 treatment rooms. There is also a heated indoor pool, whirlpool and gym.

### Long Beach Lodge Resort
1441 Pacific Rim Highway
Tel: 250 725 2442
www.longbeachlodgeresort.com
In a great location overlooking the sea, the hotel offers rooms in the lodge or self-contained two-roomed rainforest cottages, all with double soaker baths. Fireplaces are well used by those who come winter-storm watching.

### Wickaninnish Inn
Osprey Lane , Tofino
Tel: 250 725 3100
www.wickinn.com
Voted one of Canada's top 15 hotels by *Condé Nast Traveller*, this popular hotel overlooks Chestermann Beach, which is the only beach in the area with accommodation. Opened in 1996, it has 75 rooms and suites with soak tubs near the window. Guests come in winter for storm watching. The spa has three indoor treatment rooms and has been rated as one of the top two spas in Canada. There are

many appealing design features, such as the use of driftwood to make seats. The restaurant espouses slow food. Closed first two weeks of January.

### Aerie
600 Ebadora Lane, Malahat
Tel: 250 743 7115
www.aerie.bc.ca
In 2006 this hotel, at the entrance to the Cowichan Valley in the south of the island, was elected North America's premier hotel by *Travel and Leisure*. It stands in grounds of 32 hectares (80 acres) 500 metres (1,500ft) above sea level with views over the Saanich Peninsula and San Juan Islands from the 10 rooms and 25 suites. It has an indoor swimming pool, spa, tennis court, beauty centre, fitness facilities, daily yoga and tai chi, cooking classes and a host of activities that can be arranged for guests.

## Expensive

### Abigail's Hotel
966 McClure Street, Victoria
Tel: 250 388 5363
www.abigailshotel.com
Heritage hotel with faux timber framing, European furnishings, luxurious bathrooms and wood-burning fireplaces. Abigail's has been carefully modernised with air conditioning, and it is renowned for its gourmet breakfasts. In the evening, canapés are served in the library.

British Columbia

### Coast Bastion Inn
11 Bastion Street , Nanaimo
Tel: 250 753 6601
www.coasthotels.com
Bland tower overlooking the harbour, but if you need to stay in Nanaimo this is its best hotel. Facilities offered include gym, sauna and whirlpool.

### Swans
506 Pandora Avenue, Victoria
Tel: 250 361 3310
www.swanshotel.com
A high-ceilinged boutique hotel decorated with over 1,500 original paintings, sculptures and antiques and close to the Inner Harbour. The 29 suites, some with two-storey lofts and kitchens, are all individually designed. It has its own brew-pub and bistro.

### Tauca Lea Resort & Spa
1971 Harbour Drive, Ucluelet
Tel: 250 726 4625
www.taucalearesort.com
Almost entirely surrounded by water, the unobtrusive blue colour-washed buildings house large attractive suites with fireplaces. Some have hot tubs on balconies, with glorious views over the peaceful tree-lined Ucluelet Inlet. The resort has been carefully designed, even down to using gravel rather than tarmac so that the trees

**BELOW:** the grand Empress Hotel.

would receive enough moisture. It has a good restaurant overlooking the harbour as well as kitchens in the suites, and there is an exceptionally lovely spa with slate-lined walls.

### Moderate

**Canadian Princess Resort**
1943 Peninsula Road, Ucluelet
Tel: 250 726 7771
www.obmg.com
The *Canadian Princess*, a former hydrographic vessel permanently moored here, has been incorporated into this harbourside resort which specialises in

salmon and halibut fishing expeditions and boat trips. The rooms in the fishing lodge are larger, but the small cabin rooms on board the ship are considerably cheaper. Open from April to mid-September.

**Hospitality Inn**
3835 Redford Street
Port Alberni
Tel: 250 723 8111
www.hospitalityinnportalberni.com
The 50 air-conditioned rooms have high-speed internet, and there is an indoor pool, restaurant and pub.

**The Inn at Tough City**
350 Main Street, Tofino
Tel: 250 725 2021

www.toughcity.com
Quirky brick-built hotel overlooking the harbour with antiques and eclectic memorabilia, stained glass, fireplaces, hardwood floors, good seafood restaurant and waterfront patio.

**Strathcona**
919 Douglas Street, Victoria
Tel: 250 383 7137
www.strathconahotel.com
This characterful refurbished 1913 building has a Victorian-style pub, volleyball court and rooftop lounge as well as several restaurants within the building.

**Travellers Inn Downtown**
1850 Douglas Street, Victoria

Tel: 250 381 1000
www.travellersinn.com
This 78-roomed hotel has good-sized rooms with king-size beds and air conditioning; the upper rooms have a small patio. Free digital cable viewing and high-speed internet. There is a free shuttle bus to and from the Inner Harbour.

### Inexpensive

**Clayoquot Retreat**
120 Arnet Road, Tofino
Tel: 604 725 3305
Three newly-built ocean-front rooms with open-air hot tub and delicious breakfast.

# GULF ISLANDS

### Luxury

**Galiano Inn**
134 Madrona Drive
Galiano Island
Tel: 250 539 3388
www.galianoinn.com
The island's only waterfront inn (with a restaurant and spa) has been a special place to stay for a century, first as a home, and from the 1930s as a guesthouse. The gourmet Atrevida restaurant uses local organic produce whenever possible, and the hotel's spa offers a unique "Blackberry Vinotherapy massage" using an oil produced on the island.

**Hastings House Country Estate**
160 Upper Ganges Road
Salt Spring Island
Tel: 250 537 2362
www.hastingshouse.com
In an idyllic position

overlooking Ganges Harbour, this hotel is one of North America's finest and the kind of place you're really reluctant to leave. The Relais & Châteaux hotel has 18 enchanting and individually designed suites spread across sensitively adapted buildings dotted around the 9-hectare (22-acre) grounds. The Manor House itself was built by a descendant of Warren Hastings (first governor-general of British India). The Swiss chef produces outstanding cuisine using local produce, some grown in the hotel's kitchen garden. You can indulge yourself even further at the hotel's spa.

### Expensive

**April Point Resort & Spa**

900 April Point Road
Quathiaski Cove
Quadra Island
Tel: 250 285 2222
www.aprilpoint.com
This sheltered waterfront hotel has stunning views of the ocean, an Aveda spa and a sushi bar as well as a restaurant. The 49 rooms include a variety of cabins and suites. Whale watching and salmon fishing expeditions can be arranged. The island is just a 10-minute crossing from Campbell River on Vancouver Island's northeast shore.

**Poets Cove Resort & Spa**
9801 Spalding Road
South Pender Island
Tel: 250 629 2100
www.poetscove.com
Large seafront hotel with 46 rooms in the Arts and Crafts-styled lodge or in cottages

British Columbia

Vancouver

and villas. The Aurora restaurant serves West Coast cuisine, and the Susurrus Spa (meaning "whispering sound") has six treatment rooms with steam cave and waterfall leading down to an ocean-side Jacuzzi. The hotel offers a variety of activities such as

### PRICE CATEGORIES

Guide prices for a standard double room in high season:
**Luxury:** more than C$250
**Expensive:** C$175–250
**Moderate:** C$100–175
**Inexpensive:** under C$100

diving, kayaking and biking, as well as an outdoor pool.

### Moderate

**Salt Spring Vineyards**
151 Lee Road
Salt Spring Island
Tel: 250 653 9463

www.saltspringvineyards.com
Two attractive rooms have been created at this quiet vineyard, with private bathrooms and kitchenettes. There is an open-air hot tub from which to enjoy the great view. Reasonably priced romantic getaway.

**Tsa-Kwa-Luten Lodge**
1 Lighthouse Road
Quadra Island
Tel: 250 285 2042
www.capemudgeresort.com
Set in a forest, this imaginatively designed lodge offers sea views from all 35 rooms. Seafood restaurant.

### Inexpensive

**Firesign Art & Design Studio B&B**
730 Smiths Road, Quadra Island. Tel: 250 285 3390
www.firesignartanddesign.com
Small B&B (three rooms with kitchenette) close to beaches and hiking.

# THE SUNSHINE COAST

### Expensive

**A Woodland Garden Inn**
1214 Lysander Road (off Krause), Roberts Creek
Tel: 604 740 0322
www.awoodlandgardeninn.com
The three sumptuous suites have private entrances, fireplaces and garden views with old-growth forest as a backdrop. A gourmet breakfast is served in the suite, and spa treatments can be arranged. It is close to beaches and hiking trails.

### Moderate

**Salmonberry Lodge and Spa**
1111 Grandview Road, Gibsons
Tel: 604 886 7375
www.salmonberrylodge.com
An unusual boutique B&B which offers a range of spa treatments. It is an eight-minute walk to Secret Beach and hiking trails.
**Lund Hotel**
1476 Highway 101, Lund
Tel: 604 414 0474
www.lundhotel.com
This charming period

seafront hotel lies at the very top of the Sunshine Coast, gateway to the famous Desolation Sound. Most of its 31 en suite rooms have ocean views and it has a restaurant, pub and balconies for enjoying the view. Diving, golf and biking and other activity packages available.

### Inexpensive

**Around the Bend**
5174 Sunshine Coast Highway
Sechelt

British Columbia

Vancouver

Tel: 604 885 4071
www.aroundthebendbb.com
Both en suite rooms have great ocean views, and guests have the use of a huge circular lounge. The beach is just across the road.

# WHISTLER AND SQUAMISH

### Luxury

**Fairmont Chateau Whistler**
4599 Chateau Boulevard
Tel: 604 938 8000
www.fairmont.com/whistler
This huge 550-bedroomed resort in a characterful building includes a Vida spa, complimentary health club, its own mountain golf course and academy, three superb restaurants and all the luxury and amenities that one would expect from a Fairmont hotel.

**Four Seasons Resort Whistler**
4591 Blackcomb Way
Whistler
Tel: 1 888 935 2460 (North America only)
www.fourseasons.com/whistler
The 273-roomed hotel lies at the foot of Blackcomb Mountain. Its generous-sized rooms all have wood interiors, gas-burning fireplaces and all the usual mod cons and electronic facilities. Residence suites have well-equipped kitchens, fireplaces and private terrace.

### Expensive

**Adara Hotel Whistler**
4122 Village Green
Tel: 604 905 4009
www.adarahotel.com
Whistler's newest and trendiest boutique hotel, the gay-managed Adara attracts an upscale gay and lesbian crowd. It has a year-round hot tub with mountain views and a summer-only outdoor pool.
**Cedar Springs B&B Lodge**
8106 Cedar Springs Road
Whistler
Tel: 604 938 8007

British Columbia

Whistler
Vancouver

www.whistlerbb.com
The eight rooms offer a high standard of comfort with varying permutations and prices.

### Moderate

**Cascade Lodge**
4315 Northlands Boulevard
Tel: 604 905 4875

This popular condo-hotel has a variety of comfortable units, from studios to two-bedroomed apartments. It has a large year-round outdoor heated pool, hot tub and the ski lifts are eight minutes' walk.

**Coast Whistler**
4005 Whistler Way
Tel: 604 932 2522
www.coastwhistlerhotel.com
With its own restaurant, covered outdoor heated pool, hot tub and variety of well-equipped rooms only four minutes' walk from

the lift, this hotel offers good value.

### Inexpensive

**Mountain Retreat Hotel & Suites**
38922 Progress Way
Squamish
Tel: 604 904 7060

www.mountainretreathotel.com
In the heart of the town, this 87-roomed hotel is a much cheaper option than Whistler and only 45 minutes away. It has an internet café, playground and an indoor pool with waterslide.

# AROUND THE OKANAGAN

### Expensive

**Harrison Hot Springs**
Tel: 604 796 2244
www.harrisonresort.com
This is really *the* place to stay at this lakeside town built around tourism, not only for its unrivalled facilities but also the spectacular view over the water and surrounding mountains. The attractive Healing Springs Spa offers the usual treatments and services. People come from far and wide for the nightly dinner-dances in the Copper Room, one of the few places in BC where there's serious ballroom dancing.

### Moderate

**Manning Park Resort**
7500 Highway 3
Manning Provincial Park
Tel: 250 840 8822
www.manningpark.com
This excellent base for walking and skiing is the only accommodation in the Park, close to Lightning Lake. It has large rooms, a heated indoor pool with Jacuzzi, dry sauna and steam room. In winter there is a skating rink, and in summer courts for tennis, volleyball and basketball. In warm

weather hummingbirds hover around the separate dining-room.
**Quilchena Hotel**
Quilchena
Tel: 250 378 2611
www.quilchena.com
One of BC's most historic hotels, which opened in 1908 and is still owned and operated by descendants of the founder. It's in a glorious position overlooking Nicola Lake (which has 29 species of fish). Not all rooms have en suite bathrooms; the en suite rooms are No. 2 and the Ladies Parlour on the 1st floor; and on the 2nd floor, Nos. 14 at the back, 15, 16 and 17 on the front. The dining-room offers seriously good food, and the hotel has its own horses for riding on the vast cattle ranch that heads off into back country that will leave a lasting impression. There is also tennis and bike rental. The hotel is open between late April and the end of autumn.
**Summerland Waterfront Resort**
13011 Lakeshore Drive South
Summerland
Tel: 250 494 8180
www.summerlandresorthotel.com

An ideal hotel for families, with pool and small beach on the shore of Okanagan Lake, with swifts darting above the attractive if small area of wetland in front of the hotel. The rooms have supremely comfortable beds, and there is a small but well-equipped kitchen. Shaughnessy's Cove Restaurant is adjacent to the hotel.
**La Punta Norte**
365 Highway 97N
Summerland
Tel: 250 494 4456
www.lapuntanorte.com
This extraordinary building resembles a hacienda and is situated on a headland with fabulous views overlooking Lake Okanagan and the rugged hills on the opposite shore. All the large rooms have en suite bathrooms, private entrances, hot tubs on a balcony, air conditioning, internet and furniture that complements the architecture.

### Inexpensive

**J.J. Gillis House B&B**
2276 Garcia Street
Merritt
Tel: 250 378 4461
www.jjgillishouse-b-and-b.com
Named after the doctor

British Columbia

Vancouver — Merritt

who lived here for 43 years, this atmospheric heritage house with claw-feet baths, fireplaces and a swimming pool offers a high standard of comfort in its four rooms.
**Colonial Inn**
Highway No. 3
Colonial Road
Hedley
Tel: 250 292 8131
www.colonialinnbb.ca
This attractive timber building was the guesthouse of the Nickel Plate gold mine, and its five ensuite rooms are air conditioned, with Queen beds and free high-speed internet. It is sheltered by trees and has a large veranda.

### PRICE CATEGORIES

Guide prices for a standard double room in high season:
**Luxury:** more than C$250
**Expensive:** C$175–250
**Moderate:** C$100–175
**Inexpensive:** under C$100

# **A**CTIVITIES

# THE ARTS, FESTIVALS AND EVENTS, NIGHTLIFE, SHOPPING AND SPORTS

## THE ARTS

Vancouver's cultural diversity is reflected in the many musical and arts events and festivals that punctuate the year. Music to suit all tastes is regularly performed at half a dozen principal venues, and there is a vibrant theatre and dance scene focused on Granville Island and on the section of Granville Street between Robson and Nelson. Modern visual arts are strongly represented by the Vancouver Art Gallery and commercial galleries, of which there is a cluster on Granville Street north of King Edward Avenue.

The best sources of information are the free monthly magazine *Where* (www.where.ca), available in many hotels, the free weekly *Georgia Straight*, which is published on Thursday and can be picked up from newspaper stands around the city, and the *Vancouver Magazine* (www.vanmag.com), published, rather eccentrically, eleven times a year.

### Concerts, opera and ballet

The **Vancouver Symphony Orchestra** is the mainstay of the city's classical music concerts. It gives 140 concerts a year, many at its home, the **Orpheum Theatre** (884 Granville Street on Smithe; tel: 604 876 3434; www.vancouversymphony.ca). It also performs at other venues such as the **Chan Centre for the Performing Arts** (6265 Crescent Road, UBC; tel: 604 822 9197; www.chancentre.com), where the programme includes jazz, folk, world and new music as well as the classical repertoire, and has attracted such notable musicians as Arlo Guthrie and Alfred Brendel. It has three performing spaces, the largest being the 1,400 Chan Shun Hall, which is reckoned to have the best acoustics in the city. The VSO also performs at the **Roundhouse Community Centre** (tel: 604 713 1800; www.roundhouse.ca), where the Performance Centre occupies part of the imaginatively restored Canadian Pacific locomotive depot. The Centre hosts an eclectic programme of arts events and exhibitions.

**Vancouver Opera** (tel: 604 683 0222; www.vancouveropera.ca) holds a season of six operas between November and May, and each is normally performed on 4–6 nights, usually at the **Queen Elizabeth Theatre** (600 Hamilton Street between Dunsmuir and Georgia; tel: 604 665 3050; www.city.vancouver.bc.ca/theatres). Built in 1959 to seat almost 3,000 and with a 21-metre (70-ft) wide stage, the theatre is also home to **Ballet British Columbia** (tel: 604 732 5003; www.balletbc.com) and hosts Broadway shows, pop and rock concerts. Within the Queen Elizabeth Theatre is the smaller **Vancouver Playhouse** (tel: 604 280 3311; www.city.vancouver.bc.ca/theatres), where chamber concerts and recitals are given. Vancouver Opera sometimes performs at Surrey Arts Centre *(see page 247)* and the **Centennial Theatre** (2300 Lonsdale Avenue; tel: 604 984 4484; www.centennialtheatre.com) in North Vancouver. With 705 seats and an orchestra pit for 25 musicians, the Centennial includes classical concerts and ballet as well as comedy and film in its varied programme.

### Church concerts

Regular concerts are held in the glorious setting of **Christ Church Cathedral** at 3pm every Sunday and on other occasions (690 Burrard Street; tel: 604 682 3848; www.cathedral.vancouver.bc.ca). Music societies periodically hire other churches as concert venues; see the arts listings for details.

### Out of town

Up the Sunshine Coast at the small community of Pender Harbour, the **Music Society** (www.penderharbourmusic.ca) has monthly concerts from Bach to boogie-woogie, a Chamber Music Festival on the third weekend in August and an annual Jazz Festival on the third weekend in September. On Salt Spring Island in July and August, the **ArtSpring** (tel: 250 537 2102; www.artspring.ca) hosts concerts ranging from Mozart to the rhythms of Guinea and folk musicians from Cape Breton.

## Theatre

The **Arts Club** (1585 Johnston Street; tel: 604 687 1644; www.artsclub.com) is the largest theatre company in western Canada, performing in a 425-seat auditorium at its Granville Island base, and at the historic **Stanley Theatre** (2750 Granville Street, at 12th; tel: 604 687 1644; www.stanleytheatre.ca). Shows range from classic dramas and comedies to premieres by Canadian playwrights. The **Carousel Theatre** (1411 Cartwright Street; tel: 604 685 6217; www.carouseltheatre.ca) on Granville Island stages a wide range of plays and theatrical experiences. Also on Granville Island are **Performance Works** (1218 Cartwright Street; tel: 604 687 3020), which presents world dance and music, and the **Waterfront Theatre** (1412 Cartwright Street; tel: 604 685 1731), which hosts visiting productions.

Located within the Queen Elizabeth Theatre is the 668-seat **Vancouver Playhouse** (600 Hamilton Street between Dunsmuir and Georgia; tel: 604 280 3311; www.vancouverplayhouse.com), where six plays are performed between late October and late May.

A converted 1906 fire station is home to the **Firehall Arts Centre** (tel: 604 689 0926; www.firehallartscentre.ca), a 150-seat auditorium with an outdoor stage for summer use. Besides productions from the resident Firehall Theatre Society, it is home to over 25 other arts organisations and hosts over 300 theatre and dance performances each year. In Kitsilano, the highly regarded

**Blackbird Theatre** company puts on a series of classic plays between September and May at the 350-seat Vancouver East Cultural Centre (315-2228 Marstrand Avenue; tel: 604 734 5273; www.blackbirdtheatre.ca).

The **Theatre at UBC** (354 Crescent Road; tel: 604 822 2678; www.theatre.ubc.ca) puts on a season of classics, established contemporary works and new Canadian theatre as part of an interdisciplinary training programme at the university.

The **Centre for the Performing Arts** (tel: 604 602 0616; www.centreinvancouver.com) is the most striking theatre building in Vancouver, but it has had mixed fortunes as a venue since its opening in 1996. It hosts popular theatre, musicals and spectacles, but its stage is dark for most of each month.

The **Surrey Arts Centre** (13750-88 Avenue, Surrey; tel: 604 501 5566; www.surrey.ca) is principally a drama theatre but also attracts visiting concerts.

Besides **Bard on the Beach** (see page 248), the summer months see plays performed at the Malkin Bowl in Stanley Park by **Theatre under the Stars** (tel: 604 687 0174; www.tuts.bc.ca). On Salt Spring Island, the **ArtSpring** (tel: 250 537 2102; www.artspring.ca) in Ganges hosts plays, concerts and exhibitions.

**BELOW:** dancers at the Firehall Arts Centre.

## Cinema

Besides the printed arts listings, there are two websites which give details of screenings, www.movies.vancouver.com and www.cinemaclock.com. Largest of the central multiscreens is the **Cinemark Tinseltown** (88 West Pender Street; tel: 604 806 0799) on the edge of Chinatown, which shows foreign films as well as new releases at its 12 screens. The **Paramount Vancouver** (Famous Players) (900 Burrard Street by Smithe; tel: 604 930 1407) has nine screens, and **Granville 7** (Empire Theatre) (855 Granville Street; tel: 604 684 4000) has seven.

Cinemas likely to include arthouse films in their programme include: **Hollywood Theatre** (3123 West Broadway by Balaclava Street, Kitsilano; tel: 604 738 3211), which has double bills; the non-profit **Pacific Cinémathèque** (1131 Howe Street, by Helmecken; tel: 604 688 3456), which has various festivals, and screens the films made by the Independent Filmmakers' Society; **Park Theatre** (3440 Cambie Street by 19th Avenue; tel: 604 709 3456); **The Ridge** (3131 Arbutus Street by 16th Avenue; tel: 604 738 6311); **Vancity Theatre** (1181 Seymour Street; tel: 604 683 3456); and **Vaneast Cinema** (2290 Commercial Drive, near East 7th Avenue; tel: 604 251 1313).

Among the neighbourhood cinemas, the ones most under threat from commercial redevelopment (such as Point Grey's Varsity Theatre which closed in January 2007), are the **Denman Cinema** (1737 Comox Street at Denman, near Stanley Park; tel: 604 683 2201) and **Dunbar Cinema** (4555 Dunbar Street; tel: 604 222 2999).

At Canada Place is Vancouver's one **CN IMAX** cinema (tel: 604 682 4629), showing the kind of films that best exploit its unique 3-D properties.

## TICKETS

Tickets for many events can be obtained from Ticketmaster (tel: 604 280 4444; www.ticket master.ca), which has half a dozen outlets downtown and others in the suburbs. Last-minute tickets can be bought from Tickets Tonight (tel: 604 684 2787 [listings]; www.ticketstonight.ca) Tues–Sat 11am–6pm at the Touristinfo Centre, Plaza Level, 200 Burrard Street.

## FESTIVALS & EVENTS

**JANUARY:** the **Polar Bear Swim** at 2.30pm on New Year's Day is not for the faint-hearted. More than 1,500 people go for a plunge in English Bay, a tradition that dates from 1819. The object is to swim to a buoy 90 metres (98 yds) from the beach, in water that is generally between 3–8°C (37–46°F).

**JANUARY/FEBRUARY:** the precise date of the **Chinese New Year Festival** depends on the lunar calendar, but the festival entails 15 days of celebrations in and around Chinatown, including a Sunday afternoon dragon parade.

**FEBRUARY:** Granville Island is host to a three-day **Winterruption** festival late in the month, when the Coastal Jazz and Blues Society lays on a varied programme of music, plays, films, workshops for children and adults, and culinary events.

**MARCH–APRIL: Vancouver International Dance Festival** (www.vidf.ca) sees performances by internationally acclaimed dance companies and master classes by leading teachers.

**APRIL:** the **Sun Run** (www.sun run.com) on the third weekend of the month is Canada's largest 10-km (6-mile) road race, with over 17,000 competitors running or shuffling the course that starts and ends in BC Place Stadium.

**MAY:** the **International Marathon** on the first Sunday of the month is also Canada's largest marathon.

**MAY/JUNE:** the **International Children's Festival** (www.vancouver-childrensfestival.com) in Vanier Park features storytellers, mime artists, jugglers, clowns and musicians entertaining over 70,000 visitors.

**JUNE:** during the first week of the month, the **Vancouver Garden Show** (www.vancouvergardenshow.com) is held at the Van Dusen Gardens with over 200 stands.

**JUNE:** on the third weekend, the **Dragon Boat Festival** (www.adbf. com) is a race in False Creek between brightly painted canoes with prows like dragon heads and sterns resembling tails, with up to 150 teams of 80 paddlers.

**JUNE:** for 10 days from the third Friday of the month the **Vancouver International Jazz Festival** (www.coastaljazz.ca) offers concerts and free outdoor jazz and blues performances at David Lam Park, Gastown and Granville Island, where the City uncaps the nozzles on the high-pressure saltwater pumping station, and everyone gets to play in the water.

**JUNE–SEPTEMBER: Bard on the Beach Shakespeare Festival** (www.bardonthebeach.org) sees four plays performed under a 500-seat tent in Vanier Park.

**1 JULY: Canada Day** is celebrated with fireworks around the city, but primarily at Canada Place where the bangs start at 10pm.

**JULY: Vancouver Folk Music Festival** (www.thefestival.bc.ca) is held in mid-July at Jericho Beach Park, where seven stages are set up for over 100 performances; this two-day event attracts musicians from all over the world, and there's a special programme for kids.

**JULY: Dancing on the Edge Festival** (www.dancingontheedge.org) sees performances by over 100 dance artists from across Canada and the US, mostly at the Firehall Arts Centre.

**JULY:** the **Chamber Music Festival** (www.vanrecital.com) has

gained a fine reputation for the concerts which are broadcast nationally by CBC Radio.

**JULY–AUGUST: Vancouver Early Music Festival** (www.earlymusic.bc.ca) is held in the UBC Recital Hall.

**JULY–AUGUST: Vancouver International Comedy Festival** (www.comedyfest.com) takes place on Granville Island over 12 days.

**JULY–AUGUST: HSBC Celebration of Light** (www.celebration-of-light.com) is a fortnight of firework displays by competing countries, choreographed to music and set off from a barge in English Bay. A local radio station broadcasts the music, and Vancouverites mass in Vanier Park to get the best view.

**JULY–AUGUST: Pride Week** (www.vanpride.bc.ca). Vancouver Pride celebrations are centred on the fancy-dress parade that takes place along Denman Street.

**AUGUST: Festival Vancouver** (www.festivalvancouver.ca) organises up to six classical, jazz and world music concerts and events a day over 12 days at venues throughout the city.

**AUGUST–SEPTEMBER:** the **Pacific National Exhibition** (PNE) (www.pne.ca) at 2901 East Hastings Street is almost a century-long tradition. The 17 days of the country fair feature a fairground, trade shows, concerts and displays such as canine acrobats, motocross champions, pig races, horse-riding, sky diving and a marketplace with over 225 exhibitors.

**LATE AUGUST/EARLY SEPTEMBER: Classic Boat Festival, Victoria** (www.classicboatfestival.ca). Classic wooden vessels assemble in Victoria's harbour for this celebration of craftsmanship afloat.

**SEPTEMBER:** the **Fringe Festival** (www.vancouverfringe.com). Over 100 groups from around the world put on 500 offbeat performances in and around Granville Island.

**SEPTEMBER: Vancouver International Film Festival** (www.viff.com). In the last week of the month, over 300 films from 50 countries are screened at venues across the city.

**ABOVE:** live entertainment at the annual Salt Spring country fair.

**OCTOBER: Vancouver International Writers & Readers Festival** (www.writersfest.bc.ca). Over 11,000 people attend 40 events over five days, including readings and workshops. It has attracted such big names as J.K. Rowling, Margaret Atwood and P.D. James.

**21 DECEMBER: Lantern Parade.** A children's lantern parade along the seawall to Granville Island for fireworks and activities at Performance Works.

**DECEMBER: Christmas Carol Ship Parade.** During the first three weeks of December, boat owners and charter companies decorate their vessels with colourful fairy lights and promenade around False Creek and the harbour. The boats, some of which offer dinner with or without carols, gather nightly at Coal Harbour at 7pm.

# NIGHTLIFE

Vancouver is much like any other western city of comparable size, with numerous places to pass the night hours. Because restaurants are generally seen as good value, eating out is very common, though the distinction between restaurants, cafés, bars, clubs and pubs is much more blurred than in many countries.

## Live music

There are some outstanding venues for live music in an informal setting. Clubs come in and

out of fashion, and websites such as www.clubzone.com and www.clubvibes.com give the latest feedback. Some, like **Sonar** (66 Water Street and Abbott; tel: 604 683 6695; www.sonar.bc.ca), change their spots according to the time of day; until about 9pm it's a piano lounge serving bar food, but after then becomes a dance club with live bands spanning jazz to techno. For live hardcore blues, the **Yale Hotel** (1300 Granville Street, just north of bridge on the east corner with Drake; tel: 604 681 9253; www.theyale.ca) has been the favoured bar for years.

There are several good jazz venues, though Vancouver has recently lost two of its best jazz clubs, the Purple Onion and the city's oldest, Hot Jazz (www.hotjazz.ca); sadly its Main Street club closed in November 2006 but it is looking for new premises. It leaves a hole for those seeking swing, Dixieland and New Orleans sounds. With an emphasis on promoting Canadian music, though also hosting international artists, **The Cellar** (3611 West Broadway; tel: 604 738 1959; www.cellarjazz.com) has become deservedly popular; it also offers an imaginative restaurant menu. Nightly performances accompany pasta and pizza at **Capone's** restaurant and live jazz club (1141 Hamilton Street, off Davie; tel: 604 684 7900; www.caponesrestaurant.net) in Yaletown. **O'Douls** (the Listel Hotel, 1300 Robson Street; tel: 604 661 1400; www.odoulsrestaurant.com)

has become a favourite with jazz lovers for its varied programme and good food. Considerably cheaper is **Calhouns Café** (3035 West Broadway, Kitsilano; tel: 604 738 1959), which offers jazz on Sunday and Tuesday evenings.

One of the oldest and best-known venues for live music is the striking **Commodore Ballroom** (tel: 604 739 7469; www.hob.com), which has attracted such illustrious and diverse performers as Dizzy Gillespie, Emmylou Harris and Dire Straits. It had C$3.5 million spent on it in 1999, so it's the antithesis of a blues dive, and has probably the city's finest-sprung dance floor, which dates from 1929 and complements the Art Deco decor. For jazz in an elegant setting, try **900 West Lounge** in the Fairmont Hotel (900 West Georgia Street; tel: 604 669 9378), but expect to pay for the privilege.

## Pubs and bars

Because of the way restaurants, cafés, bars, clubs and pubs morph into one another, there are probably fewer dedicated drinking establishments per capita than in Europe. That said, Vancouver has some great bars and pubs, especially brew pubs serving first-rate beers *(see page 122)*. For useful listings and reviews, visit www.vancouverpubs.com and www.vanmag.com.

The **Yaletown Brewing Company** (1111 Mainland Street at Helmcken; tel: 604 681 2739; www.markjamesgroup.com) occupies a stylishly adapted former warehouse and serves eight special brews produced on the premises, which include a restaurant.

Close to Waterfront Station is the **Steamworks Brewing Company** (375 Water Street; tel: 604 689 2739; www.steamworks.com), a microbrewery which produces a dozen good beers and serves pub fare. It has good views over Burrard Inlet and the mountains, and an open fire in winter.

On Granville Island and part of the eponymous hotel is the **Dock-**

side **Brewing Company** (tel: 604 685 7070; www.docksidebrewing.com), which produces eight beers. Its lounge is smart, and there's a waterfront patio which has terrific views over False Creek. So has the **Arts Club Backstage Lounge** (1585 Johnston Street; tel: 604 687 1354), which serves good beer and sustaining nachos.

The pre-eminent Irish pub is **Doolin's** (654 Nelson Street; tel: 604 605 4343). It has 16 beers on tap, including Guinness and Kilkenny, and Celtic music from 9pm from Monday to Thursday. In Gastown is the **Irish Heather** (217 Carrall Street; tel: 604 688 9779), a gastropub run by Irish people serving Guinness and 140 varieties of whiskey in the Shebeen Whiskey Bar.

If you're visiting Lynn Valley in North Vancouver, call in at the **Black Bear** (1177 Lynn Valley Road; tel: 604 990 8880), located in a newly built Craftsman-style house, which serves great food. Also in North Van is the **Raven** (1052 Deep Cove on bus route 212; tel: 604 929 3824), which has 26 beers on tap, good food and an open fire in winter.

The **King's Head** (1618 Yew Street, Kitsilano; tel: 604 738 6966) is an English-style pub which also serves breakfasts and has quieter spaces upstairs. Other Kits favourites are **Elwood's** (3145 West Broadway; tel: 604 736 4301), which serves well-kept beer and above-average pub fare, and **Bimini's Tap House** (2010 West 4th Avenue; tel: 604

732 9232) which turns from a pub to a club for the weekend.

For elegant surroundings, hotel bars are the best bet, particularly when they're as stylish as Yaletown's **Opus Hotel** (322 Davie Street; tel: 604 642 6787). More traditional with cherrywood panelling is the **Bacchus Piano Lounge** (845 Hornby Street; tel: 604 689 7777) in the Wedgewood Hotel. For the best views over the city, go to the **Cloud Nine Lounge** (1400 Robson Street; tel: 604 687 0511) on the 42nd storey of the Empire Landmark Hotel. It rotates 6 degrees every minute, so sip the martini slowly.

## SHOPPING

The epicentre of Vancouver's downtown shops is the intersection of West Georgia and Granville streets, on which the two famous department stores of **Hudson's Bay** and **Sears** are located. The former is adjacent to the Pacific Centre mall at 633 Granville Street with 200 shops as well as the upmarket **Holt Renfrew** department store.

Like most cities, Vancouver has clusters of outlets selling similar goods. **Robson Street** west of Georgia has numerous fashion and designer shops such as Armani, Zara, Salvatore Ferragamo and Banana Republic.

On the south side of Granville Bridge is a concentration of art galleries, designer furnishings and

antiques. For outdoor equipment and sports suppliers, head for Broadway east from Cambie Street. The shopping area along **Granville Street**, north from 16th Avenue as far as 7th, has attracted lots of furnishing stores and galleries. At 3002 Granville Street, on 14th, is the outstanding **Meinhardt** grocery shop, deli, salad bar and bakery.

The two great **markets** are Granville (see page 121) and Lonsdale Quay (see page 166).

The large out-of-town shopping malls include the **Lansdowne Centre** at 5300 No. 3 Road at Alderbridge Way in Richmond (reached by 98 B-Line bus) and BC's largest shopping centre with 470 shops on three floors, the **Metrotown** in Burnaby, next to the Metrotown SkyTrain station.

The main shopping street in Victoria on Vancouver Island is **Government Street**, which has numerous craft shops, such as Earth and Fire Pottery at No. 1820, as well as such upmarket retailers as Villeroy & Boch and Crabtree & Evelyn. On Sunday between 10am and 4pm a food-and-crafts market is held in Government Street between Fisgard and Pendora streets.

### What and where to buy

### Antiques

In the Rush Building at 422 Richards Street is the **Vancouver Antique Mall** with a number of specialist shops. There are other

## GAY AND LESBIAN CLUBS

**Celebrities** (1022 Davie Street; tel: 604 681 6180; www.clubzone.com). Vancouver's biggest gay dance club attracts a young crowd of gay men and women and their straight friends.
**Flygirl** (www.flygirlproductions.com). Gay women's club nights held at a variety of venues. Log onto the website for a full calendar of events.

**Lick** (455 Abbott Street; tel: 604 685 7777). Vancouver's only dance club for women.
**Nice** (364 Water Street, www.shinenightclub.com, tel: 604 408 4321). Sunday is gay night at ultra-hip Gastown club Shine.
**Numbers** (1042 Davie Street). Packed on weekends by a mainly older crowd. Nice blend of retro disco and new dance trax.

**Odyssey** (1251 Howe Street; tel: 604 689 5256; www.the odysseynightclub.com). A popular, high energy dance club with the best drag shows in town.
**The World** (816 Granville Street, www.816.ca). Vancouver's hottest after-hours dance club is very gay-friendly. The club is non-alcoholic but be forewarned, it is a hangout for the designer drug crowd.

concentrations on Granville Street between West 6th and West 14th avenues, and on Main Street between 12th and 29th avenues.

## Art

Among the First Nations shops in Gastown are the **Inuit Gallery of Vancouver** (206 Cambie Street; tel: 604 688 7323; www.inuit.com), which has a large collection of masterwork Inuit and Northwest Coast native artwork, and two sister shops, **Francis Hill's Gastown** (151 Water Street; tel: 604 685 1828) and **Hill's Native Art** (165 Water Street; tel: 604 685 4249; www.hillsnativeart.com), which feature at any time over 1,200 Native artists in a variety of media. If you want something simpler, like a First Nations bentwood box, try **Coastal People Fine Art Gallery** (1024 Mainland Street; tel: 604 685 9298; www.coastalpeoples.com) in Yaletown, where the huge collection includes prints, glass, jewellery, masks, sculpture, argillite and basketry. The largest concentration of art-and-craft shops is on Granville Island.

## Books

**Duthie Books** (2239 West 4th Avenue; tel: 604 732 5344; www.duthiebooks.com) has an excellent selection with knowledgeable staff. Travellers head for **International Travel Maps and Books** (530 West Broadway; tel: 604 879 3621; www.itmb.com). On Salt Spring Island, **Sabine's Bookshop** (3104-115 Fulford–Ganges Road; tel: 250 538 0025) has an excellent stock of second-hand books. **Sidney** on Vancouver Island describes itself as a book town, with 10 differently themed bookshops. **Little Sister's Book & Art Emporium** (1238 Davie Street, www.littlesistersbookstore.com, tel: 604 669 1753) is Canada's biggest and best gay and lesbian bookstore.

## Chinatown

Among the many shops selling Chinese goods are **Ming Wo** (23 East Pender Street; tel: 604 683

7268), a Vancouver institution with a huge assortment of cooking equipment, and two of the largest stores with a wide range of goods, **Cathay Importers** (104 East Pender Street; tel: 604 684 2632) and **Bamboo Village** (135 East Pender Street; tel: 604 662 3300).

## Chocolate

**Rogers Chocolates** produces a varied range of outstanding products. It has a branch in Victoria (913 Government Street; tel: 250 384 7021; www.rogerschocolaes.com) and two in Vancouver (1571 Johnston Street on Granville Island, tel: 778 371 7314; The Landing, 389 Water Street, Gastown, tel: 604 676 3452).

## Groceries

There are two excellent grocery stores in Yaletown: **Urban Fare** (177 Davie Street; tel: 604 975 7550), where you can have a glass of wine and sample the deli; and **Choices** (1202 Richards Street; tel: 604 633 2392), which also has a small café. The same is true of the outstanding **Meinhardt Fine Foods** grocery shop (3002 Granville Street, on 14th; tel: 604 732 4465).

## Jewellery

Outlets range from old established firms such as **Henry Birks & Co.** (698 West Hastings Street; tel: 604 669 3333; www.birks.com) and **Tiffany & Co.** (tel: 604 681 3121; www.tiffany.com) in Holt Renfrew within the Pacific Centre, to the individual studios that are prevalent on the Gulf Islands.

## Records, CDs

Hastings between Homer and Cambie is a good place for new and second-hand CD shops.

## Men's clothes

For traditional men's (and women's) outfitters, head for **Edward Chapman**, established 1890 (833 Pender Street West, tel: 604 685 6207; 2699

Granville Street near Shaughnessy, tel: 604 738 0848; and 2135 41st Avenue West, tel: 604 261 5128).

## GUIDED TOURS

Several companies offer daily sightseeing tours: **Landsea Tours** (tel: 604 662 7591; www.vancouvertours.com) for day trips and city tours in and around Vancouver, Victoria and Whistler, picking up from hotels; **Stay and Tour** (tel: 604 524 8687; www.stayandtour.ca) offers tours of Vancouver, Victoria, the North Shore and Whistler, picking up in Burnaby, New Westminster and Surrey as well as Vancouver; and **West Coast Sightseeing** (tel: 604 451 1600; www.vancouversightseeing.com) covers Vancouver, Victoria and Whistler in minibuses, one of them wheelchair-adapted.

**AIBC Architectural Tours** (tel: 604 683 8588 Ext 333; www.aibc.ca) offers expertly guided tours around the city's buildings of architectural and historic interest on Tues–Sat between early July and the end of August.

**Alfred's Guest Services** (tel: 778 388 6643; www.vancouverprivatetours.com) provides private tours around Vancouver, Whistler, Victoria and the Fraser Valley.

**A Wok around Chinatown** (tel: 604 736 9508; www.awokaround.com) takes culinary and cultural walking tours around Chinatown.

**Big Bus Ltd** (tel: 604 299 0700; www.bigbus.ca) offers hop-on/hop-off tours with open-top buses and commentary. Tickets are valid for two days, and buses run at a 15-minute frequency.

**City Talks Audio Tours** (tel: 604 710 4679; www.citytalks.ca) for Gastown, Chinatown, Stanley Park and the West End are available from the Touristinfo Centre at 200 Burrard Street.

**City by Cycle Tours** (tel: 604 730 1032; www.citybycycle.com) offers guided tours by bike starting at 9am and 2pm.

## OUTDOOR ACTIVITIES

### Climbing

The great centre for climbing near Vancouver is Squamish, where **Slipstream Rock Climbing & Guiding Centre** (tel: 604 898 4891; www.getclimbing.com) specialises in taking families and other groups of any level of experience up the faces of its private cliffs.

### Cycling

Cycling is a great way to see the city, which has a number of dedicated cycle routes. For mountain bikers, there are many great trails within easy reach of the city – Cypress Mountain, Mount Seymour, Grouse Mountain and Whistler all provide great biking terrain. Most trails open in May or June and close in September or October. *For more information on cycling, see page 234.*

### Diving

Scuba-diving trips are offered by **SeeKing Charters** (tel: 604 737 2628; www.seekingcharters.com). For diving packages at one of BC's best places for diving, Nanaimo, try **Ocean Explorers Diving** (tel: 250 753 2055; www.oceanexplorersdiving.com).

### Fishing

There are exceptional opportunities for fishing in glorious scenery. The open Pacific shores and inner coastal straits are home to Pacific salmon, giant halibut, rockfish, and a vast array of shellfish. Freshwater fishing is equally attractive: over 24,000 pristine lakes and rivers with two dozen species of freshwater sport fish, including the much sought-after, high-jumping rainbow trout. BC Tourism publishes a comprehensive guide to fishing, and a good introductory website with useful links is www.bcfishing.com.

### Golf

Vancouver has three public full-length golf courses, **Fraserview** (7800 Vivian Drive; tel: 604 257 6923), **Langara** (6706 Alberta Street; tel: 604 713 1816) and **McCleery** (7188 MacDonald Street; tel: 604 257 8191). For advance tee-time bookings at all three, tel: 604 280 1818.

### Horse-riding

From its 4-hectare (10-acre) ranch in the Pemberton Valley, just north of Whistler, **Whistler River Adventures** (tel: 604 932 3532; www.whistlerriver.com) offers rides through forests and along riverside beaches, overlooked by Mount Currie.

At Victoria on Vancouver Island, **Trail Rides** (tel: 250 479 6843; www.dutchretreat.com) organises tours around Thetis Lake Park, trail rides, riding lessons and children's riding camps. From **Alpine Stables** (tel: 250 743 6641; www.alpinestables.com) you can take 1½–5-hour rides through the southern part of the island.

### Kayaking

Most Vancouverites learn kayaking in the waters of English Bay or in False Creek, and **Ecomarine Ocean Kayak Centre** (tel: 604 689 7520; www.ecomarine.com) has been providing facilities for over 25 years from Granville Island (tel: 604 689 7575) and Jericho Beach (tel: 604 222 3565). The most beautiful environment for kayaking near Vancouver is the 18-km (11-mile) inlet of Indian Arm along which **Deep Cove Canoe & Kayak Centre** (tel: 604 929 2268; www.deepcovekayak.com) organises a variety of guided trips. They range from a few hours to several days between April and October. Up the Sunshine Coast, **Halfmoon Sea Kayaks** (tel 604 885 2948; www.halfmoonseakayaks) organises a variety of trips along the coast from Rock Water secret Cove near Sechelt, including sun-

**ABOVE:** Whistler's terrain in summer is ideal for mountain biking.

set tours. An insight into the Shishalh First Nation and their ecological practices is offered by **Talaysay Tours** (tel: 604 628 8555; www.talaysaytours.com), which runs varied trips from Sechelt Inlet, including moonlit paddles.

On Vancouver Island, **Paddle West Kayaking** (tel: 250 725 4281; www.paddlewest.com) at Tofino runs guided kayaking excursions around Clayoquot Sound, visiting places that can only be experienced in a kayak. *See also Nature Excursions.*

### Nature excursions

BC is one of the best places in the world to watch whales and bears, and there are lots of companies that offer mostly day tours to try to see them. Some are more concerned about the environment they live off than others, and there is concern about the impact of motor boats harassing whales, with some unscrupulous boat operators ignoring the guidelines for minimising disturbance. Though orca (killer) whales sometimes come right into Burrard Inlet, the west coast of Vancouver Island is a more likely place to see them. One of the companies that offers half-day tours is **Lotus Land Adventures** (tel: 604 684 4922; www.lotuslandtours.com), featuring whale-watching, kayaking and river rafting, with collection from your hotel. **Vancouver Nature Adven-**

tures (tel: 604 684 4922; www.lotuslandtours.com) offers four-hour accompanied tours up the fjord of India Arm in North Vancouver, with a salmon barbecue on an uninhabited island.

Most whale-watching companies are based on Vancouver Island, but one in Vancouver is **Wild Whales Vancouver** (tel: 604 699 2011; www.whalesvancouver.com), which has open and glass-domed vessels. **Steveston Seabreeze Adventures** (tel: 604 272 7200; www.seabreezeadventures.ca) operates from the lovely setting of historic Steveston village. In Victoria are: **Prince of Whales Whale Watching** (tel: 250 383 4884; www.princeofwhales.com); **Great Pacific Adventures** (tel: 250 386 2277; www.greatpacificadventures.com); **Springtide Whale Tours** (tel: 250 384 4444; www.victoriawhaletours.com), which boasts BC's largest whale-watching vessel; and catamaran-equipped **Wildcat Whale Watching** (tel: 250 344 9998; www.wildcat-adventures.com).

The island's west coast is the most atmospheric place to see whales, in much wilder scenery than on the east coast. Most of the companies are based in Tofino: **Remote Passages** (tel: 250 725 3330; www.remotepassages.ca) also offers kayaking to wilderness trails and bear-watching; **Jamie's Whaling Station** (tel: 250 725 3919; www.jamies.com) takes tours from Ucluelet (tel: 250 726 7444) as well as Tofino to watch bears, sea lions and whales and also offers sea kayaking.

## Paragliding

There is no shortage of fantastic locations for paragliding and hang-gliding, both on the mainland and Vancouver Island. Covering both is **Blue Thermal Paragliding** (tel: 250 588 2647; www.bluethermal.com), while based in Victoria is **Vancouver Island Paragliding** (tel: 250 514 8595; www.viparagliding.com). Both offer training and tandem flights.

## River cruises

**Paddlewheeler Riverboat Tours** (tel: 604 525 4465; www.vancouverpaddlewheeler.com) at 810 Quayside Drive, New Westminster, operates lunch, dinner and themed cruises up the Fraser river using modern sternwheelers.

## River rafting

Among the companies offering whitewater river rafting are: **Canadian Outback Adventure Company** (tel: 604 921 7250; www.canadianoutback.com), which offers rafting and whitewater rafting near Squamish, with hotel pick-up; **Reo Rafting Resort** (tel: 604 461 7238; www.reorafting.com) has been operating rafting trips on four BC rivers for 25 years, based on a 10-hectare (25-acre) wilderness site at the water's edge; **Whistler River Adventures** (tel: 604 932 3532; www.whistler-river.com); and **Sunwolf Outdoor Centre** (tel: 604 898 1537; www.sunwolf.net), which has riverside cabins for those who want longer rafting trips.

## Sea excursions

Several companies offer pootles around the harbour and English Bay: **Accent Cruises** (tel: 604 688 6625; www.accentcruises.ca), **Harbour Cruises** (tel: 604 688 7246; www.boatcruises.com) and **Vancouver Cruises** (tel: 604 681 2915; www.vancouvercruises.com).

On Vancouver Island, **Pacific Kayak** (tel: 250 725 3919; www.tofino-bc.com/pacifickayak) offers kayak cruises and charters through the myriad inlets off the west coast around Tofino as well as hiking and camping.

## Skiing

BC's largest tour specialist for skiing and snowboarding, with guides on all tours, is **Destination Snow** (tel: 604 532 1088; www.destinationsnow.com). See also Winter Sports, page 178.

## Swimming

There are open-air swimming pools at Kitsilano Beach (see page 129) and a summer-only pool at Second Beach in Stanley Park. Close to Burrard Bridge and downtown is the indoor **Vancouver Aquatic Centre** (1050 Beach Avenue; tel: 604 665 3424). Besides an Olympic heated pool, there are paddling pools, diving tank, sauna, whirlpool and gym.

## Tennis

The most attractively sited courts are a bank of 17 near the entrance to Stanley Park off Beach Avenue. They and all other municipal courts are used on a first-come, first-served basis, except for six of the Beach Avenue courts which can be pre-booked between May and August (tel: 604 605 8224). There are 20 tennis courts in Queen Elizabeth Park (West 33rd Avenue and Cambie Street) and other courts at Kitsilano Beach Park, near the sailing centre at Jericho Beach Park, and on Granville Island.

## Windsurfing

In Vancouver equipment can be rented from **Windsure Windsurfing School** (tel: 604 224 0615; www.windsure.com) on Jericho Beach. However, the place to go is the west coast of Vancouver Island (www.surfingvancouverisland.com), where many boarders take jobs just to be near the genuinely awesome rollers that pound the sand. Canada's only all-women surf school, **Surf Sister** (tel: 250 725 4456; www.surfsister.com) provides year-round daily lessons at the beaches south of Tofino.

## Zip-trekking

For a great adrenalin rush, try zip-lining across the Fitzsimmons Creek Valley suspended from a wire in a safety harness with **Ziptrek Ecotours** (tel: 604 935 0001; www.ziptrek.com).

# A - Z

## A HANDY SUMMARY OF PRACTICAL INFORMATION, ARRANGED ALPHABETICALLY

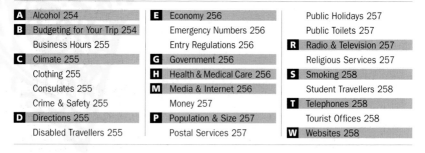

## A lcohol

BC's legal drinking age is 19. Photo identification is required to purchase alcoholic beverages or enter nightclubs serving alcohol. Alcohol can be purchased in government liquor stores and at privately owned cold beer and wine stores.

## B udgeting for Your Trip

For visitors from western Europe, Vancouver will seem good value for money, assuming of course that exchange rates do not alter significantly. But it is important to remember that prices are almost invariably quoted without tax, and these are not inconsiderable. There is an 8 percent tax on accommodation plus a 6 percent

federal goods and services tax (GST). For other purchases, there is a 7 percent provincial sales tax (PST) and a 6 percent GST. It used to be possible for visitors to claim a refund of GST, but in 2006 the government announced that the refund facility would cease from 1 April 2007.

Like most cities, there is a huge variety of accommodation and eating places, to cater for everyone from the city trader with money to burn to the student backpacker watching every dollar. Staying and eating away from the centre can be cheaper. Bear in mind that very little is free – there is not the same approach in Canada to museum funding, for example, so expect to pay for admission to everything, though concessions are

available for seniors, students and children.

Canada's first **Smartvisit Card** attractions pass is now available for visitors to Vancouver. The card allows unlimited entry to over 50 top attractions, tours and outdoor adventures in Vancouver, Victoria and beyond, such as the Vancouver Aquarium, Capilano Suspension Bridge, the Museum of Anthropology and the Vancouver Art Gallery, for either two, three or five days. The card is available for both adults and children (5–15), and comes with a free map and guidebook. Tel: 604 295 1157 or 1 877 295 1157 (toll-free within North America); www.seevancouvercard.com.

Careful planning can minimise the need for public transport within the central area: the

## CLIMATE CHART

### Vancouver

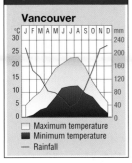

- ☐ Maximum temperature
- ■ Minimum temperature
- — Rainfall

whole downtown area can be walked, and visits outside it can be concentrated on days when a TransLink DayPass is justified.

### Business Hours

Working hours are normally Monday to Friday 8am–6pm, though banks and post offices have shorter hours. Shops are usually open seven days a week from 9/9.30am–6pm with late opening to 9pm on Thursday and Friday. There is no shortage of 24-hour corner stores and chemists. Restaurants are open for lunch from 11.30am or midday and dinner from 5pm.

### C limate

Vancouver enjoys a mild climate, and snow on the streets is very rare. But rain is another matter. The seemingly incessant rain between December (the wettest month) and March can depress even seasoned Vancouverites, but rain in the city translates into snow in Whistler. Though the average summer temperature is 20°C (70°F), it can be appreciably hotter in July and August. The transition from an Indian summer/autumn during October can be quite sudden. Winter temperatures average 2°C (35°F). For weather information, tel: 604 664 9010; www.vancouver.weather.ca.

### Clothing

Dress code in Vancouver is very casual. Only at the very best restaurants might you feel more comfortable in a jacket and tie, but you are almost certain to see someone in open-neck shirt. Shorts and T-shirts are barred in some smarter restaurants. Comfortable walking shoes, some lightweight waterproofs and an umbrella are advisable.

### Consulates

Greater Vancouver has 53 consulates. Australia, tel: 604 684 1177. Ireland, tel: 604 683 9233. New Zealand, tel: 604 684 7388. South Africa, tel: 604 688 1301. UK, tel: 604 683 4421. USA, tel: 604 685 4311. For a full list see: www.british columbia.com/information.

### Crime and Safety

Canada is very much safer than its southern neighbour. Few people own guns and even fewer carry them (usually just in back-country where you might encounter a bear), and muggings are at a low level. Property crime, however, is high though falling, according to the Vancouver Police. Take the usual sensible precautions against petty crime by making it difficult to pickpocket your possessions, avoid dodgy areas after dark and if you do hire a car, don't leave anything of value in it. Car crime is a sufficiently serious problem for some noble souls from rural communities to act as voluntary car-park minders at local tourist attractions.

### D irections

The grid system with property numbers running into the thousands takes some getting used to, particularly as the number gives no clue as to where it is located on a street that might stretch for miles. For example, it

would be helpful if 55XX Knight Street was at 55th Avenue, but it isn't – it's at 39th Avenue. So you need to deduct 1600 from the block number to get the avenue number. That's because east–west block numbering starts in single digits either side of Ontario Street, which runs north–south just east of the city centre. Addresses east of Ontario are referred to as East Broadway or East 23rd Avenue, and the same for those to the west. To make life easier, most public addresses add "on X" or simply say "2nd and Dunbar", which tells you the nearest cross street. Streets run north–south, avenues east–west. Avenues are generally numbered, the exceptions being Broadway (which should be 9th) and King Edward (which should be 25th). All streets are named, as are all roads in the downtown area.

### Disabled Travellers

Vancouver has a good reputation for providing accessibility for the disabled. The airport, for example, provides amplified handsets at ticket and service counters, low-mounted flight information monitors, public address systems displayed in written form, tactical guidance maps and accessible lavatories. Accessible taxis are available, and bus transportation can be arranged by calling the Airporter (tel: 604 273 8436 or 800 668 3141). Nearly all bus routes are operated by accessible vehicles, and the willingness of Vancouver bus drivers to help those with

### ELECTRICITY

110V, in common with the US, so appliances built for 220/240V perform poorly. Sockets accommodate plugs with two flat or two flat and one round pins, so an adaptor is required for the use of European appliances.

boarding difficulties is exemplary. All SkyTrain stations except for Granville Street are accessible. For accessible taxis, tel: 604 255 5111 or 604 871 1111. Most coach and ferry services are accessible, as are most of Rocky Mountaineer Vacations' trains (tel: 604 606 7245). Public buildings have to be adapted for wheelchairs, and street corners generally have dropped kerbs. In the UK, contact **Holiday Care** (tel: 0845 124 9971; minicom 0845 124 9976; www.holidaycare.org.uk) for free lists of accessible accommodation in Canada.

# E conomy

As BC's largest city and Canada's largest port, Vancouver's prosperity has always stemmed from trade in the raw materials that have been the mainstay of the provincial economy, together with shipment of wheat to Pacific markets. Each year the port ships over C\$43 billion in goods with over 90 countries, and much of the city's office space is occupied by companies involved in this trade: forest product and mining companies, and the complementary banks, accounting and law firms. More recently, biotechnology and software development companies have been set up in Vancouver, and the city has become a major location for shooting films and television programmes, fostering the various studio support functions. Large industrial estates support a wide range of manufacturing and wholesale companies.

## Entry Regulations

Visas are not required for short-term visitors from western Europe or Australia and New Zealand. Visa requirements do change, and a check can be made on the Canadian Immigration Centre website (www.cic.gc.ca). Among recent changes made by

**EMERGENCY NUMBERS**

911 Police/Fire/Ambulance
604 717 3535 Vancouver City
Police (non-emergency)

the US government is that everyone, including US citizens, travelling by air or train between the US and Canada must present a current passport; a birth certificate and photo ID are no longer valid proof.

# G overnment

The City of Vancouver derives its powers directly from the BC legislature and government through its own Vancouver Charter. The city government is made up of a mayor, city council and professional bureaucracy. The mayor is the city's chief administrative officer and is elected separately from the nine city councillors. Elections for all ten positions are held every three years, and all represent the entire city. Council meetings are held on three Tuesdays a month, and in those weeks three standing committees meet, also made up of all members of the council. Because the composition of the council and committees are one and the same, debate usually takes place at committee stage. The city is also a member of the Greater Vancouver Regional District; this organisation of cities and municipalities co-ordinates common services such as transport, sewage, water and economic planning. City and region do not always see eye-to-eye on these issues; for example, the city takes a more progressive view on the provision of public transport and discouragement of commuting by car. For most of the period since World War II, the right-of-centre Non-Partisan Association (NPA) has been in power. In the last elections, in November 2005, it regained power after a period in office of the Coalition of Progressive Electors, which came

to power on a drug harm-reduction platform. It is the recent NPA closure of the safe injection sites which the Coalition had set up that has increased the number of drug users on the streets. Generally speaking, the west of Vancouver votes conservative or centre-right while the eastern side votes to the left. In the Legislative Assembly of British Columbia, Vancouver is represented by ten members, currently five each from the BC Liberal Party and the BC New Democratic Party (NDP).

# H ealth and Medical Care

No reciprocal healthcare arrangements exist between Canada and other countries, so it's most unwise to travel without adequate health insurance, and medical treatment can be very expensive. Details of clinics, doctors and hospital emergency rooms can be found in the Yellow Pages. If you are travelling in backcountry, you need to learn about and guard against various risks. Worst of all is Rocky Mountain spotted fever, which is a nasty disease transmitted by hard ticks producing symptoms of fever, headache, muscle pain and rashes. It can be fatal, so early diagnosis is important. Other diseases include tick-borne Lyme disease, mosquito-carried West Nile virus, and Hantavirus from the droppings and urine of infected rodents. Even seasoned travellers in Asia may find mosquitoes a trial from June to October in areas with standing water. A mitigating measure is a tripling of the daily recommended vitamin B complex for a couple of weeks before travelling.

# M edia and Internet

Vancouver has two major daily papers: the broadsheet *Vancouver Sun* (www.vancouversun.com) and the tabloid *Province* (www.vancouverprovince.com). Both focus on BC stories, so European readers in

TRANSPORT

search of pan-Canadian and world news may prefer the Toronto-based *Globe and Mail*. The weekly *Vancouver Courier* (www.vancourier. com) has in-depth and interesting articles about the area's history and other themes. A free monthly magazine, *Where* (www.where.ca), is found in many hotels and provides invaluable information for tourists, with listings of attractions and restaurants, but Vancouverites rely on the free weekly *Georgia Straight*, which is published on Thursday. There is no shortage of internet cafés and most major hotels offer internet access.

## Money

Canadian dollar notes (paper bills) come in five denominations: $5 (blue), $10 (purple), $20 (green), $50 (red) and $100 (brown). There are six coins: 1¢ (the penny), 5¢ (nickel), 10¢ (dime), 25¢ (quarter), $1 (loonie, because it features a Canadian bird, the loon, on its face) and $2 (toonie, which features a bear). A better rate of exchange is usually obtained from banks. ATMs are common but often carry a surcharge for cash advances, and it is rare for MasterCard,

Visa and American Express cards to be unacceptable.

## P opulation and Size

The City of Vancouver's population is just over 582,000, while that of Greater Vancouver is over 2.17 million. The area of Greater Vancouver is 284,400 hectares (702,780 acres).

## Postal Services

The main post office is at 349 West Georgia Street and is open Mon–Fri 8am–5.30pm, supplemented by facilities in branches of Shopper's Drug Mart, Pharmasave and some other shops.

## Public Toilets

Lack of public toilets is a subject the Downtown Vancouver Business Improvement Association has been complaining about for years, with just two for the city centre, at Main and Hastings and Victory Square. Action has recently been taken with the installation of automated public toilets at such locations as the intersection of Commercial and Broadway, and Pigeon Park at

**BELOW:** news-stand in Waterfront Station.

**New Year's Day** 1 January
**Good Friday and Easter Monday**
**Victoria Day** third Monday in May
**Canada Day** 1 July
**BC Day** first Monday in August
**Labour Day** first Monday in September
**Thanksgiving** second Monday in October
**Remembrance Day** 11 November
**Christmas Day** 25 December
**Boxing Day** 26 December

ACCOMMODATION

Carrall and Hastings. They are time-limited to 10–15 minutes, after which a device in the unit warns the user that the door is going to open and someone will be checking the facility.

## R adio and Television

The Canadian equivalent of the BBC is CBC – Canadian Broadcasting Corporation – which tries to uphold standards. CBC Radio One (690AM) has the best, commercial-free news as well as programmes about public affairs, while Radio Two (105.7FM) has classical music and arts programmes. Pop of various genres can be found on CFOX (95.3FM), CISF (90.1FM), JACK-FM (96.9FM), The Z (95.3FM), 101 ROCK 101 (101FM), CO-OP RADIO (102.7FM) and Xfm (104.9FM). The University of British Columbia has its own eclectic radio station, CITR (101.9FM). CBC television has a mix of news, drama, documentaries and films, and the local television station is BCTV. There are dozens of cable channels, most with insufferably frequent commercial breaks.

ACTIVITIES

## Religious Services

Christ Church Cathedral has weekday services with holy communion at 12.10pm and at 8am and 10.30am on Sunday.

A – Z

## S moking

Smoking is not permitted by law in public buildings, on public transport, in shopping malls, and in most restaurants, pubs, nightclubs and casinos. Some restaurants and other establishments have designated smoking areas such as patios or outside heated seating areas.

### Student Travellers

With two universities and many colleges, Vancouver has a large student population. Always travel with a student card, as many attractions, cinemas and theatres offer discounts. Pick up a copy of the *Georgia Straight* for listings.

## T elephones

There are still plenty of public telephones, which are equipped for the hearing-impaired and take coins (25¢), credit cards and (usually) prepaid cards. Local calls cost 25¢ from a public phone, but are free from private phones, though rarely in hotels. The 604 area code has been around for decades and has to be dialled for such numbers. Long-distance calls must be prefixed by "1", which on public phones gets you through to an operator, who will tell you how much money needs to be put in. Cheap rate is between 6pm–8am, and many businesses offer toll-free numbers, prefixed by 1 800 or 1 888.

### Mobile Phones

Tri-band mobile phones allow you to make and receive calls providing your contract covers Canada. It's worth checking the cost of calls and text messages. If you need to make a large number of calls or are on an extended stay, it may be better value to obtain a local phone from companies such as Bell, Fido, Rogers or Telus, which have numerous branches around the city.

### Tipping

It is customary to add 15 percent to the pre-tax total at restaurants, though if you are a party of six or more some restaurants automatically add a service charge. Tip porters a dollar per item of luggage, chambermaids two dollars per day for stays longer than two days, and tour guides a dollar an hour. For taxi drivers, round up the fare by 10–15 percent.

### Tourist Offices

**Australia:** Integra Tourism Marketing, Level 5, 68 Alfred Street, Milsons Point NSW 2061; tel: 61 2 9959 4277.
**UK:** British Columbia House, 3 Regent Street, 3rd Floor, London SW1Y 4NS; tel: 020 7930 6857.

### Tourist Offices in Vancouver

The principal Tourist Info Centre in Vancouver is in the **Waterfront Centre at Plaza Level** (200 Burrard Street; mid-May daily 8am–6pm, Sept–May Mon–Sat 8.30am–5pm; tel: 604 683 2000), where there is a huge collection of brochures and leaflets, besides free booking and ticket purchase, discounted admission to many attractions and activities, and currency exchange.
**Tourism British Columbia Office** also has an office in Vancouver (12th Floor, 510 Burrard Street; tel: 604 660 2861).

### Tourist Offices for BC

**Tourism British Columbia:** Tel: 604 435 5622; www.hellobc.com
**Nanaimo:** Beban House, 2290 Bowen Road, Nanaimo; tel: 250 756 0106; www.tourismnanaimo.com
**New Westminster:** 601 Queens Avenue, New Westminster; tel: 604 521 7781; www.tourismnewwestminster.org
**Powell River:** 111-4871 Joyce Avenue, Powell River; tel: 604 485 4701; www.discoverpowellriver.com

**Richmond:** 11980 Deas Thruway, Richmond; tel: 604 271 8280; www.tourismrichmond.com
**Salt Spring Island:** 121 Lower Ganges Road, Salt Spring Island V8K 2T1; tel: 250 537 4223.
**Squamish:** 38551 Loggers Lane; tel: 604 815 4994; www.adventurecentre.ca
**Vancouver Island:** 203-335 Wesley Street, Nanaimo; tel: 250 754 3500; www.islands.bc.ca
**Victoria:** 812 Wharf Street, Victoria, BC, V8W 1T3; tel: 250 953 2033; www.tourismvictoria.com
**Whistler:** 4010 Whistler Way, Whistler; tel: 604 932 7231; www.tourismwhistler.com

## W ebsites

www.tourismvancouver.com – the official tourism site of the city
www.hellobc.com – travel information and ideas for the whole province
www.coastandmountains.bc.ca – travel information for much of Vancouver's hinterland
www.allianceforarts.com – weekly events calendar
www.ticketstonight.ca – tickets for arts, theatre, music, festivals and sports
www.city.vancouver.bc.ca – city government's site, with links to many activities and events
www.gayvancouver.bc.ca – directory to gay events, accommodation, etc, and local news
www.sport.bc.ca – introduction to sports
www.canada.com/cityguides/vancouver – lists attractions by category
www.bowenisland.org/visitors – information about the island
www.galianoisland.com – information about the island
www.mayneislandchamber.ca – information about the island
www.saltspringday.com – attractions, accommodation and services
www.saturnatourism.com – information about the island
www.gibsonschamber.com – information about the Sunshine Coast village

# FURTHER READING

## General

**Richard and Sydney Cannings**, *British Columbia: A Natural History* (1996). Two scientist brothers write about the province's topography, geology, biology and natural history.
**Richard C. Bocking**, *Mighty River: A Portrait of the Fraser* (1997). On the province's foremost river.
**Jacqueline Windh**, *The Wild Edge* (2004), a photojournalist's portrayal of Vancouver Island.

## Literature and Biography

**Margaret Atwood & Robert Weaver (eds)**, *New Oxford Book of Canadian Short Stories in English* (1995). Broad collection of stories about the country.
**Malcolm Lowry**, *Hear Us O Lord from Heaven Thy Dwelling-place* (1962). Lowry's novella on his years living on the west coast.

## History, Art and Architecture

**Pierre Berton**, *The Great Railway* (1972). A well-illustrated history of the Canadian Pacific Railway.
**George Bowering**, *Bowering's BC: A Swashbuckling History* (1996). A candid look at the founders of BC.
**Douglas Coupland**, *City of Glass* (2003). Well-illustrated, wry profile of the city and its art, architecture and landmarks.
**Chuck Davis**, *The History of Metropolitan Vancouver* (2007), A very detailed year-by-year history of the city.
**Harold Kalman**, Philips Ron and Ward, Robin, *Exploring Vancouver* (1993).

**Ken Liddell**, *This is British Columbia* (1958). A whimsical look at the province by a staff member of the *Calgary Herald.*
**Donald MacKay**, *The Asian Dream: The Pacific Rim and Canada's National Railway* (1986). The story of Canada's railways.
**Robert McDonald**, *Making Vancouver: 1863–1913* (1996). Academic study of the city's foundation and meteoric growth.
**Peter C. Newman**, *Caesars of the Wilderness* (1987). Best-selling account of the Hudson Bay Company's colourful history.
**Barrie Sandford**, *The pictorial history of Railroading in British Columbia* (1981). Evocative pictures and extensive text about BC's railway and interurban lines.

### FEEDBACK

We do our best to ensure the information in our books is as accurate and up-to-date as possible. However, some mistakes and omissions are inevitable, and we would welcome your feedback on any details related to your experiences using the book "on the road". The more information you can give us (particularly with regard to addresses, emails and telephone numbers), the better.

We will acknowledge all contributions, and we'll offer an Insight Guide to the best letters received.

Insight Guides
PO Box 7910
London SE1 1WE
United Kingdom
email: insight@apaguide.co.uk

## Travel Memoirs

**Jan Morris**, *O Canada: Travels in an Unknown Country* (1992). A coast-to-coast journey.

## Outdoor Activities

**Jean Cousins**, *Easy Hiking Around Vancouver: An All-Season Guide* (2005).
**Charles Kahn**, *Hiking the Gulf Islands* (2004).
**Mary and David Macaree**, *109 Walks in British Columbia's Lower Mainland* (2002).
**Dan & Sandra Langford**, *Cycling the Kettle Valley Railway* (2002).
**Teri Lydiard**, *The British Columbia Bicycling Guide* (1984).
**Greg Maurer**, *Mountain Biking Adventures in Southwest British Columbia* (1999).
**David Payne**, *Island Cycling* (1996), a guide to cycling on Vancouver Island and the Gulf Islands.
**Darrin Polischuk**, *Mountain Biking British Columbia* (1996).
**Simon Priest**, *Bicycling Vancouver Island* (1992)
**John Acorn & Nancy Baron**, *Birds of the Pacific Northwest* (2002).
**Greg Dombovsky**, *Diver's Guide: Vancouver Island South* (1999). Guide to 50 of the best dives.

## Other Insight Guides

The *Insight FlexiMap: Vancouver,* which has a rainproof finish, makes a good companion to this guide. *Insight Guide: Canada* is also useful if you're planning to travel beyond BC's boundaries. *City Guide: Seattle* is ideal if you're heading south across the US border. The third Canadian title in the Insight series is *Toronto.*

# ART & PHOTO CREDITS

akg-images 17
All Canada Photos 39
Hamid Attie Photography 8TR, 231
B & Y Photography/Alamy 128
Bettmann/Corbis 19, 24, 27R, 28,
Courtesy of Bishop's Restaurant 135
Trevor Bonderud/British Columbia Photos 111B, 222
The Bridgeman Art Library 21, 30
Private Collection/The Stapleton Collection/The Bridgeman Art Library 30
British Columbia Photos/Alamy 53, 54
Chris Cheadle/All Canada Photos 52, 60, 141
City of Port Moody 147, 154, 155
David Cooper/Firehall Arts Centre 40
Shaun Cunningham/Alamy 224
Keith Douglas/Alamy 123
Firehall Arts Centre 247
Courtesy of Floata Seafood Restaurant 105
Bruce Forster/Getty Images 87BR
Fox Photos/Getty Images 26
Chris Harris/All Canada Photos 47
Al Harvey/All Canada Photos 38, 99B
David Heath/All Canada Photos 46, 219B
Russ Heini/British Columbia Photos 216
Robert Holmes/Alamy 142B
JTB Photo Communications, Inc/Alamy 125
Kevin Judd/Cephas Picture Library 230
T Kitchin& V Hurst/All Canada Photos 56L, 194B
Anthony Lambert 142T, 153T, 161T, 219T, 220T, 220B, 221, 223, 225T, 225B
Randy Lincks/British Columbia Photos 204, 208, 211
Don Mackinnon/Stringer/Getty Images 43
John E Marriot/British Columbia Photos 56R
Gunter Marx/Alamy 151, 160
Cathy Muscat/Apa 5T, 6T, 9BR, 35, 37L, 79T, 83T, 89, 111T, 113T, 124, 130T, 130B, 131T, 133, 169BR, 194T, 196T, 196B, 201B, 238, 249, 251
Macduff Everton/Corbis 170
Ben Martin/Time Life Pictures/Getty Images 29
Gunter Marx Photography/Corbis 50, 217
Borchini Massimo/4 Corners Images 83B

Kevin R Morris/Corbis 214B
PhotoBliss/Alamy 226
Wolfgang Pölzer/Alamy 195T
Dale Sanders/British Columbia Photos 48
Courtesy of Sequoia Grill 114
Terry Smith Images/Alamy 55
Courtesy of Shangri-La Hotels & Resorts 117TR
Michael Snell/Alamy 205
Sotheby's/akg-images 18
Ulana Switucha/Alamy 101B
Tim Thompson Title page, 2/3TC, 3BR, 4T, 4C, 5B, 6B, 7T, 7BL, 7BR, 8BL, 8BR, 9TL, 9CL, 10/11, 12/13, 14, 31, 32, 33, 34L, 34R, 36, 37R, 41, 42, 51, 57, 61L, 61R, 62/63, 64/65, 68, 70, 71, 73T, 73B, 74T, 74B, 75T, 75B, 76T, 76B, 77T, 77B, 78, 79B, 80, 81T, 81B, 82, 88, 91T, 91B, 92T, 92BL, 92BR, 93, 94, 95T, 95C, 95B, 96T, 96B, 97L, 97R, 98, 99T, 100, 101T, 102T, 102B, 103T, 103B, 106, 108, 109, 112T, 112B, 113B, 115T, 115C, 118, 119, 120, 121, 122, 126, 127, 129, 131B, 132, 133B, 138, 146, 148, 149, 150, 153B, 156, 157, 158, 159, 161B, 162, 163, 164, 165, 166T, 166C, 168T, 168C, 168BL, 168BR, 169BL, 171T, 171B, 172T, 172B, 173T, 173B, 174T, 174B, 175, 176, 182, 183, 185T, 185B, 186BL, 186BR, 187T, 187B, 188, 189, 190T, 190B, 191, 192, 193L, 193R, 198, 199, 200, 201, 202T, 202B, 203, 206, 207, 210T, 210B, 212T, 212B, 213, 214T, 218, 227, 229, 234, 237, 242, 252, 257
Time Life Pictures/Mansell/Getty Images 23
Courtesy of Top Table Restaurant Group 58, 59, 140
Vancouver Public Library 22, 25, 27L
Dean Van'Tschip/All Canada Photos 45, 209
Jeff Vinnick/Getty Images 139
Rich Wheater/All Canada Photos 44, 49
Peter M Wilson/Alamy 143
Woodfall Wild Images/Alamy 195B
Lawrence Worcester/Lonely Planet Images 144
Underwood & Underwood/Corbis 16

86/87: Edward G Malindine/Topical Press Agency/Getty Images 86BL; Douglas Miller/Topical Press Agency/Getty Images 86TL; Tim Thompson 86CR, 86BR, 86/87TC,

87TR, 87BL
116/117: Anthony Lambert 116/117TC; Tim Thompson 116TL, 116CR, 116BL, 116BR, 117BL, 117BR
136/137: Barry Bland/Alamy 137TR; Chris Cheadle/British Columbia Photos 136/137TC; Cathy Muscat/Apa 136BR, 137C; Tim Thompson 136TL, 136CR, 136BL, 137BL, 137BR
178/179: British Columbia Photos 178TL; Annie Griffiths Belt/Corbis 179C; Rob Howard/Corbis 178BL, 179BR; Petr Josek/Reuters/Corbis 179TR; Randy Lincks/Corbis 178/179TC; Gunter Marx/Alamy 178BR, 179BL

## ACKNOWLEDGEMENTS

Many thanks to the following for help of all kinds: Emily Armstrong, Peter Armstrong, Charlie and Kelly Avison, Graham Bell, Ulrieke Benner, Louise Bourchier, Jamie Bray, Stephen Brown, Peter Bueschkens, Cindy Burr, Sarah Clark, Nancy Derry, Michelle Dunn, Greg Evans, Mike Fairfield, Kristine George, Volker Grady, Amanda Haines, Wendy Hartnell, Gillian Kainola, Laura Kingston, Jo-Anne Leon, Kate Colley Lo, Sarah MacIntyre, Heather McGillivray, Brian and Debbie McKinney, Shirley McLaughlin, Don McPherson, Anita Marron, Bruce K. Mason, Ian Maw, Jim Mockford, Ken Nakano, Bonny O'Connor, Larry Orr, Heather Oughtred, Jerry Parks, Dianne Quast, Jo Ann Reynolds, Kevan J. Ridgeway, Gillian Rose, Guy and Hilde Rose, Mika Ryan, Jennifer Rhyne, Michael Shirrif, Nim Singh, Darlene Small, Melita Swan, Joan Vogstad, Tia Way, Heidi Weisling, Tamara Whittaker and Inge Wilson. Thanks also to Sarah Falkingham and Rachel Grieve at goshpr, Josie Heisig and Carla Mont at Tourism British Columbia, Michelle Edington at Tourism Victoria, and Wendy Underwood at Tourism Vancouver. Special thanks for their hospitality to Bernadette Kowey and Bill Havens, Judith Reid and Scott Sudbeck, Paul and Sue Baran, and Sue Alexander and Annabel Hawksworth.

Map Production: Neal Jordan-Caws, James Macdonald and Stephen Ramsay

©2007 Apa Publications GmbH & Co. Verlag KG, Singapore Branch

Production: Linton Donaldson

# VANCOUVER STREET ATLAS

The key map shows the area of Vancouver covered by the atlas section. An index of street names and places of interest shown on the maps can be found on the following pages. For each entry there is a page number and grid reference.

## Map Legend

| | | | | | |
|---|---|---|---|---|---|
| Expressway with Junction | ⊖ Border Crossing | Expressway | —Ⓢ— | SkyTrain |
| Expressway (under construction) | ✦✦ Airport | Highway | Ⓟ | Car Park |
| Divided Highway | ✝✝ Church (ruins) | Main Roads | 🚌 | Bus Station |
| Main Road | ✝ Monastery | | ❶ | Tourist Information |
| Secondary Road | ⌘ Castle (ruins) | Minor Roads | ✉ | Post Office |
| Minor Road | ∴ Archaeological Site | | ✝ | Cathedral/Church |
| Track | ∩ Cave | Footpath | ☪ | Mosque |
| International Boundary | ★ Place of Interest | Railway | ✡ | Synagogue |
| Province/State Boundary | ⌂ Mansion/Stately Home | Pedestrian Area | ⚔ | Statue/Monument |
| National Park/Reserve | ※ Viewpoint | Important Building | ⌷ | Tower |
| Ferry Route | ↰ Beach | Park | ⌷ | Lighthouse |
| | | | ⛳ | Golf Course |

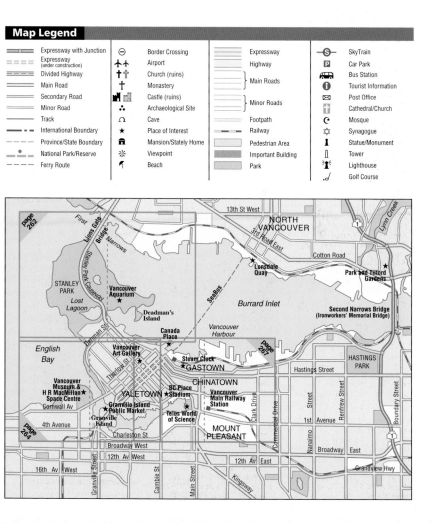

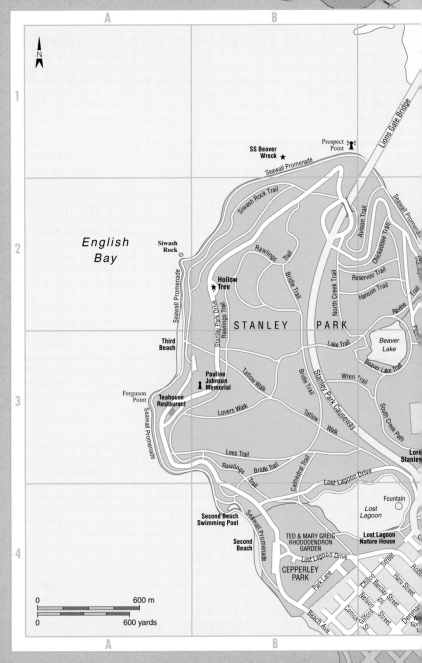

N

English
Bay

A

B

1

2

3

4

SS Beaver
Wreck ★

Prospect
Point ⚓

Lions Gate Bridge

Seawall Promenade

Siwash Rock Trail

Avison Trail

Chickadee Trail

Seawall Promenade

Siwash
Rock ○

Rawlings Trail

Bridle Trail

North Creek Trail

Reservoir Trail

Hanson Trail

Ravine Trail

Pipeline Trail

★ Hollow
Tree

Seawall Promenade

Stanley Park Drive

Rawlings Trail

STANLEY    PARK

Lake Trail

Beaver
Lake

Third
Beach

⚓ Pauline
Johnson
Memorial

Tattow Walk

Bridle Trail

Stanley Park Causeway

Wren Trail

Beaver Lake Trail

South Creek Path

Ferguson
Point

Teahouse
Restaurant

Lovers Walk

Tattow    Walk

Seawall Promenade

Lees Trail

Rawlings Trail

Bridle Trail

Cathedral Trail

Lost Lagoon Drive

Lord
Stanley

Fountain ○

Lost
Lagoon

Second Beach
Swimming Pool

Second
Beach

Seawall Promenade

TED & MARY GREIG
RHODODENDRON
GARDEN

Lost Lagoon Drive

Lost Lagoon
Nature House

CEPPERLEY
PARK

Park Lane

Chilco Street

Barclay Street

Nelson Street

Comox Street

Gilford Street

Haro Street

Roth...

Denmar...

Beach Ave.

0          600 m

0          600 yards

A

B

Jacobs Rd

1st Street

McGuire Avenue

Silverwood Crescent

Golf Range

Lower Capilano Road

Vancouver Wharf

**Capilano Indian Reserve**

McBride Street

Garden Ave

Bowser Ave

Philip Ave

1st Street

Welch Street

Welch Street

Redwood Street

Pine...

Wood Cres

Pemberton Ave

Lloyd Avenue

Mackay Road

MCKAY-KIWANI PARK

3rd St

1st St

**North Vancouver**

McKeen Avenue

**NORTH VANCOUVER**

*First Narrows*

*B u r r a r d*

*I n l e t*

**Coal Harbour**

Lumberman's Arch

Variety Kids Water Park

Miniature Railway

Children's Farmyard

Vancouver Aquarium

Vancouver Park Pavilion

Mallard Trail

Malkin Bowl

Brockton Oval

Stanley Park Horse-Drawn Tours

Brockton Cricket Club

**Brockton Visitor Centre**

Stanley Park Drive

Seawall Promenade

**SS Empress of Japan Figurehead**

**Girl in a Wetsuit**

**Brockton Point Lighthouse**

Brockton Point

**Totem Poles**

**Nine o'clock Gun**

Hallelujah Point

Robert Burns

Vancouver Rowing Club

Seawall Promenade

**Deadman's Island**

**Royal Vancouver Yacht Club**

H.M.C.S. Discovery Navel Training Centre

DEVONIAN HARBOUR PARK

**Westin Bayshore**

Hastings Street West

Pender St

Robson Public Market

HARBOUR GREEN PARK

**Harbor Air Seaplane Terminal**

**Marina**

**Vancouver Convention & Exhibition Centre Extension**

**Canada Place**

SeaBus Route

D

E

D

E

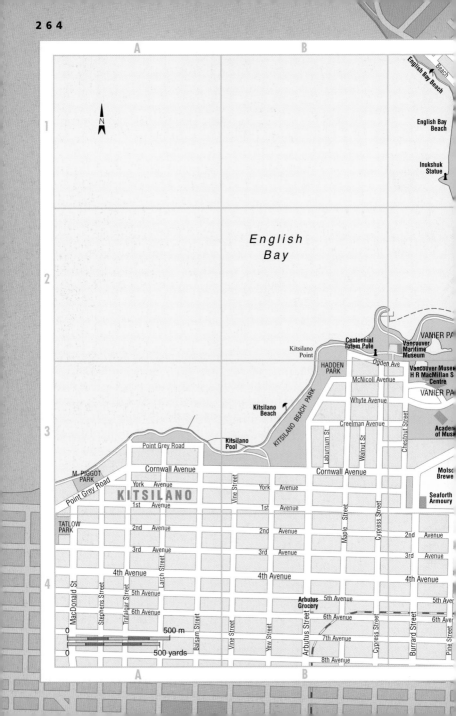

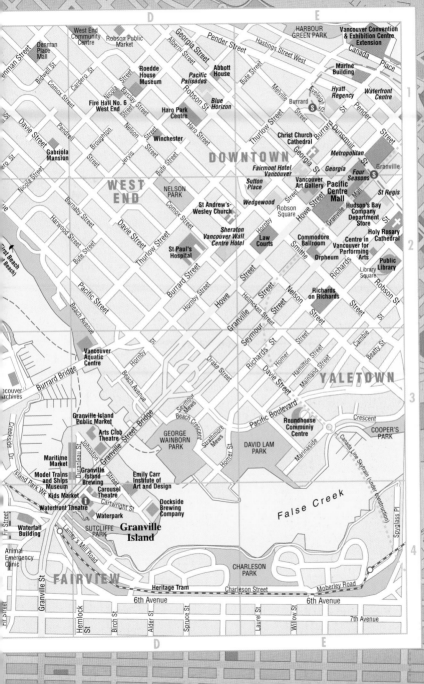

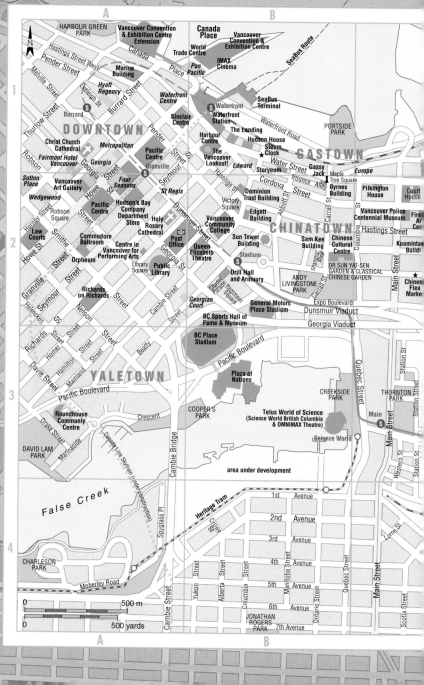

Port of Vancouver
Vanterm

Waterfront Road

Stewart Street

Rogers Street

BC Sugar
Museum

Powell St

Pandora St

Alexander Street

Powell        Street

OPPENHEIMER
PARK

Cordova        Street

Franklin Street

Vancouver Aboriginal
Friendship Society

Hastings Street

**STRATHCONA**

Hastings        Street

**(EAST END)**

Pender        Street

Pender Street East

Community Centre

Ray-Cam
Community
Centre

Frances Street

Russian
Peoples
Home Hall

Georgia Street

**WOODLAND
PARK**

Adanac Street

Georgia        St

**MACLEAN
PARK**

Prior Street

Venables Street

Atlantic St

**STRATHCONA
PARK**

Parker        Streer

Napier        Street

**Britannia
Community
Centre**

Malkin Avenue

William Street

**GRANDVIEW
PARK**

Charles Street

Greyhound
Terminal

Kitchener Street

Terminal        Avenue

Evans Avenue

Grant Street

Graveley Street

1st Avenue

Industrial Avenue

2nd Avenue

3rd Avenue

**MOUNT
PLEASANT**

**GRANDVIEW**

4th Avenue

Great Northern Way

5th Avenue

5th Avenue

St George St

Guelph St

Carolina St

Fraser St

6th        Avenue

6th Avenue

**CHINA
CREEK
PARK**

VCC/Clark

Clark Drive

Grandview

Highway

Commercial Street

Commercial        Street

Clark Drive

Vernon Drive

Campbell        Avenue

Hawks        Avenue

Heatley        Avenue

Hawkes        Avenue

Princess        Avenue

Jackson Avenue

Raymur Ave.

Raymur Avenue

Glen Drive

McLean Drive

Vernon        Drive

Clark        Drive

Odlum        Drive

Cotton        Drive

Woodland        Drive

McLean Drive

Woodland Drive

Vancouver
Main Railway
Station

HASTINGS
EAST

# STREET INDEX

# GENERAL INDEX

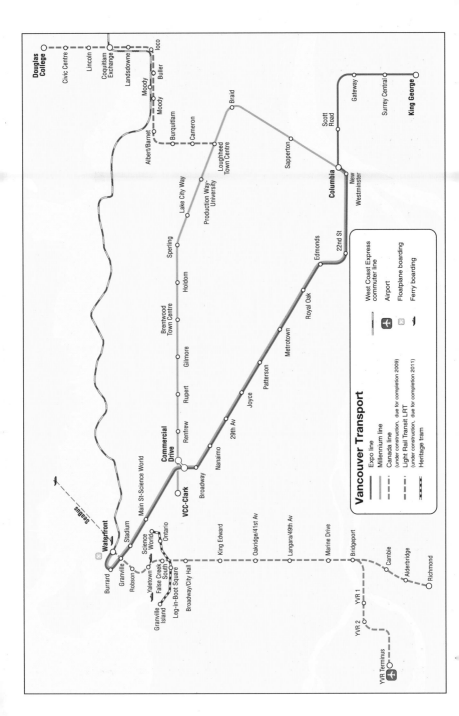